W9-ADJ-634

Africa View

THE PASTORAL LIFE.

EVENING ON THE MBUGWE FLATS, TANGANYIKA. THE FLOCKS OF CATTLE, GOATS AND DONKEYS ARE BEING DRIVEN HOME FOR THE NIGHT.

DT425
H8
1968

AFRICA VIEW

by

JULIAN HUXLEY

Illustrated

GREENWOOD PRESS, PUBLISHERS
NEW YORK   1968

DEC 16 1968

127651

Copyright, 1931, by Julian Huxley

First Edition

Reprinted with the permission of
Harper & Row, Publishers

Reprint edition, 1968

LIBRARY OF CONGRESS catalogue card number: 68-23300

Printed in the United States of America

C O N T E N T S

v

CONTENTS

ILLUSTRATIONS

vii

ILLUSTRATIONS

Africa View

Chapter I

INTRODUCTION

In 1929 the Colonial Office Advisory Committee on Native Education asked me if I would go out to East Africa to advise upon certain aspects of native education. I was very ready to do so, and accordingly set sail from Marseilles in August, landed in Tanganyika Territory early in September, and spent the next sixteen weeks travelling hard through considerable parts of the four East African Territories, with even a dash into the easternmost part of the Belgian Congo, and finding that the reality was even more interesting than my anticipation of it.

Various of the kind people I met in Africa asked me (sometimes, I have imagined, not without a note of apprehension) whether I intended to write a book about my travels—or trip, for my journey certainly does not merit the more honourable term. The question indicated that anybody with the least pretensions to writing was in the habit of making a journey to Africa the occasion for a book—a conclusion which may be substantiated by a look at the "Travel" shelves of any big library. Is there any occasion or excuse for adding to the list, and for adding to it as the result of only four months in the country?

On the last point I feel some assurance. Into those four months I have crammed whole cargoes of vital experience. I have convinced myself very speedily of the utter inade-

quacy of my knowledge and ideas about Africa; I have
marvelled at her variety and the variety of her peoples; I
have had problem after problem thrust forcibly upon my
attention, from witchcraft to the latest refinements of applied science, from prehistoric archæology to modern politics, and I feel that anything which I may be able to do to
interest people at home in the variety of Africa and the
interest of her problems will be worth while.

On her variety I may perhaps here suitably insert an
article I wrote for *The Times* when the vivid new impressions were still crowding themselves upon me:—

"I have been two months in Africa—or rather in one
small portion of Africa. For the four territories destined to
become the Federation of East Africa—Uganda, Kenya,
Tanganyika, and Zanzibar—are together far smaller in
size than other single African units such as the Anglo-
Egyptian Sudan, or the Belgian Congo. And, naturally,
I have only been able to see a fraction of this fraction of
the continent. Yet the first and most powerful impression
of those two months is one of almost unbelievable variety.

"As I write I look over the Kabale valley in Western
Uganda, across to steep but rounded hills. They might almost be bits of the English Lake District: I have been
vividly reminded of Shap Fell, of Saddleback, of Fairfield
seen from Ambleside. They are greener than the Lakes
hills, one must admit; and much of them is cultivated;
and the valley bottom is a great papyrus swamp; and the
people are black Bakiga, half-naked and very industrious,
who live in little villages of windowless beehive huts. But
the landscape is strangely un-African.

"Last week's picture was Entebbe. Green lawns, dotted
with magnificent trees, slope down to the Victoria Nyanza;

little egrets stalk in flocks through the grass, like white runner ducks rendered magically graceful; hornbills call in the trees; cormorants and darters sun themselves on the shore; lake terns and lake gulls fly overhead. There are perennial breezes and perennial beauty.

"Another week back, and Kampala provides the picture. Here is the commercial capital of Uganda; here is the high-water mark of missionary effort in equatorial Africa; here the Central African native has advanced furthest along the roads of political, commercial and educational development. Two really fine cathedrals crown two of the town's seven hills; the Baganda women, their lovely shoulders bare above their long bright robes, walk along the streets with natural grace and natural dignity; motor omnibuses do a roaring trade from the outlying districts. Round about, in every direction, are hills whose rich and never-changing greenery cloys the eye; there are cotton, banana groves, coffee, maize, sugar-cane; and among the plantations nestle the native dwellings—for the most part not mere huts, but real houses with windows and three or four rooms and often a little patch of flowers before their door. Perhaps the most strik-ing impression I take away from Kampala is of service in the Church of England Cathedral. Five or six Europeans and five or six hundred natives; a choir of fifty who sang a Bach chorale with great feeling; a sermon which I longed to understand, preached with much vivid gesture by Ham Mukasa, one of the aristocracy of the native kingdom, a noble-faced old man who has twice been to England and has written a book about his travels there.

"Back another week and I am in the Eastern Rift Valley, that strange gash across the face of the earth, with its steep parallel walls and its barren floor, pimpled with volcanoes

3

new and old and large and small, dotted with lakes both fresh and salt. Here is Elmenteita, a lovely name for a lovely lake. With its low craggy hills, wooded here and there, it is not unlike the head of Windermere. There is one difference—its shores are bordered with a line of pale coral pink, clear enough even from ten miles away; and the pink —but I will leave it to a later chapter to reveal the cause of those pink borders.

"A week before that again, and I am journeying from Nairobi to the Mara river, in the western part of the Masai Reserve. Here are herds of Masai cattle and goats; here is a Masai village, fenced with thorns to keep cattle in and lions out, the huts of extreme squalor, the people wholly untouched, save in the way of prohibitions, by our civilization. A magnificent giraffe eyes us from over a thorn-bush; he lets us motor up over the plain to within thirty yards, then makes off with his strangest of slow gallops. He moves like a ship, but he is a ship with legs. In a zoo, giraffes look merely odd. Here among the thorn-trees one understands their rationale. There, a mile off the road, is a big herd of game—several thousand head; there are zebras (pleasant, vulgar creatures) and gnu and hartebeest, ugliest of antelopes, with groups of gazelle here and there. And now a couple of ostriches dash across our bows, going a good thirty miles an hour, with magnificent leg-action. They, too, look merely silly in captivity; but here the big eye on the watchtower neck, the long leg and the potent thigh, all reveal themselves as suitable, harmonious with the creature's life and surroundings.

"The thorn-scrub country, to those whose taste does not run only to the rich and the cultivated, has a memorable beauty. The brown rolling plains are dotted with

4

acacias, in greener and more graceful reminder of the umbrella pines of Italy; the dry hillsides are covered with thick scrub, out of which rise the dark and strange shapes of huge candelabra euphorbias; here and there a river intersects the plain, and then the dry earth blossoms into a ribbon of rich greenery, full of doves and singing birds. Everywhere there are beasts and birds. A band of russet impala see us and make off, punctuating their progress with fantastic bounds and springs; exquisite Thomson's and Grant's gazelles feed over the plain or shelter from the heat of the day under the sparse trees; there are wart-hogs, bush-pig, eagles and vultures, bustards and francolins, sandgrouse and secretary-birds, packs of big tabby mongooses, huge field-mice, lizards, and the innumerable band of insects.

"The size of it all is impressive, too; fifty miles, a hundred, a hundred and fifty—all Masai Reserve, with the thorns and the game and the sparse nomadic people.

"In completest contrast with that, there is the previous week's picture from the other side of Nairobi. Settlers' lands, cool and green under grey skies, with coffee and maize and many trees. It is a soft and pale green, and the scenery might be almost anywhere in England. And beyond them, the Kikuyu Reserve, a lovely and fertile region for the most part, innumerable valleys among green hills, where this rather strange and gnome-like race of agriculturists live. And beyond again, if you are lucky one clear morning, there are the snows and pinnacles of Mount Kenya itself, towering above the enormous and spreading shoulders of the mountain, all mantled yet with primeval forest.

"I am overrunning my space, and still I have not said

5

half. There are the appalling stretches of dense thorn-scrub covering hundreds of miles of the heart of Tanganyika. There are the bare hills and plains of the pastoral people near Tabora and near Kondoa. There is Old Moshi, with Kilimanjaro hanging aloft in a fantastic vision of snow seen through bananas and palms. Kilimanjaro is gigantic. One day we went up through the forest-belt—a long and steady trudge of over four hours; and when we emerged through the tree-heathers on to the open moor, the peak still seemed as far away as ever. There are the Usambara Mountains, the beautiful wooded range running down towards the coast. They are not high, but receive the full force of the monsoon; and so their slopes are covered with the luxuriance of true tropical rain-forest. From the Research Station at Amani one walks straight into such a forest. There are perhaps fifty frequent kinds of forest tree, their trunks often rising over a hundred feet without a break, their crowns up to two hundred feet in air. Ferns and mosses and orchids grow profusely on their trunks and branches, and enormous lianas hang looped and pendulous upon them.

"Then there is the coast, with its coconut palms, its mangrove trees on stilts, its swarms of fiddler-crabs brandishing their single bright hypertrophied claws, its big ports with wharves and great liners, its native fishermen in their outrigger dugouts. And there is Zanzibar, unique place, with its lucent groves of every spice and every fruit the tropics know; its bazaar not African at all, but oriental of the Near East.

"And the people are as varied as the country—Europeans, Arabs, Indians, Africans; and the Africans, though the ignorant persist in classing them all as merely 'blacks,' 'natives,' or even 'niggers,' show more variety of physical type and way of life than is to be found in all Europe.

"On top of all this variety of nature and man there impinge Western civilization and Western industrialism. Will their impact level down the variety, insisting on large-scale production to suit the needs of Europe and Big Business, reducing the proud diversity of native tribes and races to a muddy mixture, their various cultures to a single inferior copy of our own? Or shall we be able to preserve the savour of difference, to fuse our culture and theirs into an autochthonous civilization, to use local difference as the basis for a natural diversity of development?"

My article, I see, ended with a query. That, too, is very African. One's impressions, continuing their existence within one's brain, have a way of growing long tails which then curl up and over and turn into so many marks of interrogation.

How far is the native African capable of improvement, of profiting by education? Is indirect or direct rule the better expedient? Do we intend ever to give African natives the vote? Can we free tropical Africa of malaria, sleeping sickness, plague, relapsing fever, dysentery, and the rest? Will tropical agriculture on a modern commercial scale ever succeed, ever be more than a well-accepted invitation to innumerable insects? Can the white man live in the tropics not merely as an individual but as a reproducing race? What, in the name of Galen, *is* sunstroke? Will the black races blindly copy the white, or will they develop a new civilization of their own? To federate, or not to federate? Is Christianity a good religion for the African? Is Africa in for another period of the violent geological disturbances which thrust the rift escarpments one, two, and three thousand feet above the rift floors? Should we aim at making English or Swahili the *lingua franca* of our Eastern African colonies? Who were the prehistoric inhabitants of tropical Africa, what the series of events by which the present tribes reached their existing stations? Will game and game reserves continue to exist on the grand scale, or must they dwindle and disappear before modern firearms and the white man's economic greed? Can the native succeed in ousting the Asiatic from his entrenched position in the economic system of East Africa? Will the different powers among whom Africa is divided ever meet to discuss over a friendly table means for assimilating their diverse systems of treating subject races? And so on, and so forth. . . .

The queries crowded upon me as I travelled. If I venture opinions on some of them, it is only because of opportunities of talk with settlers and officials, with doctors and foresters, scientists and business men, administrators and native chiefs, missionaries and sportsmen. At least I have heard all sides, and have thought about what I heard.

The view I have had of Africa, even if it be a partial and limited one, is vivid and real enough. And Africa is so important for the world's future that any honest impression of her variety and her problems deserves to be set down—that is my excuse for this book.

In writing it, I have deliberately adopted what may seem the hybrid method of interspersing a diary record, based on the notes which I took from day to day, with chapters on particular topics. The vividness and variety which are the joy of travelling tend to evaporate in the process of boiling down and arranging in orderly sequence; while the impressions of single days can never attain the solidity of the ideas which reflection crystallizes out of many isolated experiences. So I have tried to make the best of both methods.

If I were to mention everyone who deserves my thanks, the list would be over-long; the hospitality of the Colonies is proverbial, and I can only thank my numerous hosts and helpers collectively. I must, however, specifically mention the Governors of the three mainland Territories and the Resident of Zanzibar—Sir Donald Cameron, Sir Edward Grigg, Sir William Gowers and Sir Claud Hollis—for their interest and their hospitality; Mr. H. S. Scott, Mr. C. J. Morris, Mr. Isherwood and Mr. Hendry, the Directors or Acting Directors of Education in the four Territories, for their unstinted help; Mr. R. T. Mason, of the Tanganyika Education Department, who accompanied me and looked after me through the Territory; Mr. C. F. M. Swynnerton, Director of the Tsetse Research Department of Tanganyika, Mr. Gardiner, Director of the Forestry Service of Kenya, Mr. Clarke, Acting Game Warden of Kenya, and Mr. C. Pitman, Game Warden of Uganda, for showing me many things I should never otherwise have seen; Mr. and Mrs. Leakey, for the hospitality of their Archæological Camp; Mr. John Russell, of the Uganda Education Department, who accompanied us to the Parc National Albert of the Belgian Congo; Mr. J. E. T. Philipps, District Commissioner of Kigezi, Western Uganda, whose unrivalled knowledge of the district was invaluable for our Congo trip; Monsieur Du Buisson, Administrateur at Ruchuru, for facilitating our movements in his district; and Monsieur Hemeleers, Conservateur of the Parc National Albert, for a great deal of help and hospitality. Without the kindness and interest of these gentlemen, I should have done, seen and appreciated far less.

Nor must I forget to thank Count G. de Grünne of Brussels, and Monsieur J. M. Derscheid of the Société Internationale pour la Protection de la Nature, Brussels, for aid, without which I should never have visited the Parc National Albert; the Hon. W. Ormsby-Gore and Major A. G. Church, for much useful advice before starting; and last but by no means least, Lord Passfield, for his friendly interest. Mr. Ormsby-Gore, Major Church, Captain Walter Elliot, Professor R. Coupland, Mr. C. F. M. Swynnerton, and Mr. L. S. Leakey have all been good enough to read portions of my book in typescript; and their advice has been most valuable, and I am very grateful for it. I must also thank all those who have kindly allowed me to reproduce photographs of theirs. Specific acknowledgments are made on the plates. Where no acknowledgment is made, the photograph has been taken by me or by my wife.

Some portions of the book have appeared as articles in the *Times*, the *Cornhill*, the *Nineteenth Century*, the *Saturday Review*, the *Contemporary Review*, the *Atlantic Monthly*, and *Harper's Magazine*; I would like here to make my acknowledgment to the Editors of these journals and magazines.

· · · · ·

Such a book as this does not pretend to give more than a personal impression of what happened to strike a single traveller. For any conspectus of history or anthropology, any general treatment of economic or political problems, the numerous standard works must be consulted. I may perhaps especially mention Lord Lugard's classical *The Dual Mandate in Africa*, which is the basis of modern principles in our Colonial Administration; Major Church's *East Africa: a New Dominion*, which is admirable on sci-

entific, economic and political questions; Professor Selig-
man's recent volume in the Home University Library
Series, *The Races of Africa,* which is a mine of anthropological information and a triumph of compression; on history, Sir Harry Johnston's *Opening Up of Africa* in the
same series, and I. L. Evans' *The British in Tropical
Africa*; Dr. Norman Leÿ's *Kenya,* which may perhaps envisage questions rather onesidedly, but must be read and
digested by anyone anxious to see daylight as regards Native Policy in Africa, and, with H. E. Egerton's *British
Colonial Policy in the Twentieth Century* and S. H. Rob-
erts' *History of French Colonial Policy*, will give a good
idea of colonial policy in general; R. L. Buell's exhaustive
treatise on *The Native Problem in Africa*; on education,
the Report of the Phelps-Stokes Commission, and Victor
Murray's *School in the Bush*; on all aspects of one territory,
Sir Harry Johnston's great work on the Uganda Protectorate; Prof. J. W. Gregory's *The Great Rift Valley*, admirable combination of exciting travel and interesting science;
E. W. Smith's celebrated book, *The Golden Stool*, which
will help the stay-at-home to grasp the necessity of understanding the institutions and methods of thought of those
we set out to rule; and that useful compendium of facts,
the *South and East African Year-Book and Guide*. And
there are, of course, many books dealing with single tribes,
special aspects of geography and natural history, as well as
innumerable accounts of travel and sport, which can be
found in any good library. I hope that the readers of the
following pages may be prompted to follow up one or other
aspect of Africa in these further sources of information.

Meanwhile it is perhaps worth while reminding my

readers of a few salient facts which will help to illuminate
what comes later.

East Africa, then, consists of the Colony of Kenya, the
Protectorates of Uganda and Zanzibar, and the Mandated
Territory of Tanganyika. These have an area of over
680,000 square miles—nearly eight times that of Great
Britain; and a population now probably numbering over
eleven millions. Of these eleven millions, only about 30,000
are Europeans, and about 100,000 Arabs, Indians, and
Goans; the rest, some 99 per cent., are native Africans.
There are very few private unofficial Europeans in Zanzibar and Uganda, a moderate number in Tanganyika, and
a large number, relatively speaking, concentrated in the
Central Highland region of Kenya. Some parts of the country, notably the north of Kenya, are semi-desert and populated with extreme sparseness, and much of the rest of the
territory is distinctly underpopulated, but here and there
the native population reaches a high density. In 1927 the
value of imports and exports was about £22,000,000; this
figure was more than double that at the end of the war,
and the amount is still steadily increasing. Both European
production (notably of coffee and sisal) and native production (notably of cotton, ground-nuts and spices) are
important.

Many of the Indians were encouraged to enter the country to help build the Uganda Railway, the Africans not
being then sufficiently trained to undertake any skilled
labour. All through the early days of the country they
have provided the bulk of the skilled workmen and the
small traders, and have filled most of the clerical and subordinate professional positions. If it is true that the presence of this third racial element seriously complicates the

East African problem, it is also true that East Africa would never have developed to her present level without it.

White settlers have been encouraged to come out under various schemes, such as cheap land and assisted passages. A great influx took place just after the war, but the post-war boom was followed by a severe slump, in which many were ruined. At the moment, a movement towards larger estates and an opposing tendency towards more intensive settlement are fighting for supremacy. A serious difficulty has been the inflation of land values, with consequent speculation in land.

So much for the skeleton of fact concerning population and trade. Politically, although the four territories have different status, there is not much difference in administration. A Governor or Resident is the real Executive, directly under the Colonial Office, and in Tanganyika the affairs of the Mandate must be annually reported to the League of Nations. The Governor is assisted by a Legislative Council, some of whose members are official—the heads of various Departments of Administration, *ex officio*; the rest unofficial—either nominated by the Governor, or elected by the non-native residents (as in Kenya). In all cases there is an official majority.

Chief among the burning political questions are these:— Firstly: should the elected representatives of the non-native residents in Kenya have a majority in the Legislative Council and so make the first and most important step towards self-government, if that term can be applied to the government of a country by the representatives of a small immigrant minority? Secondly: should Indians and Europeans be on a common electoral roll, or elect their representatives separately, Indians voting on an Indian Electoral Roll,

Europeans on a European one? This, like the first problem, is only acute in Kenya. Thirdly: should the four territories be federated under a Governor-General, or continue their more or less independent ways as at present? And then there is the most urgent question of all—that of Native Policy. The Duke of Devonshire, as Colonial Secretary, laid it down in 1923 that "the interests of the native should be paramount, and this has been reaffirmed by the present Secretary of State in a recent much-discussed memorandum. Is that a right principle, or not? And in any case, what precisely does it imply in practice?

One more word, and I have done with this catalogue. To frame a Native Policy you need to know something about the natives; and the great majority of Englishmen at home and many of those on the spot are lamentably ignorant of both the racial and the social anthropology of the African. Let me, therefore, with extreme brevity remind my readers of a few facts.

First, that the primitive and probably related peoples surviving in the shape of Bushmen, Hottentots, and Pigmies were once far more abundant and widespread than now over Equatorial and Southern Africa, and formed the sole population of various large regions. The present population of Africa is due to a series of immigrations. The true or full Negro is not found in East or South Africa; he ranges across the Southern Sudan to the West Coast. The Bantu group appears to consist of Negro stock with a varying but often considerable mixture of Hamite—straight-nosed and lighter-skinned peoples akin to our own Caucasian type. Then there are the half-Hamites, still lighter and less negroid in feature, of whom the Masai are a good example; and the full Hamites, who only enter tropical Africa in its northeast corner.

The Bantu invasions of Southern Africa apppear to have taken place well within the last thousand years, perhaps within the last five hundred; and the same is true of the invasions of more or less Hamiticized stocks like Masai and Kikuyu in East Africa, and those who established themselves as the ruling caste of the notable African king-doms in Uganda, Ruanda and the Congo.

The most important point to realize is that not one of the East or South African tribes is pure Negro; all have a Hamitic admixture, and some are in blood and physical type as closely akin to men of Southern Europe or the Near East as to the Negro of West Africa.

Social Anthropology is a more complicated business. It is not, however, unfair to say that most Europeans ignorant of that science are as prone to dismiss the Africans as the merest savages, as those ignorant of racial anthropology are to class them all together as "niggers." As a matter of fact, all the peoples of Africa, save perhaps the Pigmies and Bushmen, have an elaborate social organization which contains many admirable features. They have their systems of law and justice, of ownership, of council, of morals, of village and tribal administration, even in some degree of education, and very notably of mutual aid. Sometimes large and elaborate kingdoms with a more or less feudal organi-zation, and even with official historians, have come into existence. But the basis of organization is the clan, and the outlook which results from this fact, as well as many other of their ideas, are so alien to our own that many Europeans never enter the African's mental atmosphere, never grasp the proper meaning of their institutions and ideas. This attitude will overlook the one half of native life, and find the other half ridiculous or incomprehensible.

Finally, in the matter of history, let us remember that until the present century the natives of Africa have met with little but greed, hostility and exploitation on the part of the European and Asiatic invaders of their country; and that even now things have not everywhere changed for the better. In the second place, let us remember that the partition of Africa among the European powers is an affair of the last fifty years, and that adequate administration in most regions has only begun during the present century. The problem of administering native races in a comparatively primitive state of culture is indeed a new problem; we cannot be expected to have solved its manifold difficulties in a few decades. The most important lesson of history for Africa is to go slowly.

But an introduction must not stand in the way of what it is to introduce, and I must get on with my book. My main purpose in writing it, apart from the selfish one of embodying my own memories and clarifying my own thoughts, has been to interest people at home in this extraordinary continent and our share in the responsibility for its development. If I have in any measure succeeded in that, I shall count the labour of writing it well spent.

Chapter II

THE JOURNEY

To view Africa one must get there: I feel the journey as an integral part of my African experience, introducing me at the ports of call to mediterranean Africa and desert Africa, as the ship swung me down over the degrees of latitude to the real Africa of the tropics. Besides, I was reading about Africa all the time—all the books I had had no time to read before; and as most of the passengers were returning to life in Africa, we talked Africa a good deal too. So these random notes will perhaps serve to bridge the enormous gap between the European and the African worlds.

The Straits of Messina. Still Europe, but a bit of Europe very different from beer-drinking Britain. The antique Roman spirit of which the new Italy is so conscious expresses itself in an electric sky-sign on the Messina seafront spelling out with letters of fire a message of welcome—in Latin! I wonder at what or whom the Latinity is directed. It can scarcely be the American tourist: I expect it is really at the Fascists' own projection of *Italianità*, bombinating in the vacuum of a lamentably unclassical modern world.

We have just steamed through the Lipari Islands, Stromboli grimly smoking. Nobody on board seems to know or to care that the islands are crowded with political prisoners, miserable deportees of the Fascist Government, at the mercy of the local commandant's whims and passions. I reflected that Stromboli might be taken as a symbol of Italian political life—forces subterraneously pent up, yet irrepressibly finding an outlet. I hope it may be so; but then I reflected further that Stromboli behaved in just the same way during Italy's most inept periods of liberal parliamentarianism as well as under Fascism, during the Risorgimento as well as while she lay under the Austrian yoke; and doubtless during the times of classic Roman freedom too. So Stromboli may be a symbol, but symbols are dangerous things, very untrustworthy substitutes for thinking.

Eastern Mediterranean. This is a French ship. There is none of the organized pleasure of an English boat—secretary of sports, secretary of entertainment, won't you make up a game of shuffleboard, here's Mrs. Blank would like to play deck-tennis, of *course* you play bridge, won't you recite at the performance for the crews of the second class. Blessed relief!

It has another advantage—that the bathrooms are never crowded as on an English ship. To be quite honest, I have not yet seen them used by any one save the English and American passengers.

The disadvantage is the handshaking. Why do French people expect you to shake hands afresh every morning? And some of them seem to repeat the process after each meal. I fear I have taken to mere bowing, thereby doubtless confirming the English reputation for coldness and incivility; but I really can't go on with the contact ritual.

A French rat has eaten a hole in the very English flannel trousers of one of my compatriots. He has gone to the Captain to mention the damage. A reparations account is to be rendered. The British are a great nation.

We have passed under the south side of Crete. What magnificent precipices upspringing out of the sea! The island rises steep to 8000 feet; and I see from the chart that close off shore there are depths of 11,000 feet. So from sea bottom to island top is a rise of 19,000 feet within a few miles. Crete must have stood still more magnificently during the ice age, when the surface of the landlocked Mediterranean lake lay a couple of thousand feet lower, and the tops were more often snow-capped.

Our boat is taking a battalion of Senegalese to Madagascar. They are mostly rather small, and pronouncedly negroid, not to say simian, in type, broad-nosed and prognathous; but if they cannot be called good-looking, they seem kindly, amiable fellows enough. The French officers use their soldier servants as nursemaids for their children; it is a peculiar, somehow pathetic sight to see rather untidy negro soldiers wheeling pasty-faced little French girls round the promenade deck in baby-carriages.

The French on board, officers included, make a picture of idyllic bourgeoisie. The unmarried girls are a model (pre-war model) of feminine propriety; they would not dream of speaking to a strange man without being regularly introduced, and always stick, or are stuck, very close to Mamma. The contrast between them and our three American young ladies is astonishing. Miss America is alarming in her self-possession, her untireableness, her freedom and unconventionality, her precocious sangfroid and capability. She gives me the same qualm as I once received from seeing a successful New York revue—a feeling of helplessness in face of a portentous and unrealized human energy: if ever that energy, organized and canalized, spills

19

over beyond the borders of the United States, the rest of the world will just be annexed.

A young Briton aboard, for all that he dresses smartly and thinks himself very knowing, and in spite of an extra year or so, is like a child compared with these girls. What is it in our upper-class education which causes such an arrest of personality, so that perhaps half of our young men arrive at manhood, as Mexican axolotls do at their maturity, while still in the tadpole stage?

This other French-speaking girl, no one could accuse of backwardness; but then she has a good dose of black blood in her, and her precocity is a purely physical fact. Her mother is a mountainous and horrible half-caste who has captured (*en troisième noces*—astonishing!) a poor little French *officiel* from Madagascar.

Then there are some Belgians aboard, for so huge is the Belgian Congo that it is much quicker to get to its eastern parts through British East Africa than from the Atlantic coast. They give an efficient impression, but all on a small scale, in a petty way. With them is a big Swede, who, like many other Scandinavians seeking for adventurous outlets, has given his life in service to this huge strip of Africa which the accident of an astute monarch bestowed upon Belgium. He is like a tower among the Belgians; looking at him and them, you begin to believe in the great Nordic fairy-story.

Port Said. I could hardly tear myself from the spectacle of coaling ship. Good-bye to Europe now! What magnificent figures of men, these Arabs—tall, lean, horribly muscular, all dressed in long black shifts, all grimed, all shouting and gesticulating under the flares. A truly hellish scene; but how sadly unpicturesque it will be when all the liners run on oil fuel.

The touts in the street, with their cigarettes, shawls, indecent postcards and cheap knick-knacks, are as unbearable as gadflies. They all speak at least half a dozen languages fluently—proof of the worthlessness of languages in themselves as mental discipline, for any nastier specimens of human mind it would be hard to discover.

The one redeeming feature of their pesterings is the names they bestow on the ladies of the party. If you will not buy what they offer, you become Scotch: "All right, Mrs. M'Gregor; yes, you come from Aberdeen?" I wonder if there is a corresponding style for non-buying Germans; or do they too become Scoticized?

If on the other hand they wish to flatter, the lady is generally addressed as *Mrs. Langtry*. One of our passengers recalled that the Cairo donkey-boys, thirty years ago, used to call their favourite donkeys Lily Langtry. That was in her heyday; but that the tradition should last to 1930— what rare persistence of the fame of beauty long after it had faded! Will she last on in legend indefinitely, like Helen or Cleopatra?

Gulf of Suez. To-day is my first sight of a true desert land. Here are mountains with not one blade of grass: sometimes they plunge straight into the sea, sometimes there is a strip of more or less level land. But the particles into which the mountains are blown, heated or frozen away, cannot cohere without water and plants to bind them together; and so rivers of sand sift slowly down the dry gullies, and the level foreshores are covered with shifting useless material and not with soil.

It is strange suddenly to realize the immensity of this

barren double belt of desert that girdles the world here above the tropics, and again below, down south. Its size is the penalty we pay for living in a geological epoch with much land high out of water, and a sharp zoning of climate from tropical heat to polar ice-caps. The world was very different in other ages, like Eocene or Jurassic, when palms grew in Greenland, cycads in Spitzbergen; but what monotonous subtropicality then, what portentous and never-ending green luxuriance . . .

Red Sea. The Red Sea in August—I have never experienced till now what heat could be, and do not want to experience it again. Then I see the stokers wandering about on deck to cool themselves a little, like Judas out of hell on the iceberg for his one day a year, and feel ashamed of myself.

Our Kenya settler has been wearing shorts and a short-sleeved bush-shirt for some days now, to the considerable disapproval of the French contingent, who regard him as improperly dressed, even for the deck. When he came into the dining saloon thus attired, the chief steward with his waxed mustachios firmly intimated that a coat was *de rigueur* for lunch; but at breakfast pyjamas are allowed, even for ladies, which I gather is unheard of on British boats. *Autres pays, autres mœurs.*

Indian Ocean. Those people who assert the real autonomy of the human soul ought to take a long sea voyage. Robbed of the usual variety of outer stimulus, the spirit gradually flags and sinks. So, only more suddenly, did the legendary cab-horse when deprived of the support of the familiar shafts. After days confined to the same ship, the same few people, the same eternal sea, especially if stormless like ours, the same games, the same food, a horrible

22

sluggishness and apathy descends upon one's life. Books
are not so interesting, and one cannot read so long at a
stretch; all one's plans for working off arrears of writing
dribble away to nothing or next to nothing; conversation
palls. One eats a great deal, dozes half the day and sleeps
badly at night. And all because of the increasing monotony; so Pavlov's dogs went off to sleep when a single
stimulus was long repeated.

The fact is, of course, not merely that body and mind are
inseparably one organism, but that organism and environment are one interlocking reality. Mental existence is a
process of interaction; and you can as well try to think of a
flame without oxygen, or terrestrial life without the sun, as
of a truly autonomous soul. I am a slightly different creature on board ship from what I was in Europe; and I
shall be different again in Africa.

Approaching Mombasa. We spent last night cruising
slowly round beyond reach of the reefs, and those of us
who were new to Africa got up early, as we were told we
would be entering Mombasa harbour before breakfast. But
it is now past midday, and Mombasa is only just in sight.
Were we really some sixty nautical miles out in our reck-
oning? I dare not ask. But it is the sort of thing that could
not happen in Europe; here, with the long low line of
palms and other tropical greenery distantly visible above
the uninhabited white beach, one accepts it more easily.

Chapter III

PORTS AND ISLANDS

Mombasa, Sept. 3rd. It is impressive to sail into Kilindini and see here, in the heart of the tropics, a fine harbour with berthing accommodation for five large ships, as well as anchorage for innumerable others. The dozen or so great electric cranes tower up against the mangroves and palms. The liner slides in to her moorings with a score of brown kites about her, wheeling and banking with sharp oblique movements of their forked tails; and on the primitive native fish-traps by the far shore there sit big-headed kingfishers the size of missel-thrushes.

There is just time enough to see the town and to get shown round the island before sailing again for Tanganyika Territory.

Innumerable travellers and tourists have penned their descriptions of Mombasa, and it must be acknowledged that expectations are fairly realized. There is the palmfringed coast as you approach; the old harbour with its native craft; the new port with the last word in modern commercial equipment and warehouses; the coral beach; the beautiful façade of the new Government House by Baker; the green golf-course along the shore; the trees of kinds never dreamed of in temperate lands—extraordinary candelabra spurges, ancient and astounding baobabs. There is the famous seventeenth-century Portuguese fort, the Arab

24

and Portuguese houses, the teeming if shoddy bazaar, the cosmopolitan feeling, blend of Arab, negro and white. There are the banana groves and the mangrove swamps, the husky black negro men and their buxom black women, the native canoes and the great liners.

It is all very much what the globe-trotter feels he has a right to expect of the tropics; and in addition, the European quarter, all along the breezy shore, is lovely. But when you go to the back of the island, you see that there is another side to the picture. The native quarter is untidy, dirty and ramshackle. The negroes live in insanitary-looking huts of wattle and daub, often crowded, dumped over-close and without planning. The Europeans have as much air and view and space as they need; but behind this attractive façade is a slum. Though, as I understand, conditions have been a good deal improved in late years, it is still a slum, and contrasts as painfully with the attractiveness of the European quarter as do the poor quarters of Chicago with Riverside Drive. In Chicago or London, the line between façade and slum is drawn by riches as against poverty. So it is in Mombasa too, but in addition the line delimits colours; the rich or at least the comfortable are all white; the poor and uncomfortable are all black.

One is told that all this is inevitable on a little island like Mombasa. I do not think so. It has been inevitable because we never took steps to prevent private gambling in land values. Land on Mombasa Island is worth hundreds or even thousands of pounds an acre. No one seems to have dreamt that the administration might take over all the land and utilize it to the best advantage of the community instead of allowing its appreciation to go into private pockets; this would have been Socialism, while the other way is Business. The result of course is that it is good business to crowd native huts or tenements together so as to leave other land free for other and more profitable purposes. The health authorities are beginning to intervene, but can only introduce their "socialistic" reforms by buying out Business.

As a matter of fact, speculation in land values seems to be one of the very few profitable ways of utilizing land in Kenya—at any rate far more profitable than putting in the hard work needed to make it grow crops for the world. They manage these things better in Nigeria, I gather.

The local Medical Officer of Health told me that his greatest difficulty was with the Indians, who make up about half of the 20,000 of the island's population. The negroes are willing to learn and have a natural barbaric cleanliness; the Indians do not want to change any of their ways, and combine an ancient civilization with squalor. Similar statements were repeatedly made to me later during my wanderings about the relative sanitability, if I may use the word, of Indians and Africans.

On the way back to the ship, I could not help smiling at the native coastguards, whose Gilbertian uniform consists of a white "sailor suit" with shorts, from which protrude bare black legs. My companion failed to see anything funny in them; I suppose when I leave I shall regard this and all the other partial adaptations of white ways to black people as perfectly normal.

ss. General Duchesne, Sept. 4th. En route for Dar-es-Salaam, I spent a long time last night gazing down into the third class, where sat a perfectly superb dark brown lady, attired in a pale blue silk with a black wrap. These framed her face—blue over the chin, black over the forehead—so that at first she gave the air of an exotic Mother Superior. Then suddenly the surprising nether fact impinged on my startled eyes—from this conventional get-up emerged tight blue trouserettes, pleated, protruding at the ankle into broad blue frills, and leaving the black feet bare.

The harbour of Dar-es-Salaam is in its way more remarkable than that of Mombasa—its entrance so narrow that you would give it the go-by if you did not know of the long reach of sheltered anchorage within: and manœuvring up the narrowest bit of the channel calls for the highest ranges of the pilot's art.

Station Hotel, Dar-es-Salaam, Sept. 4th. My letters miscarried, no one was expecting my arrival, and I had to find a bed in a hotel. This was awkward, as the Tanganyika Exhibition is in full swing, and the place is packed. Eventually, I found a room in the fifth of the town's six hotels, an amiable but casual sort of place kept by a German and his stout wife. I talked my best German at dinner to a young fellow whose family had bought back (after the war) what they could afford of a large estate. It seems hard; but I recollect that my African Handbook gave some figures as to the cost of the East African campaign. Yes, here they are: cost to British and their native allies (excluding that incurred by the Belgians), £72,000,000. The victors can hardly be blamed for taking something.

This bull-necked young man contrasted forcibly with a Scotsman who turned up later, very much the worse for liquor, introduced himself and invited me to have a drink. When I left him, he had just ordered three bottles of beer to take to bed with him, explaining that "Dar-es-S'laam was thirshty place in the mornings."

. . . . .

The first night in a wholly new country, when every trifling experience strikes with the force of novelty, is always strange and vivid. Here, there were the black waiters at supper, with scarlet and yellow jackets over long white robes; the velvety sky and its southern stars; the traffic policemen on boxes at the cross-roads, ·impressive but strange with their black physique, their jersey and shorts, high red fez, and puttees over bare feet. There were the rows of Indian shops, swarming with Indian children, the little boys already in long trousers, the girls in long skirts, and all with round spangled caps; they look strangely anaemic and as it were unsatisfactory by the side of the robust and cheerful blacks. There are the avenues of flamboyant trees, with their flaunting masses of flowers, orange-scarlet in colour, fantastic in shape. There is the feeling of a life new and uncrystallized, in which black, brown and white men are mingling on new and uncertain lines. The latest Western business methods, African temperament, the missionary spirit and the spirit of adventure, Indian trading pertinacity, League mandates, money-grabbing commercialism, British administrative tradition, negro superstition, European science and medicine—they confront each other in strange jumble and tangle. It is the early embryo of African town civilization that one sees here, as different from its future self, whatever that may prove to be, as is the thing we are three weeks after conception—whitey-pink, microscopic, and gill-slitted, from the adult man.

Sept. 5th. Yes, my letters had miscarried; but now all is set to rights, and I am the guest of a charming host and hostess. I am installed in a guest-house which I share, amusingly enough, with two Oxford dons whom I know well. They have just made the journey by car from Rhodesia. And the fourth guest is a man I have often wished to meet, Swynnerton, naturalist and man of science, once Game Warden of Tanganyika and now in charge of the new Anti-Tsetse department.

In the morning to the Exhibition, and learnt a good deal about the Territory. This is the first thing of the kind to be held in Tanganyika since the war. But the Germans in their time had also organized an Exhibition, which was duly opened a day or so before the outbreak of war. That was fifteen years ago; but the natives have long memories. I am told that scarcely a soul came to the weekly market in Dar-es-Salaam this week; they were afraid that this Exhibition also would be the opening event in a war. The behaviourist would see in this a good example of an elaborate conditioned reflex. In any case, it is a pretty piece of reasoning. Levy-Brühl would have us believe that the savage's mind is alogical, works along different lines from ours; but this is logic, though based, like so much of primitive magic, on the false premise that mere association is causal.

Dinner at Government House. We spent a great deal of money after the war in building a new Government House to impress the population with our superiority to the Germans, although we neglected for years the scientific and medical services they had so well begun. The architectural result is mixed. The building's oriental style is in the glare of daylight just not distinctive and distinguished enough to prevent associations with Wembley or the White City; but at night, when detail is lost in the soft starlight, and hidden lights, salmon. pink, illuminate the porticoes, it achieves an undeniable effect.

A house-party of important personages from Kenya;

good talk (Sir Donald Cameron is not only a good Governor, but a good conversationalist and a good host); amusing charades after dinner—my second African evening is very different from my first.

Sept. 6th. A visit to a mangrove swamp has helped to complete my biological education. It is a lesson in the force and luxuriance of tropical life, driving organisms into marginal and specialized occupations. The mangroves are green trees which, by means of turning their roots into stilts, invade the tidal mud. Their seeds germinate without falling off, and the seedling, nourished by its parent, grows into a heavy, dart-like structure, which, falling one day into the mud, dibbles itself in, and starts life ready planted. This amphibious vegetation has its amphibious animal inhabitants. There are plenty of hermit-crabs, and scuttling swarms of fiddler-crabs, so-called because of the male's one absurd enormous claw, almost as big as the rest of the body, which he often holds in front of the body as a fiddler holds his instrument. The male's other claw is a tiny thing, used to spoon nutritious debris into the mouth, and both the female's claws are such small spoons. When the males first abandon their microscopic free life near the surface of the sea, they are like the females. Then comes a stage when both their claws show a slight enlargement. The strange fact seems to be established that now their future right- or left-handedness depends entirely on accident. Lobsters and crabs, when their claws are damaged, shed them by snapping them off at a special performed "breaking-joint," afterwards growing a new one. If one of the young male fiddler's claws be thus lost, what regenerates is a small, female-type claw, while the other one continues its masculine growth. It goes on growing steadily

SOME SMALL AFRICAN ANIMALS.
ABOVE, A LARGE PRAYING MANTIS FROM WESTERN UGANDA.
CENTRE, A MALE FIDDLER-CRAB FROM A COAST MANGROVE
SWAMP, WITH EYES ON STALKS AND ONE CLAW ENLARGED.
BELOW, A MUDHOPPER FISH; THE ELBOW-LIKE BEND IN THE
FORE-FIN IS CLEARLY SEEN.

THE SNAPPER SNAPPED.

THE AUTHOR PHOTOGRAPHING MUDHOPPER FISH IN A MANGROVE SWAMP NEAR DAR-ES-SALAAM.

(*Photo. by Professor Henry Balfour, F.R.S.*)

throughout life, at a rate about half as much again as the body. If a fiddler-crab were to get as big as a big eating crab, its claw by that time would be ten or a dozen times as heavy as all the rest of itself. That, we may surmise, is one reason why all fiddler-crabs are small.

There are several kinds of fiddlers here—medium-sized, black-and-white, with a pinkish scarlet claw; bigger ones, white-patterned on blue, with crimson claws; and little ones with ivory claws. As a human being passes, the crabs see him with their long-stalked mobile eyes (though doubtless they see him only as a moving shape), and react by brandishing their claws back and forth in an almost military but wholly ridiculous manner, a gesture to which they owe their German name of Beckoning Crabs. As the moving shape approaches closer, they dart sideways into their holes. It is an amusing sight to see them emerge again, sideways of course and very cautiously, out of their burrows, with their eyestalks held obliquely to get as much view as possible.

I have always been interested in fiddler-crabs, because they are among the least elaborately organized animals which practise courtship. It used to be thought that the hypertrophied claw served to carry off unwilling females, or to fight with rival males; but although they do fight now and again, the chief use seems to be advertisement—advertisement to passing females that here is a desirable male—*the* desirable male. The little creature stands tiptoe, brandishing his coloured claw in air; too often the female crab walks on, no more interested in the claw and all it implies than are we in nine hundred and ninety-nine of every thousand advertisements which bombard our senses.

But the thousandth time, again like us, she is in the right mood, and the advertisement has its effect.

But even more interesting are the mud-hopper fish. These—Periophthalmus is their proper name—are truly amphibious. Their eyes too are set well up above the head, to get a good view, and, like a chameleon's, are separately movable. Their fore-fins are bent forward at a sort of elbow-joint so that their flat expanded ends can be used as feet, with which, aided too by their tail, they hop over the mud, or climb the mangrove roots; they will even die if kept too long submerged. I knew all this before from books of travels. But what I did not know is that they are capable of running over the surface of the water: they spread their fins to the full, and flap, flap, flap, off they hop five or ten yards, like animated aquaplanes. There are very few other creatures that can utilize the actual surface for their support—water-skaters are the most familiar example; but among vertebrate animals, so far as I know, only the Divers and Loons and some kinds of young ducks are also capable of the feat.

The mud-hoppers proved to be the most aggravating brutes to photograph. My attachment for close work only began to focus at under three feet. The little mottled creatures would almost always let me come to five or even four feet; I pushed the camera forward—oh, so gently!—but at about three foot six they would be off, hop, hop, hop across the mud, till I was dizzy with heat and stooping. But at last I got something which was just tolerable—to find afterwards that my companions had been busy snap-shotting me snapshotting the elusive fish.

Sept. 7th. In Africa every one begins the day with an early morning cup of tea. We in the guest-house make a pleasant habit of drinking ours (brought at dawn) out on the terrace in our dressing-gowns. The sun is just risen above the Indian Ocean; the air, still fresh, shakes the coconut leaves together with a strange rustling, more metallic than vegetable in sound; the bulbuls strike up their morning song; the kites float along, adjusting their course by sharp sideways twists of their forked tails; on a favourite tree not a hundred yards off sit herons, grey and purple, ibis and egrets, waiting for the tide to uncover the flats. It is the most lovely time of the tropical day, better even than the soft evening.

I had an hour's talk with the Governor to-day. He has a mind that drives its way through facts with the aid of ideas and principles; a mind for concentrated action on the matters that arouse its interest. And when the swift penetration to the mental goal has been accomplished, humour, illuminated by the most attractive and disarming of smiles, is allowed to enter the field. The two do not mix—the penetration is of the pure intellect, the humour has its own place and season: the result is a rapid and stimulating variety of moods.

In the afternoon, I crossed to Zanzibar. The little steamer was captained by a remarkable-looking man, a burly Arab in pea-jacket and lamb's-wool fez, every inch a sailor; he might almost have passed for a master mariner from southern France.

The Zanzibar Residency is a cool and pleasant place, overlooking the sea. In the big hall are some of the finest chandeliers I have ever seen. Their only drawback is that a certain kind of small finch will nest in them (windows are always open in this heat), preferring leaves of glass to real foliage. On one occasion, as the lady of the house

33

was advancing to meet a visitor, one of the finches laid an egg smack on the floor between them. . . .

Zanzibar, Sept. 8th. More variety last night. A British cruiser has been here for a week, combining the duties of patrolling the area with those of providing entertainment to the population. The final cricket-match took place yesterday afternoon; the farewell dance last night. The ship's officers came in fancy dress, all got up with red beards (of the hayseed frill variety), and in their sailor servants' clothes, as pirates. Sir Claude Hollis, the Resident, preferred bridge to dancing; and we played at a table in the illuminated gardens. The Navy, it appeared, grudged this absorption in cards, and proceeded to dance round us in single file, singing. But the bridge party was unmoved.

I have rarely seen such an attractive lot of young men as these officers were (one of them was not merely attractive but had a strange feminine beauty, so that I thought him a very lovely girl dressed up as a boy). On the other hand, I have rarely seen young men who still looked such complete schoolboys. They gave the impression of knowing and caring about nothing outside their own homes, their own ship, the outlook of their own class, the routine of their own profession: they were immature. Immaturity has many charms, as we perceive in puppies, colts or lioncubs; but it should not usurp the place of maturity. Looking at these boys, I felt that the British Empire was a very nice Empire. But it is not enough for Empires to be nice; they demand seriousness, free intelligence, and the determination to understand the minds of other nations and of other races. Meanwhile our education is inclining us to sport, to a distrust of intelligence when applied to immediate and practical ends; and is moulding us to a type which is innocently but none the less insolently Narcissistic —it takes itself for pattern and cannot trouble to see that any other types could be really admirable. I compare these nice boys with young men of the same age and standing I have known in the United States. The Americans are more primitive; but they are also much more grown-up. They will have mixed with many more types of men, have fewer unconscious prejudices, be more interested in things in general. Most of them will have paid for their own higher education by working with their own hands or brains in the vacation or even in the term. They will be crude, but they will not be ashamed of their own enthusiasms. They will be very partially educated; but they will still want to be learning. They are not so nice, but they have a more vigorous and more varied vitality.

This evening, a pleasant drive with Sir Claude Hollis, the present quiet and efficient holder of the Residency, to whom Zanzibar owes its wonderful roads, its Clove-growers Association, and its harbour extensions.

The island is of extraordinary beauty: but the beauty is oriental rather than African in its effect. One drives mile after mile through plantations of cloves, their leaves lucent in the evening light. Then there are huge coconut groves; and scattered plantings of almost every other tree yielding spice or fruit or stimulant that the tropics can show. Tea; cocoa; oil-palms, with stems so slender that their fruit must be picked by young boys; dark spreading mango-trees; mangosteens; oranges, lemons and limes; cinnamon; and many another. I was half-sorry, half-relieved to find that the celebrated durians were not in season.

They are the West Indian fruits whose smell is so nauseating that a single one makes a room almost insupportable; but yet are said to be the most delicious eating. Alfred Russel Wallace, in his *Malay Archipelago*, had inflamed me with a desire to overcome olfactory repugnance and try one. Their consistence and flavour, he says, is indescribable; yet he essays to describe it. "A rich butter-like custard highly flavoured with almonds gives the best general idea of it, but intermingled with it come wafts of flavour that call to mind cream-cheese, onion-sauce, brown sherry, and other incongruities. Then there is a rich glutinous smoothness in the pulp which nothing else possesses. . . . It produces no nausea or other bad effect, and the more you eat of it the less you feel inclined to stop."

Here and there are large stone buildings, once lived in by prosperous Arab clove-growers. Now, however, with the decline of the industry and with the curious apathy that descended on most of the Zanzibar Arabs after the abolition of slavery, they are deserted by their owners, and turned over to the use of an overseer. The effect is a melancholy one; an era has passed, a phase of the eternal social organism has decayed.

Poor Zanzibar has been hard hit these last years. All of the world's cloves, and almost all of its vanilla flavouring (manufactured out of clove oil), used to come from this one small island. But now other countries are attacking her monopoly of clove-growing, and the chemist is making synthetic vanillin. There is, however, one bright spot on the horizon. The natives of certain of the smaller East Indian islands have started to smoke large cigarettes made partly of tobacco and partly of powdered cloves. The

mixture sounds a powerful one, and I do not think that
the authorities at Zanzibar are smoking any of this brand
themselves; but they hope very much that the vice (I think
it deserves that title) will spread.

On board the German boat, bound for Tanga, Sept. 9th.
What other memories of Zanzibar are there to record before I return to the continent? First a visit to the Museum
under the guidance of its curator and almost its creator,
the veteran Dr. Spurrier. Quite apart from his long service in Zanzibar and his interest in the country's history
and products, he deserves commemoration as a link with
the past: his father was born two years before the outbreak of the French Revolution!

I liked the Museum. I liked too the style of the ticket-
ing and description of the exhibits. An enthusiastic eth-
nologist had put down various native beliefs as if they
were statements of accepted fact. Thus for instance:
"Leaves, flowers and fruit of the so-and-so tree. Under this
tree the Resurrection will take place. Used for soap." *Will
take place* is good.

Perhaps the most interesting single exhibit was an object
used up Somaliland way in certain religious ceremonies.
It is a typical trident of Neptune; it is used only by a small
community of sea-coast natives; and only in ceremonies
concerning the sea. One would like very much to know
how this isolated bit of ancient Greece came to survive in
tropical Africa.

Then there was a visit to a native school, where a native
medical assistant gave a short talk on hookworm, spoke of
the best preventive measures against it, and demonstrated
living hookworms and their eggs to the children through

the microscope. As a result of such education, and a strong propaganda in favour of building latrines with cement floors, Zanzibar hopes to rid itself in a few years of most of the burden of constant debility caused by this blood-sucking internal parasite. At night there was the crying of the bush-babies—the little lemurs that live in the trees; and in the early morning a bathe in the Indian Ocean, with the striped zebra-crabs scuttling in and out of the rocks; there were the outrigger canoes, used by the fishermen hereabouts and all along a big strip of the East African coast, but nowhere else in the continent. They seem to have come, like half the population of Madagascar, from Malaya or Polynesia, a marvellous early thrust of the far-eastern world to westward.

There was a reception by the Sultan, a dignified man with charming manners, at which we sat round the wall and drank coffee and sherbet in the intervals of polite talk. There was the Bazaar, where one found it almost impossible to believe that this was Africa and not the Near East. There was a stroll through one of the native quarters, rewarded by the unpleasing but interesting sight of a family in which several of the children were albinos, with blotchy pink skin and pale blinking eyes. There was a native fisherman all but naked on the shore, with the true athlete's figure—magnificent shoulders above fine-built waist; watching him I asked myself a question that was to recur throughout my African months—why does a good physique look better when the skin over the muscles is black than when it is white? There is some mixture of animal glory and bronzed statuary grandeur in the strong black body besides which the white, however powerful his muscles, however well-proportioned his limbs, seems bleached and artificial, his nudity unnatural.

Physical geography is in some ways the pleasantest of the sciences. It is so concrete. This morning I read Stockley's pamphlet on the geology of Zanzibar and Pemba, the two islands which make up the effective Sultanate of Zanzibar. One would imagine that these two islands, both about the same size and shape, both lying at about the same distance off the coast, were similar also in their origin and geological structure. On the contrary, they are entirely different. When I crossed to Zanzibar on Saturday, the sea-bottom was never a hundred feet below me. To-night we pass through the Pemba channel; one cannot anywhere sail from Pemba to the mainland without passing over a depth of eight hundred feet or more. Zanzibar is of quite recent rocks; the bulk of Pemba is made of much older strata. Zanzibar is geographically a bit of the coral formation which here fringes the mainland: slight subsidence and the scouring of currents have given origin to the shallow channel by which it is now isolated. But for the formation of Pemba we must look to the same forces which have produced the Red Sea and the great Rift Valleys of Africa. There has been prodigious faulting: rocks originally continuous have been fractured along two parallel lines and the centre bit forced down (or the two sides forced up) to make a long, narrow, steep-sided trough. Pemba channel is such a trough: both its mainland and its island coasts sink almost sheer till they reach its nearly level bottom; and the same happens where the eastern coast of the island fronts the Indian Ocean.

The separation of Zanzibar from the mainland is geologically very recent—some time during the ice-age, almost certainly well under half a million years ago; Pemba was rifted off in the Miocene, at least ten million years ago. This difference in time of insulation is reflected in their animal inhabitants. More kinds of mainland animals are absent from Pemba than from Zanzibar. But of the animals which do exist on Pemba, many more have been modified into distinctive species or sub-species than is the case on Zanzibar. Evolution is a secular process; it takes time, and time on the geological scale: and on Pemba animals have been isolated from crossing with their continental congeners for at least twenty times as long as on Zanzibar. An intensive survey of the mammals, birds, snakes, lizards, butterflies and flowering plants of the two islands in comparison with those of the neighbouring mainland would be an exciting piece of scientific research. Any wealthy friend of natural history could not find a better object than the financing of an expedition of this kind, for there can be very few other regions where two neighbouring bits of country have been isolated for known but different lengths of time; the results should really throw light on one of the most interesting problems of biology—the rate at which new species evolve.

Chapter IV

RESEARCH: THE AMANI INSTITUTE

Amani, Sept. 10*th*. Since my last entry, there has been a crowded twenty-four hours. Entering Tanga harbour, the sight of blue distant hills was a reminder that here I was to leave the sea and the palms and heat of the coastal strip for the continental interior.

And now the tropical coast is a thing of the past; and so is the German liner, so spick-and-span, with bugle-calls for meals and smart stewards—but with no possibility of obtaining bath or breakfast at any but the fixed and punctual hour; and Tanga, hot little commercial port.

After a glimpse of the town and a brief inspection of the Government Town School, away we sped in a box-body car, myself, my companion Mason of the Tanganyika Education Department, and all our baggage, driven by an efficient young German. The car, of course, was American. It is a regrettable fact that even the so-called Colonial Models of British make will not stand up to African conditions like the American cars. This journey in an English car would have necessitated constant gear-changing, even in a Morris Isis; we had to change down no oftener than in a British car on British roads, though we encountered mud-holes and sand-draws and the most erratic and often violent gradients.

After leaving the coastal strip we traversed dry country,

with sisal and kapok plantations; and then entered the foot-hills of the Usambara mountains, a lovely broken landscape.

Confused shouting, singing, and drum-beating from a native village attracted us; we walked up and found a native wedding in progress. The couple had been married at a neighbouring mission church, and the bride had just gone off to her future home, heralded by the customary gun-shot. But the festivities were in full swing, centred round some professional entertainers. A couple of negroes were sitting on the ground, each beating a little drum and singing. And there were two dancers. The chief dancer was an amusing figure. He wore wisps of Colobus monkey fur on arms and legs, and to his trousers were attached bells, jingling to his movements like the bells of Morris-dancers at home. The old felt hat he had on his head would perhaps have taken off from his appearance, had it not been overshadowed by three huge ostrich feathers ar-ranged in Prince of Wales style. In his mouth he held a whistle, on which, as the spirit moved him, he blew pierc-ing blasts. An amusing creature, he minced, capered and grimaced, and eventually squatted right at my feet, look-ing up with a pleasant impudence, head tilted on one side, and an assumed solemnity of grimace over a suppressed grin—the expression one would imagine in a mediæval jester. When the time came to take up a collection, he pranced round the circle, stretching his neck forward, tak-ing his money with protruding lips, and pouching it in his cheek.

The women guests were very gay in handsome cotton prints, yellow and scarlet, black and white, light and dark blue. There is no doubt that these imported fabrics give the African new possibilities of beauty. It was a cheerful scene; one of the traits I like most at first contact with the Africans is their obvious capacity for enjoying life.

Later we stopped at a little station of the Universities' Mission to Central Africa, and were given tea by its pleasant and kindly staff. This area of East Africa is more or less reserved to the U.M.C.A., while others are under the sway of the Church Missionary Society, or of the Church of Scotland Mission, and so on. This delimitation of areas doubtless has its good points in preventing squabbles and what without irreverence may be called interdenominational armaments competition; but it is curious to reflect that, in proportion as missions are having an influence on the growth of a new native culture, they are imposing a bias to ritualism and catholicism in one whole region, to straightforward "C. of E." in another, and to puritanism, nonconformist protestantism, or fundamentalism in still others.

The hills get larger, with more forest on their slopes. The road gets muddier. We follow a stream in a ravine up to an old sawmill. And then comes the formidable climb to Amani itself. The road zigzags 2000 feet up the steep face of the mountain, a narrow track, with eleven hairpin bends. A good deal of work has recently been done on it; and the bends can now be negotiated in one, whereas in old days you had to back before you could get round, a quite terrifying experience in wet weather. But what it was like in its original narrow state, and after years of neglect during and after the War, I hate to imagine. I was told that when the East African Parliamentary Commission of 1924 visited Amani, they were told that it might be safer to walk up; that, inspired by Major Church, they insisted on being driven; but that long before they were up, even he was wishing he hadn't.

Up, up, up, the forest growing richer and wilder all the way—till finally we come to green meadows, plots under cultivation, cattle pasturing, Indians sawing tree-trunks, African labourers walking home (two thousand feet down every night, two thousand feet up again every morning), and at last the well-built stone house of the Director—and the view.

Amani, 6 a.m., Sept. 11*th.* This is assuredly a lovely place. I woke to an orange light in the sky, and leapt out of bed to see the dawn. Two palms stand just before my window, silhouetted black against the east. Ten miles away, a Sacred Mountain, where animal sacrifices are still performed as by the ancient Hebrews, on a sacrificial stone near the summit. But now the summit is veiled in misty clouds, drifting slowly northwards. Over and through the clouds, orange light: between the sacred mountain and us, a deep valley with buttress upon buttress of forested mountain, in different shades of green and indigo, as light and distance takes them. A bulbul is singing his curiously elementary but sweet-toned song in the near trees, and another answers farther off; more accomplished but softer songsters make an accompaniment, with a sub-accompaniment, if I may use the word, of the universal insects, cicadas and grasshoppers and the like. Now and again a hornbill interrupts with grotesque note and still more grotesque shape against the sky. But the forest on the hills that it covers—how beautiful!

We walked out yesterday in the last of the daylight, and in two minutes were in a road tunnelling through the primeval forest. The trees run a hundred to two hundred

Professional Entertainers at a Native Wedding in the Foothills of the Usambara Mountains, Tanganyika. One of the Drummers is Sitting Astride His Drum. The Cotton Prints of the Women and Children Are Very Rich.

Natives Making Molasses; between Kikori and Kondoa, Central Tanganyika. The Juice is Squeezed Out of the Sugar-cane by Means of a Wooden Mill, and Then Evaporated in Large Earthenware Pots Over These Earth Ovens.

feet high—mostly about a hundred and fifty. Many of the stems gleam white in a way curiously characteristic of Africa as against other continents. No two trees that you see seem to be the same kind.

And everywhere the marvel of the epiphytes. Huge lianas up to an inch thick are festooned upon the trees like gigantic bell-ropes, and take the eye right up sixty, eighty, and a hunded feet before they reach any support. One has the impulse to pull the rope in expectation of some simian flunkey answering from the unknown upper storeys.

Then there are the birds'-nest ferns which catch debris within their thick crown of leaves; there it turns slowly to humus, so that they manufacture their own soil, make their own beds. Here is a network of fig-stems interlacing over the trunk of a great tree. One day the fig will be a great tree itself. It began life as an epiphyte, from seed dropped by a bird in some lucky crevice of bark up near the light. Then it sent down thin ropes of roots that felt their way down the supporting tree's trunk to the ground. Now they are growing large, anastomosing, intertwining. Finally they will make a complete cylinder and will choke the host within; it will die, and be replaced by fig. In the West Indies they call them Scotch Attorneys: the old sugar-planters often left their estates in the hands of "attorneys"—business managers; and as often as not the estates ended up in the hands of the attorney, especially, one gathers, if he hailed from North Britain.

Then there are trunks plastered with huge leaves of arum-like creepers—but these were all introduced by the Germans from South America before the War. Here, however, is a home product and a very remarkable one—the only kind of cactus that is indigenous to Africa, and a cactus that grows as an epiphyte high above the ground. The place of ordinary cactuses in Africa is taken by the spurges; it is they that in the dry country have grown prickly and taken on the form of candelabra.

There is not a great deal of true equatorial rain-forest in East Africa: for its proper African development you must go to the Congo basin. But here, on the east side of these low mountains exposed to the moisture-laden winds from the sea, is a perfect sample.

After dark, in the train, Sept. 11th. Amani was founded as a biological research station by the Germans. It went nearly derelict after the War, and would have slid altogether back and been engulfed by the jungle again if it had not been for the energy and devotion of one man. Mr. Rogers, the present Superintendent, a man from Kew, was for three years the only white man there. With a small staff of natives, he kept the plantations and plots going and held the wild greenery at bay. Mr. Ormsby-Gore, on his East African trip, found him there still solus, and referred to him in his report as the Uncrowned King of Amani.

It was Mr. Ormsby-Gore and Major Church who insisted that the place should be re-established as a research institution; and now it is the centre for fundamental research in agricultural problems (which include most things from soil science to the biology of locusts, from fungus diseases to plant heredity) for the four East African territories.

The chief effort of the Germans lay in making small plantations of every conceivable tropical plant of any utility, up and down the slopes of the mountain, on which of course every possible variety of temperature and moisture could be found. This our authorities regard as more spectacular than useful; and though they intend to keep up these plantations as an exhibit, they are concentrating more upon research. In this field it is surprising how small was the scale on which the German laboratory was planned. We have more than doubled the research accommodation.

Under Dr. Nowell as Director, the Station is now embarking upon its definitive career. It is lucky he is an all-round man. They have had to construct their own hydro-electric plant; they make all their own furniture and laboratory fittings, as being cheaper, quicker and more satisfactory than getting it done through the Public Works Department; they are so isolated that they must have their own motor workshop; they print their own labels, and have even a native trained in bookbinding to bind their scientific periodicals. And of course they have their own farm.

The great drawback of Amani is its isolation. It is no light journey to undertake from any other centre of research or administration. The mere distance is bad enough; but the approach through the foot-hills can be impassable in wet weather. Visits and return visits between members of its staff and the staff of other institutions will have to be organized, and a regular liaison system carefully worked out if it is to achieve its maximum usefulness.

It is indeed pretty certain that if the Germans had not chosen Amani as their site, we should not have fixed our research station there; after the War the country was much more opened up, and a wider choice was possible. On the other hand, it is quite possible that if the old German station had not been in existence, we should have done nothing whatever towards establishing an inter-territorial research laboratory. And so, since a live dog is better than a non-existent lion, and a laboratory in an inconvenient situation is a good deal better than no laboratory at all, we can be reasonably content. In passing, since the Germans did accomplish such notable pioneer work, it would seem a gracious policy, as well as one of practical value, to invite a German worker to a place on the research staff.

Meanwhile a good deal of hasty criticism has been passed on Amani by public opinion in East Africa. "What has Amani done for African agriculture?" is the sort of question you hear asked; and unofficial members of the Legislative Councils demand that its subvention shall be cut down or discontinued altogether.

The answer to such criticism is that no one who was not either foolish or uninformed would expect Amani to have done a great deal for the practice of African agriculture in the very few years since it was re-established under British control. In the first place, the necessary new laboratories have only been finished this year, and the full complement of staff has only just been made up. In the second place, how can anyone expect pure scientific research to have its repercussions in practice in a year or so? The effect of scientific research of a fundamental nature is and must be slow but cumulative. If anyone wants proof of this, let him study the history of the Dutch Research Station at Buitenzorg, in Java, and the progressively expanding benefits which it has conferred upon the prosperity of the tropical possessions of Holland. (An admirable account of some aspects of this work of the Dutch, by the way, is to be found in Mr. Ormsby-Gore's report on his visit to Malaya and the East Indies.) Amani is at the present moment just embarking upon its full career. Important work has already been begun on virus diseases of plants; on a soil survey of East Africa conducted according to the latest principles (which we owe primarily to Russian scientists); a study of the migration of insects, which it is hoped may help in the understanding of locust visitations; the breeding of varieties of plants, disease-resistant and suitable to local conditions; and other subjects. But in the nature of things the work is only just beginning. If, five years from now, it has not begun to justify its existence, it will then be time for criticism and overhaul.

It was with regret that I left Amani's strange combination of cool air and tropical luxuriance. After once sticking in the mud and once puncturing a tyre, we caught the train by minutes, and are now puffing inland, with the Usambaras dark against the moonlit sky on our right, and a fountain of wood-sparks from our funnel, towards Moshi and the largest mountain in the western part of the Old World.

Chapter V

MOSHI: A GOVERNMENT SCHOOL

Moshi. We are staying here with the Headmaster of the Government School and his young wife, fresh out from England. The school is at Old Moshi, on the site of the old German post on the lower slopes of Kilimanjaro. The coming of the railway has taken the business and traffic of the place to New Moshi, a rather unpleasant tin town, recalling the less finished parts of the American Far West, old German post on the lower slopes of Kilimanjaro. The snow cone of Kibo (as the higher of Kilimanjaro's two craters is called) hangs miraculously over us; fifty miles to westward is the lovely shape of Meru, almost as high as Mont Blanc, but never snow-covered and needing the addition of a Ben Nevis to overtop Kilimanjaro. At sunset, when the Masai steppe beyond is plum colour, and the fine cone of Meru deep violet against the orange sky, the view is unforgettable.

Moshi School is typical of the larger Government schools of the Territory. It is a boarding-school for the whole of the Province; most of the couple of hundred boys are between 10 or 11 and 18. They are divided into five "Tribes," corresponding to Houses in an English public school, with big boys as prefects. Each Tribe comprises dormitories, kitchen, dining-room, and sitting-room. These are all of an African simplicity. The dormitories are oblong sleeping huts, with eight or ten iron bedsteads with a strip of canvas for mattress. (Some visiting settlers complained that this was pampering the native.) The dining-room is a large thatched shelter without walls, where the boys squat about in groups on the floor (there are no tables or chairs) and eat their dinners of maize meal or cooked bananas. Even College at Winchester five hundred years ago, with its wooden platters and the rest, cannot have been so primitive.

But all is clean and neat. The boys are cooked for, but themselves tidy their huts, fetch firewood, and wash their own clothes. They wear shorts and a white jumper with the giraffe, emblem of Tanganyika, on the pocket. They have a cheerful look, and hold themselves better than the average native child. This is because of the daily drill given in all Government schools. It is a delightful sight to see the boys exercising under their instructor, an ex-sergeant-major of twenty-one years' service with the King's African Rifles, and as typical a sergeant-major, in spite of his black skin, as you could wish to find. They are really very keen, and march with an almost exaggerated swing. Out of hours you may often see boys amusing themselves by drilling each other: all the words of command are in English, and the spectacle has its funny side. The school itself is a good but ugly stone building. There the boys learn the three R's, geography, and a little history, and science, hygiene, handwork, and agriculture. They have big school gardens where they must put in a definite amount of work. In addition there are workshops in which the apprentices, making up the technical side of the school, learn carpentry, metal-work, tailoring, or mason-work.

Each school "Tribe" may comprise only boys from a

single real tribe; or may consist of contingents from a number of tribes which are smaller or less partial to education. For instance, though they cater for most of the Masai area, there is only one boy of this tribe in the school—the Masai have remained till now almost untouched either by Missions, or Government, or Western Commercialism. Change may be on its way, however. An important Masai elder recently visited the school, admired the building, and asked how much it cost. On being told ten thousand pounds, he answered, "Is it for sale? Because if so I'd like to buy it and give it to my son." And he could have bought it, too, as he owned cattle worth many times that amount.

In the afternoon I went for a stroll by myself. The huge flanks of the mountain are scored with valleys, steep-sided and green, like Devonshire coombes magnified about three diameters. The more fertile slopes are covered with the banana-groves and coffee-plantations of the local natives, the Chagga. You see no villages, as they build their huts singly in their own holdings.

Turning off the road, I made along a native path. This was the first time I had walked alone in the African countryside. Meeting groups of black men along the path, coming upon a neatly-thatched beehive hut in the midst of monstrous-leaved bananas, with black life in full swing, and an uncomprehended language sounding in my ears, I found myself subjected to a curious feeling, not of fear but a mixture of shyness and nervousness, quite irrational. After a few days, familiarity banished it. I wonder whether others have the same experience the first time they step right out of their own civilization and century?

As I came homewards, at every turn of the road I met

Chagga women walking slowly uphill with enormous bundles of grass on their heads. On enquiry, I found out that this was to feed their cattle. Instead of Mahomet going to the mountain, the mountain (or rather the plain!) is brought to Mahomet. The cows are kept in dark huts, and never let out. Here on the mountain flanks the country-side, where it is not intensely cultivated, is all woodland and there is no pasture. So every morning the women walk down to the plains, cut enough grass for the cattle, and carry it home again. Those who live at the lower levels may only have to walk ten or twelve miles; but others cover twenty or more every day.

Apparently the habit of keeping the stock in huts (where, by the way, their hoofs grow long and claw-like for lack of walking), and of fetching their food instead of driving them down to pasture, was due originally to fear of Masai cattle-raiders. It persists, partly no doubt just because it is the custom, but also, I understand, because the Chagga are afraid that their beasts would catch certain diseases on the plains. That it is not solely stupid conservatism is shown by the fact that on the opposite side of the mountain, where these diseases are not feared, the custom has been given up.

Next day I learned many things in talk with Dr. Gutmann, the German missionary and anthropologist. Over the coffee and brown rolls and strawberries (or something like them) served by his wife, a quiet smiling German Hausfrau of the old type, in his parlour, and again at talk in his book-lined study, we might have been in a country Pfarrenhaus near Heidelberg before the War. Then a look out of window showed the enormous African plain with ranges of hills disappearing hull-down over the horizon.

Of Gutmann himself I wrote in my notes at the time, "He looks like a cross between Shakspere and a bearded Saint, lit with an intellectual gleam." He first came to Kilimanjaro twenty-eight years ago, and has been here ever since save for the five years after the War when we refused all Germans entry into Tanganyika.

It is interesting and reassuring to find that after all this experience he still believes that the African continent can be won as an ally for the ideas of Western civilization, and that the African can benefit thereby. But he is disquieted over many things.

He thinks our censorship of films hopelessly inadequate. Most natives love travelling; and young men from his district often go off to enjoy themselves in Mombasa or Tanga, the best part of two hundred miles on foot, as we might go off to Brighton for a week-end. There they see the most lurid films, and when they come back often put their new illumination into practice. Highway robberies and murders have notably increased in the last few years.

Afterwards we inspected the native girls' school which the Mission has started at the request of the Government. Gutmann is a little afraid of the influence of schooling on girls. At the moment, it appears, there is a healthy balance between the initiative of the men, who, finding that coffee-growing pays, are anxious to grow more and more coffee, and the conservatism of the women, who are traditionally responsible for food-supplies, and insist tenaciously on keeping enough land under bananas to provide for the family even if the coffee failed. Gutmann seems to fear that education may make them less willing to do the work of the banana plantations, and more prone to listen to the men's arguments, with the consequent danger of

54

the Chagga coming to rely wholly on their one commercial crop, and then being helpless if over-production causes coffee to slump (as is only too possible in our modern world with its fantastic lack of economic regulation).

This is perhaps the place to say a few words about coffee-growing by natives. There is in Kenya, of course, the strongest opposition to any such competition of the black man with the white settler; and although I imagine that natives could not be prevented from growing coffee if they really wished, the official discouragement of the practice has been great enough to ensure that none of them do so.

The chief grounds of objection put forward against coffee-growing by natives are as follows: First, natives would not look after their plantations properly, and therefore weeds and especially insect pests would multiply there and constitute a danger to the whole industry. Secondly, the quality of their coffee would be poorer and so would give a bad name on the world-market to all East African coffee. Thirdly, if natives grew and sold coffee, this would constitute a serious temptation to native pickers on white estates to steal some of the berries and dispose of them through native growers.

There are, of course, two kinds of coffee, *robusta* and *arabica*, the latter more difficult to grow but fetching considerably higher prices. The white coffee-plantations are almost all *arabica*; and the above objections are made chiefly to the growing of this variety by natives. In addition, by way of belittling the existing native coffee industry in Tanganyika, it is frequently asserted (it was so asserted to me by a prominent man in Kenya) that the native *arabica* coffee industry would never have come into existence there if the already developed German plantation with *arabica* trees in bearing had not been made over to natives after the War.

After what I had seen with my own eyes near Moshi, I found it difficult to believe many of these statements when I heard them made in Kenya, and wrote for information to Dar-es-Salaam. And the facts provided me by the Government authorities there dispose altogether of most of the allegations. The matter is so important, involving as it does the whole question of native versus white production, and the prejudice and misrepresentation engendered by the clashing of economic interests between races, that it must be discussed.

The last point, that the growing of coffee by natives in Tanganyika, and notably the growing of *arabica* coffee, which is the chief crop in the Kilimanjaro district, was only made possible by the natives being given ex-enemy plantations, is simply not a fact. Natives began growing coffee some time before 1913. In 1921, before any ex-German plantations had been handed over, there were 125,-000 native-owned coffee-trees on the slopes of Kilimanjaro. And the total ex-enemy coffee-bearing land later handed over to the natives accounted for about six per cent. of the native coffee crop in this area in 1926.

The most serious allegation is that cultivation by natives is so much less efficient than cultivation by whites that it encourages the spread of weeds and pests. To investigate this charge the Government called in their expert in agricultural entomology. As the result of his inspection he stated that in the Kilimanjaro area the condition of the native plantations was very high, whereas that of the white settlers' plantations was definitely inferior to the natives'! In the same way, the actual prices obtained for native *arabica* coffee give the lie to the second allegation. In general they equal those given for coffee from white plantations, and in some cases have exceeded them.

There remains the question of stealing. Small pilfering may be occasionally practised, but so long as white and native plantations remain in different areas it can assuredly not be on a large scale. Transporting large quantities of coffee is not simple: a ton of coffee, be it remembered, is equivalent to about forty full head-loads, so that a reasonable amount of watchfulness should prevent any serious loss.

Petitions have been addressed by white settlers in Tanganyika to the Governor asking that native coffee-growing shall be prohibited. As he pointed out in reply (in 1926), he had no power to prohibit natives growing any crop they liked on their own lands, and in any case felt it was right to encourage the prosperity of the colony by encouraging native production. There were in 1929, by the way, over 12,000 native coffee-growers on Kilimanjaro, and about 200 white planters. The number of native planters was less than 600 in 1922, 8000 in 1926; and the number of coffee-trees grown by them has risen from 180,000 in 1922 to 2,500,000 in 1929. In 1923 there was organized the Kilimanjaro Native Planters Association, which includes over ninety per cent. of the native growers in the region, and helps production by co-operative storage and marketing, and by disseminating advice. Another province of Tanganyika, Bukoba, where *robusta* is chiefly grown, in 1925 accounted for more than one-quarter of the total weight and nearly one-quarter of the total value of coffee exported from Tanganyika, Kenya and Uganda together.

The recent Report of the Agricultural Commission in Kenya, while recognizing that regulations against coffee-growing by natives cannot be legally or morally upheld, publicly repeats all the allegations as to pests, poor quality of crop, and theft, and ends up by recommending that no one should be allowed to grow coffee unless he pays a minimum licence fee of £10 annually. This of course would automatically rule out the growing of coffee by the vast majority of natives—an ingenious but glaring example of racial discrimination. But enough of racial friction and statistics. It was at any rate agreeable to be in a region where the evidences of native initiative and prosperity were so high as on the slopes of the Great Mountain.

Moshi was one of the few places in East Africa where I was able to show to native school-children three educational films with which the Empire Marketing Board, interested to know more about the value of the cinema for educational and propaganda purposes, had provided me. These had been deliberately chosen to represent three levels of difficulty of comprehension by the natives. The first was entitled "Cotton-Growing in Nigeria." This represented people like themselves, engaged in familiar occupations. The second, "Fathoms Deep Beneath the Sea," was a picture of marine animals taken at the Plymouth Aquarium. It was straightforward and comprehensible in that it dealt with the ordinary activities of animal life, but difficult inasmuch as many of the animals shown were of types quite different from anything familiar to a landsman (sea-anemone, octopus, etc.). The third was the well-known film "The Life of a Plant," which represents the life-cycle of a nasturtium speeded up several thousand times. In this, not only were many unfamiliar details of botanical structure and process introduced (anthers, pollination, etc.), but technical devices were employed to produce wholly unfamiliar kinds of results. For one thing, microscopic pictures were used to show structures far below naked-eye vision; and, still more radical, the speeding-up device introduced a tempo whose meaning could only be appreciated by an intelligent and novel use of the imagination.

In the morning, I gave a short talk to the boys on the speeded-up films. As the only cinema was at New Moshi, the boys were paraded at six o'clock, and marched down the five miles to town to the music of the school band. All except a few, however, had lorries to take them home again. I arranged with the headmaster to have the boys write essays on what they had seen, and the sample of these which were sent on to me I shall always cherish. The spirit was willing, but the English was weak; and the impressions of the march were clearly as vivid as those of the cinema. I cannot forbear from giving some extracts:—

Stanislaus (!) on the fertilization of flowers:

"And then how flowers can bear. First of all the bee take a little medicine in a masculine flower on his feet and put in a woman flower and it can bear the seeds."

Another boy (Standard V.) on the same subject:

"One of it were showed the flowers from the beginning up the top and how the flowers married."

M. Juma, Nyangarika Mbagha, deserves to be quoted in full, even though he does give so much less space to the cinema than to the other incidents of the day:

"On the 13th of September, when we were reading in our classes, our Headmaster came with one European stranger who has been sent by the Government to see our school. The Headmaster said to us that, "This stranger wants to talk a bit with the standard VI., V. and the Standard IV. in our class room." Then we went out to one room and set down. The stranger said [not in these precise words. J. S. H.] "Look at here my boys! There is a cinema to-day which I will show in New Moshi place, and this cinema is of many wonderful things, etc."

"Therefore when 4 o'clock was over, we were ordered by our Sgt: Major to stand at our parade ground in order to make practice of drill. By and by our band boys stood towards us, and we began march from here through to New Moshi with our march band. Having arrived at New Moshi the people of there looked us with much wonder for our best approach march.

"Having arrived in the cinema's house, we were quiet.

"The first cinema which was shown to us was the cotton which is obtained in the part of Africa called Nigeria, and how the people of Nigeria pick up the cotton. And how they separate the cotton seeds from the cotton by the way of ginning machines. And how they weave clothes.

"The second one was the different kinds of fishes and animals which are living in the water, and how these fishes and animals are caught by the fishermen in the sea.

"The last one, namely the third one was the flowers which are changed male into female by the way of bee; and how the bee make honey by taking the flowers. Oh! I was happily pleased to be shown these pictures.

"At last good night was said. Then Mr: P. J. Chandor said, 'three cheers for our provesor, Heep, Heep Hurrah.'"

Here is an extract from Maruma's essay:

"But the one which was suitable to me, was the picture of how the people of Nigeria grow cotton.

A GOVERNMENT SCHOOL

"We found that the people of Nigeria are now civilized as I saw the women picking the cotton from the pods and put in the sacks, and how they gin it by machines called gins. Also how they tie in bales, and how they make clothing. All these were shown to us. And we were pleased with them.

"After we had been shown the above mentioned, we were stated that nobody is allowed to go in disorder; therefore then Sergeant redressed the boys and return us back to Old Moshi. But as we were a good number of boys, we hesitated the town's people as we had drums and fluits.

"We ourselves passed without any hesitation."

I like the conscious pride of the last sentence.

And here is Mghoja's effort: "On the 13th September there came Professor from England who had a cinema show to us. Therefore we have started in our ground march with drums and music. At five o'clock all the headmasters, teachers and even cookers were followed behind of us, on account of good singings good drums and very nice clothes of boys were washed well. Then many motor cars, round us about. So we reached house cinema. There we have been given good chairs to sit on them. But the first picture is about plants and flower. Ah! I wonder for these wise English people they can draw a picture plants, how it grows, how we plant, how we can get good flowers, and how the bees go into flowers to take something from flower to flower. I was pleased indeed when I saw those bees do so. It is wonderful. Second thing about the water on the ocean how getting rain and all the kinds of fishes. Therefore I saw one fish about eight feet [*i.e.* Octopus. J. S. H.]. Ah! I wonder of it.

"This it gives me much please to give many thank to these wise English people for their good knowledge."

And finally the very flattering conclusion of another boy: "We praise this Professor that God gives him another cinema and come to Africa to show us again and we beg to God that go reaching him up to England and he will come to Africa again."

These extracts must not be judged at their face value. Most of the boys had only done English for a year or so, and were not at all at home in the language. The headmaster wrote to me that he was quite surprised at the interest and comprehension many of the boys showed; and felt, as I did, that the cinema could be a most important instrument for awaking the young African mind.

Chapter VI

KILIMANJARO

Sept. 12th. In the clear exhilarating morning, above the dry plains and the scrub, rises Kilimanjaro, white and faint in the far sky. It is beautiful, but at first a little disappointing with its blunt top. At this distance (it is over fifty miles away) one cannot grasp its size; lacking that majesty, it has terribly the air of a pudding with white icing, thrown on very slapdash, dribbling over its sides. But as we draw in to Moshi, realization begins, though even here our eyes deceive us; we lack the right scale to measure the mountain until our feet and long hours of climbing have taught it to us. Each of the dribbles of icing turns out to be a glacier, forced down by pressure from a huge snowfield above. That darker belt round its sides must be the forest zone; and a rapid calculation shows that this must extend for over four thousand feet of vertical height. You could stow Ben Nevis away between the forest limits, starting above the enormous cultivated slopes below; and then pile two more Ben Nevises above and yet not have reached the top. It is not beautiful as Fujiyama is beautiful, or Vesuvius before the last great eruption truncated its pure cone obliquely; but in addition to its wonder of equatorial snow, it is very majestic and has real grandeur.

How lucky we are to live in a period of the earth's history when its scenery is interesting! The facts of geology show that through perhaps three-quarters of geological time the lands have lain at a low level, planed down by the forces of denudation into dull undulations with slow meandering streams. Only at long intervals has come rejuvenation. Geophysical forces which we do not fully understand have come into play. They have raised the continents, crumpled up their edges to build enormous mountain-chains, released volcanic forces. Climate is sharpened, glaciers and ice-caps form; from the new heights of land, water pours off with new violence, to excavate gorges and to carve deep and lovely valleys in the ancient plains. The countenance of our planet, which over vast ages had been expressionless, almost featureless, is suddenly young again, mobile, exciting. Earth has had her face lifted.

We live just after one of these rejuvenating revolutions. Through this accident we are privileged to possess our Alps and Rockies, our Himalayas and Andes; to this we owe our rift valleys, our canyons, our mighty volcanoes—all new, not yet worn down to stumps and cores, Etna and Aconcagua, Orizaba and Kilimanjaro; it is this we have to thank for the scooping of ice that formed the fjords and dug down to make a land of mountains out of an old plain, as in Scotland; and the moraine-damming of valleys that made us our biggest and our loveliest lakes —Como and Superior, Geneva and Windermere. Our descendants a million generations hence will be much to be pitied. I wonder if they will cherish traditions of our Golden Age, of the pristine beauty when man's world was young?

Sept. 13*th*. We are staying at Old Moshi, five miles up the volcano's slope, a thousand feet above New Moshi and the railway in the plain. Here the mountain rises over us, an unreal apparition above the fertile valleys rich with palms and banana groves. Perhaps it is most wonderful at night. You sit out on the verandah in the scented air, seeing the lights of the town below and of the cars on the road from Arusha; you turn your head, and there the mountain hangs in the tropical night, the snows shining as if with their own light. Every time it comes with a shock, unexpected, infinitely improbable in such a place.

To-day we had the first direct taste of its size, when we went to pay a visit to Dr. Gutmann. The mission is another thousand feet above Old Moshi: and the forest zone, that to us yesterday seemed to begin so soon above the plain, is not reached till you have climbed fifteen hundred feet more. All this country (all belched out of the volcano) slopes quite gradually, and is dissected into ridges and deep valleys, sometimes so steep that they cannot be cultivated. But all the available land is rich with crops. Little beehive huts sit shaded in banana groves, there is coffee, there is maize; it is a land of plenty, girdling the base of the great hill, up to where the rain-forest allows.

Sept. 15th. And now we have had our complete demonstration of Kilimanjaro's bulk. Yesterday soon after sunrise our host took us in his car up the five miles (and two thousand five hundred vertical feet) that separated us from the base of the forest. The road, by the way, was made by the Chagga people themselves to facilitate the marketing of their coffee. The District Officer suggested the main line for them, and they did the rest themselves, gauging the gradients by eye. The various chiefs, meeting in conclave, agreed on co-operation and each turned out the men required for the section allotted to him. The result, in spite of the difficult hilly country, is an excellent road, with steep gradients in parts but perfectly motorable: an admirable example of what the African can do if he cares. There a guide and five porters awaited us, and we plunged into the forest track. It was still early, and the morning freshness was still on everything. We brushed through herbage wet with mist and dew, with flowers everywhere, and into the thick wood.

The mountain is more or less terraced—a long, gentle slope with occasional sharp pitches, then a bit of level or even a descent, then an up-slope again; and all in the dripping forest, with only the rarest of peeps through. It is very silent. An occasional hornbill gives his honking cry; there are sparse birds in the bushes; once we saw a blackish squirrel and once a monkey. Well up in the forest was a native beehive—a hollow log suspended to a tree, visited perhaps once a year by its owner to extract the honey.

In reality, the wood must be full of animals; but it is so vast, they so quiet and so nocturnal that you only know of their existence through their footprints; and of these there are abundance. At one spot I saw a strange sight— the great spoor of an elephant, like the imprint of a tray, pressed down into our muddy path, and within its outline the unmistakable pug of a leopard, and the bifid print of a buck's hoof as well; unfortunately it was far too dark to dream of photographing it. The tree-ferns here and there are lovely, and the tall bush begonias with creamy flowers, and the Cambridge-blue peas. And as for the balsams at ground level, they are magnificent—spurred and delicate-winged, of white, pink and crimson, and one of scarlet-orange with yellow spots. Here and there are the very un-lobelious green spikes, six or eight feet high, of mountain lobelias, and at one place we passed a patch of tree-heather.

Yet perhaps the most interesting sight in the forest was a work of man's, not of nature's—the leats or furrows which the Chagga tribe have made to bring water down to irrigate their crops.

These are troughs or ditches connecting the cultivated lands with the springs high up in the forest zone, often two or three hours' hard going from the highest villages. Some of them are over ten miles long. Where they run straight down the face of a gentle slope their construction is simple enough; and the erosion of the water soon eats them out into safe runnels, five or six feet deep. But often they must be run along the side of the hill, across a steep slope, and then they must be skilfully engineered and very carefully banked. Frequently the elephants trample down the banking, and the tribesmen, notified by the cessation of the flow, must make off into the forest to find and repair the damage.[1]

In certain quarters where it is the fashion to disparage the capacity of the African, it is often asserted that the Chagga and their Masai neighbours learned this hydraulic art from white men. This seems definitely not to be the case. Though documentary evidence is naturally lacking, there is proof of one big Masai furrow having been dug the best part of a century ago. Further, the distribution of the water to the crops is regulated by an elaborate and detailed customary law, administered by what can only be called a "Water Rights Association"; such an organisa-

[1] Much information on the subject is to be found in Mr. C. C. F. Dundas's book, *Kilimanjaro and its People*.

tion and such a body of elaborate custom obviously dates back for many decades, if not for centuries. Each individual cultivator has his share of water, both as to quantity and time, regulated with the greatest nicety; and Mr. Mitchell, the Commissioner for Native Affairs, tells me that he knows of no case of dispute between individuals which has not been settled without white intervention, through the Water Association or the local native court. Altogether, there seems little doubt that the irrigation system was developed by the local tribes without any aid from Europeans.

At length even the furrows are left behind. We continue (puffing and blowing, I confess, for after three weeks of shipboard and the hospitalities of two African capitals, I am not in the primest of training) up through the forest. Even here, however, the natives sometimes come on their own errands. Dr. Gutmann said that for certain kinds of cattle sickness, Chagga men would march right up to the snowline, over 16,000 feet, and bring down snow-water as a remedy. And later Mr. Swynnerton assured me that the natives used to go up above the forest zone to fetch a special long grass for thatching purposes. When there they lit fires and burned the woodland, so that the forest belt must have been shrinking gradually both from above and below, what with these burnings and the steady advance of cultivation upwards from the plain.

Finally the trees begin to break. There are clearings, with red-hot pokers growing in them, then bushes of a honey-scented white-blossomed heather, then an open swampy level (not unlike a marsh in the heather county of Surrey) with Lady's Mantle and aromatic marsh herbs; then a final scramble, and we were out on a vast expanse

CONTRASTS OF EAST AFRICAN SCENERY.
ABOVE, AT THE COAST. VIEW FROM MY WINDOW AT DAR-ES-
SALAAM. (*Photo. and copyright reserved by Professor H. Balfour,
F.R.S.*)
BELOW, IN THE UPLANDS. A STREAM IN THE KIKUYU RESERVE
NEAR NYERI, WITH WEAVER-BIRDS' NESTS SUSPENDED OVER THE
WATER.

THE INTERIOR OF THE CRATER OF KILIMANJARO.

IN THE CRATER ARE 4 OR 5 SNOW-MASSES, EACH SEVERAL HUNDRED YARDS LONG, WITH PRECIPITOUS SIDES. ONE OF THESE IS SEEN IN THE MIDDLE DISTANCE. (*Photo. by J. W. Stauffacker, Narok, Kenya Colony.*)

of tussocky grassland. The two peaks are both in sight, the snow-capped modern crater of Kibo to the west, and just in front of us Mawenzi, the jagged black remains of a much older vent; between them runs the interminable saddle, over which antelopes and even elephants will pass, though it is nearly as high as Mont Blanc.

All is different here. The most lovely immortelles spangle the grass, white and faint roseate and deep pink, and another yellowish sort; there are friezias, and a pink ground heather. The going is very hard over the coarse tussocks; and the grass is full of unpleasant ticks. At last we reach our destination—a hut built by an enterprising German before the war, and, though now windowless, at least well-roofed. The snows of Kibo seem no nearer than they did from Moshi—what a heartbreaking mountain in its sheer size. I am rather ashamed of feeling so puffed and exhausted; but the guide informs us that he reckons five hours good going for this 4500-foot climb, and we have only taken four.

Lunch, at which a little stone-chat comes to pick up crumbs, as friendly as a robin. After lunch, a sleep. Then up a little to see the view and the sunset.

At about 11,500 feet (nearly 8000 more to the top—what a thought!) we stop and sit. The huge expanse of coarse Alpine meadowland is all around us, and very impressive is its sharp delimitation against the dark forest margin. It is only invaded where there are valleys; up these there grow tongues of forest, far above the tree limit elsewhere. Below, far away, the plain, with the Usambara mountains dwindling along it, and here and there volcanoes rising out of its waste and expanse of scrub. The immortelles all about us are most beautiful. Birds are much more abundant than in the forest. In a patch of bushes near by I see my first sun-bird—exquisite creature, black with sheen and gloss all over, emerald sheen on the crown, blue-green on the wings, slender curved beak for probing flowers, fantastic forked ribbon-like tail. Finches and warbler-like creatures abound; and soaring over to inspect us came a pair of huge African ravens, bigger-beaked and broader-tailed than ours and with white nape.

On our way back we came on a gully full of tree-groundsels, those unreal-looking inhabitants of high African mountains.

The night is cold, with squalls of rain, and sleep is fitful. It is strange to wake and listen to the porters, over at the other corner of the hut, talking in a language which even my seasoned African companion cannot understand.

Up at dawn and off before eight. Close to the upper limit of the forest, there is a frightful crashing in the trees—an elephant. The porters make as if to throw down their loads and bolt; but luckily the great beast makes away from us. Lower down we see a tree with branches broken and bark all rubbed away where an elephant had been practising his tusks. This had not been done when we passed yesterday.

My companion drew my attention to the fact that he had seen no bamboos in the forest. Afterwards I found that this was one of the peculiarities of Kilimanjaro. Every other high mountain in Africa possesses a broad bamboo-zone, Kilimanjaro not. But why not? I respectfully leave the puzzle to the botanists.

We go down a third again as fast as we came up, and emerge from the wood at 11, to find a very welcome car wating to take us back to civilization.

That same evening we set off for Arusha.

Chapter VII

THE REAL AFRICA

Sept. 16*th.* I have been glorying in the variety of my African experiences; but only to-day have I seen Africa—the Africa that thrilled my boyhood, the country of bush and big game, primitive tribes and thorn-scrub and volcanic hills.

Arusha—I quote the placard in the admirable hotel—is the halfway station on the Cape to Cairo road; 2450 miles from Cairo, 2450 miles from the Cape. We set forth from Arusha's pretty parkland in the direction of Cairo. The road gets worse and worse; we average less than twelve miles an hour in our Chevrolet lorry. Soon we are in the thorn-bush savannah—scanty trees on great rolling downs of yellowing grass, strewn here and there with lava-blocks. It is the beginning of the game country. There stand three ostriches, two cocks and a hen. We stop, and off they go at a smart trot, tail-plumes ludicrously erect, but the great naked thighs striding along with a wonderful impression of efficiency. When they stop, the watchful eyes, perched up on the erect periscope of the neck, peer at us over the thorn bushes. Then a herd of impala grazing in the distance, and a gnu beyond them, a little black speck in the brown landscape. Soon after, two impalas silhouetted against the sky on a rise of the road; they see the car and with a marvellous bound leap into the bush. A little russet duiker, inquisitive and huge-eared, watches us pass. In a thorn-tree grove a herd of zebra stands resting, lazily flicking with their tails; fat, sleek, pleasant creatures, yet rather vulgar—donkeys in football jerseys, as the little boy said. Behind them are a pair of kongoni, strange ugly antelopes with bent horns and a back sloping down from the withers. A jackal slinks off into the bush. Three lovely roan antelope, almost as big as cattle, but of aristocratic build, with their black and white faces and regular horns, allow us to walk within sixty yards.

And the birds—how exciting to a bird-lover fresh from Europe! Rollers, azure and soft buff; glossy starlings bright with purple-blue sheen; weaver-birds, as big as thrushes, a flash of black and white wings with brilliant patch of ochre on the rump; a flock of guineafowl, looking very much a part of Africa and not the ridiculous creatures one would expect from knowing them only in European poultry-yards; big plovers, looking very like the brown sandy soil until they get up and fly off with flashing white on their wings.

The bush hornbills are comic birds; they flap up with quick beats of their wings, then tilt down as if their long beak overbalanced them, and so on, *ad lib*. Doves are everywhere—large turtle-doves; smaller dark grey doves, plump with black bands across their tails; tiny slender doves with long pointed tails, twisting and turning as they rise, like living arrows. Shrikes abound too, perched on the look-out for insects; their black-and-white conspicuousness argues immunity from enemies. One big one is amazingly like a magpie built on a two-thirds scale.

And all the birds of prey . . . The wild glory of them, so nearly lost from civilized countries like England, was summed up in the sight of a fine male Bateleur eagle who crouched, tearing at some carcass, by the roadside. The red-orange on his face and claws, the handsome pattern of his plumage, gave him a barbaric glory; and when at last he rose, his nearly tailless, broadwinged silhouette, floating effortlessly into the sky, made a mock of aeroplanes.

Nor was human interest lacking. First it was occasional groups of natives walking south, loaded with pots and pans, umbrellas, bundles of clothes. These were men who had come up from Southern Tanganyika to work on European estates, and were now returning—on foot, across several hundred miles of bush—to their families with the proceeds of their labour. The negro seems to love travelling, and combines profit with the Chaucerian longing to go on pilgrimage. There is a much greater movement of Africans over the face of Africa than most people realize.

Then there was a white man to pass the time of day with, an official of the Public Works on the job of repairing the road, in camp with his wife and baby. The other day, his wife sent the native boy running to say that a lioness was in the kitchen, so he came back and shot it: *African-issimo!*

A lovely wooded mountain rises from the rift floor on our right. It is an old volcano, with one of these haunting names the Masai give—Essimingor. Leaving this behind, we see a big expanse of glistening white on our right bow —the broad sheet of salt rimming Lake Manyara, now three-parts dried up. The lake lies under the Mbulu scarp, which here makes a western wall for the rift, while the eastern wall is represented only by a gentle terracing. Then suddenly we are out on a broad plain—the Mbugwe flats— and in every direction huts and cattle are seen. The whole area of a distinct tribe, the Wabugwe, is here in view at once. They are semi-pastoral people, but not nomadic, since they cultivate as well. The huts are very strange—long, low and rectangular, well made, with flat roofs on which food and gear are piled, and floor sunk a foot or two below the level of the ground; and their entrances all face in one direction, west by south—why?

Seeing the trailing herds—mixed herds, like those of Job, cattle, goats, and donkeys—being driven across the plain, I felt suddenly that I realized more fully the life of the Hebrew patriarchs. What was Abraham but a whiter and more religious Masai? A good deal more, no doubt, but still these African pastoralists do help biblical realization.

I was told later by an anthropologist that the plains-living Wabugwe and the Wambulu on the scarp above have developed an interesting mutual relationship concerning twins. The Wabugwe believe, like most African tribes, that the birth of twins is exceedingly unlucky, and expose the unfortunate pairs of infants to die in the bush. The Wambulu, on the other hand, have no such prejudice, and as their birth-rate is rather low, like adopting children. Somehow the custom has grown up that the Wabugwe expose twins at definite spots on the border of their neighbours' territory, and these come down, take the children, and bring them up as their own. Thus everybody is happy, and the mixture of blood, which has been going on steadily in Africa since history began, is taken a little step further.

Out of this primitive scene we ran into a little village—strange contrast. It was full of untidy Indian shops plastered with signs—Texaco, B.P., Somebody's Biscuits; a Government hut where a black clerk was receiving tax-money; groups of natives gossiping, some in nondescript European clothes, others in primeval skins; a negro sewing away at a sewing-machine under his Indian employer's eye, another negro hacking away at the carcase of a buck.

The flocks on the plains may make you think of Abraham, but it is difficult to connect villages like this with Ur of the Chaldees. Yet, though on a lower level, there is a parallel; commerce and the settled life is here invading the nomadic and barbarian world.

On and on, in spite of bodies getting numb with jolting on the lorry's hard seats. A pair of great bustard: a flock of crested cranes. We are right under the wooded scarp: Hanang, handsome eleven-thousand-foot volcano, lies ahead. The road gets more wooded. Just before sunset we are stopped by a couple of half-naked natives armed with miniature butterfly nets. These are the tsetse-fly control. They catch the numerous flies (devils to bite!) in the car, and one of them enters something in a penny notebook. Tsetses always make for moving objects—an adaptation to their dependence on the blood of antelopes and other game; they thus collect in cars, and are often transported from infested to uninfested areas by motorists—another example of the unexpected effects of civilization. These fly patrols are an attempt of the Tsetse Department to prevent this; unfortunately, I was told, white motorists often refuse to stop at the request of the native "fly-boys." The white man in the tropics too often looks down on the ignorance and foolish habits of the black. But what of the deliberate flouting of Government regulations by white men who ought to know better?

Dusk is falling: we do not know the exact road: the local Sultan is away: no one knows the way to Kikori: it is all

very African. By great good-fortune we find a white man—
a German settler on his way to his coffee estate fifteen hundred feet up on the escarpment. He gives us a boy to act as
guide (who to-morrow will cheerfully walk back the
twenty-five or thirty miles), and off we go into the dark.
Green eyes of hares and plover shine at us; nightjars get
up from the convenient flat resting-places provided by the
road; twice we pass close to where natives on the slopes of
Ufiumi Mountain are burning bush, and the orange flames
are lovely in the blue-black night. It is a weary way over
a bad road. At last, after ten hours' driving at an average
of 11 m.p.h., we see a light—Kikori, the entomological
station.

I knock at a door. A voice says come in. There on a bed,
pale and big-eyed from dysentery, is a young man. He is
Nash, one of the research workers. Three years ago I
shared lodgings with him when we were both working at
the Plymouth Laboratory: and I had no idea he was here.
Tents are ready for us; and we are ready for bed.

Sept. 17th. Guy Marshall is here, head of the Imperial
Bureau of Entomology in London; and Lamborn, in control of tsetse-research in Nyasaland, come to inspect the
Tanganyika tsetse-research on the spot; and Swynnerton,
Director of the Territory's Tsetse Department. It is a remarkable and interesting fact that these three men, all
distinguished scientists and all influential in the practical
field, one of them occupying the most responsible post open
to an entomologist in the Empire and perhaps in the
world, began as amateurs, and have none of them had any
special scientific training. I spend the morning with them
and Phillips, head of the Kikori Station, listening to and
discussing a long scientific report which Nash gets up

from bed to read. It is curious to foregather thus, a band of biologists, in the heart of Africa, 150 miles from any railway. However, it undoubtedly makes one's ideas about the tsetse much more vivid and real to imbibe them in the midst of a huge tsetse area, where one may expect to be bitten any moment by one of the brutes. But the tsetse and its problems deserve a chapter to themselves.

Chapter VIII

THE TSETSE FLY

"The tsetse fly," remarked the Provincial Commissioner, "is one of the two chief curses of East Africa; and the other"—but to say what he considered the other to be would be indiscreet. However, he was certainly right about the tsetse. Tanganyika Territory is three times the size of the United Kingdom. Two-thirds of the huge area is tsetse-ridden, and the fly is making advances every year. It is advancing in Rhodesia and Nyasaland too. It is bad enough in Uganda; and, though the White Man's country in Kenya is without fly, the rest of the colony has plenty and to spare. As Major Church forcibly put it in the House of Commons, "Are we going to surrender these huge tracts of country to the domination of an insect?"

For when the tsetse appears at the borders of native cultivation and a few cattle grow sick, the people generally take fright, desert their homes, drive their beasts away in search of fly-free country—and in a few years there is no trace of cultivation more. The bush has spread over all the former clearings; the bush provides the best home for tsetse; thus the insect has consolidated its gains, and can begin making fresh advances into new country.

Now the malaria mosquito is bad enough; but malaria does not drive cultivation out of a country like the fly-disease of cattle, nor does it kill wholesale like the tsetse

of human sleeping-sickness. And finally it is a more orderly
and controllable creature. It must live half its life in water;
and there, by various methods, you can get at it. But the
tsetse refuses to behave in a clean-cut way. It lives in very
varied situations and sucks the blood of very various animals. It does not lay eggs and expose its brood to long
dangers, but matures a single grub within itself, which,
within a few minutes of being deposited, transforms itself
into a tough resistant pupa. It is not confined to any one
kind of breeding-place; anywhere with a little shelter, and
not too much sun and not too dense shade, will serve. And
there is not merely one, but half a dozen kinds of tsetse-
fly; and several of them will convey the trypanosomes of
cattle disease or of sleeping-sickness with complete impar-
tiality, either separately or both at once. Tsetse live largely
on game. But you cannot, even if you wanted to, exter-
minate all the game in the country; and anyhow they may
also suck the blood of crocodiles and other reptiles and of
birds. Tsetse live chiefly in bush. But you cannot readily
destroy tracts of bush as big as France; and even if you
could, you could never keep the areas clear—the bush
would reinvade them.

Luckily, the tsetse will not fly far afield on his own; and
he will not breed in country that is actually cleared and
under cultivation. So there are two main ways of attack
open. You can clear infested bush, settle it with natives,
and take certain precautions to ensure that bush (and
therefore fly) shall not reinvade the cleared area. Or you
can destroy the fly in a certain area, without necessarily
destroying the bush, and between fly-free and fly-infested
regions put in a barrier that will prevent the insect from
getting across again. To accomplish these effectively, you

must know as much as possible about the habits of your fly; you must know as much as possible about the habits of your bush; and you must be able to control the habits of your natives.

As in other fields of applied science, there are three kinds of necessary work. There is pure research. For years this may seem only academic, the amassing of knowledge for knowledge's sake; but one day one bit of knowledge is sure to prove the key to control. There is the testing of the best way to apply what knowledge you have got—field tests, experiments, work on a large enough scale for the practical man to pronounce on its value in actual practice. And there is the practice itself, the final clearances and settlements. All three lines of work are being actively pushed forward in Tanganyika to-day. At Kikori, in the bush country 100 miles south of Arusha, there is a remarkable centre of pure research. Three years ago a single young entomologist was sent up there. He lived alone in a wattle hut for nine months, finding out a good deal about the intimate habits of the fly, and varying this by encounters with game of various description, from lion and rhino to buffalo and every kind of buck. Now there is a well-equipped little laboratory, a number of field stations where elaborate meteorological readings are taken thrice daily, and a staff of half a dozen European workers.

One experiment has concerned the seasonal and diurnal habits of tsetse in different kinds of country. The entomologist and a couple of "fly boys" go a series of rounds, week after week, at various times of day, and catch every tsetse they can find. By this means a mass of information has been gleaned about the breeding and dying-off of the flies, the way they collect not only where game are, but

SCIENCE IN THE BUSH.

IN THE CENTRE, A NUMBER OF NATIVE ASSISTANTS, ONE OF WHOM IS MARKING TSETSE FLIES WITH SPOTS OF PAINT FOR FUTURE IDENTIFICATION. ON THE RIGHT, ANOTHER NATIVE ASSISTANT HUNTING FOR TSETSE PUPÆ. (*By courtesy of Mr. C. F. M. Swynnerton. Director of the Department of Tsetse Research, Tanganyika.*)

THE BENEFITS OF TSETSE RESEARCH AND RECLAMATION.

NATIVE CATTLE PASTURING IN THE CLEARED AREA NEAR SHINYANGA. FIVE YEARS AGO, THIS REGION WAS ALL TSETSE-INFESTED BUSH. (*By courtesy of Mr. C. F. M. Swynnerton, Director of the Department of Tsetse Research, Tanganyika.*)

where game have been, the differing behaviour of male and female, the effect of bush fires on the adult fly and its pupae. And some of this knowledge is already suggesting new methods of practical control and is ruling out others.

Another experiment in which hundreds of flies were caught, marked with spots of paint, and released, some with their eyes varnished, others with their antennae varnished, others with both varnished, has pretty conclusively proved that the tsetse hunts by sight alone; he goes for moving objects of a certain size. Smell only comes into play once he is close, or perhaps not until he has settled.

In a third ambitious experiment, certain definite areas are visited thrice daily; rainfall, evaporation, wind, temperature, and so forth are read, and a five-minutes catch of fly is made. Every fly is painted with three spots of paint, whose position and colour indicate the place, day, and hour of its capture—and then released. By this means we shall learn how far and how quickly fly stray away from one locality to another, and whether they behave differently in different kinds of bush and different kinds of weather. A host of other work is being begun which should at last give us detailed knowledge of the tsetse's history.

It is also giving us a knowledge of the bush, for the stations have been carefully chosen in different kinds of vegetation, grading down from the thick woods of the hill-slopes almost to the open grasslands of the Masai steppe that you see from the laboratory rolling its barren buff expanses away to blue volcanic chains on the horizon. Meanwhile, at another station tree-poisoning experiments are being carried on. You can burn the grass and cut the smaller trees, but poisoning will be quicker for the larger ones, and will prevent their growing again from the stool.

At Shinyanga, 200 miles to the westward, the field tests are going on. Can you successfully catch out all the fly from a patch of bush you have isolated by clearances? What is the maximum width of open ground which fly will cross? We are pretty certain it is less than a mile, but will a quarter of a mile do? Will a fence keep game from crossing, so that, once an area of bush is rid of fly, infected game from neighbouring areas will not stray in and reinfect the cleared area? Is repeated burning of grass and undergrowth enough to rid bush of fly, or must you cut as well? Can you not make a barrier against fly even more effectively by planting a strip of trees too dense and shady for them than by clearing a strip, which will then have to be cleared again and again as the years pass?

To answer these questions Nature is being interrogated by experiment. A fence of green poles about 8 feet high has been built, eleven miles long. The only breaks in it so far have been made by giraffes that were being chased by lions. Some kinds of poles take root and grow. The live hedge thus produced is what you want; so here is a strange experimental garden—rows and rows of large poles, of small branch sections, of twigs, belonging to many different species and planted at different seasons, to determine the best material and method for the fence.

The research workers at Kikori had shown that fly collect in small clear places in bush to look for game. So here in one area a series of small clearings have been deliberately made, and native boys with bird-limed boards on their backs walk or bicycle up and down them every day. The flies dash for the moving object and are caught. This may prove an excellent method of freeing of tsetse isolated patches of bush several square miles in extent. Then there is the thicket problem. Burning bush-country will get rid of many fly; but the fire spares the denser thickets, and here the insects stay unscathed and repopulate the bush next year. Hand-cutting of thickets over a large area is a formidable task; so a lorry has been fitted out with a pair of saws converging diagonally to a point in front of its bows, and with this Boadicea's chariot attempts are to be made on the fly harbourages.

Some of these experiments are certain to be fruitful. Meanwhile two methods have passed beyond experiment into practice. One is the freeing of bush from fly by thorough burning. You wait on and on to the very end of the dry season until the grass is bone-dry, and then one day when the wind is strong you make a great burn. If there are not too many refuges in the shape of thickets, this, repeated for two or three years, reduces the fly to negligible numbers or to nothing. The great difficulty here is that even with careful supervision casual natives are likely to start fires too early, which will prevent the burning being thorough enough.

The other is clearing the bush itself, followed up as quickly as possible by settlement. In certain areas where natives have been ejected from their homes by the advance of the fly it has not been difficult to persuade them to co-operate, and by this means several hundred square miles have been reclaimed from bush, game, and tsetse for the growth of cattle, crops, and men.

In Tabora and Mwanza provinces, in Western Tanganyika, you may come on bands of a thousand men thus engaged in cutting down the thorn-scrub. They are working, by order of their chiefs, to rid the country of tsetse-fly and make it fit for cattle and so for men. It is worth while looking into the story, to see how surprisingly the fate of its different characters—men, crops, cattle, insects and bush —is linked together in one dramatic unity.

On one side of Shinyanga, where these big clearings are slowly driving the tsetse out, is a sea of bush. Old men remember when much of this was still open country inhabited by an abundant population and their cattle. What happened to them when the fly ejected them and the thorn trees covered their fields? They crowded into the open country that lies on the other side, north and east, and extends almost up to the Victoria Nyanza. This increased the population. Meanwhile, the white man had come into the land, and was stopping war and raids; was killing wild beasts; was beginning to check the ravages of disease. For this reason also the population increased in the open areas. It increased so much that it began to alter the character of the country; and now disaster looms ahead unless steps are taken quickly to prevent it.

Practically every tree for miles has been felled, save only the strange, majestic baobabs. In some villages the natives have to go twenty or thirty miles to get wood to build their huts. Unless encouraged or commanded, the African hardly ever plants trees—he merely cuts them down. Herds of cattle and goats are everywhere. They are so numerous that next to nothing remains of the grass. The whole district is over-grazed; one wonders how the cattle live at all. And if one year the rains hold off a little too long, they do not live; they have no reserves, there is nothing to eat, and they die by hundreds. Meanwhile the natural covering of the soil has grown thin or has even disappeared. In the dry season the hot winds sweep over the plains, parch the ground, and blow the soil away. In the wet season the rains, no longer retained by the sponge of vegetation, wash it away. As further result, the country becomes poor and the cattle concentrate more and more on the grass that is left. This is a vicious circle.

In consequence, you see patches of mere sand where once was rich grass, ugly runnels and miniature gorges cutting back and back into what was smooth rolling downland. That is erosion; and erosion will continue at an ever-growing speed unless the vicious circle be broken at some point or another. One way is to make clearances or to free bush areas of fly, and send cattle back into these fly-free areas. (Here erosion links on to tsetse again.) This is being done; but it hardly relieves the pressure. The natural increase of the flocks is so great that tsetse clearances can at most take up the surplus. Erosion links up with forestry, too. The only way in which erosion can be directly countered is by planting trees. Woods along the watersheds and belts of trees along the upper edges of the valleys—these would break the wind, hold the moisture in the soil, affect the climate.

Then erosion interlocks with water supply. There are huge areas where cattle would live well if only there was water for them; there is food, but not drink. The beasts cannot go more than a certain distance from water-holes; therefore, the concentration in these areas is kept unduly high; and, therefore, over-grazing and erosion set in. Wells and dams are the solution—dams where the ground slopes, wells and deep bore-holes where the surface is too level for dams.

But up till now only a fractional beginning has been made with tree-planting and water-supply; and the herds increase and multiply. Why not sell the surplus stock, you

ask. Why not, indeed? But this is where erosion hooks on
to the Africans' economics and traditions. The cattle-keep-
ing African does not want to sell his beasts. He reckons
wealth not in money but in head of stock. His social
standing is estimated by the number of his beasts, as the
social worth of the peasant girl in some parts of Europe
is estimated by the number of petticoats she wears. You
begin to appreciate early Old Testament psychology when
you see a cattle-loving African tribe. Even so did Job
reckon up his possessions; even so did Abraham feel
about his flocks and herds.

Just as one shilling is as good as another, though one
be old and worn and the other fresh from the Mint; so
one beast is as good as another, though one be small and
the other big, one scraggy and the other sleek. Each is a
unit. Cattle, in fact, are just cattle; they are not distin-
guishable by quality unless actually diseased or deformed.
Thus, though there is a big demand for beasts to go to
the meat factory at Mwanza and be turned into meat
extract or salted and dried meat-rations for labour gangs,
for beasts to be driven over to the Katanga mining area in
the Congo to feed the workers there, and for half a dozen
other purposes, the supply falls far short of the demand. A
certain beginning has been made; but the cattle are, as it
were, squeezed out of their owners—there is no natural
economic flow of beef. Criticism of the Cattle Standard in
pastoral economics still meets with the same intolerance and
scorn from the African as does criticism of the Gold
Standard in the City. The two systems are equally sacro-
sanct. One wishes that a committee—say, Mr. M'Kenna,
Mr. Keynes, and Professor Pigou—could be sent out to
report on African economics; the tribes might be suffi-

ciently impressed by them to give ear to their recommendations. Plans are, it is true, being made in some districts to make a stock census, and then to exercise some form of compulsion or indirect pressure to insist on the sale of surplus bulls and steers. Somehow or other, in any case, the deep-rooted sentiment and old traditions of the native must be broken down or altered before over-grazing can stop.

Then, of course—and only then—the science of animal-breeding can step in. But it will link on to the problem firmly enough, once the tribes think of their herds in terms of money value and not merely as so many head; for then they will inevitably come to consider quality before quantity.

On the other hand, it is of no use their thinking of quality before the grazing and the water-supply have been dealt with, since improved stock would simply die on the fare which the native cattle now get. Soil science, too, comes in, for in many parts there is a deficiency of one or other mineral salt in the soil, and big rapidly-growing beasts would feel the pinch quicker than the small slow-growing African cattle of to-day, just as a quick-growing child will suffer much worse from rickets than a stunted one.

And even bees enter the story. They do not link up directly with erosion, it is true, but with sleeping-sickness. However, sleeping-sickness is an affair of tsetse, and tsetse has immediate bearings on erosion, so they all come into the one interlocking system. The natives have a primitive system of bee-keeping. They hang their hives here and there in trees; and the hives are mere hollow logs. When they want to take the honey, they make a huge fire under the tree to smoke the bees off, and sacrifice the whole population of the hive to get the honey. One is reminded of Elia's essay on Roast Pig. In so doing they often start premature grass fires, which prevent the tsetse workers from making their thorough burns later; and when sleeping-sickness is about, and the medical authorities are trying to round up the people into concentration areas in clearings, the bee-keepers will slip off into the fly-infested forest after their honey, and so may get bitten and bring back the trypanosome to the concentration camp.

Who would have thought that sleeping-sickness control involved the improvement of native bee-keeping? Yet until you can persuade the native to use better hives, in which taking the honey does not mean the destruction or driving away of the bee community, and to put them all round the edge of a clearing instead of off in the bush, you have left a nasty loophole through which the enemy may creep in and bring your elaborate scheme of control to naught.

But so it is in every field. The medical man, fresh from English hospital wards, as likely as not finds himself clearing bush, or trying to persuade natives to leave their homes as sleeping-sickness creeps up. The veterinary officer will discover that it is just as important for him to study native customs and to get at the back of the African's mind as it is to prepare and dispense the best of sera against disease. The agricultural official, in the absence of sufficient forestry staff, must turn forester himself. The geological department has in the past not unnaturally concerned itself mainly with mapping the country for valuable minerals; it is finding that it must organize another branch whose main duties will be to find and store water and to check erosion. The forester is trained at home to think primarily in terms of timber and of cash profits. Out here he must devote at least as much attention to schemes of tree-planting whose main aim is to benefit not forestry but agriculture and stock-raising.

And the administrative officer—but one shudders to think of the variety of duties which he is called upon to perform, and the immense background of knowledge which he ought to have to help him in their performance.

Chapter IX

MPWAPWA: INTERLUDE WITH A TUTELARY
SPIRIT

Mpwapwa and its Training College was our next objective. It took us nineteen hours to get there: twelve on the road, two resting, four by the night train, and another hour's drive up. I have only space for a few outstanding incidents of the day. One was a visit to a native rock-shelter, covered all over with rock-paintings. Most of them were either paintings of hands, or curious gridiron-like objects, their square compartments filled with dots. There seemed to be some arithmetical meaning in them, since in each compartment the dots were in tens or multiples of ten. One with two elongated compartments had 100 in all, but was not quite correct in dividing them up, giving 54 to one side and 46 to the other.

These drawings were all, it seems, quite recent, but Nash has found a number of old paintings, including some very interesting hunting scenes recalling the spirited Bushman drawings of South Africa. It seems certain that the Bushmen once ranged widely over Africa, and were gradually pushed south by the successive waves of Negro, Bantu and Hamitic invasion.

Then there was an interesting scene in one native village we passed, an ingenious sugar-mill, consisting of a movable post with a capstan and a fixed post, the two beautifully cogged with spiral cogs—no light feat when cut out of tree stems with rude knives. Four men worked the capstan; a boy passed bits of sugar-cane through between the posts and collected the juice in a pot. The pots of juice were then evaporated over an earth oven, and thick molasses was the result.

Later, climbing a little range of hills we saw a queer sight—a valley containing a river of pure sand, which had poured out into the plain below, expanding there to form a gradually increasing sand delta. This, and the fantastically carved ravines we afterwards saw, are results of the erosion due to overgrazing by too abundant cattle, which is ruining the district.

Then there was the sight of a really big native village, seat of the local Sultan; and Kondoa, administrative centre for the district, with a regular "village green," but dotted with baobabs in place of oaks.

Later we drove suddenly through thick low scrub—a dreary country, extending for hundreds of miles, with an extremely sparse native population. My companion had once journeyed five days on foot through this everlasting bush, with hardly a glade, to visit a school. A queer flowering shrub with flowers like red and green toothbrushes (*Combretum*) was everywhere.

One is apt to imagine that these enormous stretches of bush, dense or sparse, which cover so many thousands of square miles in Central Tanganyika, are all part of the natural original vegetation—how could they be anything else, one thinks, in such a wild country? Certainly I had imagined this, but talks with Swynnerton and other ecologists convinced me of my error.

Man, with his cultivation, his cattle and his fire, has profoundly altered even this area. The general tendency under human influence, it seems, is for rain-forests to disappear and to give place to bush or grassland; for dense scrub-thicket to give place to a looser thorn-bush. The hunter does not clear; but when man at the cultivating level comes along, he embarks on shifting cultivation, and patches of forest are cleared. These do not have time or opportunity to regenerate forest when they are temporarily abandoned for new clearances, and rarely develop further towards their natural climax than the dense bush stage. Meanwhile the same process is going on where dense scrub is the natural vegetation. Once the bush is at all opened up, grass grows below and between the trees; and then man can begin to burn. And with annual burning a radical change takes place in the trees. A ruthless natural selection is set up, and only those species survive which have (or acquire) by means of thick bark, or special chemical substances in the bark, a resistance to the flames.

Once the bush is all opened up, cattle can be introduced, and they and the fires between them prevent the bush from ever regenerating to its full density again; and where settlement is more intensive, of course, the forest and bush may be cleared away altogether.

Thus in many regions, so long as man is absent or only in the hunting stage, the natural climax of vegetation may be rain-forest or dense bush-woodland. But the same regions, if agricultural man arrives on the scene, will have their climax altered towards open scrub, and eventually, with increasing density of settlement, towards bare grassland.

The huge luxuriant rain-forest of the Congo basin is not so amenable to change; whereas in East Africa huge areas have been radically altered by the presence for a millennium or so of the black agriculturists, he has made only a negligible impression on the Equatorial forest to the west. How negligible may be realized from the fact that, in spite of the African's passion for cattle, there are no cattle at all in the true forest area. Here the black man has been unable to alter Nature's climax; this is being reserved for the greater technical skill of the European—with what results, good or evil, it is still too early to say.

The drive up from the railway station to Mpwapwa in the moonlit small hours was superb. Had one but control, like Joshua, over the heavenly bodies, one would frequently command the full moon for Africa. Under its rays the landscape becomes a breathless wonder of silver and black.

Mpwapwa is a pleasant place on the edge of the hills in the Central Province of Tanganyika. Stanley, on his way to find Livingstone, camped under a spreading, heavy-foliaged tree in the village. The Germans had one of their fortified administrative posts here (now replaced by a British District Officer's friendly-looking little office); the road is still there which they made and planted with vegetable barbed wire in the shape of formidably-spiked sisal, and on a hill a few miles off is one of their heliograph towers. Here, too, they plumped down their main veterinary station; the English have taken over the laboratory, and are now moving the headquarters of the whole veterinary department here from the capital, over two hundred miles away. Here the present administration has also built its lymph laboratory, where a quarter of a million vaccination doses are kept in reserve, and whence the whole territory, three times the size of the United Kingdom, is supplied with vaccine for the campaign against small-pox.

And we have started a big educational venture at Mpwapwa. Not only are there a local elementary school and a central school where boarders come from all the Central Province, but it is the only Government centre in the territory for the training of native teachers. And besides the fields and steadings of the local tribe, there is also a big native village where was once an important station on a main slave-trade route. Slaves from all parts of the territory and from far-off Congoland beyond the Great Lake got left here for one cause or another, so that it is a much mixed little African cosmopolis, with Indian shops to boot. The main Tanganyika railway passes only twelve miles away, close under the mountains that bound the opposite side of the narrow plain, and a good motor road runs from the railway to the town. There are two excellent tennis-courts, and the rudiment of a golf-course. Mpwapwa is thus a busy modern place, as much exposed to the disturbing swirl of civilization's current as any of the smaller townships of Africa.

In the morning I saw over the veterinary laboratory, where vast quantities of anti-rinderpest serum are made and bottled (it looks very much like rather turbid beer) for shipment far and wide, and where they study the unpleasant trypanosomes that wriggle their way through the blood of cattle and keep cows and horses out of the half of tropical Africa. In the afternoon I had a long conference with the staff of the school over the teaching of science to the African schoolboy and future schoolmaster, and about five, as the sun was softening downward to the west, the headmaster and I, putting on the regular outdoor kit of shorts and open-collared shirt, went for a walk.

MPWAPWA

We headed for a little rock pinnacle that rises just beyond where the cultivated plain gives place to the hills and their mantle of scrubby woodland. It was a fine little fifty-foot needle of hard rock, and my climbing instincts were aroused. I found my way to its base through the tangled, thorny copsewood, noticing vaguely that the way was roughly barred by a small tree and a branch or two that had been cut and put in the obvious approach between two big boulders. The little climb was easier than it looked, and I was quickly on top, looking over the brown plain and purple hills, parched and waiting for the short rains. Suddenly a loud and peculiar hoarse hissing broke out from just below where I was sitting. I thought of giant wasps or tropical hornets—nor without some alarm, for descent in a cloud of stings would have been not only unpleasant but dangerous. But my anxious eye fell not on a swarm of insects but on a solitary reptile—a huge monitor lizard, about four feet long, in a crevice of the rock: I had stepped right over the place without noticing its inmate.

There it was, its scales like tiles upon its trunk, and rising up on its neck into bosses like heavy leatherwork. It looked up at me with a cold malignant eye, darted its flickering tongue, leaden and forked, out of its hard mouth, and hissed with raucous intensity.

This was the first big lizard I had seen wild, and I became seized with an intense desire to catch it. Having decided that its bite might be dangerous, I made a running noose with my garter and prepared to lasso the beast. But on this he turned, and slowly began to creep into a crack. I seized his tail, and there was a struggle, pull devil, pull baker. Once in a crack, he wedged himself with extraordinary firmness, and it was only after two or three minutes that I got him out.

This was no ordinary monitor. The average specimen, so I am assured by those who know his habits, would have been round and away in a flash. He would have protected himself by vicious and swift snapping, and would have lashed with his tail so intensely that I should never have been able to get him out, or hold him, ignominiously dangling, when I had done so. Doubtless he was an aged creature, who had lived in this rock fortress for decades, scores of years, even a century—we know little of reptilian spans of life. His near fore-paw was badly scarred, with several of the clawed toes bitten off.

Then came the problem of descent; unencumbered I had found the ascent easy, but to get down with only one hand for climbing, while trying to prevent that ugly head from coming within snapping distance of my person, and those powerful fore-quarters from wedging themselves in a crevice, was another matter. However, I succeeded: if ever (which is unlikely) I become a candidate for admission to the Alpine Club, I shall record that brief but anxious descent.

My companion came up to inspect my capture. He too noticed the barring of the approach to the rock, and suggested that the place was a holy place, and the beast a holy beast. So we let it go, but not until after an interesting demonstration of the east with which reptiles can be hypnotized, or put into the catalepsy which is the evolutionary forerunner of the true hypnotic state. While we were talking, the beast was struggling to make off; to put him at a disadvantage I twisted his tail to turn him over on to his back. At once his movements ceased; I found I could release my hold, and he would still lie there, breathing deeply. Put over on to his belly again, he at once woke up; but if rapidly twisted into the supine position and held still there for a few seconds, he at once became immobilized. Doubtless Aaron's rod had been tricked into the same physiological state, and I recalled playing the same game with the amusingly ugly Horned Toad lizards of the western United States, much to the astonishment of some Wyoming cowboys, whose exclamations of "Gee!" and "Wal, I swan!" were redoubled as I succeeded in piling three of the lizards into a grotesque edifice of catalepsy-struck reptilian flesh.

Just down across a patch of cultivation was a little *tembe*, one of the steadings in which the local people, the Wagogo, live. They are square, with buildings all round (or on three sides, with a thorn hedge on the fourth). The cattle are driven in at evening into the central space, and the gate barricaded. In the buildings lives a whole patriarchal family—the grandfather with his wife or wives, the sons with their wives and children; and there are compartments too for the chickens and the goats.

The patriarch of this *tembe* was a little man in the forties or fifties, with a curiously Tartar face, low and broad, with highish cheek-bones, and a little stringy moustache hanging Chinese fashion round the corners of his mouth. He was a nice little fellow, with humour in every wrinkle of his face, and quick gesticulations of his hands. He was dressed in a low red fez, an old brown golf sweater, and a little cloth kilt. One of his daughters-in-law sat wrapped in a cotton dress, the other, a fine figure of a girl, naked to the waist, with a necklace of English beads, busied herself about the place. As the little man talked, I was reminded of the Italian peasant life I had got to know near Padua during the War. These people were black and pagan; their life was more primitive, their belongings fewer and cruder, their outlook more limited. But there was the same simplicity, the same feeling of a human stock rooted in the soil. There was the same acceptance of life, its drudgeries, pleasures and vicissitudes, that I had learnt to know there, an acceptance for the most part contented, sometimes tinged with humorous resignation.

He showed us his room—wattle and daub, mud floors, no windows, but clean. There were two beds, with skin mattresses; a nicely-carved stool; a stone worn smooth by the grinding of interminable maize, with a skin mat on which the women could kneel while they ground it; a big board for playing *bau*, the African game which is played over half the great continent—he played *bau* with his sons in the evenings, he told us, after the work of the day was done.

My companion, after a little general talk, threw out a feeler about the monitor. "By the way," he said, "when we were up at that pinnacle over there, we saw a great lizard among the rocks."

"Ah yes," said the little Mugogo man. "Yes, there is a big lizard up there. He looks after all of us in the neighbourhood. We get pretty good crops, thanks to him." He speedily changed the subject.

Afterwards I made some enquiries. It seems certain that monitor lizards are rare in the district; and that this particular specimen was of great age. The rocks were striking to look at, and there was nothing else like them for some miles round. They might well have been chosen as phallic symbols; anyhow, it appears that striking rocks are not infrequently selected as places where certain of the initiation ceremonies are gone through. And certainly the obvious approach to the base of the rock had been deliberately barred.

There seems no doubt that it was a sacred place, and the monitor a sacred beast, a tutelary creature to which some divinity attached. I wonder if he is accorded offerings of food. In any case, I hope that his forcible capture and dethronement to the base of the rock will have no evil effects. I left him vainly trying to get the hinder half of his body into a too-narrow crack. May he by now have found his way back to his tabernacle at the summit, there to live long years more. May the people of the neighbourhood not fail in their belief in him so long as he lives. May our rule in the Territory not cause a collapse of all their simple living, but cause it to evolve into a richer and more stable peasant life.

．　　．　　．　　．　　．

We went on homeward in the gathering dusk. Across from the next mountain, a couple of miles away, came the rhythm of drums, inviting to foot it, with accompaniment of shrill whistles and occasional bursts of singing. So home, to dine, and play bridge until it was time to catch the night train up country. . . . A varied day. My companion's only regret is that he had no camera to snap me silhouetted against the sky, with the ancient beast dangling in indignity from my hand, on the summit of the sacred rock. He says it was a funny sight.

Chapter X

THE ETON OF TANGANYIKA: TABORA SCHOOL

The Government School at Tabora has been called the Eton of Tanganyika. This is a loose phrase, for Eton may produce a large quota of the statesmen of the Empire (even in these democratic days, about a fifth of the House of Commons are old Etonians, and a couple of years back the Speaker, the Lord Mayor, the Lord Chancellor, the Governor of the Bank of England, the Head of the Metropolitan Police, the Dean of St. Paul's, and I think the Governor-General of every Dominion, had all been at Eton), but she does not do so officially, so to speak.

Tabora School, however, is a Government School, officially entitled "for the sons of chiefs," and its official aim is to prepare these future native administrators of the Territory for their tasks.

This is not to say that no other boys are taken, but preference is given to the sons or near relatives of Chiefs and Headmen. Here at Tabora they are given the standard educational grounding, as well as a taste for football, a good deal of discipline, and a real *esprit de corps*. In addition, special attention is given to what may be useful to them later. For instance, they are taught the use of ploughs; and already an old boy of the school has introduced ploughing into his father's territory. They are given a course in accountancy and bookkeeping so that they may understand the working of their Native Treasuries; and some instruction which will help them in their law-dispensing functions.

The school has had a career often seen in pioneer ventures. It was started through the initiative of local officials, without much central support. But the Governor soon became enthusiastic, and now the school is the spoilt darling of the Education Department. A sum of nearly £30,000 has been voted and more promised, to build permanent buildings; and these are now nearly ready. The old school-buildings stand to one side—pleasant and unassuming, thatched and white-washed, with a central flower-garden. The new school is a two-storey building of stone, light grey, standing round three sides of a square; it is perhaps over-simple, but dignified with its round arcading. Its great hall, a really lovely room, is the largest room in the Territory.

The casual traveller finds himself assailed by a certain amount of doubt as to whether the new school is not too ambitious. There is, for one thing, a purely financial doubt. Is it wise to spend this relatively huge sum on a single educational institution, when the Territory's education service cries out for all-round expansion? At the moment, only about one native child in ten is receiving any schooling at all; only about one in twenty-five any schooling worthy the name.

There is also a purely educational doubt. Is it wise to make such a jump all at once, to put the boys in surroundings so different not merely from any to which they have been accustomed, but even from any which they can hope to build up for themselves when they inherit authority? Will you not tend to disorganize rather than develop, to foster discontent instead of slow progressive change? It is hard to say. But it is relevant to remember that to many English lads of the fourteenth century the grandeur of Winchester and New College must have been infinitely beyond anything they knew in the surroundings of their village homes; and that to have enjoyed for a spell of life a perfection otherwise out of reach may stabilize the growing mind, and, if it lead to discontent, only to that divine discontent out of which development proceeds.

In any case, some of the results seem good enough. I myself later saw a recent product of the school very efficiently helping in the work of clearing tsetse-infested bush —work which demands the handling of men and a considerable amount of detailed organization; and I heard good reports of the character and energy of several others. Furthermore, the experiment, under the enthusiastic guidance of Mr. Lacey, the Headmaster, has been most definitely begun. In such a case, any doubts one has should not be allowed to interfere with the most whole-hearted prosecution of the work; they should remain in the background, as purely intellectual questions to which the experiment itself will in due time give its answer. That is, I suppose, the application of the scientific method to practical affairs.

Indeed, one of the excellent features of Tanganyika's youthful Department of Education is its willingness to experiment. For example, in complete contrast with Tabora is the Government School at Malangali, in the southern part of the Territory. Unfortunately I was not able to see this school, as it was vacation time and there was no one there; but the Headmaster, Mr. Mumford, has written a most interesting article on the school in a recent number of *Africa*, and with this, and talks with Education Officers

A Dance-festival at Nzega, Tanganyika.

Above, a Man's Dance. The Leader is in the Centre; All the Rest Wear White Robes and Form a Circle, Clapping Their Hands and Occasionally Leaping or Bobbing.

Below, a Mixed Dance. The Performers Are Got up with Bead Head-dresses and Neck-frills. (*Photos. by Mr. Alleyne, Nzega, Tanganyika.*)

THE ETON OF TANGANYIKA.

ABOVE, ONE SIDE OF THE NEW BUILDINGS OF TABORA SCHOOL
FOR THE SONS OF CHIEFS, APPROACHING COMPLETION.

BELOW, SOME OF THE SENIOR BOYS, OUTSIDE THE OLD BUILD-
INGS. (*Photos. by Mr. Whybrow, Headmaster of Tabora School.*)

© *C. Whybrow.*

who know the place, it was possible to get a reasonable idea of its aims and methods. Briefly speaking, Mumford's chief aims have been, first, to build up a school on the basis of native ideas and native methods; and, secondly, to introduce new ideas and better methods wherever possible, but gradually, and in simple forms which can be immediately applied by the boys when they return to their homes.

The school is divided into Tribes, which do not merely serve as useful subdivisions, to correspond with Houses in an English public school, but actually have a tribal basis, and are organized somewhat on the true tribal pattern. The school as a whole is organized on the same plan, with a council who decide minor matters of discipline. The council is presided over by the boys who have been chosen as heads of the several tribes; these are called Leaders of the Young Men, which was an actual title and position in the original tribal organization. To ensure that this system shall not be mere make-believe, but that there shall be continuity with real tribal tradition, he has arranged that there shall live at the school an elder of each tribe from which the boys are drawn. These old men instruct the boys in tribal tradition and history, and advise on points of custom and law, thus acting like the chosen elders who advise the chief in law and other matters, but with the additional role of historians and teachers.

Twice a week, in the evening, all the boys and the masters gather round a huge fire. On one of the two days, the boys discuss any subject they choose, addressing questions to the old men, the native teachers, or the European master present. On the other, there are entertainments, the different tribes vying with each other in singing, dancing or acting.

In accommodation and equipment, the principle has been to take indigenous methods and improve them. The buildings, for instance, have windows, but are constructed on the plan of the local native *tembes*, and are built of mud or sun-dried brick. The same is true of the instruction provided. In agriculture, both native and introduced crops are grown, both native and European methods adopted, the aim being again to modify and improve existing practice rather than to inculcate an entirely new practice. Every boy brings his own cow and calf to school, and learns improved methods of milking, butter-making and so forth. The result is a huge pride in the school stock, and a great interest on the part of the parents. So, too, history and geography are linked on to what the boys know and learn of their country and traditions, and native songs and handicrafts are encouraged; while in sport, spear-throwing, dancing and other native recreations have their place on the same footing as European games like football.

Mumford himself sums up the difference between Tabora and Malangali thus. Both aim at putting the feet of the African on the path of progress; however, while Tabora can hope for quite large advances, but only in comparatively few cases, Malangali can hope for advances of lesser degree, but diffused over a large number of boys. The general opinion among those with whom I discussed the matter in Africa was that the Malangali system was excellent for areas remote from white civilization, but would not work close to a town or to an area of white settlers. The Tabora system, on the other hand, while well suited for training picked individuals for the special new duties which science and modern methods of administration demand, would not be suitable in the present state of the country for the general run of the population.

Of other schools of intermediate grade in the Territory, besides these two very dissimilar institutions, there is the Normal School for teachers at Mpwapwa; the school at Moshi, which on the whole is a less developed and less specialized version of Tabora; the straightforward town school at Tanga; the town school at Dar-es-Salaam, now rather in a transitional state; and in addition to these Government schools, there is all the variety to be found in the Missionary institutions.

We are thus in Africa remaining true to our national characteristic of experimenting with educational methods, as opposed to the Latin system, most strongly exemplified in France, of centralization and uniformity.

Chapter XI

SOME PRINCIPLES OF INDIRECT RULE

Before I left Dar-es-Salaam, Sir Donald Cameron had insisted on a modification of my itinerary in order that I might see more of Shinyanga and other places in the Wanyamwezi country, as object-lessons in the principles and practice of Indirect Rule.

For this alteration of my plans I have been very grateful. I must confess that "indirect rule" had previously only a very hazy meaning for me. After seeing it working in a particularly interesting form at Shinyanga and Ngudu, I was made more able to grasp the significance of what I afterwards read about it; and so, what with my visit, Lord Lugard's *Dual Mandate*, and the extremely interesting memoranda on Native Administration issued by the Tanganyika Government under Sir Donald Cameron's signature,[1] I feel I am beginning to understand something of this peculiarly British contribution to the methods of colonial administration.

The principle of Direct Rule is that native peoples are to be administered, their taxes collected, their disputes settled, their schools and hospitals, seed farms and irrigation works, and other social and economic services provided, all by the interposition of the Central Government,

---

[1] No. 1, Principles of Native Administration and their Application; No. 2, Native Courts; No. 3, Native Treasuries: Dar-es-Salaam, 1926.

working through agents appointed directly by it. In territories like those of Central Africa, this of necessity means that local administration must be put into the hands of paid headmen appointed by Government, who accordingly come too often to be looked on only as tax-gatherers and tools of a remote and arbitrary power, alien to the actual life of the people, their ideas and customs, their aspirations. Under these circumstances, the tribal organization, with its customary law and its traditions, will tend gradually to disintegrate, or to be forced underground and take the form of anti-Governmental organizations and secret societies. Policies of direct rule were followed by the Germans in Tanganyika before the War, and by us in Kenya until the establishment of native councils in very recent times.

The policy of indirect rule, on the other hand (I quote from one of the above-cited memoranda) is "the principle of ruling through the native chiefs, who are regarded as an integral part of the machinery of government, with well-defined powers and functions recognized by Government and by law, and not dependent on the caprice of an executive officer." And then follows a rider: "It must be clearly understood that the policy of the Government is to maintain and support native rule (within the limits laid down) and not to impose a form of British rule with the support of native chiefs, which is a very different thing."

Indirect rule, in fact, means the employment of the existing institutions of the country for all possible purposes to which they are adequate, their gradual moulding, by means of the laws made and taxes imposed by the Central Government and of the guidance given by the administrative officers, into channels of progressive change, and the encouragement within the widest limits of local traditions, local pride and local initiative, and so of the greatest possible freedom and variety of local development within the Territory.

The principles of indirect rule were first fully worked out in Nigeria under Lugard's governorship. There, however, large and important kingdoms and emirates were already in existence; already linked on to world-civilization by means of their Mohammedanism; and with their own highly-developed if not always admirable systems of law, taxation and government, their own traditions and history often extending far into the past. The method of ruling through these existing agencies was in many ways the line of least resistance. The chief novelty was the insistence as a matter of principle on the wide freedom given the local organization to keep its own traditions and basic ideas and to develop along its own lines, with the minimum amount of central despotism, however benevolent, or tutelage, however well-meaning.

The special interest of the application of these principles in Tanganyika lies in the fact that in this territory even the most advanced native institutions were on a far more primitive plane than those of northern Nigeria, or even than the more developed systems in neighbouring parts of Central Africa, such as the elaborate kingdoms of the Baganda or the Banyoro to the north in Uganda, or the Watusi to the west in Belgian Ruanda. Here in Tanganyika it would have been far easier than in Nigeria to ignore the native tradition and social structure, and to impose our own methods and systems from above.

Up till 1925, although the British Government in Tanganyika had decided against any system of purely direct rule, it had not really thought out whether it was going to embark upon indirect rule in the full sense, or upon the compromise policy of using native chiefs and native institutions to introduce our British methods according to a system devised in a Government office at the capital. The real difference between true indirect rule and the imitation article is whether the system is home-grown, authentic local produce, or is imposed from outside, take-it-or-leave-it, stamped with the manufacturer's name—"British Government."

In Tanganyika, since 1925, the unit of Governmental organization has been, wherever possible, the Native Authority, working on conjunction with the white district officers. And the Native Authority consists usually of a Chief and his Elders; but the importance of the Council may vary greatly from place to place, and in some cases government is carried on by a Federation of chiefs.

The areas over which these bodies exert their authority vary greatly in importance, from little districts of less than a thousand inhabitants up to Sultanates of perhaps a quarter of a million. The natural tendency has been towards the amalgamation of the quite small districts into larger units and federations, as giving greater efficiency and economy of administration.

The chiefs are not appointed by the Governor: they are recognized by him, which is a very different matter. Sometimes a chieftainship is strictly hereditary; in other cases the people elect, or we had better say select, their chief; and there are various grades of latitude between the two extremes. In general, the Government reserves to itself the right to refuse to acknowledge a particular individual as fit to hold office; but this is only exercised in extreme cases.

This, then, is the first great difference in practice between direct and indirect rule: in the one case the chief is a creature of Government, a mere appointee, in the other the traditional representative of the people. The second great difference concerns the payment of the native authorities. Under the direct system, the headman or chief is paid a salary from headquarters. Under the indirect system, he is not paid at all by the Central Government. On the contrary, he is looked upon, in regard to the finance of his district as in regard to his own status and appointment, as the repository of local independence. In the old tribal days, the normal state of affairs was for chiefs to receive from their subjects either tribute or service (or both). Under the system of indirect rule, this bond of economic duty between people and chief still receives recognition, but it has been regularized and modified, both in relation to the existence of central authority and to new conceptions of the duty of the local ruler to his people. The essential point is this— that although the Central Government fixes for each district the amount of the native tax (hut and poll tax), this is collected by the native authorities and paid into their own treasuries. A certain percentage is then paid over by the Native Treasuries to the Central Government as their contribution to the business of general administration; and a certain fixed sum (varying with the size and importance of the district) is further paid to the chief as his "civil list," and as salaries to various officials of his Native Administration. In this way the people feel that the chiefs belong to them, while the chiefs are brought to realize that they are no mere puppets of the Central Government, but an integral part of the administrative and economic organization of the Territory.

After these amounts have been paid out, a considerable

proportion of the tax-money (in all save a few backward districts where the tax so far has had to be fixed very low) remains unspent. In addition, the Native Treasury receives other revenue from fines and fees imposed in the local native courts, and from various minor sources such as market dues, salt royalties, and so forth.

How is the spending of this balance controlled? Here is the third essential of indirect rule. Under direct rule any surplus of money from native tax would probably go straight into general revenue, and in any case would be expended by the Government according to schemes planned out at headquarters. (Some centrally-planned schemes of wide application are always necessary; where indirect rule exists, the Government can carry them out with the aid of the fraction of the tax-money passed on to it by the Native Authorities.) But here the balance in a Native Treasury is regarded as being entirely under the control of the local Native Authority, to be expended as the Chief and his Council think fit for the benefit of the district. Not unnaturally there will be need for many years of guidance and advice from the District Officer; and his sympathetic and even forceful influence may sometimes be needed to prevent extravagance or folly. But he has no official control, and the system does in practice work out as it was intended —as an encouragement to foresight and an increased sense of responsibility on the part of the Native Authority, and as an enhancement of local patriotism and general interest in the development of the district.

Fourthly and finally we come to the administration of law. Under direct rule, an overburdened white man attempts to deal with the legal affairs of tens of thousands of natives. In spite of finding his energies overtaxed, he knows, if he reflects a little, that only a fraction of the accumulated litigiousness of the people actually finds its way to him. Either violent or illegal means of settling disputes must be increasing, or the old traditional methods of native justice, although unrecognized by white authority, are dealing with the bulk of cases out of his sight, below the surface.

This latter state of affairs seems undoubtedly to have been going on in Kenya before Native Councils were created. Among large tribes like the Kavirondo only an infinitesimal number of cases come up to be tried in the white man's courts. Now Africans are fond of going to law, and we have no reason to think that the Kenya tribes suddenly changed their character in this respect. In any case, it is certain that the elaborate system of native land tenure has continued to work through the ancient machinery without any organic connection with "Government." Very luckily for the future of the country, the traditional native institutions tenaciously continued to live a subterranean life, waiting until circumstances allowed them to sprout fully again above ground.

But under the full system of indirect rule, not only are Native Courts recognized, but they are recognized as the mouthpieces of local law and custom, only to be interfered with or modified if these conflict with certain fundamentals of white justice. Thus the law which regulates the dealings of a native people with each other is no more imposed upon them from without than is the chief who rules them; it is their own law, an indigenous product.[1]

[1] In the Musoma district I was given an example of how under indirect rule the natives get the law they like, and not an alien code. The people here are very frightened of witchcraft, and take great precautions to conceal their excrement, nail-parings, and so forth, for if an enemy

As time goes on, attempts will naturally be made to approximate the various local codes, thus avoiding obvious difficulties such as the trial of a stranger according to laws wholly different from his own. Meanwhile, in some districts the interesting experiment is being carried on of recording in writing the local common law, as well as the decisions of the Native Courts. In this way, since writing is the parent of large-scale coherence, an autochthonous legal system, closely adapted to local conditions and yet far more elaborate than the original tribal code, may gradually develop.

Here as elsewhere some control must be reserved to the representative of the Central Government; and the District Officer, in addition to being the first Court of Appeal from the Native Court, has the duty of examining the records kept by the Clerks of the Native Courts as he goes on tour through his area, and the right of revising sentences or ordering the rehearing of cases where he thinks fit.

That will suffice to give some idea of the principles of the system as it has been operating in Tanganyika for the past half-dozen years. In the succeeding chapter I shall try and clothe some of these bare abstract bones with flesh and blood by describing something of what I actually saw myself. Before ending this present chapter, however, a few

---

got hold of such products of their bodies, there would be no limit to the harm he might do. Recently a man was caught stealing another man's urine. The presumption was that he wanted it for magic purposes, and the Native Court inflicted the heavy fine of 10s. And the District Officer, when he went through the records, upheld the judgment. According to certain standards, he was wrong to confirm what he knew was based in error; but granted that the Territory has embarked on the policy of indirect rule, he was perfectly correct.

more words are necessary on the peculiar conditions in parts of Tanganyika.

There are some parts of Tanganyika Territory where the German method of ruling through paid headmen or akidas, coupled with the policy of deliberately discouraging the old tribal organization (a policy which appeared to have been vigorously practised in some parts of the colony, hardly or not at all in others) seemed to have broken down the spirit of tribalism and its institutions. In the southern coastal area of Lindi (I am citing the Report on the administration of the Tanganyika Mandate in 1927 issued by the Colonial Office to the League Council), the forty years of direct rule, combined with other detribalizing influences such as the penetration of Arab culture, seemed to have destroyed all trace of the original social system. Investigation showed, however, that the tenacious conservatism of the people had retained a clan or family group system, and that in the heads of the various family groups (who still dealt with the apportionment of land) there lay to hand the raw materials for native administrations under an indirect system of rule. In spite of months of investigation by District Officers, followed by explanation and promises of a change of system, the people refused to believe that the old paid headmen (who had to be continued in office until new officials could be appointed) would ever really be replaced by men representative of popular institutions. When finally the change was effected, and native administrations were actually formed, ruled by Councils of Family Heads, collecting their own taxes, and trying cases in their own Courts, the people became enthusiastic. One member of a Council summed up the situation by saying, "You have given us back our country. We are men again." Since then very notable progress has been made in shouldering the new responsibilities and in recovering the spirit of independence so long suppressed.

Then in some regions there exist tribes whose organization is such that it is impossible to use it as a basis for an efficient system of indirect rule. Back from the southeastern shore of Lake Victoria, for instance, as I was told by a friend who is Administrative Officer there, is a tribe organized so completely on the age-group system that the Elders have no say in affairs. Each age-class consists, of course, of all the young men initiated at one time; and a new class is inaugurated about every seven years. The affairs of the tribe are in the hands of the senior age-class of warriors—young men from about 25 to 32 years of age. At the conclusion of their time, they pass on to the Elder stage and hand over the reins of office to the age-class below. This meant a complete lack of continuity, and was always liable to lead to the warriors making the best of their short term of office by practising extortion. The United States has been finding the Spoils System unsatisfactory: it is equally unsatisfactory for Africa. So the old organization, in its existing form, had to be suppressed, and one deliberately set up which was more adapted to modern conditions when peace not war is the rule, and the tribes are not sovereign entities but parts of a larger community.

There still are, I believe, a few backward or difficult communities in Tanganyika among which it has not yet been practicable to introduce indirect rule. But their number is decreasing year by year. Year by year, too, the responsibilities of the existing Native Administrations are being enlarged, and, through adjustments of tax, the amount of money which they have at their disposal for their people's advancement is being increased. Every administration has its faults: doubtless our administration of this Mandated Territory is no exception, but at least no one can deny that we are putting into practice and carrying out, with a thoroughness and rapidity which has surprised even the warmest partisans of the system, one important duty laid upon a Mandatory Power—the development of the native inhabitants along lines fitting them to take over more and more of the government of their own country.

Chapter XII

INDIRECT RULE IN OPERATION

A nasty blow to the system of indirect rule was the recent Saidi case at Tabora. Sultan Saidi, chief of one of the largest Native Administrations in the country (with headquarters just outside Tabora), recipient of the greatest consideration from its white administrators, from the Governor down, was found to have been guilty of the wholesale embezzlement of the Native Treasury funds in his charge. The details of the extremely ingenious method by which he circumvented the safeguards to the system do not concern us here, nor the question whether the European officers whose duty it was to administer those safeguards had not been a little negligent or at least perfunctory. What concerns us is that he had, during a series of years, misappropriated about £10,000—a huge sum for an East African chief. When arrested, he had scarcely anything to show for his lapse. Much he had been forced to give to his accomplices, active or passive, most he had simply thrown about in a desire to cut a grand figure—a sheer stupidity of largesse. Kenya, of course, rubbed its hands over the case; phrases such as "This is what comes of giving responsibility to natives," "the inevitable outcome of the system of indirect rule," and a general attitude of "I told you so," filled the Kenya newspapers.

It is a good thing to face a failure or so at the outset. It cures undue optimism. The sad case of Sultan Saidi may have been needed to demonstrate that we are none of us perfect, not even if we have black skins; but I do not see that by it the whole system of indirect rule for East Africa stands condemned.

Later, when I was the guest of Sir William Gowers in Uganda, that shrewd and capable judge of human character told me of the difficulties he had had as an official in Nigeria a quarter of a century ago when indirect rule was first being launched on the country. Some even of the keenest and most influential sponsors of the scheme were extremely reluctant to push the principle to its logical end when it was a question of putting financial responsibility on the chiefs. The chiefs would not be up to it; they would peculate and bring the whole scheme down in ruins; they could not be expected to have the same ideas about honesty as a white man. Gowers, however, insisted that the vital point in indirect rule was the assumption of responsibility by the Native Authorities; that there was no more reason for refusing them responsibility in money matters than in matters of law or government; and indeed that, if the chiefs were not to have money to spend on their own responsibility, the system would be hollow and sham, and would fail of its purpose because it left the native still in leading strings as regards the chief source of material power.

Lord Lugard in his writings stresses the same point: if we seriously believe in the value of responsibility as a means of educating the African, we must not be afraid of the African making mistakes. If he did not have the chance of making mistakes, he would not be enjoying real responsibility. Besides, *Humanum est*—we ourselves are not immune.

There is also a further, more subtle influence which must be guarded against. It is the reluctance of a maturer mind to allow those of less mature judgment the freedom to err. And this reluctance is intensified when the mature man has a sense of responsibility for the immature, and still more intensified when he is fond of them, proud of them, anxious for their success, or in any other way emotionally concerned about them. It is, in fact, the same influence which makes it so difficult for parents to let their children alone, and prefers for them a safe, uneventful, but repressed and incomplete development to a more vital salvation attained through pain and error. But it is most important that the vicarious hope and pride and ambition of the parent, or of the white man *in loco parentis* to the black, should not be allowed to defeat their own ends; and one of the most important as well as the most difficult tasks for an administrative officer in a district where indirect rule is well under way will always be to efface himself and give his charges their head.

In any case, it is irrational and unhealthy to expect a higher standard of honesty in native chiefs than in European aldermen or politicians, just as it is to expect a more perfect morality from one's children than from oneself and one's adult friends. The real believer in indirect rule and the progress of the African will never be lenient to dishonesty or oppression, but he will know that offences must come; and when they do, though it be pain and grief to him, he will console himself by remembering that "it is better for a man to go wrong in freedom than to go right in chains."

Just at this time the trial of Saidi was being held at Dar-es-Salaam. The news of his acquittal on a legal technicality arrived at Tabora the day after I did, and I was witness of heartfelt blasphemies against the Law and all its ways on the part of long-suffering Administrators. I understand, however, that Saidi, though free, is not allowed to return home, and that the district is doing well under his successor. Since my return I have seen the Provincial Commissioner's Report for 1929. In it he writes: "The magnificent rains which are falling are accepted by the people as a visible sign of the return of the rightful line, and, given a good harvest, the position and popularity of the new chief should be assured." In Africa there is something to be said for Providence.

Even at this awkward time native affairs went smoothly on under the impetus of the old organization. I visited the central Native Court and heard a case decided. On our entry the crowd of listeners in the court-house (a big thatched building, with its walls pierced so as to leave it half open to the air) rose and, bowing slightly, clapped their hands. This hand-clapping is the charming form of salutation here in vogue. Strong is the effect of association! This apparent applause automatically made me feel as if I had done something worth while, and I walked up the gangway experiencing the sensations of a successful prima donna without having had to earn them.

We took our seats on the dais; the four judges, who with natural and dignified courtesy had risen and greeted us, sat down again, the case went on, and I had an opportunity to look about me. The President of the Court was a very fine-looking old man whose big oblong face testified to an admixture of Arab blood with the Bantu stock.

Then there was another elderly man, also grave and dignified, and a muscular, powerful young fellow, more purely negroid. The last of the four, to my intense surprise, was a woman; and not an old woman either, but a woman of twenty-five or thirty, with an aristocratic cast of features and a very decorative cotton print swathed round her slim body. When the time came to give judgment on the case (a straightforward affair of stealing goats) she spoke in her turn, with perfect assurance. I later ascertained that in this area it is quite customary for women to be on the Councils of Elders; and one whole district is in charge of an ancient and extremely efficient woman chieftainess. Even in Africa the rule appears to hold that, of the women who do succeed in attaining power, a disproportionate number are of outstanding character or ability.

The verdict was given. The defendant, a trifle grumpily but very promptly, stepped forward and paid over to the clerk of the court a little pile of silver shillings. The clerk entered up the case in the court book—date; plaintiff, John Doe; defendant, Richard Roe; charge, stealing four goats; brief reasons for the judgment; the fine. The record was there for the District Officer to see when he comes on inspection.

It is naturally more agreeable to dwell on successes than on failures; and I expect the Provincial Commissioner was glad to take me off with the dawn next day to see Shinyanga, one of the star turns of indirect rule.

We halted half-way, at Mzega. What delightful unexpectednesses await one in Africa! Our host, the District Officer, was an elderly man, intelligent-faced, small and frail-looking; you might be pardoned for associating him with literary bachelordom in a Kensington flat. By way of

contrast, however, his verandah was adorned with eleven
leather quivers, all containing poisoned arrows. He had
confiscated them ten days before from a band of natives
who were illegally slaughtering game. As a matter of fact,
he is a man of adventurous life. His elephant-hunting ex-
ploits have made him almost legendary in the country. I
had previously heard the story of his being invited to join
a condescending Personage for some elephant-shooting. "If
I get one this time," said the Personage, "it will be my
eleventh." "Really," replied the little man; "if I get one,
it will be—let me see—my sixty-seventh." And there was
a charming tale of his being confronted, while coasting
down a steep bush track on a bicycle, with a huge bull
elephant. He could not stop; a collision would be, undoubtedly, disastrous. Automatically, he rang his bell; and
the elephant, snorting, turned and fled back into the bush.

But native administration is my theme, and not elephants. A Ngoma or dance-festival had been organized for
my benefit; and it was evident that under indirect rule the
people had lost none of their zest in life. There was a
women's dance, a men's dance, and a mixed dance—a
regular three-ring circus. The performers in the mixed
dance belonged to a special sect which is said to have some
of the objectionable features of a secret society. The men's
dance was very extraordinary, in that the circle of dancers,
instead of appearing as one would expect in perspiring
semi-nudity, were all dressed in the white nightdress robe
you associate with house-boys in East Africa. These long
khansis were, of course, introduced by the Arabs, and the
wearing of them at a dance was another example of the
strong Arab and Mohammedan influence still persisting

hereabouts, an influence dating from the days when Tabora was the inland metropolis of the slave-trade.

Whatever the originating influence, the effect produced by long white robes upon the persons of excited negroes, hopping rhythmically up and down with bodies bent a little forward, shouting the while, emphasizing the time by hand-clapping, and occasionally in a frenzy of enthusiasm leaping forward to do a brief *pas seul* and pirouette in the ring, was peculiarly grotesque. And the incongruity was heightened by the appearance of the dance-leader—an enormously tall, raw-boned man, with frizzy hair, loose joints, over-large features and an unpleasant expression, who, with next to no clothing, but his face plastered with light yellow earth, wore himself out, shouting hoarsely, in acrobatic violences.

It is curious, by the way, to see the familiar psychological and physical types of Europe reappearing in Africa. This man's general appearance and quality of disagreeable loutish leadership and power through impudence could easily have been matched in an East End gang or the leading spirits of some minor insubordination in a dockyard town. Indeed, you can recognize all the variety of our temperamental types among Africans. The black skin, negro features and other racial characters are as it were a garment; beneath this, the variations of ductless glands, nervous constitution, inborn psychological bias, body-build and the rest see to it that the same range of human variety is realized, the same gallery of types created, in Africa as in Europe. One soon ceases to think of the Africans as so many "natives" or "negroes"; they become just people, as full of individuality as a European crowd, but happening to have dark skins and differently-formed lips and noses.

So on to Shinyanga. I have already spoken of Shinyanga
as the place in which so much has been accomplished in
the reclamation of bush from the sinister empire of the
tsetse-fly for the use of man and his beasts. It is the headquarters of the European administration of the district.
Indirect rule has worked well here for a combination of
reasons. In the first place, the local tribe, the Wasukuma,
are an industrious and intelligent people, with a large
number of able chiefs. Secondly, the District Officer has,
by his rare blend of energy and tact, got the chiefs to move
faster than of their own initiative they would have done;
it makes all the difference, especially at the outset, for
Africans faced with new vistas to have at their elbow a
white man whom they can trust, who can give them technical advice, who can help them in their thinking and
planning. Thirdly, there is complete harmony between the
representatives of the several Government departments—
notably Administration, Agriculture and Tsetse Research
—and all are co-operating actively to help the Native Authority; not merely is there no jealousy or friction, but, I
gathered, none of the fuss of formalities such as too com-
monly clogs the machinery of collaboration. So often, in
Africa as elsewhere, the spirit is willing, but the red tape
is strong.

And here perhaps I may insert a parenthesis on Imperialism. I feel I must do so somewhere, and this is a
good opportunity. I saw the light in the good old days
when

> Every boy and every gal
>   That's born into the world alive
> Was either a little Liberal
>   Or else a little Conservative.

124

INDIRECT RULE IN OPERATION

Personally, I was born a little Liberal, and imbibed, with complete unconsciousness, together with the idea that Protection was wicked and nonconformist morals somehow good, an attitude, not quite amounting to hostility but definitely grudging, towards Mr. Kipling's poetry and the Empire in general. The basis of such imbibed beliefs was of course completely irrational, like being Oxford for the boat-race; but as Mr. Trotter reminds us in his *Instincts of the Herd*, it is usually unreason which gives tenacity to beliefs. However, reality is a powerful solvent; and contact with the actual work of the Empire and with men who, like my hosts here, M'Mahon the District Officer and Stiebel the Provincial Commissioner, are engaged upon the details of that Imperial work, do produce a changed attitude. The traveller in Africa, without indulging either the false sentimentality of jingo imperialism or the false shame of doctrinaire little-Englandism, can simply feel proud of belonging to a nation which does a difficult job, demanding such unselfish devotion, honesty and hard work, and does it on the whole so well. Undoubtedly, our men have their defects compared with those of other Empires, such as the French or the Dutch. But these defects are perhaps mainly defects of intellectual attitude and limited outlook; in the routine of practical administration, our average of performance seems to stand the highest. If a contact with a bit of the British Colonial Empire has not yet made me a full-blooded devotee of *Kiplingismus*, it has certainly shown me the way to a spirit of Liberal Imperialism.

The headquarters of the Native Administration is at Ibadakuli, a few miles away. Here you find a big central building for assemblies and the trying of cases, and near

by are a series of smaller buildings which are for the accommodation of the various Chiefs and Headmen of the
Sukuma Federation when they come in for meetings. Close
by is the school. This was of the usual residential type,
but with little round thatched huts for the boys' sleeping-
quarters instead of the usual big rectangular dormitories.
Each hut holds eight boys; they cannot be said to be
pampered, as they sleep on army boards; but everything
is beautifully clean, and the huts are having concrete floors
laid down, as precaution against spirillum ticks. There was
the usual technical side, which included a tailor's shop;
here the boys who were learning a tailor's job made various
garments for the tribal messengers and other functionaries. The great pride of the school is its band. I am told
that nowadays when a chief wants to give an entertainment he asks for the school band instead of arranging the
usual dance to a tom-tom accompaniment. Such, rather
regrettably, is progress.

A little way down the road again was a considerable-
sized experimental farm, in which a great variety of crops
were being grown. Some of the plots contained familiar
crops grown under various methods; others contained crops
not generally cultivated in the district, including new kinds
of beans, whose suitability or the reverse was here being
determined. An interesting feature was the plots of Sudan
grass and other grasses, whose seeds will be planted to
check erosion. On the farm was the first plough I had
seen in Africa, busily at work with six oxen and a native
ploughman. From hoe and digging-stick to plough: the
African is just taking a step which for us lies far back in
pre-history.

And over against the farm was the new seed-store—

a nice-looking modern building, concrete-floored, in which large quantities of tested seeds are kept ready to be sent out to native cultivators as required. A group of black figures busy among a pile of dead-white cotton made a vivid picture.

There is also a stock-farm, which I was unable to see; and the making and selling of ghee (clarified butter) has been embarked upon. And of course the excellent roads, apart from the first-class and trunk roads, are local products.

Remember that all these are ventures of the Native Administration, due to its initiative and financed out of the local money in its treasury; remember too that all this has grown up in little over five years of indirect rule; and you must acknowledge that the system has its points. Nor is this all. In some ways the *pièce de resistance* is the medical centre; but as this is partly the result of private white initiative, it stands in rather a different category.

Mr. and Mrs. Maynard are American missionaries; in addition, Mrs. Maynard is a medical woman. They have lived here for some time, devoting most of their attention to the health of the population. They started a tiny hospital with a few beds and an out-patients' room that was always full; they started a leper colony; they started a maternity and child welfare centre. This was all done without any subvention. Then the District Officer persuaded them and the chiefs that it would be a good thing for all parties if the medical centre had some official connection with local government; and with considerable enthusiasm it was affiliated to the Native Administration, with voted moneys for an extension of all the buildings.

Quite good results are being got at the leper hospital,

over which a keen-looking native had charge; the general
hospital is a model of neatness; in the out-patient department about three hundred people are dealt with every day.
But the maternity hospital is the most fascinating. It is
equipped with the utmost simplicity and the minimum of
expense; there are no luxuries, only cleanliness, efficiency
and a happy spirit. A group of women smiled at us from
the steps. Some were still expecting their babies; one had
had hers that very morning at seven, but was up and about.
(The women here are encouraged to get up if they feel
like it. In some other East African maternity clinics, I
understand, the white matrons have rigidly enforced the
lie-abed principles of Europe; but the native women chafe
under these regulations—and, what is more, seem not to
need the rest.) Mrs. Maynard told me that here in Shinyanga they had just as many complications and difficult
deliveries as at home, but that when labour is normal the
women recover from it with astonishing elasticity and
speed. On the other hand, the Indian women who come to
the clinic make a terrible fuss.

When maternity work was first tried, the women viewed
it with great suspicion. Very luckily, one of the most important chiefs believed in it, or at least in Mrs. Maynard,
and sent his favourite wife to have a baby under her care.
After that, there was as steady a flow of expectant mothers
as there was of abdominal operations in England after
King Edward's appendicitis.

At either end of the little building was a baby-room.
There was not money or space for separate cots; so in
each was one enormous cot, much broader than it was
long; one held a crop of six, the other of seven little black
creatures, all less than a week old. (I say black, but their

tint varies greatly at birth, some being already almost as dark as they will ever be, others a mere grey-brown, which will deepen later.)

And for all this there is but the one doctor, the solitary Mrs. Maynard. How does she manage it? She has only managed by adding yet another to the list of her activities: she trains native girls to help her. She takes girls at fourteen or fifteen, and makes them pledge themselves to stay with her and not to marry for at least three years. They start on the simpler and more menial work, but long before their time is up they are good nurses, quite capable of dealing with a birth, administering an injection, and so on. Owing to the spectacular success of the treatment of yaws by bismuth, injections are all the rage among the local natives, and for the least complaint they come in demanding, not highly-coloured and nasty medicine—that is old-fashioned—but the needle-prick: puncture is the panacea. However, for a long time the natives demurred to having their injections given them by a native nurse, and insisted on the overworked Mrs. Maynard. Finally the District Officer, having occasion to be injected for some prophylactic reason, had it done *coram publico* by one of the black girls. After this, there was no further difficulty.

These native girls, who have been trained to the cleanliness, tidiness and efficient compassion of the wards, look charming. They may have lost the barbaric and semi-nude fascination of pristine Africa, yet their simple uniforms do not look in the least unbecoming or incongruous on them as, alas! European clothes ordinarily do on negro womankind, but confer the grace of suitability. Under the nurse's headdress the black faces acquire an appearance of added breadth, a look of solid kindliness. At the moment there are seven of them—including one whom Mrs. Maynard helped to bring into the world.

As the girls grow up, they marry, and new ones must be trained to fill their places. But their usefulness is not diminished; for, under the proud title of District Health Visitors, they become centres of enlightenment in the villages. Mrs. Maynard broke her usual routine of continuous work to give us a cup of tea in her pleasant little house, with wide verandah giving a view over the rolling plain. It was a delight to talk to her, for here, you felt, was someone who was not only doing useful work, but happy in her existence.

The visit ended with a crowded assembly in the Court-house, at which I had to make a speech. What it was like when it reached the auditors' minds, I don't know, as it had to be twice interpreted—first into Swahili by my host, then into Sukuma by the official interpreter. Doubtless it was skilfully rephrased to suit the African mind, for it received a generous meed of applause.

This difficulty of language is a very real one. In Tabora and Mwanza provinces, the Wanyamwezi-Wasukuma group of tribes comprise more than a million people, and therefore nearly a quarter of the population of the Terri-tory. Yet I was assured that there was no white official in the country who was really at home in the language. This, of course, comes largely from the constant transfer of men from one district to another. Further, no encourage-ment, direct or indirect, is given to men to learn a local language; everything is concentrated upon the *lingua franca* of Swahili. In the present state of affairs this is very likely inevitable. It is none the less unfortunate: you cannot be really at home with the inside of people's minds unless you think in their own language.

As we sped home in the car, it was delightful to see the men and women working in the fields throw down their tools and scurry towards the road, stopping to bow and clap hands and shout greetings to the *Bwana Shauri*. (Bwana Shauri, the usual appelation for a District Officer, is not easily translatable. For *Shauri* means affairs, but also *affaires*; it means legal cases and casual disputes, and also business discussions. If you were cynical you could translate Bwana Shauri as the Lord of Fuss—if a little bit pompous, as Controller of Affairs; and both would have truth in them.)

Next day we were motored to Ngudu, the headquarters of the Bukwimba Native Administration. Ngudu is in Mwanza Province, so I was handed over to another hospitable Provincial Commissioner, who was even more energetic than my previous host, and motored me sixty miles —or was it eighty? anyhow, a good three hours—before breakfast. Here at Ngudu the same general features of a young, keen and intelligent Native Administration were repeated. One difference was the amount of afforestation being practised; large and small plantations of yellow-flowered cassia were being made, and we passed a mile-long avenue of cassia which a chief had planted along the track from the main road to his house.

Another difference was that whereas the Sukuma district is ruled by a federation of chiefs in council, Bukwimba, though also a federation, has its council dominated by a Head Chief. This important personage is Chief Massanja; his own chieftainship contains 70,000 people, and the Federation nearly 200,000. He greeted us—an interesting-looking man of about 40, dressed in very well-cut European clothes (in spite of the Government's encouragement of native robes for chiefs and headmen). He became chief when quite a boy, and has recently celebrated the twenty-five-year jubilee of his rule. In the court-house, where we presently went, is a large chair or throne, presented to him by the Governor on that occasion. It looked uncomfortable, but was very imposing. The fact that its arms are carved to represent elephants will give some idea of its rather over-powering grandeur. He was also the recipient of the much-coveted King's Medal, and of a £500 Buick (a much more magnificent car than that of any white man within two hundred miles) presented by subscription of his subjects. They had wanted to give him a British car, but Britons, it seems, will be Britons, and no guarantee of delivery within three-and-a-half months could be obtained from certain firms who shall be nameless; so the order, as often, went to America. (In other cases it goes to Germany, or to Japan. I was reliably informed that the Germans, having discovered that the African likes a clock whose ticking really *is* ticking, manufactured a loud-ticker alarm-clock especially for the African market. With works which can be heard for a hundred yards, and the additional embellishment of a coloured picture which moves across the clock-face at each tick, it is killing all rivals. And the Japanese take trouble to suit the African's taste in cotton-prints, while our people too often adopt a take-it-or-leave-it attitude, won't split bales, and altogether seem to prefer not to make a sale unless it is in the approved manner.)

The Native Courts fascinated me, and I was glad to find the Ngudu one in session. Chief Massanja sat in his elephant-armed chair of office, his colleagues on either side. They were all in European dress, and therefore looked commonplace to European eyes. I suppose the glamour of white civilization is so strong as to make them look dazzling to the eyes of their compatriots; but trousers and grey felt hats—when they might have been wearing long white robes with embroidered jackets and some turbanish headdress! On a bench against the opposite wall were a couple of native policemen, and four or five old men—the learned elders, repositories of tribal law and custom, to be consulted by the judges in case of need: one was very old and shrivelled, another with a yellow tint in his black and a queer Mongolian cast. The case was people this time, not goats. The plaintiff accused the defendant of committing adultery with his wife and getting her with child. The defendant was a handsome but very barbaric-looking creature; comparing him with the plaintiff, a rather slinking, unpleasant little fellow, one could not feel too harshly against the wife. Then there was the woman herself, small and not unattractive, with a six months' baby at her breast; her father; and a witness for the defendant: they all stood in a row in the front of the court. While they were giving the evidence, one of the native policemen opposite bothered me: he would keep on interjecting conversationally, 'M'm —m'm—lamu . . . m'm . . . m'm, m'm, lamu—m'm . . . ,' and so on. I whispered to the District Commissioner at my elbow to ask why he did this, and found that he was only keeping up an old tradition of the Wasukuma. When cases are being heard, there is always a man deputed to mumble thus—in order to make the witnesses feel at ease and to stimulate their flow of language. An admirable notion!

They all spoke, the woman at great length. The old men were consulted; the judges conferred. Result—*guilty*: the defendant had been caught in the act (very direct evidence is apparently needed here, evidence after Justice Merivale's heart, none of your mere hotel-bill stuff); and he was condemned to pay five head of cattle to the plaintiff.

Back of the court-room was the office. In it two negroes were busy typewriting, and there was a large safe containing huge numbers of shillings from court fines and hut-tax, waiting to be taken to the bank. And with that glimpse of order and prosperity in our minds, we took our leave.

Motoring on to Mwanza, my mind was full of the native life I had seen in the last few days. And now, as I put my notes into shape, it is full also of other kinds of native life which I have seen, talked about and read of elsewhere.

There do seem to be two main channels along which the stream of native African life can flow. One channel is that of Indirect Rule, some of whose results I have just been recording. The other is the channel of Economic Least Resistance, which would assimilate the African peoples to Western civilization as an economic appendage, a new kind of proletariat, black-skinned and concerned with raw materials instead of white-skinned and concerned with manufacture. For it seems clear enough that unless more deliberate attempt is made to organize native society, it will not develop but simply collapse in contact with the powerful and corrosive forces of supra-national economics. Nor is the attempt to do so either unnatural or sentimental, as some *Realpolitiker* would have us believe. Young children would not develop properly if they had to stand alone in a world of adult competition; they need the "unnatural" artifice of a home, the "sentimental" assistance of maternal devotion or some substitute for it. Different conditions are needed for the development of strength and capabilities, and for their exercise.

"The young District Commissioner of thirty years ago surveys in his old age with astonishment and dismay the work of his hands: the orderly and reputable society he knew and ruled by a word or a gesture is gone, and, jostled in the streets of a corrugated iron city by those who were accustomed to fall on their knees when he walked abroad, he asks himself in bitterness if it was for this that he has laboured all his life, for this tattered rabble of malodorous and ill-disciplined savages." So "P. E. M." in a pamphlet on Native Administration.[1]

The criticism seems just, after one has seen the native quarters of East African towns or the labour-lines of unprogressive settlers. Do not let us forget that the African in contact with modern ideas and economic forces is in a very different plight from any member of a Western civilization, even the humblest and most down-trodden. We have our ponderous system of ideas, rooted in centuries of tradition, actualized in powerful institutions. There are new ideas and forces that threaten the stability of our world, but for one thing they have sprung out of the tradition of that same world, and for another they are not organized; our world is not in contact with another and more powerful world of existence. Whereas the world of the African native is in contact with a world whose forces are immeasurably more powerful, whose science is a greater magic, whose ideas are on an altogether different

[1] Dar-es-Salaam, 1927.

135

plane of coherence and continuity. And his old life, in its undeveloped form, has no place in his new world; his tradition seems to have no relevance to the new ideas. So smash goes the old tradition before anything else is built up to take its place. And the native social organism disintegrates into a mere tissue-culture of isolated human cells, cultivated in a rich but unhealthy broth that is a by-product of Western Capitalism, instead of growing coherently in the blood of their own tradition.

The only way open to counteract this disintegration is to strengthen the existing native social organism and give it a fillip which will rouse it from its century-long drowse of arrested development, and set it growing into something stronger. And I confess that to achieve this, some variation or other on the theme of Indirect Rule seems the only possible method.

This is not to say that Indirect Rule is a panacea. For one thing, towns will come (though one is sometimes tempted to add, but woe unto them through whom they come). And in East African towns, Indirect Rule in the strict sense will not work; for it bases itself upon existing tribal institutions, and these are dumb when confronted with a town.

It may be that something analogous to the mediæval guild system will prove to be the best way of making the first big step out of chaos in African towns. It is certain that the African needs some organization which will appeal to his strong social solidarity and group loyalty; and that, in the present stage of his development at least, he is very susceptible to the influence of symbolism and ceremonial, both of which can be made to play a considerable part in a guild system. He already possesses something analogous in his widespread dance organizations, and it should not be impossible to extend the idea to industry.

Whatever the solution may ultimately prove to be, something must be done if we are not to find ourselves responsible for the growth of slums and a parasitic proletariat in Africa: and although various beginnings have been made to cope with the problem, none have as yet taken us very far. There is, however, a danger inherent in the very nature of Indirect Rule which needs considering—the danger of making too much of a good thing, of making a fetish instead of a stepping-stone (if I may mix my metaphors) of existing native institutions. It can never be our aim, save perhaps with a few out-of-the-way peoples whose fate in unrestricted contact with Western ideas would be simply to wilt, degenerate and disappear (the Congo pigmies seem to be an African example), merely to preserve a human zoo, an Anthropological Garden. It cannot be our aim, for it would not work. Our mere presence in Africa makes it in the long run impossible; the fact that we are encouraging native production and native education, permitting the entry of white capital, missionaries, and science into Africa, makes it doubly impossible.

From this angle Victor Murray, in his *School in the Bush*, criticizes our policy in certain parts of Northern Nigeria, where the administration has been discouraging or forbidding the establishment of schools other than the traditional Koran schools, where the chief aim is the learning by rote of the Holy Book, on the ground that the areas are Mahomedan. The implication is that the people ought not to *want* Western ideas, and should in effect be protected against them, even though a progressive minority are quite anxious for them and for our methods of education.

A not dissimilar danger is that of perpetuating practices which are really transitional, in a form which becomes rigid because written and Governmentally-sanctioned. Written law and established order confer many benefits; but they are capable of producing dead hands which may lie heavy on living existing systems.

And there is, of course, the ever-present danger of allowing too much latitude to the representatives of the existing tribal system, the chiefs and headmen, without giving the common people sufficient opportunities of education and development, or sufficient chance of making their voice more effectively heard in local affairs through some democratic development of the system. This concentration on the administrative machinery instead of on the spirit of indirect rule may lead to corruption and oppression, and the last state may be worse than the first.

But every experiment has its difficulties. The watchwords of those responsible for the experiment of Indirect Rule should be gradualness, so that all that is good in tribalism may have a chance to strike firm root under the new conditions; freedom for orderly change, so that healthy development may run its course unhampered when the time is ripe; and, when change is in the air, an insistence on correlation in change, so that one activity does not outrun another and unbalance native life, but schools keep pace with economic progress, and the general spread of ideas be not left behind by technical efficiency in law and administration.

But you never can keep long to one subject if you are travelling rapidly through Africa. That evening I was leaning over the rail of the lake steamer, talking with a young American with horn-rimmed spectacles and a strong likeness to Harold Lloyd. He was a member of the Metro-Goldwyn Company, which had just, at fabulous expense, been making a talking film of Trader Horn on the shores of a little lake (whose freedom from crocodiles is fortunate, but completely mysterious) close to the north-west shore of the Victoria Nyanza. He was responsible for the sound-recording apparatus. A party of them were just going up to the Serengeti plains to do some wild-beast scenes; and then he was to be left alone in Africa for six months or a year to collect a "Library of African Noises.". . .

> The world is so full of a number of things,
> I am sure we should all be as happy as kings.

Stevenson was certainly right in the first line. But then there seems to be a *non sequitur*: bewilderment, or despair, could equally follow. At the moment, gentle amusement and a strong desire for bed were my chief feelings; and I slept greedily and thankfully for an unconscionable time.

Chapter XIII

TABORA TO MWANZA: VARIA

I have already said a good deal about Tabora and the road to Mwanza in the last chapter. But I would not be true to my purpose of giving a view of African variety if I did not set down also a few scattered incidents from my diary.

Tabora. Besides the Government School for the Sons of Chiefs I went over the White Fathers' Higher Seminary, an imposing brick building whose construction is not quite finished. The Father in charge was a Frenchman, bearded, of course, cultivated and efficient. The Seminary, like other Seminaries, trains candidates for the priesthood; here the candidates are naturally all black men, drawn from Tanganyika, Kenya, and Nyasaland. Another Higher Seminary has existed for some years in Uganda, and over thirty black priests have already been fledged from it. Counting from the beginning of their time in a bush school, the candidates must have had over twenty years of education before they can be ordained. And the vast majority fall out by the way; of those who begin with the intention of becoming priests, at the very most five per cent. achieve their aim. During the last six or seven years of their course, the medium of instruction is—Swahili? No; English? No; Latin, just as it would be in Rome or Maynooth, I suppose.

TABORA TO MWANZA: VARIA

From the point of view of Roman Catholicism this is entirely logical; but to a humble scientific humanist it did, I fear, seem merely preposterous. The Father in charge told me with pride that when a year or so ago a notable Catholic scholar from Louvain visited East Africa, he engaged in a Latin disputation with a student of the Uganda Seminary, and that in respect of rhetoric and Latinity the African proved the better man.

From the Seminary we went on to see ex-Sultan Saidi's palace—a large quadrangle, with rooms papered and furnished in European style, and over the way another big building for his main stock of wives. In the courtyard was the stump of a tree, with its branches cut back so that it looked like a hat-rack in the rustic style. But instead of hats it was hung over with the skulls of lions. These lion-trees are a feature of the region. Each chief has one; whenever a lion is killed in his district, the skull is brought in and with appropriate rites hung on its peg by an official whose major duty is to perform the ritual on these occasions. It must be admitted that such a violent juxtaposition of incompatible religions does provide a new sensation for someone accustomed to the comparative uniformity of a European country in this respect.

And then we visited the house, now in ruins, in which Livingstone and Stanley once lived for some months; a monument nearby commemorates the strangely-assorted pair.

Tabora town was well worth a visit, with its animated market-place. In the centre of the square was a sort of loggia in which a packed crowd of natives sat and drank native beer—all very orderly and pleasant, if a little strong-scented to white noses. Among them was a troupe of professional dancers (this, too, I understand, is due to Arab influence) with white bead headdresses or ostrich-feathers on their heads. I enjoyed a stall which combined the functions of an Old Curiosity Shop with those of a rag-and-bone merchant. In it you could buy almost anything as long as it was scrappy enough, from leopards' claws to bottle-stoppers, from dilapidated iron bedsteads to broken china. The proprietor was an ex-corporal of the King's African Rifles; his very military salute when he bade us farewell was a little spoilt by the very unmilitary rags he was wearing.

Then there was the pleasant European Club, with the inevitable golfers and tennis-players drinking the inevitable sun-downers and talking the inevitable gossip; and the official dinner (with real ices—great rarity in these parts; the necessary ice comes out of the refrigerating car on the twice-a-week train) which prolonged itself with bridge and vingt-et-un till after midnight, for all that we had to breakfast at 6.30.

So goodbye to Tabora. On the road to Shinyanga I cherish the memory of a rather large out-school, and the nice little black brats, with exceedingly alert faces, rolling their eyes round to look at the visitors while standing stiff at attention. Asked if I would like them to perform in any particular field, I inquired if they could sing. Oh yes, they could sing: and in a moment I was almost deafened by the strains of *Clementine*, rendered with the metallic nasality prevalent in East Africa. Verse succeeded verse— all in Swahili, of course—until at length I ventured to say that it would be nice to test them in arithmetic (or indeed anything rather quieter). The intense earnestness of the performance had made me want to laugh; luckily, however, I had restrained myself, for when I asked my host why this tune had been selected as a representative of Western musical culture, I was told that it was the Territory's National Anthem.

"Tanganyika, Tanganyika, oh my *dar*ling Clementine. . . ." It must be admitted that the word Tanganyika fits well into the melody; but all the same, what a barbaric tune to have chosen! I feel that the Germans could never have been guilty of such a musical insult. And the worst of it was that the little chaps so obviously found Clementine to their taste, and sang it with the greatest gusto.

Shinyanga. I have elsewhere spoken of the remarkable tsetse-clearing operations here. It was astonishing to sit on the District Officer's verandah, looking out on the new settlement, and the new railway, and the open plain beyond stretching for some miles in every direction, and to be told that five years ago this was all bush, and tsetse-ridden bush at that. And it is wonderful to see along the roadside native villages and herds of cattle where five years back no human settlement was possible. Faust crowning his life by draining a marsh does not strike one as a very romantic or exciting end to Goethe's great drama. But when you come to a country in which man has to fight with Nature for the mere right to live, human successes in that fight assume a very high value, and thrill one in a way almost impossible for the dweller in an old and long-tamed country to understand.

The old post, built by the Germans, and containing as usual a strongly-fortified boma, lies ten miles away. It is there that the headquarters of the practical side of tsetse research are stationed; and the place swarms with the wicked, sharp-tongued brutes. There I found poor Swynnerton suffering from a triple bill of malaria, bilharzia, and relapsing fever—a veritable museum of tropical diseases, caused by three very different kinds of parasites, and conveyed by three very different kinds of hosts, one by an insect, one by a mollusc, and one by an arachnid. He seemed to be congratulating himself on not having sleeping-sickness as well. If you will work as hard and expose yourself to as many risks as he does, you will still from time to time incur these penalties of tropical life. He was just going on to Mrs. Maynard's care at Ibadakuli. I later heard that she kept him two months, but turned him out a fit man.

That night, before going to my bed in the little guest-house in the garden, my hostess told me not to be worried if the dog (a very large Airedale) paid me a visit during the night: it was his habit to inspect sleeping visitors. I was very glad that she had not forgotten to warn me. The hyenas had been making their ghostly whining laugh close by as I walked across; and there is always, I suppose, the off chance of a leopard. When in the small hours I awoke suddenly to hear an animal breathing and padding about in my room, I confess that the first reaction was, quite instinctively, fear: but then, after one bumping heart-beat, I remembered the dog.

The country all hereabouts is not very exciting—low rolling hills, covered with thick bush where there is tsetse, browsed unpleasantly bare where there is not. But as you pass northwards, the granite tors so characteristic of the southern shores of the Great Lake begin to appear, some very fine, some merely fantastic. The villages are mostly circled with a hedge of manyara spurge, which gives them a picturesque look.

After these primitive kraals, and the spectacle of native

self-government, it was a contrast to arrive at a great hole in the ground where digging for diamonds was going on —the Mabuki Mine. It was a symbol of another kind of civilization, with its ugliness, its efficient machinery, its amiable horn-rimmed business-faced manager (who produced for our inspection several thousand pounds' worth of diamonds in a Gold Flake tin), its shifts of native labourers leading a life that has only come to Africa with this generation. It is curious and pleasant to know that when they have exhausted the pipe, and all the machinery and the white business-men and engineers have packed up and gone, the workings are to be converted into a reservoir for the water-supply of the black population.

For the last stretch into Mwanza, the road was bordered with big cassias, planted decades ago by the Germans— a fine avenue, twenty miles long.

Mwanza itself is a busy little town, and growing rapidly more busy with the traffic of the new branch railway and the excellent road from the south. It is said to be unhealthy, but is pretty, with green vales and granite eyries, and of course the Lake. This is my first sight of the Victoria Nyanza, and it is lovely, though very different from my imaginings—soft and mild, with kindly bays and promontories that recall Devon rather than suggest the heart of the tropics. Then one is told that there is no bathing; and the thought of crocodiles puts a genuine African tang into the pretence of Devon. And my host was recently held up in his car, not fifty miles away from Mwanza, by a procession of zebra and buck, thousands upon thousands of them, dribbling across the excellent motor-road: more African flavour.

Even here, in the couple of hours before my boat sails,

I am kept busy—first digging my boxes out of the luggage office, then inspecting the recently-started town school. It is impressive to see the difference between the tidy, well set-up boys who have been there the six months since the school was opened, and the dirty little ragamuffins, fresh from the streets, who have just come. Native schools are, if anything, more necessary in town than country.

On board at last. The boat steams out past the illusory Devon headland into the open lake. I have only been just over three weeks in this astonishing Africa; but these three weeks have been lived hard and packed full. How hospitable everyone has been, how interesting every hour of every day! yet I cannot truly say that I am sorry to have before me two whole days of shipboard, with no schools, no dinner-parties, no lorry-journeys, no mountain-climbing, no sight-seeing, no scientific conferences, and a cabin to retire to and even sleep in whenever I feel so disposed. And I shall need it before beginning all over again with Kenya.

Chapter XIV

THE GREAT LAKE; AND A WHITE ESTATE

Sept. 28th. I had always visualized the shores of the Victoria Nyanza as low and rolling, swampy and papyrus-fringed. So they are, over a large part of the lake's huge circumference; but this morning we pass under a lovely mountain, rising three or four thousand feet above the water (which already lies close on four thousand feet above the sea). It is handsomely sculptured, and in the grey cloudy morning has an air as of Ben Cruachan or some other fine Scottish peak overlooking a northern sea-loch.

The country here must be very fertile; stockaded villages of beehive huts are all along the lower slopes. And an island just off the coast is unusually populous, suggesting the crowded East Indies rather than undermanned Africa. So to Kisumu, the port at the terminus of the old railway, which has suffered a good deal from the building of the new line to the north which takes the railway right into Uganda. Then by train to Koru, where I enjoy the hospitality of fellow-passengers on the boat, the manager of a big sisal estate and his wife

Sept. 29th. We are getting up into the hills here, and the air is fresher. The view in the morning is lovely—a wooded mountain to the north, eroded remains of a volcano; green rounded hills to east and south, looking like English downs, but magnified about six diameters (and

the grass on them enlarged disproportionately); to the
west the broad valley leading out towards the lake; and at
my feet a garden full of flowers and flowering shrubs.

There were many new things I saw during the day.
The sisal itself is curious enough. Many people find it
hideous; I would rather say bizarre. These great aloes,
with their huge bayonet-pointed leaves and the cande-
labrum-like fruiting-spike that is a sign they are finished
commercially, all planted in regular formation over square
miles of country, appear a highly-industralized vegetation,
and produce a modernist effect on the eye.

Then there was the mill. In all up-to-date factories
you get the impression that it is the machines which really
count, the astonishing, expensive, elaborate machines,
while the human beings are merely their servants or even
their slaves. But here the contrast was peculiarly forcible
between the marvellous decorticators which manipulated
the leaves so as to slice off just that thickness of their
substance which contains the long fibres, and the ragged,
happy-go-lucky natives who tended them.

But not all the natives are so raw. The power station
(that and the dam and the flumes put up by my host
with no aid save what African labour he could get) was
looked after by a little hunchback Kikuyu. Though quite
untaught, he had shown a natural aptitude for tools and
machinery ever since he first came as a lad to the estate;
and now he could safely be left for weeks at a time in
full charge of the electrical machinery. All minor repairs
he could do himself; and if anything went seriously wrong,
he could be trusted not to tinker, but to send for the
Bwana.

In contrast with this was the Lumbwa man who acted

ABOVE, AN ARAB DHOW BEING SCRAPED
AND PAINTED ON THE EAST AFRICAN
COAST. LARGE NUMBERS OF THESE DHOWS
PLY REGULARLY BETWEEN ARABIA AND
EAST AFRICA.
BELOW, THE "LION TREE" IN THE COURT-
YARD OF A SULTAN NEAR TABORA. ON IT
ARE SKULLS OF LIONS KILLED IN THE
NEIGHBOURHOOD. (*Photo. by Mr. Whybrow,
Headmaster of Tabora School.*)

© C. Whybrow.

WORKING FOR THE WHITE MAN.
KAVIRONDO MEN ON A SISAL ESTATE IN KENYA, FEEDING THE
DECORTICATING MACHINE WITH SISAL LEAVES.

WORKING ON HIS OWN.
A NATIVE BLACKSMITH IN UGANDA. HE IS WORKING A PAIR OF
STONE BELLOWS BY MEANS OF STICKS ATTACHED TO TWO
PIECES OF GOATSKIN.

as herdsman to the draught-oxen. The Lumbwa are in the main a pastoral people, so that for cattle-herding you do not have to train your men; you find your specialists ready-made. This fellow was still the untouched native; and his wife, a comely creature with brilliant white teeth, chatting with a visitor from the Reserve in the doorway of her hut, might just as well have lived a thousand years ago for all the difference that contact with machines and motor-cars and an Imperial people had made to her appearance or habits.

One of the rather ramshackle huts in the native workers' lines was a little bigger than the rest, and had two sticks, nailed together crosswise, protruding from its thatch. This was the church made by the Christianized workers on the estate. There was also a school. Here, as on many estates, the provision of a schoolmaster had been found to pay; the workers came more readily and stayed longer. The schoolmaster had evening classes for the men, taught the women and children during the daytime, and held services on Sunday. What he taught was only reading and writing and a little arithmetic, with catechism and hymns thrown in; but, be it always remembered, to the African that means admission to a new world. We find it hard to put ourselves back the paltry few thousand years to the time when our countries, like Africa, were still illiterate. We also find it hard to remember—or convenient to forget—that we rulers of the modern roost did not discover written language for ourselves: that was achieved by darker-skinned and more Oriental people than the Nordics. We had to be taught it then, as the Africans have to be taught it now. We have certainly been changed as a result (we tend to think the change has been for the better); we can have no conception of what change it will in time bring to them.

My host was more broad-minded than many white employers in Kenya. He frankly said that he thought the shortage of labour had in the long run been good for the white settlers, because it had forced them to take an interest in labour-saving machinery. It had also forced them to pay more attention to the diet and housing and education of their native workers, because when labour was expensive you had to think twice before you employed it wastefully; and this, too, in the long run had paid.

On the other hand, I could not help but be struck, in this my first glimpse of the white uplands of East Africa, by the contrast between the native conditions here and in the advanced Native Administrations I had just left in Tanganyika. It was the atmosphere rather than anything tangible. For one thing, there is here the ill-regulated untidiness of the uprooted African, the neither-one-thing-nor-the-other feeling, of human beings truly belonging to no stable order, neither the tribalism they have left nor the white civilization for which they are working. Their clothing has neither idea nor tradition behind it—just scraps of European clothes; untidy, often ragged, whatever they fancy and can afford, or even anything European they can pick up. They live in ramshackle labour lines, which look as if they had been put up only to be taken down again as soon as possible, with no suggestion such as a genuine native village gives, however primitive or dirty it may be, of home. They are kicking off many of the restraints of tribalism without really emancipating themselves from its more pervasive ideas; their mental life would

seem to be as patchy and promiscuous an affair as their
clothing. And though conditions on this estate seem to be
excellent, as evidenced by the fact that my host never has
a real labour shortage, and that many of the men come
back year after year to work for him, you miss the signs
of personal contact. In the Wanyamwezi and Wasukuma
country, every Government official whom I saw gave good-
day to every native he passed; and the natives would come
running to the roadside to get their greetings in—not because they were forced to, but with gusto and smiles. Here
we walked through groups of labourers without there being
any recognition from either party that the other existed—
no sign of hostility or glumness, but just a curious remoteness, an indifference to any possible human relationship between white and black.

As against orderly development there, here you felt a
makeshift social life that might collapse into real disorder-
liness of existence. As against a human bond between black
and white, you felt a relation that was almost solely
economic.

One cannot get away from one's feelings; and that is
the feeling I had then and was constantly to get again in
Kenya. Nor, I am sure, was the feeling ungrounded. On
the other hand, it is perfectly true that many natives learn
a great deal from contact with white men and white men's
methods; that the treatment of native labour is steadily
improving (though in some cases it still leaves much to
be desired: I heard horrifying stories from reliable sources
of exploitation, callousness, and even cruelty by isolated
white men); and that the establishment of native councils, together with the work of schools and of various

Government departments, is making it possible to establish order instead of chaos in the life of the natives.

As elsewhere in East Africa, the real hope lies in the characteristics of the African himself. There are qualities of virility, of cheerfulness, of adaptability about him which make it difficult to be too gloomy about his future.

Chapter XV

NAIROBI

Sept. 30th. My chief discovery to-day is that many carriages on the Kenya Railway have bottle-openers built in, so to speak, to the wall of the lavatory compartments. I don't know whether this is a recent innovation, or a survival of more robust times; it is at least interesting.

The rest of the day passes pleasantly, watching the scenery and the people, black and white. Huge rounded grass-covered hills, with deep valleys; rolling upland plateaux, here covered with crops, there with forests spreading down from the heights. Well-dressed white women at the stations, and bronzed and virile white men looking like the product of a cross between the breath of the American Wild West and the adventurer spirit of Elizabethan England, garbed in the get-up which is East Africa's contribution to world-fashions, the bush-shirt—khaki shirt and coat in one—, shorts, and broad-brimmed felt hat, double-layered, to keep off sunstroke. At the stations, too, Indian stationmasters, amiable and officious, with their long-robed wives and their gaudily-dressed, noisy little children; and Africans touched by the breath of Europe, some well turned out in European clothes, but most quite regrettably garbed in a patchwork caricature of the West—felt hat, white jumper, khaki shorts, bare legs, and a British warm; a gaudy pull-over with ragged cotton trunks; and every other

153

combination you can think of. And finally a good sprink-
ling of original Africa—*Ur-Afrikanismus*; a Lumbwa
woman (or was she a Nandi?) in handsome furs; two
warriors with spears; a Hamite of sorts helping to load
pigs into a truck, his garb of skins, fastened only at the
neck, flapping behind him as he rushed after the squeak-
ing porkers and revealing his sinewy black nakedness for
all and sundry to see; groups of coffee-coloured Kikuyu
women, their skulls indented by the straps on which
their heavy burdens are supported, the brown of their
voluminous skin garments set off by the bunches of mauve
bangles at their ears and round their necks.

The gradients are terrific, the train slow, and darkness
falls just before we get a sight of the Great Rift.

Nairobi, Oct. 1st. One doesn't get much breathing
space in Africa. Dawn came after the train had climbed
out of the Rift. I had just time to get a look at this
green, upland, and most un-African country, before arriving at Nairobi soon after eight. Then a glimpse of the
town as I drove through—new buildings springing up on
every side, good shops in plenty, more motor-cars per head
of white population than anywhere else in the world, big
hotels and offices. Imagine a rapidly-growing small town
in the Western United States, but Britannicized, and acutely
conscious of being the only real European city within a
huge territory; then pepper its streets with rich tourists,
big game, up-country settlers in for business and a good
time combined, native house-boys doing shopping; Kikuyu
women in skins and bangles, always carrying heavy loads,
Indian merchants, half-naked Masai warriors with ochred
hair plaited into pigtails; and you will have a faint idea of
Nairobi.

NAIROBI

Mr. Scott, the Director of Education, was my host to-day. I was allowed a bath and breakfast; but as soon as that was over, a programme for my stay was produced, and I was there and then taken off to the Jeanes School a few miles outside the town.

It seems rather a pity that education burdens its terminology with terms like Jeanes School and Dalton Plan, for they are meaningless to the uninitiated. A Jeanes School (the term is taken from the Southern States of the United States, where the original Jeanes started the idea) is a school for giving special training to selected rural native teachers. The teachers will have already been teaching for some time, and are selected on the basis of their record. When they have received their Jeanesification —the course here lasts two years—they go back to their districts, and there, in addition to teaching in their own schools, are put in charge of a group of out-schools. These they visit, teaching a little, giving advice to the local teachers, introducing new ideas and new methods, and altogether acting as the much-needed leaven in the lump of African elementary education in remote districts.

A very important fact is that the teachers bring their wives and families to the Jeanes School; the wives, too, are trained in various domestic and hygienic ways, and add appreciably to the quantity and quality of the leaven on returning to their districts. The two chief members of the staff here are Mr. Dougall, who was once a Presbyterian missionary, and Mr. Benson, who was once a Harrow master. They both say that they find their job at the Jeanes School far more interesting than their previous work. There is accommodation (in rows of funny little concrete houses) for fifty teachers. The year previous they had forty-four; this year forty-nine, most of them married and in residence with their families. At the moment all of them are Christian converts, whose work lies in Mission Schools; but as time goes on the authorities anticipate that there may be pagan teachers as well, chosen from schools on large settlers' estates, where religious qualifications are not necessarily demanded. As in most places, there is a certain amount of difficulty caused by the presence of both Catholics and Protestants; but their mere co-existence in a single institution more than counterbalances this.

I felt that the place was one of the most interesting and hopeful things I saw in Africa; it was so enlightened, so unhampered by tradition, so practical. Two women are detailed to help the teachers' wives: one is a Froebel teacher who instructs them in cooking and housework, knitting and sewing; the other a woman trained in infant-welfare work, who deals with health, maternity and the care of children. In addition, the fact that the women live here in well-built little houses of improved pattern, and that they have two years' opportunity for discussion with each other and the European staff, makes a notable difference to their outlook—in all probability relatively more than the change effected in the men's outlook.

The men, on the other hand, start at a higher level. I will not bore my readers with details of curriculum, but will pick out some especially interesting points. As the Education Department's Report for 1928 says, "It is a principle of some importance that nothing should be done for the teachers [at the Jeanes School], or given to them, which they are capable of making for themselves." Accordingly they are instructed in the making of most of the furniture for their houses, the simpler school equipment, and much of what is needed for the agricultural work of the school.

Agriculture is rightly a feature of the place. In addition to typical school gardens and their private plots, the teachers in residence work a ten-acre community farm. This is run on a profit-and-loss basis, so that the men learn practically how to cost, market, and keep accounts.

This practical side is also fostered by the Co-operative Shop, again run by the teachers themselves, with advice from the European staff. Here they have managed to keep down prices below those of the usual shop run by an Indian trader, and yet to make a profit. The African finds it very hard at first to grasp the principle of interest on a fixed capital, the need for a sinking fund against depreciation, and other financial ideas. He may learn about them from books in an abstract way; but when he becomes co-partner in an actual business concern like this shop, the abstract ideas become living realities. Such work as this is vitally necessary if the African is ever to hold his own with the Indian as trader and shopkeeper.

On the more academic side, much attention is rightly given to the principles of hygiene and agriculture. I was interested to be told that the two Europeans responsible for these respective subjects had found it impossible to teach them properly without a considerable foundation of general biology; and discovered, on comparing notes, that they had been duplicating over three-quarters of this foundation. The absolute necessity of agriculture and hygiene for Africa, and of scientific foundations for agriculture and hygiene, constitutes one of the strongest arguments for making general biology an important part of the native African curriculum.

Other subjects are not neglected; and of course the men do a good deal of practice teaching. A strong point is the amount of thought given to the activities concerned with recreation and self-expression—handicrafts and drawing, acting and story-telling, singing and games. In the first years of the school's existence, opposition was found on the part of some of the teachers to the native folk-songs and games, which they, as Christians, felt to be something on a lower level, something to be put behind them; and even after this had been overcome, and the men gone back to their districts, sometimes, I was told, there was opposition or tacit resistance on the part of the white missionaries to such "heathen" practices. But this attitude is rapidly passing away.

I was particularly interested in the success which the acting seems to have achieved. Most Africans have an inborn talent for comedy and burlesque; and with proper training they can get a good deal out of more serious dramatic performances. Last year the Jeanes teachers presented five scenes from the history of East Africa, from the voyages of Vasco da Gama to the Great War. Native music is intermixed with negro spirituals and English songs, and football with the native games. Once a week there is a community meeting of all connected with the school; sometimes a visitor is present and gives a lecture or a talk, sometimes the men pool their stock of tribal folk-tales, sometimes they swap native riddles, and so on.

The training is in a sense expensive, for it means removing a good teacher from his teaching for two whole years, but undoubtedly in the long run it pays. Something of the same sort can be achieved by shorter vacation courses for groups of selected teachers, such as are organized in Uganda, for instance. The essential is to get a number of good men together, and imbue them with new keenness and provide them with new ideas and methods; but the intensive year's or two years' course during which the teachers' wives as well as the teachers themselves are imbibing the new spirit is bound to yield the fullest returns.

The most notable and exciting fact about native education in Africa is that it exists—this new feature in the life of a continent—and that it is rapidly growing; next to that is the fact that so many interesting and pregnant experiments are being tried, experiments modern in spirit and generous in idea. The fruit of them, in a generation's time, cannot but be rich and varied. I came away from the Jeanes School full of pleasant and hopeful feeling.

. . . . .

Nairobi: later. The European School is a handsome erection of Baker's. The pillars which the architect has put at regular intervals across the open entrance-hall prevent it from being used as a playground, which I understand was the wish of the school authorities; but they certainly give a fine effect, collegiate and dignified, as of the space below Wren's great library at Trinity, Cambridge.

The hall is a good room, too; but one cannot say that the mottoes have been wisely chosen. There are two, in big black letters along the top of two of the walls. One reads (I quote from memory): "O God, help me to win. But if in Thy inscrutable wisdom Thou willest me not to win, O God, make me a good loser." This appears to embody a rather out-of-date view of the Almighty, and a wholly out-of-date view of educational aims. The other is as follows: "Love of England, gratitude to one's country, is the happy duty of us all."

This is a really beautiful expression of natural patriotism; the unwisdom of choosing it was a purely political unwisdom. It rather surprised me to learn that it was a quotation from the works of Mrs. Alice Meynell; but it did not surprise me at all to hear that the large and vocal Scotch section of the Kenya white population (the Scotch section of every colony is always large and always vocal) objected very strongly to this use of *England* in place of *Britain*. No matter that it was quite clear what Mrs. Meynell meant; nor that *Britain* is an awkward modernism, associated with politics, popular oratory and flag-flapping, while *England* calls up an actual countryside, green and real, with valleys, towns and hills; nor that, if you want nowadays to be logical and complete, you should say *British Commonwealth of Nations*. The fervid Scots are not to be appeased. They have written privately to the headmaster of the school; they have organized deputations to the Director of Education; they have indited a great number of letters to the East African *Standard*; and now they are threatening, I understand, to take the matter to His Majesty's Secretary of State for the Colonies. It will be interesting to know how this international incident will end; and it will also be interesting to see what further quotations, if any, will be chosen for the two walls at present blank.

The school is a pleasant school, with an excellent headmaster and a nice-looking lot of boys and girls in it. But the standard is not yet very high. It is a depressing fact, for instance, that boys from the Indian school are passing examinations which have not yet been even attempted by children from the European school. And who can tell what will happen to black education in another two generations? Where twelve million negroes are given full educational facilities, the pick of them are likely to reach a very high standard.

The curriculum is being improved in many ways; but one has still no feeling that the school is in any real way a *Kenya* school—rather than a London school, or a South African school. They appear to do these things better in Southern Rhodesia, where a real attempt is being made to adapt education to Rhodesian conditions.

White settlement in Kenya will depend, more and more as the years pass, on two essential things: an understanding of the peculiar scientific problems of the country—afforestation, tropical agriculture, tropical insects, tropical hygiene and the rest; and an understanding of the natives—their customs and tribal organizations, their ways of thinking, their needs and wishes. Education need not be parochial, but it should be adapted to regional needs; at the moment, white education in Kenya seems more adapted to home examination syllabuses. In especial, little or nothing is being done to foster a better and more scientific understanding of the African natives and the problem they create.

I know that our educational system at home is being radically overhauled, and that much of it, notably the secondary school, is coming in for a good deal of severe criticism; and I realize that a colony with a few thousand whites must almost inevitably follow the home pattern in most things. None the less, I am haunted by a phrase in Church's book on East Africa. If, he says, we do not take steps to reform the education of white children in tropical Africa, "we may within a few years be faced with a grave problem, that inherent in the political ascendency of an ignorant white minority over a well-educated black majority." The danger is less now than when he wrote; but I do not feel that it is by any means past.

    •   •   •   •   •

In the evening, a concert at the European School by two South African ladies who are touring East Africa. Beethoven, Schubert, Debussy—hearing good music well played, one suddenly realizes that one is starved of such things. The African country is often exciting in its strange beauty; but I think of Italy with its hill-towns and monasteries, or England with its old villages and country houses. Here even in the towns there is lamentably little that is attractive; the buildings that think they can call themselves *Architecture* are too often the ugliest. There is scarcely any music—and indeed little inducement for musicians to come; when these same ladies later gave a public concert in Nairobi, about twenty people found time to desert their golf and tea and bridge! There are no picture-galleries. There are scarcely any plays, and those almost all got up by amateurs. You can go to the movies; but you will see an even greater majority of bad films than at home. Anyone to whom music and the visual arts have much to say makes a real sacrifice in coming to the tropics.

In its little towns, East Africa is not unlike the middle west of America fifty years ago. There are the same wide untidy streets, the same cross-country tracks that serve for roads, the same abundance of corrugated iron, the same general air of unpleasing temporariness. The Middle West has now risen to riches, and with riches to town-planning and subscription concerts, art galleries and pride in beautiful buildings. In another fifty years East Africa may have trodden a similar road: or, as Mr. Belloc says, "Or else it may not: I cannot be positive which."

.   .   .   .   .

Staying at Government Houses gives one a sensation of reflected grandeur. Staying at Government House in Nairobi is also very stimulating, as Sir Edward Grigg is a man of the most wide-ranging interests, who excels in the broad scope of his ideas. Architecturally, the exterior is not one of Baker's best bits of work—not on a par with his Government House at Mombasa, for instance, or his Indian School here—but the interior is very fine. One great room in particular is truly noble in proportions. However, it is difficult to please all tastes. My hostess, at a recent reception by the Governor, commented to another lady of Nairobi on its beauty. "Yes, it's naice," she was answered; "but not so naice as the New Regent Cinema at Braighton."

Sir Edward Grigg has been heavily citicized for spending so much money on the two Government Houses, here and at the coast. However, if Nairobi really wants to be the capital of a federated East Africa, the existence of this fine building, simply asking for a Governor-General's occupancy, may turn the scales in its favour.

For almost every other reason, however, Arusha would be better as the capital. It is central; it is in beautiful country; it is politically in Tanganyika, but socially and economically it half belongs to Kenya, so that neither Territory would feel very jealous. It has no awkward historical associations, nor is it the main focus of the financial and political interests of the settler party of East Africa, as Nairobi is.

Mombasa has also been suggested, but Mombasa, quite apart from its physical remoteness from Uganda, belongs to a world alien to the most of East Africa, the world of the tropical coastal strip. Then it is the seat of the most powerful purely commercial influences in the country. And finally, it should be a principle for the future development of Africa to get away from the old idea of coast versus hinterland, and to centre things up-country. Mombasa cannot help standing for the idea that all that matters in Africa's life is to be measured in terms of exports and imports; an up-country capital would be more ready to take the wider view that is needed.

But to return to Government House at Nairobi. It is approached through a rather forlorn expanse of meadow. A formal avenue had been planned, but it was difficult to find trees that would grow well in the rather barren soil. I made the suggestion of Candelabra Euphorbias, but it was not well received. Hideous, gloomy, grotesque, were the epithets that burst from all lips. But I still think there is something in it. The candelabra tree belongs, intensely, to Africa; its very strangeness breathes of the African bush; its fantastic gloom is not without true dignity. Could you alternate these giant spurges, rigid and sombre, with some brilliant-flowered tropical tree like the Flamboyant, your avenue of dark green and violent scarlet would be not merely unique, not merely emblematic of Africa, but striking and in its own African way (like a savage Masai warrior) truly handsome. But I fear the European associations are too strong; the omnipresent desire to make everything as like home as possible will never allow my African avenue to be planted.

Chapter XVI

MEDICAL WORK IN KENYA

Oct. 2nd. A whirlwind of a morning, a medical whirlwind. Perhaps *whirlwind* is wrong. Dr. Patterson, the
Deputy Director of Medical Services, is more like a very
strong monsoon or some other steady blast than a whirlwind. He has principles and all-embracing theories as to
the functions of a medical service in tropical colonies, and
he gets his principles put into practice. He can explain his
principles, too, and does so at length, quietly but remorse-
lessly; I expect that has a good deal to do with his success
in carrying them into effect.

I am shown films of health campaigns, plans and models
of the ideal native house, maps of native locations, statistics of infant mortality, tables of proper and improper
diets for the perusal of white employers of labour, propaganda leaflets for natives (all in Swahili) about malaria
and hookworm.

But I carry away a fairly definite impression (as well
as a stack of pamphlets). Contrary to one's preconceived
notions, natives living their old tribal life are not living
healthily. We have known for some time that the noble
savage was a figment. The attractiveness of savage life
is so, too—the last blow to the Golden Age idea and the
romanticism of Rousseau. Carefully-collected statistics in
one tribe showed the mortality of children less than a year

old to be over forty per cent. (not per mille! ours in Britain, by the way, is only seven per cent.); and they rarely live to be very old. Their houses are insanitary; they live so as to make disease-transmission easy. Their diet is often unbalanced—the eaters of animal food like the Masai, surfeited with blood, milk, and meat, lacking vegetables, tend to rheumatism; the vegetable-eaters would be stronger and more resistant if they got more meat (the craving for meat in the Congo jungle seems to have been one prime cause of Congo cannibalism); many tribes are chronically short of essential mineral salts, so that you may see children in the native markets spending their cents not on sweets but on raw salt, thus satisfying the instinctive biochemical urge of their organism. "Noble savages," in Africa at least, are more parasite-ridden than pet dogs. In their blood they have malaria parasites, bilharzia, trypanosomes, filaria; they have tape-worms, round-worms, and hookworms in their intestines. Clean out these drainers of life-blood, these sappers of energy, and the native would be reborn on a new level of energy. . . .

So we have the Ideal Homes which Dr. Patterson is trying to get built in the Reserves—four-roomed, with windows and a kitchen. But who will find him cheap roofing material which shall be rat-proof? So, too, he has general schemes for raising the natives' production and standard of life; for only thus will you combat malnutrition and the apathy it breeds, and give new incentives to living. He has his plans all drawn up for properly-planned native locations in the towns, in place of the present disgraceful slums; the settlers like to call it pampering the nigger, but they are wavering here and there under his arguments. He makes propaganda for giving a decent physiological diet to native labourers. The old idea that a native does best on nothing but maize-meal dies hard (perhaps because if true it would be not only cheap, but a pleasant physiological proof of the radical difference between black man and white!), but it is dying. Employers are beginning to realize that it is very poor business to pay wages to men who have no strength or stomach for their work, and who are always going sick because they lack normal resistance.

Perhaps most impressive, because so all-embracing and on so large a scale, was the Department's campaign in the Digo country near the coast, whose population were riddled with hookworm. You cannot be very efficient or energetic if dozens of hookworms are clinging on to your internal surfaces, steadily sucking your blood. Thus success in such case would be spectacular; on the other hand, as America knows, it is not so easy to get rid of hookworm even among a white population.

However, the Medical Department tried it. Luckily, Patterson arranged for the expedition to take a baby cine-camera; and on the film the work re-lived for me. I saw a couple of white doctors, with skilled native dressers, moving their camp from village to village, examining every one—a whole population submitted to medical examination. Nor was the examination perfunctory; it was Harley Street medicine—or at least Wimpole Street medicine—in the bush. And it took two years. They treated a trifle of 49,000 people. They gained the confidence of the coast Arabs, and were even invited by the Arab men to examine and treat the Arab women. They gained the confidence of the white sisal planters, and persuaded them that it paid in the long run to build concrete houses for their labour, and to put in sanitary arrangements. Most important, they gained the confidence of the Digos themselves. They got them to understand about hookworm, and how it could only be prevented by the use of latrines; they got the latrines dug, nearly nine thousand of them—no light task in a country of coral rock; most surprising of all, they got the Digos to use the latrines they had dug. And already, in less than two years from the end of the campaign, the white settlers report an increase in the efficiency of their labourers, and the Digos are giving proof of new tribal vitality by taking up fresh land for agriculture.

The film brought it all home to one. This will become a very important use of the cinema—the recording of special activities of Government Departments for demonstration and propaganda purposes. In the later stages of the Digo campaign, proceedings in a new village were opened by a showing of the film, with running commentary; and this broke the ice, so that the doctors could get on twice as fast with their real work. With a little training beforehand in the photography, and a good deal of skilled assistance in the cutting and titling, such films could be of enormous assistance in all those numerous cases where the understanding and the feelings of the general population need to be enlisted before a reform, be it medical, agricultural or social, can be properly carried out.

Emerging exhausted but excited from the Medical and Sanitary headquarters, I was handed over to the charge of an officer of the department to make a medical and sanitary tour of the town. Nairobi is more full of contradictions and contrasts than most towns, and the impression of this tour is vivid but patchy, like a patch-work quilt. Here is the native market—a big, tidy, modern construction, full of natives and snuff and tripe, vegetables and fowls, pancakes and grain. There is even a tea-and-bun stall. Fowls come to market in great spindle-shaped baskets carried on the head. Men may walk thirty or forty miles thus to sell their fowls: or they may take the motor-bus! Half-a-dozen motor-buses are waiting in the road outside. In the open space alongside is the goat and cattle market. Dominating this are groups of Swahilis, big fine men in bright robes, often with an Arab touch to their features. They are the great cattle-traders of East Africa. They wander round the country buying and selling cattle, now settling for months in one place, then moving on again—trader-nomads.

Untidy and amorphous are the native quarters; here and there are rudiments of planning, attempts to civilize this chaotic slum, a monument, like our slums at home, to British indifference and lack of foresight. There are a few Government-built housing quarters—some of the first pathetically unattractive, the later ones much better. There are clinics for women and children. There is a municipal brewery, in whose yeasty atmosphere monstrous old negresses were hard at work—almost the only fat women I saw in Africa: it seems a general rule that proximity to beer should fatten the human species. There is a municipal beer-shop where natives can sit and talk and drink decently. There is an Institute for meetings and recreation. But there is a great deal of slum and chaos too.

Another patch on the quilt is the Indian quarter. Here is a different kind of disorder. It is like an Orientalized Whitechapel High Street. It is curious, but everywhere I have been told the same thing—that the Indian in Africa, for all his ancient civilization, is dirtier than the African.

He is more insanitary when left to himself; and he is so bound by tradition and superstition that he is more difficult to persuade into change.

More patches, and very different ones, in the shape of the hospitals. Here is the main native hospital—two hundred beds, and only two white doctors. One patient is paralysed in the legs, not for any physical reason, but because he says he has been bewitched. My companion suggests to the doctor in charge that he should be told he was going to get a stronger magic, and then be made to sniff strong ammonia. I wonder if it was tried and if it succeeded? That is the worst of hurrying on from place to place—one never sees the end of anything.

Here is an ugly, jolly little black girl, sitting up in bed and grinning cheerfully. She had a large piece of jaw removed this very morning. What physique and vigour —typically African!

A great dispute is going on as to whether the new hospital shall be all together, white and native, outside the town; or whether the native section shall remain purely native, in the native quarter. Medically, the first seems better; but socially, from the point of view of native development, I believe the second is desirable. We want the native quarter to be proud of itself. And if the natives can think of the hospital as *theirs*, part of their city, it will help.

There were plenty of other patches in the quilt, but I prefer to think of the tea to which I gratefully relaxed myself after the long day of new impressions.

Chapter XVII

THE FORESTS OF KENYA MOUNTAIN

Oct. 3rd. After the capital and civilization, a little of
the background and the backwoods: off in a car with the
Director of the Forest Service to the forests of Mount
Kenya. The road drops steadily, the country grows drier,
with sisal taking the place of coffee. We stop at the Thika
bridge, where the river drops over a ledge in a single white
curtain. Below, the pool and gorge among the arid buff of
the general country is rich with palms, lianas and all the
paraphernalia of tropical greenery. A few hundred yards
away the Chana river, on its way to join the Thika, repeats the theme with its own falls, its own pools, palms,
and gorge.

Near the gorge were two Wakamba, busy. They had a
bit of old iron which they were converting into depilating
tweezers, those universal adjuncts of the African male, by
hammering on a stone.

At Fort Hall a Kikuyu market in full swing—a thousand natives thronging a bare hillside, chattering and
bargaining. The Kikuyu are great chafferers, and their
markets are always crowded.

Then we turn and begin to mount, into a broken country dissected into innumerable little valleys among steep
green hills. Many of the slopes are covered with bracken
—the same bracken that one can see in England, in

America, in the Antipodes, one of the puzzling ubiquists of the plant-world.

The country looks very rich, with arrow-leaved taro growing in the swamps, bananas and all kinds of crops on the slopes, and pleasant little villages everywhere. The absence of wood is rather sad. Scarcely a tree is left of the original forest, save a few sacred groves conspicuous on the hilltops. Here and there, however, the Kikuyu have taken to planting wattle, an imported tree beautiful in shape, with fragrant blossom, profitable on account of its bark; and the habit is rapidly spreading.

At last, a hundred miles from Nairobi, we reach Nyeri, the administrative centre of a province. I rub my eyes: surely this can't be Africa. You approach through an avenue of blue gums which one day, when they have added to their girth, will deserve the epithet "noble." Through the hedges one glimpses houses and gardens. The gardens are lovely at Nyeri. A leat of water has been run through the place, and with its aid you can grow anything you please. My host the District Commissioner had a fine herbaceous border, a lovely little close-mown lawn, and a well-clipped yew hedge (it was really a species of cedar, but to all intents and purposes a yew hedge). Behind the house, an orchard with grass under foot, and a couple of roomy huts for the numerous casual visitors whom a District Commissioner is expected to entertain.

Starlings bustle about in the trees—only, here they are a deep glossy blue. A black-and-white shrike sits meditatively, pouncing now and again on some insect. Early next morning I was woken by a bird-song that recalled a missel-thrush's; and then the doves began—a ridiculous and rather aggravating performance not unlike the wood-pigeon's "take-two-coos-Taffy," but hurried through over and over again at double-quick time, as if an equatorial life had speeded up all the bird's workings.

There is, of course, a golf club and a tennis club. A mile or so out is a polo ground; and right across from my orchard is a full-sized cricket field. This seems a bit of England transplanted—trees all about its smoothness, with rolling hills beyond; the white screens against the green are peculiarly convincing. On Sunday there is to be a real eleven-a-side match. Truly the British are a re-markable race. No imperialists save perhaps the Romans have ever exported their domestic habits and their recrea-tions so whole-heartedly all over their Empire. Perhaps it would be fairer to say that no other imperialists have ever had such elaborate recreations, or domestic habits so meticulously insisted upon.

It turns out that my host was at Oxford with me (these little coincidences are always turning up in Africa). After tea he takes me out to a neighbouring river, famous for its trout. It should be famous for its beauty too, slipping along in a steep valley, rich but not too rich, here running through water meadows, there through a narrow all-but-gorge, with weaver-bird nests at the ends of the branches which great trees hang over the water, and sandpipers calling and teetering on the margin. Here again it is difficult to remember you are on the Equator, and not in Gloucestershire or Somerset—till you wander up a path and come into a village of native huts no different from the villages that were here before the first white man set eyes on the valley.

Oct. 4th. Many natives in these cool heights wear a blanket fastened on one shoulder, and kept in by a belt round the waist. It looks very like a combination kilt and plaid; was this how the Scottish national costume evolved?

We make for Kenya Mountain. Just below the forest foot is some bare ground where yellow Cassia bushes simulate gorse, and the effect is not unlike a Surrey common. Then up into the forest zone. The giants of this part of the mountain forest are the magnificent red-boled camphor-trees, Ocotea. We saw one leaning at a sharp angle (a frequent habit of this species), with a branch as big as an elm horizontally protruding. The leverage on the roots must have been colossal; to withstand it, huge woody buttresses stood out from the trunk. The forest is dense, but does not give a tropical feeling, save here and there in the steep-sided valleys, whose bottoms are filled with magnificent tree-ferns. Once there is a crashing in the tops— a family of Colobus monkeys. They are fine creatures, with their thick long fur in bold pattern of white and black. As they leap from tree to tree they look, if not like the magic flying carpets of the fairy tales, at least like animated hearth-rugs.

Next day to another part of the forest, more to the north. The climate alters so rapidly as you pass round the mountain that the forest takes on a different character in each new sector; and by the time you reach the nor'-nor'-east there is scarcely any forest left, the plain's grass creeping far up the mountain. And the same is true for Kilimanjaro. The difference is as striking as between the west and east coasts of Spitsbergen, where in a hundred miles you pass from rich beflowered tundra, swarming with birds, to the grimmest high-arctic scenery.

On the way we have considerable difficulty with a

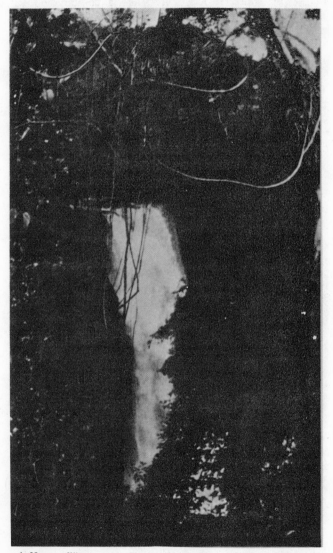

A KENYA WATERFALL. THIKA FALLS, NORTHEAST OF NAIROBI.

IN THE FORESTS OF KENYA MOUNTAIN.
A FINE PENCIL CEDAR. (*Photo. by Dr. Gardiner, Director of the Kenya Forestry Service.*)

muddy hill, and only succeed in getting up with the aid of a score of native labourers; our chains do not fit, so we call at a nearby farm to borrow some wire to fix them. The view is superb, down over a lip on to a patch of forest, and away beyond two vast plains. The forest consists of that very remarkable tree, Brachystegia, a member of the composite order, akin to our daisies and groundsels, but the only composite to have developed into a true timber tree. We are apt to think of trees as a higher product of evolution than little herbs. But the reverse is, in fact, true; herbs and grasses and suchlike small flowering plants are the crown of vegetable development. The composites are usually regarded by botanists as the highest and most advanced type of flowering plant. It is therefore to be expected that they should mostly be herbs; but why should just this one type have reverted to the arboreal? It is one of the many unsolved puzzles of evolution.

At its edges the little forest resolves itself into glades; and in these glades the owner of the farm often sees a rhinoceros family browsing. One day he saw a rhino vainly coveting the juicy leaves on a sapling; finally the beast rode the tree down between his legs and got his desire. No such lucky glimpse for us, alas! and we make off. Our progress towards the forest is delayed by a ford across a swift pebbly stream. Our wheels revolve fruitlessly, and it is only with the aid of a little caterpillar tractor, engaged on the construction of the bridge which will replace the ford, that we get over. Last week a lorry got stuck attempting to pass, turned over, and all its load floated off. Such are communications in a new land. I was reminded of a day in Texas when I spent eleven hours making twenty-eight miles in a Ford. . . .

Now we begin to mount, slowly but steadily. A few junipers appear. They are the outposts of the forest. From straggly shrubs they become tall bushes; the bushes unite into groups of little trees; the groups of trees become an open wood; and finally the wood becomes a forest, a forest of the same junipers but now magnificent hundred-and-twenty or even hundred-and-forty-foot giants. It is from these junipers, usually called pencil cedars, that the wood of lead pencils is made; East Africa is becoming a rival to the United States in this field. The pencil cedars are mixed with two very fine species of olive, and the handsome Podocarpus, belonging to the yew family, though quite unlike a yew to look at. Many living pencil cedars are rotted inside with a fungus; the foresters prefer them to die, for then the fungus will not attack them, and their wood stays in prime condition for decades!

Here is a big sawmill, the office wholly panelled, parquetted and furnished in the most lovely local woods. Beyond it we penetrate along a grassy ride into the wood. There is a handsome arboreal St. John's-wort here, while the tree-begonia, abundant in the moist forest of yesterday, is absent. Huge clumps of Loranthus, the most characteristic African mistletoe, gaudy with orange-red flowers, hang on the trees; it luxuriates much more than our northern pale-flowered Viscum, sometimes indeed cutting its own throat by killing its host.

On our return we pass a Kikuyu woman bent almost double under a huge load of potatoes. She had come into the sawmills when we were there, and had put down her load to chat with a friend. Out of curiosity I felt its weight; with both hands I could just lift it off the ground. When the time came for her to go, a man had to hoist it on to her back. Like most of her kind, she was but a small-made creature; and yet she was carrying this burden at least seven miles. Gardner tells me that such loads are by no means exceptional. The Kikuyu living near forest reserves are given permission to take out as much fire-wood as they can carry. Women go in, collect vast loads, and then, as soon as they are outside the forest, distribute it to their waiting families. Out of curiosity he weighed a few of these bundles, and found that they ran up to 250 lbs.—not a bad load for women who certainly weigh less than ten stone! I begin to believe the story told me in Nairobi of an early settler who brought up a piano in the train, and was in despair about getting it from the station to his house, till a Kikuyu woman, proud of her carrying capacity, volunteered for the job, and carried it in triumph through the streets.

Coming back we took another route, across the open plains which extend hence for miles to northward, fine cattle country, and to-day still full of game. After crossing the Guaso Nyero, a steep-banked brown river bordered with great acacias, there was game everywhere. In one broad clearing we came upon a wonderful mixed bag of beasts and birds: fifty or sixty zebra; a small herd of oryx, with their strangely-patterned face, ugly gait, and superb straight horns of which even lions go in fear; a family of ostriches; and two or three dozen Grant's gazelles with a few kongoni among them.

Suddenly we were treated to a spectacle such as only Kenya could provide. A large and expensive car emerged out of nowhere, saw us, swerved across the open ground, cut under our bows and hove to alongside, like a revenue cutter running up to a suspected coaster. Driving the car was a gentleman who might have stepped out of a film. His handsome oval face, complete with black moustache, was surmounted by an enormous Stetson hat; the usual bush-shirt and shorts (but with very smart lace-up high boots) completed his costume. If he was clearly the clever villain of the films, his companion was equally clearly the comic relief—a young fellow of astoundingly vacuous expression, with Oxford bags of a delicious puce, a shirt of green silk with brown stripes, and in one hand a revolver with an eighteen-inch barrel. . . . However, it was not a hold-up they were after: they had mistaken us for acquaintances. On hearing our destination, they said the road was hard to find, and volunteered to guide us. More cinema: for they made off at breakneck speed along the unmade track, we following as best we could, but often guided only by their dust round a patch of bush. Once, crossing a glade, a fine covey of guineafowl ran clacking off; the car was going at least thirty miles an hour, but young green-shirt emptied his revolver at them—naturally without scoring a hit.

So back to an interesting dinner-party at which were two of the three members of the commission appointed to go into the Kikuyu system of land-tenure; but of that more later.

Next day, my first sight of Kenya Mountain. Very beautiful are the snowy heights and rock peaks spiring it there, three and a-half miles up in air; and yet the mountain as a whole is a little disappointing. The base is too big (it covers an area even greater than Kilimanjaro), the angle of slope is too gentle; and so, when the true peaks do show up, they are disproportioned, dwarfed by their own immense pedestal. When you are up above the forest, they are grand enough, as the lovely photographs in Major Dutton's *Kenya Mountain* testify; yet even so they fall far short of Ruwenzori's grandeur, though Ruwenzori is not so high. This is because Ruwenzori is not volcanic, but a huge block of the earth's crust forced up into the sky. Kenya, on the other hand, is an aged volcano, its flanks eaten away and their slope flattened by millennia of erosion until the plug of lava which once stood in the vent leading up to the crater now sticks up into the air and has been dissected to make the central system of rock peaks.

Oct. 7th. Science this morning—at the Veterinary Research Laboratory at Kabete close outside the city, a building far more handsome and up-to-date than the deplorable and blowsy mother of British veterinary laboratories in Camden Town. At Kabete they have just nailed down the transmitter of heart-water, one of the more serious African diseases of cattle. It is a kind of tick. This is only a first step—there remains to study the domestic and other habits of the beast before there is much hope of preventing heart-water; none the less, it is a big advance.

Here are cultures of the germs of bovine pleuro-pneumonia. They make little white spots on the culture-plate, and yet when you look down the microscope you can see nothing. Though visible in mass to the naked eye, they are ultra-microscopic, and can only be seen singly in photographs taken with ultra-violet light.

Another triumph of the place is its new method for vaccinating beasts against the rinderpest, in place of the complicated and often dangerous method now in use, of double inoculation.

A particularly intriguing side-line was a collection of poisonous plants from Kenya. Here is Akokanthera and handsome Strophanthus, commonest sources of poison for arrows (I am assured, however, that the "poisoned" arrows of some tribes owe their lethal effects solely to dirt); and here the remarkable yellow-flowered Tribulus, usually a good fodder-plant, but deadly poison to sheep if it is both in flower *and* wet with rain!

I go home to lunch a wiser man, with my eyes fully opened to the fact that veterinary work in Africa demands as much scientific skill and as much knowledge of native habits of mind as does human medicine.

The agricultural laboratories were equally interesting; but I must not weary my readers with technical details. However, I cannot forbear recording one intriguing fact. The Government are amassing hundreds of thousands of ladybirds of a certain species, which are then to be liberated to attack the hated mealy-bug, cause of so much loss on coffee plantations. Till recently, the ladybirds have had to be fed on live mealy-bugs. But at last, as the result of the chemical analysis of mealy-bugs and much experiment, a synthetic food has been devised which seems to satisfy all their requirements. It consists of chopped eggs, radio-malt, cream, marmite, and honey. Ladybirds are one of man's few insect allies; so one likes to think of their enjoying such good food.

After tea, an unexpected jaunt. The Governor is holding a *baraza* or conference with a number of Masai chiefs to discuss the tribe's grievances concerning water-holes, and asks me to come along. The baraza is at the Provincial Commissioner's house, in a well-kept lawn bordered by flower-beds, among the marvellous sweeping curves of the Ngong hills. They are all green parkland with lovely tree-groups, the curves reaching up to a high skyline, to fall away sheer to the floor of the rift valley, for the great rift-fault has cut clean through the range of hills.

The Governor and half a dozen Europeans sit in deck chairs; facing them a long double row of Masai dignitaries, nearly forty of them, squat on the grass. There is one Moran or Warrior, a young man with hair orange from ochre and oil; the rest are Elders. The old chief in the centre with his staff of office provided by the Government, a sort of bandmaster's staff topped by a silver crown, has a rather insignificant face despite his age and his fine robes of dark blue. Indeed, I was frankly disappointed, after all I had read of the physique and handsomeness of the Masai, in the looks of most of these men; the most noticeable thing about them was their variety of physical type, running even to one squat, fattish little old man with a beard and a slightly Socratic cast of face. However, there was one very remarkable figure, a middle-aged man whose face reminded me strangely of Dürer's wonderful St. John in his "Four Evangelists" at Munich (it was half uncanny, half poignant to see the likeness obtruding itself through the dark skin and alien features); and the interpreter, wholly different but equally striking, might have been an early Egyptian statue come to life.

This was the second year of severe drought in Kenya; and there was trouble about the Masai watering their cattle at water-holes outside the Reserve. (In passing, this is not altogether to be wondered at. If you look at the boundary between Masai Reserve and the lands alienated to whites, you will see it is strangely zig-zag; and the reason for this is that the natives' area has been indented so that almost all the borderline springs are in white ownership.)

This particular dispute was complicated. The Governor

promised that they should not go short of water during the drought, and that the matter would be looked into and settled later; and he reminded them that the Government was beginning to bore for water in the Reserve, for the Masai's benefit.

They went away looking only moderately satisfied, I thought. It is indeed a pity that there is always being friction between the Masai in Kenya and the Government. There is no need for this, as is demonstrated by the very cordial relations which subsist between the Tanganyika section of the tribe and their Government. The ultimate cause of the friction seems to be the presence of white settlers. The possibility of Masai cattle spreading disease to white stock leads to troublesome quarantine regulations; and the undesirable idea of natives competing in beef and hides with whites is always in the background, adding new pressure to the restrictions.

Friction may be inevitable when white and black live different lives side by side; but it can be minimized, and there are signs that the Government is embarking on a conciliatory and constructive policy. It is indeed time, for we have, alas! no reason to be very proud of our past dealings with the tribe, including one of the few occasions on which we have broken our word to a subject people.

Chapter XVIII

A KIKUYU MARKET

The Kikuyus are one of the most important tribes in Kenya, and are at the moment in the forefront of the "Native Problem" of the Colony. In Nairobi I was repeatedly told of the unrest among the Kikuyu, and quite a number of people, alike among settlers and officials, were gloomily prognosticating actual insurrection in the near future. So I anticipated that in the Kikuyu Reserve white men would be greeted with surly looks or even actual hostility. However, these expectations were luckily not fulfilled. The Kikuyu has, it is true, a queer alien look about him, as of a gnome or other creature of slightly different breed from ordinary human beings; he seems to be by nature cunning, reserved, perhaps mistrustful (even in the early days of the opening up of the colony the tribe had the reputation of being the most difficult and shifty to deal with); but I met with no visible sign of unfriendliness, much less any overt act.

One of the peculiarities for which the Kikuyus have always been noted is their markets. Whether this be due to their bargaining temperament which makes them enjoy haggling and chaffering for its own sake, or to a love of change and company, the results are remarkable. In quite a number of places in the Reserve, markets are held once or even twice a week, and are attended by crowds of natives: it is not at all uncommon for over a thousand Kikuyu to be crowded together on such a market-ground. I was lucky enough to strike three market-days in my short trip, and brought away a very vivid impression of the activity and orderliness of these African trading centres.

The market-place is merely an open space set aside for such use, sometimes out in the open country, sometimes on a sort of village green close to a little settlement, bordered by the tin stores and ramshackle shops of Indian traders. There are no booths or tables; the goods are exposed on the bare ground, or in certain cases slung on a string between two posts. Most of the market is naturally taken up with agricultural produce; the variety of this is extraordinary, and completely contradicts the idea that the African is always content with a monotonous diet. There is millet (of at least two kinds), maize, and various other grains I did not know; beans and several kinds of peas; sweet potatoes and taro and sugar-cane; and many other kinds of produce. The vendors squat by their wares, all close together; the buyers pick their way deviously through the dense crowd and over the varied foodstuffs.

Each main category of goods has its own section of the market-ground. Over in one corner is the firewood. This is a very precious commodity, since the deforestation which the Kikuyus themselves began by constantly cutting down new areas of forest for their shifting cultivation, their goats have perpetuated by preventing the new growth of seedling trees; and their Reserve, which was once all richly wooded, is now bare of trees, save for a few sacred groves on hill summits, and patches of gum and wattle which the Government have at last persuaded them to begin planting.

A KIKUYU MARKET

Anyhow, bundles of kindling cost more in Kikuyuland than they would in London.

In another place is the salt department. For some reason the vendors of this in one market I saw were all young lads. The "salt" is largely soda, with admixture of other salts, and is a very necessary ingredient of the natives' diet. It comes long distances from the salt-lakes in various parts of the colony. Here, again, is the snuff and tobacco section; the instrument used to measure out the snuff is always a cent piece attached to the end of a stick—a unit of measurement invented by the natives and rigorously adhered to by them. On the outskirts of one market was the goat department; this was for some reason rather less crowded than the rest.

Another activity of the outskirts is the sale of produce to Indian traders. You see the old shopkeeper towering above the little Kikuyu women, bowed down with their heavy sacks, weighing the produce and paying over the shillings and cents. Perhaps you are struck with amazement for a moment at the ramifications of the world's economic system, invented by man and yet seemingly now out of man's control, which sends its tentacles into these remote equatorial villages, and dislodges Indians from their proper home to come and help thrust change upon an African tribe; then the impression fades, and the actuality of the scene takes you again.

Perhaps the most intriguing parts of the market are where personal adornment is bought and sold. Kikuyu women wear an abundance of bead rings (pinkish is the fashionable colour just now) suspended in clusters on either side of their heads. These you may see, of all sizes, dangling from a string between two posts, with

women dawdling along and eyeing them. Then there are
elaborate beadwork belts and forehead straps, adornments
for the lobe of the ear, brass neck-rings. There may be two
or three "jewellers'" stands in one market; and I was interested to find by questioning them that the prices were
identical in all.

Then there are the coils of wire which the women
wear round their legs. These, it seems, cannot be put on
by unskilled hands any more than a permanent wave can
be self-administered; and on one fringe of the market is
an expert who will ring a girl in style for a fee (so I
elicited through my companion's interpretation) of one
shilling per leg. The expert's wife and family will be engaged in preparing the wire: it is pegged down at one end,
and then pulled and rubbed to make it straight and give
it a polish. The expert himself was an oldish man who,
seated on a nice little olive-wood stool, attended to the
real business of twisting the wire in even coils round the
leg. For some parts of the operation his clients can stand,
but for others they have to sit on the ground, and, balanc-
ing themselves with their hands, hold up a leg. The process
takes time. At the beginning one girl whom I saw being
thus adorned was still there, I am almost certain, and holding up the same leg still when I left the market nearly an
hour later.

What strikes one most at a Kikuyu market is its wonderful orderliness. The market-place is as active as an ant-
hill; it seethes with humanity, coffee-coloured human beings talking, laughing, bargaining, picking their way
through squatting forms and over heaps of grain and
vegetables; there were no Europeans about, and I could
not see any native policemen; and yet there was no quar-

A KIKUYU MARKET, AT KARATINA, KENYA COLONY.
ABOVE, THE TOBACCO SECTION, WITH THE JEWELLERY DEPART-
MENT BEHIND.
BELOW, THE BEAUTY PARLOUR. A GIRL HAVING BRASS WIRE WOUND
ON TO HER LEGS BY AN EXPERT.

CONTACTS OF THE AFRICAN WITH OTHER RACES.
ABOVE, KIKUYU WOMAN SELLING PRODUCE TO AN INDIAN TRADER
ON THE OUTSKIRTS OF A NATIVE MARKET-PLACE.
BELOW, A KIKUYU MAN IN EUROPEAN CLOTHES, PHOTOGRAPHED
FROM THE TRAIN; IN THE BACKGROUND THE INDIAN STATIONMASTER
AND HIS ASSISTANT.

relling, not even a squabble or an unseemly raising of
voices, in any of the three markets I saw.

In the markets well inside the Reserve you see very few
Kikuyus wearing European dress. The women especially
cling tenaciously to the traditional costume of heavy skins,
greasy and dirty, no doubt, but warm and rain-resistant,
the bright metal round arms and legs, the pinky-mauve
bead circles bunched below the ears. There are no fashions
—only Fashion, uniform and very slow-changing. The only
variation is that a few women—a bride, or a guest going
to a wedding or a dance—will have on their best clothes
instead of their workaday ones. This means that they will
be wearing a specially good skin, clean and untorn, and
glistening a rich yellowy-brown from the application of a
mixture of grease and ochreous earth; their hair will be
shiny with the same mixture, and dressed with especial
care; and they will be wearing all their bead ornaments.

The men go in a good deal for variously-coloured European blankets. Some of the dandies carry knobbed sticks
or put a feather in their hair; it is a charming sight to see
two such young fellows strolling through the crowd, hand
in hand, a David and Jonathan couple. Many of the older
men and women as they grow wizened acquire a strange
look of ancient wisdom or distinction; many of all ages
have the queer gnome-like look which I mentioned before
as of creatures essentially incomprehensible to us alien
whites; but there are many interesting faces, many merry
and intelligent ones among the boys, many pretty ones
among the girls, though the prettiness is not according to
our ordinary European standards.

The impression you get is of an industrious, sociable
people, not in the least more brutalized or less intelligent

than uneducated peasantry of whatever colour or country. They, like you or me, are tied up with the destinies of England and the British Empire. Over and over again one wonders what will be the effect of the change that is inevitably creeping in upon them, through the suppression of their tribal wars and feuds, their gradual Christianizing and education, their adoption of better methods of agriculture and higher standards of comfort. The existence of a hut-tax enforces periodical migrations upon almost all able-bodied males, migrations to and from white men's estates and white men's cities where they may work for wages as labourers or house-boys.

One hopes that as time goes on more and more of them will be able to remain at home and build up a real peasant civilization of their own, comparable to the peasant civilization of Europe before the industrial revolution. A central island of Kenya may be a white man's country; but even now there are two hundred natives to every one European, and clearly our policy should be to encourage native production as it has been encouraged in West Africa. Once the natives reach a certain degree of prosperity, they will begin asking for the things we make, and a flow of native-produced exports from Kenya to Britain will mean a flow of British-produced goods—clothing materials and cutlery, agricultural implements and clocks, bicycles and trinkets—in the return direction.

This ideal is often supposed to be incompatible with the welfare of the white settlers, who demand a constant supply of native labour for their farms. But the two aims are not really opposed. As the efforts of the Medical Service begin to bear fruit, and better housing and higher standards of health and infant welfare become prevalent, the native population, which of late years has been more or less stationary or even decreasing, will turn and go up; and if this happens, there will be ample man-power to supply both the outside labour market and the development of a true native civilization. Increased native prosperity is the only permanent way to increased all-round prosperity in a country like Kenya.

Chapter XIX

KIKUYUS AND THEIR LAND

Up on the borders of Kenya forests I was shown a patch
of land used by the Kikuyu tribe as a sort of experimental
farm. There is nothing very remarkable in this, it might
be supposed, save a laudable desire for progress. But the
farm was in the Forest Reserve, although there was abundance of suitable land in the Kikuyu's own Reserve.

This does begin to look remarkable. The reason appears
to lie partly in the Kikuyus' peculiar custom of land tenure,
partly in the unreasoning suspicion that has grown upon
them in recent years concerning all land questions. They
could not find a way of getting the consent of the interested parties to allow any of their land to be taken, even
for purposes which would benefit the community as a
whole, and so were driven to the extraordinary expedient
of paying rent to the Forestry Department for land outside the Reserve.

This suspicious attitude towards all projects concerning
land may be irrational and indeed ridiculous in some of
its manifestations; but it is no good discussing it as just
another example of native crankiness. There would have
been no suspicion if it had not been for the acts of the
white man, who (ignorantly but none the less effectively)
rendered whole clans landless in certain districts; who by
the Crown Lands Ordinance of 1915 formally asserted that

the natives (for whose benefit the Reserves were established) had no title to their lands, all rights being vested solely in the Crown; and who by nibbling at the Reserves and refusing to fix definite boundaries created a feeling of insecurity in the native mind.

At Nyeri I met the members of the Committee newly appointed to investigate Native Land Tenure in Kikuyu Province. Talks with them interested me in the problem, and their subsequently-published report has amplified that interest. It is worth while, I think, to summarize certain aspects of the question as a striking example of the difficulties that can crop up in native administration.

The Kikuyu, then, like so many other present-day African tribes, are quite recent immigrants into their present area. They seem to have filtered in by a succession of immigrations, their first irruption dating back only about three centuries. When they first arrived, all the country was densely forested, much of it apparently inhabited by a race of pigmies, cunning hairy little hunters like their surviving relatives of the Congo, who were called Gumba, and lived in roofed-over shelters dug into the ground. In some regions the Gumba did not exist, but other purely hunting tribes (the Wanderobo) ranged through the forests; and still other regions seem to have been uninhabited.

The Kikuyu, when they first arrived, were also in the hunting stage of culture; they proceeded to buy hunting-rights from the Wanderobo wherever these existed, and to stake out hunting-claims where they did not. (The Gumba seem to have been in too primitive a stage of culture to be thus bargained with; they were gradually squeezed out of the lower lands, and eventually—unless the rumours of their survival among the forests of Kenya

Mountain be true—out of existence.) Such a hunting-territory is called a *Githaka*, and has been passed on by inheritance to the descendants of the original owner.

Very soon the Kikuyu began clearing the bush and planting crops, and the practice spread until the tribe became almost wholly agricultural; but the Githakas (the real plural is Ithaka, but I prefer easy intelligibility to pedantic accuracy) remained the basis of land tenure in the new conditions. Indeed, by that time the tribe had reached their south-western limit, round and beyond Nairobi; they had already ceased to be a hunting people, and the land they bought from the primitive hunters was bought for immediate clearance and tillage.

A Githaka may run from about fifty acres to nearly ten square miles. In its typical form it is always the property (if we may use a word which as regards land has a different connotation for African and European minds) of a group-unit. The Githaka in whole or in large part is divided up among individual "share-owners," to use the Committee's phrase, who remain in personal enjoyment of their individual holdings so long as they cultivate any part of them. The rest of the Githaka constitutes common ground for the owning group, for purposes such as grazing; but portions of it may be allotted to new individual share-owners as need arises.

The immediate control over a Githaka and its rights is vested in a man styled a *Muramati*, who is usually the senior resident representative of the clan or family group: he is the first arbiter in case of dispute, and it is he who allots undistributed land to new share-owners. But in the typical or at least the original form of the system, further control is exercised by the clan itself, through its Elders.

It is they who represent the ultimate group-owner—the clan; and their decision is necessary for sanctioning the redeemable sale of a share-owner's land (of which more hereafter) or permitting a share-owner to allow tenants on his plot.

Now—and this is of peculiar interest as an example of rapid evolution to be seen actually in progress—this system is nowhere stable, and has been changing at different rates, or even in different ways, in different regions, so that the separate districts of Kikuyu Province have quite different laws and customs on the subject. There exists, in fact, a gradient of practice running from north-east to south-west. The most unchanged custom occurs to the east of Mt. Kenya; the most altered in the Kiambu district, north and west of Nairobi, where not only has the impact of white civilization been greatest, but also marked congestion has occurred through the expropriation to white use of all the land of certain clans. This gradient of evolution goes hand in hand with an increasing density of population, which rises from fifty-two in the Meru region to nearly five hundred per square mile in the Dagoreti subdistrict west of Nairobi. (As this last figure is not far behind that for Belgium, the most closely-populated of all industrial countries, it represents a very high density for an agricultural people.)

Everywhere there is a tendency towards the decay of communal or clan control, and an approximation to the idea of private ownership. In some regions the ultimate control, instead of being vested in the whole clan, reposes in a large family group or section of the clan. Elsewhere these large family groups have given place to small family groups or even single families. In the most primitive districts communal privileges on individual holdings are still important; in the most advanced, the share-owner has individual rights over minerals, wild trees, salt-licks and many other objects that elsewhere are communal.

The result of the weakening of communal control is twofold. It strengthens the position of the shareholder as an individual proprietor; but it also strengthens the position of the Muramati as controller of individual land rights. Thus if the balance swings a little one way, it tends towards unrestricted individual ownership of small holdings; if it swings the other way, towards individual land-lordism with the share-owners as tenant-farmers.

One of the most interesting developments concerns the sale of land-rights by the individual share-owner. This is one of the fields, not uncommon in the life of primitive peoples, where the inquisitive European has to get used to standing mentally on his head, so different are the underlying ideas from those in which he has grown up.

The Githaka system always envisages the right of a share-owner to part with his land, or rather what in European terms would be called his individual cultivation-rights on it, in return for payment, which of course is in the form of the usual Bantu currency—live stock. And the purchaser then has full rights of use over the land he has "bought." But, as typically developed, the system seems topsy-turvy to us in two salient points. First of all, the intending purchaser must not open the negotiations; the initiative must always come from the would-be vendor. This, like much else in the system, derives from the fact that land and cattle alike are clan possessions. Or rather, there is really a form of dual ownership, quite unlike anything in Europe, by which land and cattle in some respects belong to the clan, in others belong to the individual. A shareholder who is short of cows or goats to make up a bride-price may ask a wealthy friend, if possible also a member of his own clan, to lend him what he needs, giving him the use of his land in return. The land transaction is merely a pledge of security, the only one possible in tribal conditions: it is only quite recently and locally that land has come to be looked upon as real wealth, and in most regions tribal custom has not altered to fit this new conception.

Secondly, the transaction is not an outright one; the purchase is redeemable. Strictly speaking, it is redeemable at any subsequent period, whether next season or after the lapse of many generations, by the restoration of the original number of cattle paid.

This, however, only obtains if the purchaser has exercised his cultivation rights. If he has never put the land under cultivation at all, but has simply let the land lie fallow and waste, then the original owner can only redeem it by paying back not merely the original number of stock which he was lent, but the original number *plus* their full natural increase. . . . This is where the European's brain begins to reel. But if, as I suggested, he stands his ideas on their head, all becomes clear. The essence of the transaction was that the purchaser obliged the vendor by lending him stock. In return for them and their natural increase, he is given a plot of land and the right of enjoying *its* natural increase. If he cultivates the land, then, when the vendor wants to redeem, the natural increases cancel out. But if he has not cultivated it, why, then he has had no advantage to set off against the natural increase of his stock enjoyed by the other fellow. It is as clear as pie, and horribly logical.

Unfortunately, it does not fit modern conditions, under which land has become increasingly an object of value in itself. This is due partly to the fixing of Native Reserve boundaries, which prevents migration in search of new land; partly to the natural increase of population; partly to improved cultivation; and partly to the introduction of currency, which always favours individualism in the ownership and disposal of property as against communal rights and clan control.

This pressure of new conditions has been greatest in the Kiambu district, where population is densest, and where the alienation of land to white settlers left whole clan sections or family groups without any Githakas of their own, thus creating a real land-hunger. The result in this district has been a profound modification of the system. Side by side with the old custom of redeemable purchase, there is the possibility of irredeemable purchase, which is implemented with special and elaborate formalities. Under this latter system, if a man pays so much stock for a bit of land, it is his for ever. And the younger men are beginning to take a European attitude about the freedom of a would-be purchaser to make overtures to a landowner. This, however, is so recent a change of view that the old men are unanimous in clinging to the idea that such an action would be a grave insult to the landowner, since traditionally it would imply that he was hard-up and short of stock to buy wives. But the changed attitude is making such rapid headway that, as the Committee write, "if the present tendencies were to continue unchecked for another · generation, it may be conjectured that in the Kiambu area the Githaka would by that time have given place to the small holding, as the unit of land-tenure."

Though the system is thus evolving rapidly—as rapidly as any European land system has ever evolved—towards individual tenure, yet various dangers beset its present and its future. The Kikuyu as a tribe deeply resent the fact that their traditional method of tenure is not officially recognized, and not unnaturally see in the existing law, by which all land rights in the Reserves are handed over to the British Crown, an arrangement by which the alien white men could manipulate matters to their own advantage if they wished. They accordingly press with unanimity for formal recognition of their system, with registration of Githakas and of all transactions in land conducted according to native law and custom.

It may be shrewdly suspected, however, that a few of the Muramati who are pressing for this reform are not doing so in the interests of the share-owners and actual cultivators, but because through it they see a prospect of becoming a privileged landlord class; and the legal registration of Githakas in the sparsely-settled north-eastern areas, over much of which they are not yet properly demarcated, might easily favour speculation in land values.

The Kikuyu might perhaps retort, Why not? The settlers next door have had great fun speculating in land values, and what is sauce for the white goose is sauce for the African gander. But the results of the process in white men's Kenya have not been so wholly admirable that we should wish them to be repeated in the Reserves; and I imagine that the Administration will take its precautions.

If, on the other hand, any provisions introduced to guard against landlordism err by excess, the process of subdivision of Githakas, which has already gone a long way in the most densely-settled districts, may run to seed and give us a patchwork of tiny holdings so small and so complicated that the benefits of individual ownership will be lost. Something of this sort seems to have occurred in some of the coast areas of Kenya, where in the space of a mere generation or so, coconut plantations have been rendered almost worthless by being split up and split up among a geometrical progression of heirs, until the individual owns only a few trees. The extent of the shares is always altering with deaths and marriages; and anyhow each inherits so little property that it is worth nobody's while to weed and cultivate, and the plantation goes to the dogs.

Then there is the danger of taking native custom and stereotyping it in the form of legal ordinances, although what happens to exist is merely a phase in an unstable and rapidly-evolving process. This is a danger of which Lord Lugard, in his book, expressly bids the benevolent administrator to beware. Luckily, the instability of the system and the need for further change are so obvious that this mistake is not likely to be made here.

Then there is the unsuitability of the system, at any rate in its typical form, for all sorts of modern developments. If redeemable purchase is the only way of buying land, and a man builds a permanent building—say a large shop or a mill—on land he has bought, then the original owner not only has the right to redeem the land at any time by restoring the stock he had received as price, but could insist on the building being removed, however useful it might be to the tribe.

Nor is there any provision, under the Githaka system, for securing land for any public or social purpose. The

Committee quote a case when some Christian Kikuyu, as recently as 1926, intended to build a church, but "were unable to hit on a method of getting a piece of land with secure tenure."

The situation is most pressing in respect of schools. In the province there are over three hundred mission out-schools "with no more secure tenure, as far as native custom is concerned, than the permission of the Muramati, which is revocable at will." And even then the Muramati has, or claims to have, the right to veto the making of school gardens or the erection of permanent buildings.

Similarly, wherever redeemable purchase is the rule, any proposal from Government or from the more advanced spirits among the natives themselves for giving up land for a township, a school, an experimental farm, or any other permanent enterprise, is regarded as an affront to tribal ideas, and rouses the tribal conscience in opposition, however intellectually cogent may be the arguments in favour of its benefiting the community as a whole. Of this I had ocular demonstration in the patch of land which the Native Council felt impelled to rent from the Forestry Department for a communal farm, because they could not go against tribal feeling and alienate it, as it were, from the clan-lands of which all the Reserve consisted. There are difficulties, too, about communal grazing rights; and, now that the existence of money is inducing a more commercial spirit, cases are cropping up where a share-owner has made over a bit of virgin forest to a fellow-tribesman only to insist on redeeming it as soon as the other man has effected the heavy task of primary clearing—a rather low trick which apparently would have been unthinkable in the old days when a friendly atmosphere surrounded all land transactions.

The Committee recommends that every Githaka should be registered; that sale in the European sense should, subject to safeguards, be legalized in the district where it is now beginning to appear, and should gradually be extended to other districts; that additional safeguards should be given to tenants (whose rights are now very precarious); and that, subject to administrative sanction, occupiers of land who are not owners may put up permanent buildings.

The difficulties in the way of obtaining land on secure title for social or tribal purposes—these were not within their terms of reference. It would seem that the natural evolution towards more truly individual ownership must simply be encouraged, and that then, with the aid of propaganda and persuasion, the tribe may be trusted to take the sensible view. It is at any rate certain that so long as events keep them suspicious as to the white man's intentions about their land, or (like certain missionary activities to which I shall refer later) can be construed as an attack on their traditional institutions, they will react by clinging unreasoningly to the letter of their existing customs.

I may have spent some time on the Kikuyu and the past, present, and possible future of their land system; but it is typical of what may be found all over Africa to-day—systems already in process of change before the white man came; the change accelerated and modified by the white man's interference and the new ideas he brought with him; old fundamentals of tribal organization and thinking, such as redeemable purchase or the cattle-standard of wealth, proving unequal to the new conditions; the dangers of *laissez-faire*, the equal dangers of imposing artificial rigidity upon the particular phase of evolution which happens to be in existence; the need for firm Governmental action; the danger of arraying native suspicions in hostility to change. Truly the African administrator needs the wisdom of Solomon and the patience of Job!

At any rate, the Committee have put the Government in possession of far fuller information than was available before. Part of the wisdom of authority must consist in amassing knowledge: and Applied Anthropology must come to be recognized as an essential part of African administration.

Chapter XX

THE EASE OF BEING MISUNDERSTOOD

To those unfamiliar with peoples at a different level of culture from their own, with languages built on different principles and ideas constructed on a different basis, a concrete example is needed to open their eyes and make them realize the difficulties and dangers inherent in trying to bridge in one span the gap between two disparate ways of living. Fortunately an East African example lay ready to hand. Mr. Leakey kindly allowed me to draw on the manuscript of a forthcoming article in *Africa*, concerning the trouble over female initiation rites which has been brewing for some time among the Kikuyi, and in the last few months has burst in storm.[1]

The facts are briefly these. Among the Kikuyi, as among so many African peoples, girls as well as boys must pass through an initiation ceremony in order to pass out of childhood to a new stage of life. All those initiated in one year belong to a special "age-class" (as all who graduate from an American college are bound together as "the class of 1910" or whatever year it may be); and these age-classes play an important and indeed essential part in the tribe's social structure.

---

[1] In the few months between the writing and the publication of these lines, the trouble appears to have died down, I gather owing to a change of attitude on the part of the missionaries concerned.

THE EASE OF BEING MISUNDERSTOOD

After initiation, boys and girls do not marry for some years, but, as in many, perhaps most, primitive tribes, are allowed and indeed encouraged to enjoy considerable sexual freedom. In this tribe, however, only a modified form of sexual intercourse is allowed to the unmarried, in which physical virginity is preserved, and the birth of children rendered impossible.

Initiation involves several things. It involves a lengthy but sporadic course of education in regard to natural phenomena; a course of "sex-instruction" which in some respects might be copied with advantage by our own educational authorities; the inculcation of various social and individual virtues, including respect for tribal elders, tribal custom and authority. And it also involves a physical operation which is the outward and visible sign of the passage from one stage of life to the next, and the endurance of which with fortitude is a fitting symbol of leaving childishness behind.

This operation in the case of the girls is usually known as "female circumcision," and consists in a mutilation of the external organs of generation. There can be no doubt that it is a cruel rite, and also one which is often harmful, for, if it is not skilfully done, considerable masses of scar-tissue are formed which may endanger the lives of the mother and the baby at the first child-birth. Curiously enough, the presence of white civilization has made the operation more cruel and more dangerous. What with squatters living outside the Reserves, girls going with their parents to live in the towns, and the general slight decay of tribal solidarity, it is now no longer practicable for the candidates to be initiated at a few central places. This means that instead of the operation being performed only by a select band of skilled old women, it is often carried out by bungling unpractised hands, with disastrous results.

A crisis has recently arisen owing to the attitude of certain missions, notably the Church of Scotland Mission, to the practice. As net result, the stand they have taken up, instead of tending to the modification or abolishment of the rite, has been regarded as unwarrantable interference, has crystallized in opposition all the reactionary traditionalism of the tribe, and has caused the rite itself to be regarded by the more jingo section of the Kikuyu as the central symbol of their tribal patriotism.

The missionaries referred to have stated that female circumcision and Christianity are incompatible. Just before I left Nairobi they were refusing Holy Communion to all Kikuyu Christians who would not declare themselves open opponents of the rite, and were insisting that all the native schoolmasters in the schools of the mission should sign a document pledging themselves to work against female circumcision. The result was a dearth of communicants, and, a good deal more serious, the closure of the bulk of the out-schools in the big area served by this mission.

(On my return to England, I found a certain grim humour in reading in the *Times* of a parallel from Russia —medical men being imprisoned for circumcising male Jewish babies, such "tribal superstitions" being repugnant to the Bolshevik authorities. Bolsheviks forbidding the hallowed Jewish practice of male circumcision: British forbidding the hallowed Kikuyu practice of female circumcision, in both cases under penalty. . . . The world is an odd place!)

Now, it might be thought that in this they were making a laudable stand. But they seem to have ridden for a fall in taking up such an intransigent attitude. And, what more particularly concerns us here, they had, without realizing it, introduced the most unfortunate difficulties and confusions into the subject by erroneous use of the Kikuyu language or ignorance of Kikuyu thought.

The first difficulty lies in the Kikuyu word *irua*, denoting female as well as male circumcision. For one thing, this is the word used for circumcision throughout the Kikuyu translation of the New Testament. Accordingly the native Christians were asking themselves, "Does not the Missionaries' Holy Book itself say 'circumcision is nothing, and uncircumcision is nothing'? Why then teach us this and then turn round and say it is a great deal, and very wicked? Why use the word as a symbol of the elect, as St. Paul does in Colossians? Why say 'circumcision verily profiteth, if thou keep the law,' as in Romans?"

For another thing, the same word is unfortunately used in Kikuyu to mean not only the actual operation, but the whole rite of initiation, including the preparatory teaching. And since Kikuyu society is constituted on the basis of age-classes, and since age-classes can only come into existence through initiation, there arise further difficulties. An attack on the operation, unless very carefully explained, can be legitimately construed as an attack on the whole idea of initiatory instruction and the age-class system behind it; (and I was elsewhere told that this same verbal confusion appears to have nullified certain efforts on the part of the Administration to get the native chiefs to agree to a modification of the rite; they thought the Government were out to destroy the basis of their society). Further, even if this obscurity is avoided, a successful attack on the operation of circumcision, without any substitution of some other permissible rite, would mean the collapse of the whole age-class system, and so the tribe's very structure and social stability.

There is another unfortunate error due to language difficulties. In the Kikuyu language there is no word which expresses what we mean by *virgin*, as there is no such thing in Kikuyu life. There are little girls below the age of sexual maturity, and there are girls circumcised and initiated but yet unmarried, who are technically *virgines intactae*, but are encouraged to practise the modified sexual intercourse to which I have referred. The word for this latter state is *Muiritu*: as will be seen, it means *demi-vierge* rather than virgin. *Faute de mieux*, however, the word virgin in the Bible has been translated *Muiritu*. So the native Christian is confronted with another puzzle. He finds the Mother of Jesus extolled and blessed in the faith he has embraced; but she is described in his Bible as a young woman who by definition has been initiated and circumcised. And now the missionaries tell him that female circumcision is wrong. He may be pardoned for a little perplexity.

The chief result of the C.S.M. campaign against the rite, apart from the regrettable deadlock with the native teachers which led to the closure of so many schools, has been to make the tribe irrationally suspicious of a plot against their liberties and traditions, and to harden tribal opinion in favour of the rite, the whole rite, and nothing but the rite, as an emblem of their patriotism.

Feeling having been once aroused, regrettable incidents have followed. Christian girls who were being educated at mission schools have been abducted and forcibly "circumcised." Others who have gone back to live in the Reserves have had pressure, often of a brutal nature, brought to

bear on them to submit to the operation. In the middle of
a service in a big mission church, a patriotic tribesman
(afterwards tried for disorderly conduct) forced an entrance, harangued the congregation, and ended by urging
them to throw off their clothes and reveal themselves as
true circumcised Kikuyu. And one missionary worker has
been murdered. The net result is that it will take years to
repair the mischief.

Leakey, from his intimate knowledge of the tribe, believes that the more progressive Kikuyu, who undoubtedly
realize the harm caused by the operation as at present
practised, would even now welcome a compromise. They
cannot consent to mere abolition, for that would cut at the
whole system of initiation. But they would agree, he thinks,
to a modification of the system. The training and instruction must be kept—they have much in them that is good,
and could be made even more valuable by slight modification of the teaching, especially in matters of sex and general morals. So should the actual ceremony of initiation—
it could be made as important a socio-religious function as,
for instance, First Communion in Catholic countries. But
an alternative operation should be sanctioned—it might be
an incision on some other part of the body, but should in
the present stage of Kikuyu evolution leave a permanent
mark and be in some degree painful; and, though the
original operation need not, and should not, be banned outright, the alternative rite should be encouraged until it
supplanted the other. An enlightened missionary spirit
would then seek not to suppress such a purged and modified initiation rite, but to blend it with its own corresponding ceremonials, with the same combination of tolerance
and good sense which in the youth of the Church fused

pagan orgies with the celebration of Christ's nativity, and submerged the mystic rites of the year's rebirth in the festival of Easter resurrection.

Other unfortunate and unforeseen consequences of the Kikuyu's contact with white civilization may be mentioned here, as further illustrations of the difficulty of dealing with problems of native morality. In Kenya it is only in the last few years that Native Councils have been set up in the Reserves. The natural result of the previous period of direct rule by paid headmen, was a weakening of respect for tribal authority and tribal tradition. This was accentuated by much of the missionary work among the tribe, since the native convert was encouraged to break with much of his pagan past, and, receiving an education which left tribal history and pride out of account, often came to despise the elders of the tribe and to laugh at their ideas and their authority. Meanwhile, however, very few found themselves willing or able to live up to the ideal set before them by the missions—an ideal exceedingly difficult for an all-but-raw tribal African—of pre-marital chastity.

The traditional system under which modified intercourse was recognized and encouraged has its faults; but at least it frowned on children born before marriage and inflicted severe punishments on the unmarried father. Since, however, British law inflicts no such penalties, young people, freed from traditional restraints, have been taking to normal sex intercourse, with a resultant marked increase in the number of illegitimate children. And, as further result, many of the new class of unmarried mothers, who naturally do not find favour in tribal society, betake themselves to Nairobi and the facile trade of prostitute.

This tendency has been aggravated in yet another way.

THE EASE OF BEING MISUNDERSTOOD

The Kikuyu, like most Bantu tribes, have the so-called "bride-price" system, whereby a bridegroom must hand over so many cattle or goats to the bride's family. This system is almost universally misunderstood and misinterpreted by Europeans as a mere purchase of wives, and our feminists often enlarge on the degraded state of societies in which women are thus bought and sold like chattels. Social anthropology, however, delving below the surface appearance, reveals the transaction in a different light. For one thing, its main meaning is not concerned with the mere purchase of individual wives, but is concerned with the stability of the enduring clan, that central feature of African social life and thought. The clan must endure; for it to endure, its men must beget children; to beget children they must take to themselves women. Women serve the clan not only as cultivators and preparers of food, but as bearers of children, and so it is only right that, when a clan surrenders a woman in marriage to a member of another clan, it should receive in return the wherewithal to recoup itself.

But from the point of view of the individual bride and bridegroom themselves, the "bride-price" is not a mere cash transaction: it is an insurance. The husband's goats and cattle are held by the bride's family as a pledge against her possible ill-treatment and as an earnest of her good behaviour. For if a wife deserts her husband without good cause, or commits adultery (the details vary from tribe to tribe, but the general principles remain constant), her family must restore the "bride-price." But if she leaves her husband owing to his maltreatment of her, then he has no claim, and loses both woman and stock.

The "bride-price" being thus a guarantee and an insurance, native custom would permit it to be paid in instalments, and this was regularly done when the two families were on friendly terms. Unfortunately, many Government officials and missionaries have taken the "common-sense" view that the "bride-price" is a true purchase price, and therefore insist on its being paid over in full before church weddings or officially-registered marriages. Thus every Kikuyu suitor, a black Jacob, has to work for years to amass the full price, and can no longer marry young; and when, as is the custom with certain missions, the bride's father has to sign a declaration at the marriage that he has received all that is due to him, he knows he can look forward to no more gifts from his son-in-law, and lays on an extortionate price, still further delaying the marriage. Native nature being what it is, a large proportion of the young Christians seek extra-marital intercourse while waiting to get married, with the result that illegitimate births are further increased, and venereal disease disastrously spread.

I have spent some time over this case of Kikuyu morals and customs, because it illustrates two points at one and the same time. It illustrates the danger of radical interference with particular native customs, however desirable it may be to alter them, because they so often turn out to be part of the warp and woof of the native social structure; pull the one thread violently out, and the whole fabric disintegrates. And it also illustrates the difficulty inherent in language and its limitations, the difficulty of making sure, when you try to explain one of your own Western ideas, that you are not making it mean something quite different to your hearers.

This language difficulty may have only grotesque results. I remember being told once by an administrative officer from Nigeria that the only way which the missionaries in one district had found to translate the term *Holy Ghost* into the local language was by two words which, taken literally, meant *White Liver.* . . . It may have awkward consequences, as in the dispute we have just been considering, or as in another Kikuyu instance where *adultery* had been translated in the Seventh Commandment by a word which did mean adultery, but adultery in one special degree only. There were several other words signifying other different kinds of adultery; and the most zealous native converts, who had been doing their best to live up to their new code of morals by scrupulously confining themselves to the kinds of adultery not mentioned in the Decalogue, were aggrieved when they were accused of grave sin by their white teachers.

Or it may have quite serious consequences. Some time ago an unfortunate white sanitary inspector in Uganda had his arm cut off by a native man who objected to being inoculated for plague. The man belonged to a peculiar native sect styling themselves the Malachites, one of whose tenets is that medical interference is wicked. And one of their reasons for this attitude, I was assured, was the fact that in the local translation of the Bible the word "witch" in the cruel Old Testament passage, "Thou shalt not suffer a witch to live," had been translated by the word currently used for *doctor*. So he was only doing his best to obey the injunctions of the Scriptures.

One of the most curious difficulties confronting the penetration of Western thought into black skulls is recorded of the Trobriand islanders, who have no inkling of the fact of physiological paternity, and for whom accordingly the father—the man in the family group—stands in no real relationship to the sons. As result, the idea of God as a heavenly Father or that of the Sonship of Christ say nothing to them, the missionaries are baulked at the outset. But this is not an African case, and I must leave the reader to follow it up in the fascinating pages of Malinowski's *Sexual Life of Savages.*

Most people like stories with a moral. The moral of this chapter at least is very simple. It is that in dealing with primitive peoples, whether your business is to govern them or to educate them, to help them towards a higher economic and cultural level or to convert them, both anthropology and toleration are needed.

Chapter XXI

NATIVE LIFE AND KENYA SCHOOLS

Oct. 8th. Up betimes, and off across the plains to Machakos, lying among the distant blue hills in the Wakamba country. Ostriches race the car, and there are the usual herds of buck and zebra, though we fail to see any giraffes.

Machakos is a tidy little place among the hills, its streets crowded with natives. The Wakamba are black in comparison with most East African tribes. Their two special peculiarities are their remarkable mechanical aptitudes, and their dental habits. Their native metal industry is well known, and they are in great demand as chauffeurs and mechanics. As to teeth, the tribal custom is for the men to have them sharply filed to a point, after the fashion so prevalent in parts of the Congo, and popularly supposed to denote cannibal propensities. As if this were not enough, they often extract their own teeth, then take those of animals, goat or hartebeest, file their ends, shape their bases, and screw them into the vacant sockets. When first I read of this in a popular book, I refused to credit it; but it is sober fact. These artificial teeth can be made to project further than natural ones, with points filed so as to protrude in a curve, giving the mouth an inhuman, dragonish, or fish-toothed look. The tooth-filing process is excruciating, and so, I gather, is the screwing-in of false teeth; but what

213

will not human beings undergo in the pursuit of *bon ton*?
Do not let us forget tight-lacing and eighteen-inch waists.

More serious than the pain is the decay of teeth and
general sepsis of the mouth which these practices promote;
and even the most ardent upholder of native customs can
scarcely regret that the habit is now on the decline.

At the Government School we saw a brilliant drill display by the older lads (mostly apprentices on the technical
side); and the workshops were a delight, clean and cool,
with slim black boys, keen-looking and attractive in their
shorts and white blouses, busy at carpenter's bench or forge,
sewing-machine or cobbler's last.

The significance of such a school dawned more fully in
the afternoon, when we visited a couple of native villages
out in the Reserve. Untidy and primeval, a few rough beehive huts on a dirty space surrounded by an irregular
hedge of thorns—these are the tribal homes, these the kind
of surroundings among which the boys in the school had
grown up. The boys may perhaps lose something of value
in return for the cleanliness, smartness and skill which they
acquire, but it is hard to think that on balance there is not
great gain.

Besides the technical branch, there is a general academic
side to the school. One very encouraging feature here was
the attention given to nature-study and to local native in-
dustries. The assistant European master had got together a
fine collection of stools, carved walking-sticks, metal-work
chains, ear-ornaments and the like, and the boys spent some
of their time copying these, instead of always working on
European models (usually not in the best taste) as is the
case in most schools.

There was one entertaining moment. My host, the Director of Education, had been attempting since his arrival in Kenya to purge native education of academic absurdities, such as giving young Africans fresh from the bush Readers which presupposed a knowledge of European climate and scenery and history, or setting them sums concerned with problems so highly germane to their lives as the papering of rooms, or the rate at which baths fill when hot and cold taps are on and the plug is out. And he was congratulating himself on having impressed upon his Department the need for common-sense in such matters. As we went through the school, however, and I turned over the pages of the boys' exercise-books, my eye was caught by the following problem: "Convert 5,555,555 Farthings to Pounds, Shillings, and Pence." Farthings do not exist in East African currency; and even in Britain the problem could hardly be said to have a vital connection with everyday life. The old ways die hard!

Lunch with the Provincial Commissioner—the usual charming hospitality of Africa which greets one everywhere; and then a drive into the Native Reserve.

The hills are of a fantastic beauty, for instead of green or withered brown they show red, violet, chestnut, purple. But this beauty is a beauty of death. The brilliant colour is the colour of the earth's flesh that should be hidden. Not only is there scarcely a blade of grass on the slopes, but over large tracts the soil has been swept away, and the subsoil or the bare rock itself lies naked to the sky.

This is all due to tree-felling and over-grazing. Not many centuries back, these hills were green with forest. As new migrations flooded the land with their black and brown human waves, new peoples penetrated the hills, hunting gave place to agriculture, and the forest was

burned and cut from the plains upwards until only a few
scattered groves and sacred trees remained. Yet grass
sprang up where the trees had grown before, and the hills
were still green, though grazed by thousands of cattle.
But after the coming of the white man, conditions again
changed. Now there were no longer any raids, so that the
population, both human and bovine, increased. The tribe
was restricted to a definite Reserve, much of which is not
suitable for cattle owing to tick-borne disease. They could
no longer ease pressure by migration, nor was pressure automatically eased by the raids of warlike neighbours such
as the Masai. Yet the immemorial attitude towards cattle
has changed less among the Wakamba even than in other
tribes; cattle for them are still the emblem of social success,
the only desirable form of wealth. A settler who has lived
for many years on the borders of the Wakamba Reserve
told me how once an old man of the tribe, whom he had
asked why his compatriots refused to sell their beasts or
to cull out the poor stock, replied, "Well, you see, we old
men like to get a little drunk and sit about and tell each
other how many cattle we've got." Where there is no possibility of talking about your score at golf, your latest car,
or your distinguished friends, this is perhaps as good a
pastime for the elderly as any other; but unfortunately it is
helping to ruin the tribe.

So the carrying capacity of the Reserve was exceeded, the
grass was eaten down here and there, the browsing pressure
of the herds of cattle was concentrated on what was left,
creating a vicious circle, until the soil was exposed without
its protecting blanket of herbage, and in many places was
washed away down to the naked rock beneath. A recent
estimate puts the stock-carrying capacity of the Reserve at

60,000 head of cattle; there are now on it 240,000 cattle, not to mention over a quarter of a million goats!

The immediate misery is bad enough; the mischief done to the land is even more serious. It is easy enough to set erosion going. But once started, it will continue at an increasing velocity; it is much harder to restore soil once it has been washed away. Two things seem urgent—to reduce the cattle to reasonable numbers; and to proceed with a broadly-conceived plan of afforestation to temper the violent run-off down the slopes and give the grass a new chance. Forestry is beginning. The native councils themselves are planting trees in the valleys; but this is mainly for fuel. The Forestry Department has begun a scheme of planting the tops and watersheds. But this is being hindered by the suspicions of the natives, who regard this as a Government dodge to filch land from them: so do harsh land policies come home to roost.

As regards the cattle situation, the recent Agricultural Commission's Report provides some interesting reading. Some of the more enlightened headmen realize the cumulative disaster that is overtaking their country, and the reasons for it; but, they say, the bulk of the tribe put it down merely to a run of bad years, and do not connect it with over-stocking. Nor would the Wakamba be willing to part with any of their beasts save under compulsion. In fact, there are reports of tribesmen who have died of starvation rather than kill any of their stock for their own consumption. It is a situation as paradoxical in its way as was the slump of the mark or the kroner. As the Report says, "The habit of raising cattle and goats as a form of social competition, without regard to their utilization, does in itself provide a purpose for existence and might be in-

217

dulged—did it not inevitably lead to the destruction of the people themselves."

The Wakamba demand more land as a remedy; and in default of a formal grant are erupting from the Reserve into various stretches of Crown Land and into other Native Reserves, naturally creating unrest and disorder. But new land, even if such were available, would be no remedy: it too, in a decade or so, would become over-grazed, under-grazed, and generally ruined. The Agricultural Commission recommends the establishment of a meat-factory, to be run at a loss if need be for a time until the danger is over; and some form of compulsory culling of the stock. Here again, however, the psychology of the "cattle-standard" of economics raises difficulty. Bulls, heifers and steers have different values, as have pound notes, ten-shilling notes and half-crowns. But all cattle of one category are equally valuable to the Wakamba, just as all pound notes, new or old, are worth a pound to us. The Mkamba knows that such and such a price is being given for a good working ox: he expects as much money for the wretchedest beast, in the same way as we should be much aggrieved if we were to find the purchasing power of an old dilapidated banknote only half that of a nice new one.

It really looks as if compulsion—combined, let us hope, with the best kind of propaganda—will be necessary: but it is quite on the cards that it will cause serious discontent. The Agricultural Commission tentatively suggests that special coins bearing the image of a bull, and pierced to be worn on the person, might be minted for use in the Reserve. They would in the first instance be paid over only for stock sold to the meat-factory, and it is suggested that the collection and display of such "cattle-coins" might take the place of the amassing of actual cattle (as baseball has been substituted for head-hunting in parts of the Philippines). It all sounds very Gilbertian; but when the initial situation is so topsy-turvy, perhaps comic remedies will help.

Here, perhaps, I may appropriately record a case which one of my hosts, a settler on an estate near Nairobi, was recently called upon to settle, and which amused him so much that he noted the details down. It well illustrates the complexity of financial transactions when your currency is alive and has the power of reproduction. John Doe and Richard Roe were two Wakamba men. We will call them A and B. Before the war, A and B bought a cow between them, each paying so many goats. The cow was looked after by B. During a famine, A went to look for work in the township; meanwhile, B killed and ate the cow. When A returned he quite rightly complained, so B gave him another cow. This new cow had a heifer calf; the two men arranged that B should take back the cow, and A should keep the heifer.

In due time the heifer, after producing three calves, and breaking its leg, died; and so did the two old men. They each left a son, however, and A's son kept the three calves. But now B's son claimed that he had the right to one of the three, and appealed to white, if informal, justice.

Verdict: all pre-war *shauris* are now washed out; A's son keeps the calves.

An incident of my day at Machakos will illustrate the effect of over-grazing on the cattle themselves. I was walking across a hillside with another visitor from England, when a herd of cattle hove in sight. They were so small that I ironically remarked, "Fine goats, aren't they?" My companion, interested in something else, cast a half-glance at them, and said with perfect seriousness, "Yes, they're really quite good goats"—a statement which well portrays their size.

Driving back to Nairobi, the Wakamba hills, illuminated by the sunset light, took on the most astonishing colours— red and burnt sienna and purple. It was hard to remember that their bright beauty was a beauty of doom and death.

Oct. 9th. Impressions crowd on one so fast in this forced draught of official visits and unofficial sightseeing that one must catch them at once if they are not to escape or be blurred. Yesterday it was the bare red hills of Machakos in their dry plains; to-day the fertile heights of the green Kikuyu country west of Nairobi. Yesterday our chief objective was a Government School; to-day the big Mission School of the Church of Scotland Mission.

It is a fine school, though not so good as some schools I saw later in Uganda. One of the most interesting facts about it is that throughout its existence—which now runs into seven decades—they have had co-education for all class work. (Outside the classroom, rules are strict; boys and girls are only allowed to meet at certain times in certain specified places.) They have never had any trouble, and believe firmly that co-education in class is better than segregation of the sexes for Africans—or at any rate for the Kikuyu.

Mrs. Watson, a splendid "old-timer," showed us over the girls' school. The girls live in dormitory "cottages" of twelve beds each; a head girl is responsible for each cottage, and has a room to herself. The cottages are issued with rations, which the girls can then cook as they prefer, supplementing them with vegetables from their own school gardens, which they are taught to cultivate by approved methods. Into the charge of each cottage are given two black babies, generally orphans, for whose well-being the girls are responsible—an excellent way of training them in the care of their own future children.

There are sixty girls in all—but a waiting list of a hundred or so who cannot be accommodated for lack of funds. Many on the list give up waiting after a few months, and either marry "heathen husbands" (I never could get used to the deliberate use by missionaries in Kenya of the depreciatory term *heathen* when they could just as well have said *pagan*: to me it is like saying *nigger* instead of *negro* or *African*), or else, alas! go off to Nairobi and embark on prostitution as a career.

Then to the very efficient-looking senior sewing-class. The girls' new pattern "Gym" dresses were rather attractive, but this is unfortunately a rare exception. Most dresses and uniforms designed for native girls at missions are hideous. I suppose it is largely a matter of money; but I cannot help thinking that the idea of feminine attractiveness as something essentially rather sinful plays a part. The Sunday-go-to-meeting dress here was an abomination of narrow-striped pink and white. And the Christian dresses are often to my mind much less decent than the original native attire of skins. More of the figure is actually covered up, but they are often cut so as to accentuate the spreading buttocks and big breasts of the African girl in a way both disagreeable and suggestive.

Then on to the Alliance High School—the sole institution of higher education in Kenya. The great difficulty at this school, I gathered, is the fact that all the boys are after some certificate or other, and certificates have a way of interfering with real education: educational troubles are much the same all over the world! Whatever the cause, the curriculum was rather disorganized.

Some local patriots would like to see the Alliance High School develop into a full-blown college, rival of Makerere in Uganda. But I am sure this would be a retrograde step: we know in this country something of the dangers of multiplying centres of higher education; and where, as in Africa, standards are of necessity so low, it is infinitely better to have one really good college for the whole of East Africa than an indifferent institution for each separate territory. The Alliance has the makings of a first-class high school; let it be content with that.

Lunch—a very pleasant affair at the house of a settler who is also in the Administration. This dual existence, by the way, is a real problem for the Government. Should it be permitted at all? The fact of a Government servant owning an estate makes it more likely that he will stay on in the country when he comes to the pensionable age, and this is desirable. But can he really pay attention to two businesses at once, even if he have a manager for his estate? And is it right that he should have financial interests tending to pull him over to the side of the settlers, who in Kenya constitute a party rather than an industry? And if the practice be prohibited, will not the prohibition be evaded by various artifices?

Meanwhile, this particular estate thrives. It is planted with tea, rather a novelty in Kenya. The conditions of climate are so different from Ceylon or China that special methods of drying the leaf have to be introduced; but the quality seems to be good.

The charming stone house with its pretty garden and,

inside, its oars inscribed with triumphs on Thames and Cam, was like an English country-house, with a flavour of Western America added in its verandahs, its newness, the pleasant wildness of the country round about, and the general pioneer spirit which it inevitably breathed.

At lunch, the three males were all old Etonians, of three successive generations. But our charming hostess and the other women saw to it that there was real conversation round the table, and not mere talk. There have been innumerable disputes as to what constitutes civilization and what are its criteria; but no one would deny a place to conversation. It is the seal of civilization, only possible where the inner man is civilized, and not merely the externals of life. At such times as these it is impossible not to sympathize with the ideal of a white island along the backbone of Africa. After all, there is such a thing as a scale of values, and the realization of values is the only ultimate aim which we can perceive for man on earth. Is it not inescapably good to be able to realize these values of ordered activity, cultivated mind, civilized enjoyment, such as I see here springing up on the soil of Africa within the tropic belt, where before was only black barbarism?

Agreed. But then one visits another African centre of our white civilization, and finds the only topics of interest to be money, golf, bridge, and gossip. Suburbia unrestrained, exalted to feudal dominion over an African population who may have been barbaric but at least lacked all vulgarity, and had the charm and the indefinable quality (as of some beautifully-adapted organism) of the unspoilt barbarian. Of a large and important section of white people in Africa, officials as well as settlers, it is not unfair to say that the *Tatler*, *Punch*, a few magazines, detective stories and second-rate romantic novels, represent their intellectual and cultural level. Think of Africans, whose fathers, however ignorant, lived a life exposed to elemental nature, to tribal war and wild beasts, their fears crystallizing out in the ritual of magic, their joys in the violent abandonment of the primitive dance—think of them now being brought up to imbibe (unconsciously but all the more insidiously) the spirit of second-hand Tatlerism. It is then that one is not quite so sure of the white-island theory and all that it implies.

Oct. 10*th*. An amusing story is going the rounds. I do not vouch for it, but there is no reason why it should not be as true in fact as it is in spirit. The story is that the Agricultural Commission now sitting, a majority of which is composed of settlers, had at first not wished to hear any native witnesses at all. The chairman had insisted, there had been threats of resignation, intervention from high quarters, and so on. Finally it was agreed that natives should be heard, but the procedure was to be such as to emphasize the proper distance between white and black: native witnesses should not shake hands with the members of the Commission like white witnesses, they should stand while giving their evidence, all questions should be put to them through an interpreter so as to avoid any back-chat or free-and-easy familiarity, and so forth.

The first witness was a Kikuyu (a very interesting man, by the way, who has over a hundred acres under maize, and uses ploughs and European methods of cultivation): after he had given his evidence, several members of the Commission grew so interested that they forgot all about the interpreter, and began an animated and friendly discussion with him, to the chagrin of the chief anti-native member.

But this gentleman's discomfiture was completed by the next witnesses—two Masai in their blankets (only one had been called—the second explained that the tribe had sent him along to see that the first gave the proper evidence), who, after looking round, chose him as the first man on whom to bear down with smiles and outstretched hands. His hand wished to remain still; but inexorably, automatically, in face of this natural politeness and friendliness, it extended itself, to be seized and warmly shaken. Then, after hand-shaking their way all round the Commission, they quietly but with dignity sat on the floor—as there were no chairs—to give their evidence. And so ended the Commission's brief ride on the high white horse.

I repeat that I have no means of knowing whether the tale is as true as it sounds. But I was at least told on very good authority that the Commission as a whole had been much impressed by the evidence of native witnesses. Most of the settler members had, I gathered, simply not known that such interesting men existed, nor that there existed, even sporadically, such a desire for improved agriculture among native Africans. They had made the natural mistake of judging all natives by those who came to work on their estates, and they had never been brought into contact with those who had the providence and ability to remain at home and earn money not by working for wages but by producing crops for sale. We are all prone to make the same sort of error. Some Americans do it, for instance, when they judge China by the Chinese proprietors of laundries and chop-suey restaurants, or Italy by the hordes of "dago" labourers.

The Kikuyu witness, I was assured, made one very interesting appeal. He asked whether the Government could not promulgate an ordinance restricting the sale and consumption of native beer to the evening. "You white men," he said, "work hard all day, and then drink in the evenings; our people often begin their drinking in the morning, and so they don't get so much work done." But it was felt that this experiment in partial prohibition, even if desirable, would be impossible to enforce.

To-day I visited the Indian School, handsomest building in Nairobi, and one of the two or three best of Baker's numerous designs in the colony. More smallness of the world: the Headmaster, brought over to this post after years of educational work in India, was of my year and college at Oxford. Great progress has been made in Indian education in Kenya of recent years. A number of the boys enter for, and pass, standard examinations like London Matriculation; and in general—regrettable but true—reach considerably higher levels than the local white children. More interesting to me than this academic precocity was the remarkable effect of drill and the Boy Scout movement upon the Indian boys. I have a great weakness for children; but I must confess that most of the Indian children I saw in East Africa did not attract me; there was something pallid and weedy about so many of them, a rather unhealthy precocity which yet amounted to nothing. Regular drill and physical exercises, which are compulsory at the Indian School, have undoubtedly improved their physique and bearing. Admission to the Boy Scouts is not easily gained; as result, the Scouts are extremely keen, and I was delighted and astonished at the physical development, the expression and the frank pleasant manners of the group of Scout Leaders to whom I was introduced. As boys like these grow up, they cannot fail to introduce new ideas and new values into the life of the Indian community of Kenya.

Chapter XXII

TOWN AND COUNTRY

October 10*th*. Another visit to the native quarters of Nairobi, made this time in the company of Dr. Mary Shaw, a capable and energetic woman doctor in the Public Health Service. Towns will certainly be the crux of the native problem in the tropics, just as they were of Meredith's too-rural philosophy. There are over ten thousand natives now in Nairobi, huddled into three separate native locations that have grown up more or less haphazard where there was space. The older dwellings are made of wattle-and-daub, and thatched, or roofed with bits of tin. They are cheap to build, but dark and dirty, and eternally in need of repair. Each of these little houses or huts is the home of several families—a regular warren. Various Government Departments have recently been making experiments in providing better housing—not always, it must be confessed, with success. Some of the single-room dwellings for unmarried labourers are completely reminiscent of prison cells, and even the two-room homes for married couples have often a discouraging institutional look about them. They are clean and tidy, however, with their brick or cement walls and floor; and the ventilating space just under the roof does not interfere with privacy, and is almost impossible to stuff up with rags, as is the usual fate of windows in a native house.

Yet even these modest beginnings of decency have been bitterly attacked in many quarters as a pampering of the native. I think many people genuinely believe that natives prefer squalor and thrive better in dirty and primitive conditions. That they really appreciate better things, however, is attested by the facts. Directly these model lodgings were put up, the native labourers began bringing their wives along to the towns. This naturally meant that they stayed longer at a time and were more contented with town life. The greater stability of labour which this brought about effected such savings that the Railway Department is, in all its main centres, embarking on these permanent housing schemes in place of its old ramshackle and really disgraceful labour lines.

But many difficulties still hang about African town-life. When wives are brought to town, where they no longer have any agricultural duties, they suffer from the lack of occupation; and we all know the dictum about Satan and idle hands. It is curious to find the problem of leisure, which is beginning to weigh so heavily on energetic married women in our labour-saving civilization, pressing equally, though in a different fashion, on their African sisters. Then many men leave their real wives to cultivate the crops at home, and take to themselves temporary wives while in Nairobi, deserting them when they go home again. Not unnaturally these women take to prostitution when thrown on their own resources. The ranks of the prostitutes are also swelled by girls from the Reserves who seek to avoid some tribal or domestic difficulty—usually a marriage which is being forced on them against their will, or an unfortunate incident in the shape of a baby before marriage —and see in the town an easy and glittering escape from their troubles. As result of all this promiscuity, venereal disease is severe in Nairobi and is spreading rapidly in the villages round about.

The Government clinics for women and children, one for each of the main native locations, are doing a great deal of good; but it is still a mere fleabite to what is needed. When they were first started, the authorities wrote round to the various Missions in and near Nairobi, telling them of the project, and asking them to encourage women to come. Every woman is asked how she heard of the clinics: incredible as it may sound, I was assured that, up to date, neither the Catholics nor any of the Protestant Missions, save the Salvation Army, had sent a single new patient. Perhaps a Government institution, being merely secular, is not to be encouraged, or perhaps it is considered that bible-classes and suchlike are more important than health; but the fact remains.

Oct. 13*th*. I must confess that Nairobi's sprawling native locations and crowded Indian quarters filled me with gloom. Why should it be necessary for towns to·be so horrible, for each new town to repeat so many of the mistakes of the old towns? It was a relief to set off with Clark, the Acting Game Warden, for a trip into the Game Reserve. We made off westwards, cheered by a view of distant Kilimanjaro (over a hundred miles away), to cross the Rift Valley.

I must acknowledge a certain disappointment at my first view of the rift. The rift walls, fine scarps though they be, are so small in comparison with the huge trough between, and even the great volcanoes in the trough are dwarfed. But my disappointment was largely due to the whole scene being so very different from what I had imagined. Once

INDIAN EDUCATION IN KENYA.

LEFT, A GROUP OF BOY-SCOUTS FROM THE INDIAN SCHOOL, NAIROBI.
RIGHT, THE PORTICO OF THE SCHOOL WITH THE HEADMASTER. (*By courtesy of Mr. J. H. Maxwell. Principal.
Government Indian Secondary School, Nairobi.*)

NATIVE SCHOOLS AND NATIVE HOMES.
ABOVE, WAKAMBA BOYS DRILLING AT THE GOVERNMENT
SCHOOL AT MACHAKOS, KENYA.
BELOW, A TYPICAL HUT IN A WAKAMBA VILLAGE. MOST OF THE
BOYS WERE BROUGHT UP IN HOMES LIKE THIS.

I had grown accustomed to the huge scale of its construction, I fell in love with it, and enjoyed it more each of the four times I subsequently saw it. And it appeals not only to the eye but to the imagination, this great gash, whose origin no man has yet fully explained, across the face of a continent. It is true, however, that the western rift between Kivu and Edward is immeasurably finer as a spectacle; and I believe that the Kenya rift itself is far grander a hundred miles to northwards.

We descended, crossed the wide rift north of the huge, gently-sloping crater of Suswa; saw many zebra and various buck, and my first giraffe; and climbed out the other side on to a pleasant tableland, wooded, and intersected here and there by deep river-valleys heading in the Mau heights to northwards. Lunch at Narok, with the District Commissioner, and afterwards to see the school there, one of the two dairying schools for Masai boys that the Government of Kenya has started.

Here, selected boys of the tribe, besides being given an elementary general education, are taught dairying and agriculture. If this experiment succeeds it may save the Masai, that fine warrior tribe, from degenerating into a sort of human zoo. At the moment, deprived by the *Pax Britannica* of any outlet for their warlike habits, still clinging to their haughty belief that all work save the tending of cattle is beneath their dignity, and yet so obsessed with the idea of cattle as wealth that they are reluctant to sell or improve their stock, they are in danger of becoming mere anthropological specimens, like the Red Indians in some of the United States Reserves. Only education of some sort can change their background. I saw some of the elders critically watching the scions of their tribe playing soccer. The force with which they kick barefooted makes one's toes ache to look at it (often, I was told, they play in a state of natural nudity; to-day in my honour they had put on their neat white jumper and shorts). Afterwards the sixty boys queued up before me and one by one placed their bowed heads in the pit of my stomach. This is the method of salutation with respect; my correct response, as I hastily discovered from the master, was to lay my hand on each woolly head in Biblical benediction. It is a charming gesture, but during its sixty-fold repetition I had leisure to reflect that perhaps it would be inconvenient to substitute it for the present methods of saluting in vogue at Eton or Harrow.

Then back a few miles to Clark's "country-house," a delightful little place with flower and vegetable gardens sloping down to the Syabai river, rapid and brown, and a path leading through the forest to a fine fall. It seemed like a wild garden in Wales or Cornwall; but my host reminded me I was in Africa by taking his gun when we went down to see the fall—in case we met a rhino or other unpleasant brute. As is usual here, visitors have a little guest-house assigned to them; I slept very soundly under my buckskin coverlet. In the morning we breakfasted with Clark's American missionary neighbours, Mr. and Mrs. Stauffacker. He had just climbed Kilimanjaro, and is one of the few who have reached the highest point of all, most men being more than content to climb to the crater rim, and save themselves the walk round to the summit, only a few hundred feet higher at the other side of the crater— a long walk, with lungs panting and heart pumping violently, at over 19,000 feet. He showed me some very interesting pictures. One was of the dead body of a leopard, mummified by the cold, which has lain for years on the crater rim, the poor beast having doubtless strayed up in a mist and been frozen to death. Another was of the extraordinary snow masses within the crater. There are several of these, a hundred feet or more in height, steep-sided and two or three hundred yards long, standing all by themselves on the bare floor of the crater like so many icebergs. One can only surmise that in seasons of exceptionally heavy snowfall the crater gets well filled, and that then a differential thawing leaves these sharply-circumscribed masses standing in isolation; perhaps the crater, though long extinct, is still kept warm from below and some parts of its floor are warmer than others.

Two days later we were back at the Syabai, having camped the intervening night by the Mara river, a hundred miles further west. That camp was a delight. Open bush country, full of game, sloped down to the brown untamed river, here running smooth between steep luxuriant banks, there open for the Masai cattle and the wild beasts to come down and drink. Beyond the river rose a wooded range of hills, recalling to me some of the hill scenery of central Texas.

After some vain attempts to push through the scrub to the river (one does not think of cars as tied to roads in African dry bush, but here the thorn-trees and the rocky ledges were too much for anything but a caterpillar-car), we found a way down and selected a site.

Clark preferred a rest, but I could not afford to waste my short African time or miss any African experience, and went on a solitary walk down river. Touracous called in the trees; gazelles showed through the scrub; one stony place was a haunt of hyaenas, for there were bones and

233

abundance of their uncanny dry white dung, looking like coprolites. All of a sudden an enormous beast appeared from nowhere under my nose and rushed off with much snorting and raising of dust: a fine boar wart-hog. I got a scare, but at the same time learnt some natural history; I had never realized before that these large and grotesque pigs live in burrows like rabbits. When taking to earth, they reverse with agility and go down their hole tail foremost, in order to be able to make a rapid and unimpeded exit.

Finally I came to a track which led across a ford—too deep and exposed for my taste, with crocodiles about. I lingered, watching swallows over the water and hearing the rustling of unknown life in the bushes; then turned for camp. Coming towards me was a solitary black man, padding along on naked feet, skin-clad, with a long spear in his hand. Again I was subject to the tame, civilized city-dweller's involuntary reaction at being confronted with the incalculable humanity of savage life. But my subconscious might have spared itself its little jump. As the fellow came up to me, he extended his arm for a handshake (the Masai love shaking hands), and with an incomprehensible greeting passed on to ford the river. I might have been passing the time of day with a country labourer at home.

Back to camp, and a bathe in some more or less crocodile-proof shallows. A little further up-stream, something had died, and a grove of acacias was covered with the waiting figures of forty or fifty crouched vultures—a heavy crop of obscene fruit.

On the way I had shot a buck; the meat tasted good by the camp-fire after the long hours of open air. It was a perfect night, and we did not trouble to pitch the tent. I slept in the car—Clark, rifle at side, on the ground by the fire. In the pungent coolness of the dawn we broke camp and were off.

We returned by a different route, across the Loita game-plains. Clark was chagrined at the paucity of game. The drought has sent them trekking elsewhere (I afterwards heard there was a huge concentration of animals far across to the eastward); but we saw more giraffes, including a couple right out on a bare plain far from all trees, with what to me at least was a wonderful variety of ruminants, and a hideous hyaena, which we failed to kill. There are amiable-minded philosophers (Sir Arthur Thomson, for instance) who assert that no living creature is really ugly. Of course, this depends on what you mean by *ugly*, and what you mean by *really*. I must confess, however, that a hyaena, however admirably adapted for the remorseless tracking down of sick and wounded beasts and for the cracking of their bones, *is* ugly—and worse, hateful and mean-looking—with his mangy colouring, cruel but ignoble face, and weak hindquarters.

They can lope for hours, but have no speed. We timed this one against the car; even in a spurt it could not do twenty-five m.p.h. There is, by the way, a widespread superstition that hyaenas are hermaphrodite. This is wholly untrue, but has a foundation in the fact that the female external organs are enormous—and look male. An animal is shot which superficial examination puts down as male; but it is in milk—hence the hermaphrodite legend. Dissection is needed to show the truth; and very few people have much stomach for dissecting a stinking hyaena.

After a rest at Clark's house, we pushed on and were

back in Nairobi soon after sunset—180 miles in the day, almost all over rough tracks. The dust across the rift was choking, and clothes and faces were plastered grey. And then a bath, evening clothes, a dinner-party that might just as well have been in London as on the Equator; these contrasts make African life so odd and vivid.

Chapter XXIII

WILD LIFE, SPORT AND SANCTUARIES

A proper Game Policy is an important item of the general statecraft of African territories, a more important item than seems to be realized by many otherwise well-informed people. It would be better to say a proper Wild Life Policy, for the pressure of events and of changing public sentiment will inevitably merge the game question in the much bigger problem of the State's attitude towards wild life in general, be it animal or plant, flower or weed, elephant or humming-bird.

Not long after my return I found a striking example of the misconceptions that may occur. I was enjoying a conversation with a man who, though he had never been in Africa, was deeply interested in African problems, and was in a position to exert a definite influence on opinion. I was talking of the difficulties presented by the Kenya Masai Reserve being simultaneously the chief Game Reserve of the colony, when I found myself rather at cross-purposes with my interlocutor, who seemed to want all the game there to be killed out. The matter was cleared up when I found that he had been firmly convinced that a Game Reserve was really a Game Preserve, in which game was kept for wealthy sportsmen to shoot!

Then there is another and subtler form of misunderstanding. The word *game* may have the dictionary mean-

237

ing of something to be shot for sport, but in Africa it connotes wild and free animal life and comes to include by accretion many animals which are technically vermin, like the hyaena, or the lion when in the wrong place, and many smaller creatures which are never shot at all. In Britain, on the other hand, game tends to connote creatures carefully tended, or preserved from overdue extinction, or even introduced deliberately, in order to provide a few days' shooting. There is about it a flavour of wealth and privilege, repressive legislation, vindictive sentences on poachers, land used for the sport of the few instead of for useful purposes or the pleasure and health of all. It has, in fact, class and party-political associations. And with various people at home, including again some capable of influencing African policy, I have found that this fringe of associations has determined their attitude to the question. "Game Reserves—I am not interested in Game: what we want is Wild Life Sanctuaries." When that sort of remark is thrown at one, it means that the party attitude about game has so distorted the man's general ideas on the subject that it is almost impossible to persuade him that Game Reserves are already Sanctuaries for Wild Life.

Then there is, of course, the same bias turned inside out, the "huntin', shootin' and fishin'" attitude of minds which have never become fully civilized, a barbarian attitude which can find in the killing of animals for sport, not an occasional vivifying escape from the routine and complexity of modern existence, but one of the most important of life's aims. With such people, brought up since childhood in an atmosphere of sport for sport's sake, it is impossible to argue. They find in the idea of wild-life sanctuaries a mere sentimentality, and those who disagree with them simply kill-joys or, more sinister, "Socialists." And finally, worst offenders of all, there are those who kill only to make money out of killing, and value wild life solely in terms of their own pockets.

It is therefore very important to clear the mind of prejudices before tackling the question of African Game Policy, and equally important to be chary of words which, like Game, have a political and social *aura* of meaning, or, like Reserve into Preserve, tempt the unwary brain by association to think of something else.

The old conception of Game Reserves was, it is true, very largely coloured by the sportsman's point of view. They were regarded primarily, or at any rate largely, as reservoirs in which game animals could thrive and multiply, and from which they could spread into the shooting areas round about to fill the depletion caused by the sportsman's rifle.

Of late years, however, what we may call the conservationist point of view has become more and more important. This regards wild animals and wild nature in general as worthy of preservation *for its own sake*: not so that they may afterwards be shot at and killed, but because the world would be poorer without them, because there are many people to whom the sight of wild animals living in untouched surroundings is profoundly stirring and indeed one of the valuable things in life. The camera and the cinema have been powerful allies of the conservationist; for with their aid a man can indulge all his sporting instincts (it is usually a great deal harder to get a good photograph of an animal than to kill it) and his desire for permanent trophies, and yet not slaughter a single creature. Many big-game hunters have virtually abandoned the rifle for the camera. A recent recruit to their number is the Prince of Wales, who devoted most of his latest East African *safari* to photography.

The ideas both of Game Preservation and Wild Life Conservation, however, have come into collision with other ideas and other forces. In the first place, there is health, both human and animal. There is no doubt that game can help the disastrous spread of rinderpest, for instance. In Africa, the most important fact in this domain is undoubtedly the fact that most of the various tsetse-flies are attached to the larger wild animals. As a result, there is a widespread and influential movement which favours the wholesale or at least widespread destruction of wild game in order to make the land safer for man and his domestic animals.

Then there has been a conflict between native development and game. Native cultivation and native stock may undoubtedly suffer very greatly from elephants, hippopotamuses, buck, lions, leopards, and other animals; and the more settled native cultivation becomes, and the bigger the area cultivated, the more acute will the conflict be, until the stage is reached (as it has been reached in densely-settled areas like those round Shinyanga and Maraza) at which all the bigger animals are pushed out of the settled area. The greatest difficulties will occur in regions like the Masai Reserve of Kenya, which is Game Reserve as well. The more the Government succeeds in its aim of making the Masai settle down, whether to dairy-farming or even to a crop-producing existence, the more impossible will it be for Masai and Game to share the single area on the same equal terms as at present.

There is a similar conflict between white settlement and

game. But here the conflict is even graver, for it is not merely agriculture, but all kinds of white man's activities, which are inimical to wild animals. His sporting propensities combined with his possession of modern firearms will ensure that in a few generations his mere existence in any density in the country will, unless counter-measures are taken, reduce the game to a very low level. Round townships the need for protecting life and property will kill off all the big carnivora. Worst of all, wherever big business in the shape of mining interests steps in, it is inevitable that buck and hippo and other sources of cheap meat for native labour will be shot out (as is happening at the southern end of Lake Albert to-day) unless something vigorous is done to prevent the massacre.

At the present moment it is, I think, fair to say that African Game Departments have not really sat down and thought out either their methods or, still more important, their objectives; they just are what they happen to be through the accident of their past and of the present men who chance to be in charge. Some concentrate upon what may be styled police-work; others go in for conservation; here and there a man with scientific leanings makes the best of the opportunities provided him by his position; but there is no definite policy shared by the several Territories.

It is a symptomatic fact that in the United States, where pioneer work in applied biology began much earlier than with us, there are a number of separate administrative branches recognized as connected with what in Africa would be called the Game Department. The first, in addition to dealing with international treaties concerning game and migratory birds, has the straightforward police duty of preventing the breaking of the game-laws by poachers, violators of close-time regulations, and so forth (though most of this detailed executive work is in the hands of the Game Departments of the separate States). It also has the equally straightforward aim of encouraging the multiplication of game animals (whether by a close season, close time for a series of years, or other means), to ensure a constant and adequate supply for the sportsman. The second concerns itself with pest control—the keeping within limits of large animals which inflict damage on crops, spread disease, or are otherwise harmful. (The control of elephants which have formed the habit of raiding crops is a simple African example.) The third deals with fur-bearing animals, and incidentally has proved a great source of profit to the country. The fourth or research branch is scientific, and studies the pure natural history of game animals—which, of course, means a great deal of study of the country they live in, the plants they eat or use for shelter, the other creatures with whose lives theirs are entangled, and even the weather. And the fifth is what the Americans call conservationist; it is organized as a separate Department, and concerns itself with America's wonderful system of National Parks.

It seems to me important that Game Departments in Africa should also come to exercise these multiple duties, and that, in order that there should be no mistake about it, they should bear the stamp of this functional variety by being subdivided into corresponding administrative branches. It is perhaps equally important to signify both the expansion of function and the new emphasis on general conservation, as contrasted with mere Game Preservation, by a change of title. "Conservation Department"—"Bureau

of Wild Life"—the adoption of some such phrase in place
of Game Department would go a long way to dispel ignorance and prejudice.

But even if the Game Departments are thus reorganized,
it will be necessary to make up our minds as to the relative importance of their various functions—in other words,
to have a general policy. And here I suggest it will be well
to take a long view. One of the most interesting tendencies
of the last half-century has been the growing interest in
wild life, beginning with the successful efforts of a few
devoted men (generally labelled cranks at the time) to
introduce legislation for protecting birds, culminating in
the astonishingly widespread interest in wild creatures
shown notably in parts of Germany and the United States,
in grandiose pieces of legislation like the establishment of
the system of National Parks and Forest Reserves in America and elsewhere, and in the rapid growth of interest in
watching and photographing birds and animals instead of
shooting them for sport or collecting their skins or eggs.

At the moment, East African Governments are making
a tidy sum of money out of game licences, and private
firms and individual white hunters an even greater sum
by outfitting game *safaris* and advising and guiding sportsmen. But only a very little imagination is needed to see
that these sums are trifling in comparison with what the
country could make by exploiting (in no offensive sense
of that word) humanity's interest in living wild animals,
in grand and strange scenery, and in unfamiliar and exciting holidays, instead of merely capitalizing its atavistic
hunting propensities. East Africa is unique in the variety
of large animals which can be easily seen there. Lion,
leopard, hyaena; elephant and giraffe; rhino and hippo;

baboon, colobus, other monkeys; ostrich and crocodile; zebra and gnu; large buck, middle-sized buck, little buck— you would be very unlucky if, after spending a fortnight exploring East Africa for wild life, you had not seen at least one creature out of each of these groups. And in no other region of the world could you approach such a list in such a time. In addition, East Africa, if not unique, stands extremely high as regards interesting and lovely scenery. Lakes, fresh and salt; rift valleys; volcanoes of all sizes; a great non-volcanic mountain; deserts and jungles; green uplands, coastal strips tropical with palms, park-like savannahs; rivers great and small—they are all here within easy compass. And finally, there are few other countries in which such striking savages, such a variety of primitive human life, can be so easily seen.

As the possibilities of Africa become realized, there is every reason to anticipate a really large stream of travellers and tourists. But to attract them and provide for them will need a certain amount of imaginative foresight. There must be some game areas set apart where mere sightseers can camp, others for those who wish to spend some time in watching and photographing wild animals. Rest-houses or camps must be provided in such places, with white guides and native trackers and porters. The fees charged for these would be so arranged as to give a profit; and if people chose to come in their own cars bringing their own equipment, they would still be charged an entrance fee and so much per day.

Similarly, camps or huts, guides and equipment should be provided for the great mountains—Kenya, Kilimanjaro, Ruwenzori (a beginning was made with Kilimanjaro before the war by private German enterprize); and if so, it may be safely prophesied that their fantastic beauties will draw men and women from all over the world.

Nor should hotels be left out of account. Already the hotel on the eastern slopes of Ruwenzori is proving a great success. There will come a time when there will be room for a big hotel on each of the three great mountains, in some striking part of both Eastern and Western Rifts, on Lake Victoria (how extraordinary even now that there should exist no hotel at Entebbe!), and on the edge of one or two of the big Game Reserves or Wild Life Reservations, as they will then be called.

It is rather sad to think of the touristification of Africa. But, for one thing, it has begun and there is no stopping it; and if it is planned for in advance, it may not only give the most intense enjoyment to people from more crowded continents, but be made to contribute to the saving of the larger wild animals and the preservation of Africa's regions of natural beauty. One serious danger is that it may lead to a cheapening and artificiality of primitive native life. Lions and giraffes and gazelles may grow tamer by being looked at; they do not become vulgarized. But there is no more deplorable spectacle than a community of human beings consciously "being primitive" for the delectation of tourists' sentimental minds, and turning out "native articles" whose manufacture and style are fundamentally insincere, because they are made merely to tempt the tourists' purses. That is sophistication inside-out, and sets a blight of inevitable degeneracy on its victims. Here is something which a wise Government will guard against.

But we do not want all Game Reserves and all mountain forests indiscriminately overrun by international tourism;

so that here further foresight is needed. To start with, there should be created a system of National Parks besides mere Game Reserves. Any of the East African Game Reserves can at the moment, I understand, be abolished by a stroke of a pen—or rather of two pens, those of the Governor of the Territory and of the Secretary of State for the Colonies: no debate in the local Legislative Council, much less in Parliament, is necessary. They are in fact purely administrative areas, to be altered or abolished as the executive for the time being sees fit.

There will long remain a place for such purely administrative reserves, as breeding reservoirs for wild life in general and game in particular; they will need adjustment as intensity of settlement increases. But in addition there should be certain areas which remain for ever safe from administrative interference as well as from the pressure of local vested interests. Such areas are National Parks. The essence of a National Park, as the idea has been developed by the Belgians in Africa, is that it is removed from administrative control, and is vested in a body of independent trustees; thus, without amending the deed of trust, no alterations in boundaries or functions can be made. The Belgian National Parks in the Congo, however, differ a good deal from those, for instance, of the United States; for their primary and indeed sole purpose is the preservation of portions of African fauna, flora and scenery in their pristine condition. The pleasure and recreation of the multitude is not one of their objects; indeed, since this would interfere with their main purpose, it is discouraged, and no one is admitted to the National Parks save naturalists and men of science and serious travellers.

Here, it seems to me, a further advance is necessary,

and I hope that East Africa may make it. There is a real danger that the National Park movement, becoming confused between the two partially contradictory aims of preservation of nature and recreation of man, will lose much of the impetus which comes of clear objectives. For there is no reason whatever why you should not aim from the outset at a system comprising both of the two distinct kinds of National Parks. The one kind might be styled National Park Sanctuaries; here nature is to be predominant and man admitted only on sufferance, as it were, to study and observe her. The other, *pace* the Belgians, are the National Parks pure and simple, where nature is preserved for the enjoyment of man; in them, certain interferences with nature will be not only tolerable but necessary, and one major interference—the presence of large numbers of human beings—is specifically aimed at. The main thing is to have some distinction of terminology corresponding to the difference of objective, so that people know from the outset what they are working for.

In many cases, perhaps most, a National Park Area would include both a National Park and a National Park Sanctuary, though the relative size and importance of the two would vary from area to area.

Before going on to deal more concretely with East African possibilities, I must refer to some objections that are often made. What is the need of National Parks, people say, when East Africa already has such excellent Game and Forest Reserves, and when its regulations preserving rare species of animals are so good and so well enforced? One answer has already been given—because the Reserves are not reserved in perpetuity, but can be cut about or abolished at administrative pleasure. The second is this.

Forest Reserves are indeed wonderful reservoirs of wild nature; but they too fall very short of the National Sanctuary ideal. They do so for the simple reason that they are under the control of men whose job it is to build up an efficient forestry business for the country; and in doing so they not only cut and interfere with nature, but usually replant with alien trees, often merely because they happen to be quick-growing. If the present general trend continues, then in a hundred years or so the entire character of African mountain forests will be altered (and the alteration in the trees will, of course, react on their animal inhabitants).

The third point may be dealt with by reference to a particular example. The southern section of the Parc National Albert in the Congo comprises all the Belgian portions of the wonderful Virunga range of volcanoes, which constitute one main home of the Mountain Gorilla. The northern halves of the three eastermost of these mountains, however, are in British territory. And the Belgians have been attempting to persuade Uganda to declare this sector a National Park, so that the whole range shall be uniformly protected. (I was told on good authority that the Uganda Government had during the past twelve months received more despatches on gorillas than on any other subject; one can only admire the pertinacity with which the Belgian authorities are attempting to "make the world safe for gorillas," as I once heard the Belgian Ambassador in London phrase it in a witty speech.)

In answer to these requests it has been pointed out that the gorilla is entirely protected in Uganda, and that as a matter of fact fewer gorillas, even proportionately to the total ape population, appear to have been killed in Uganda than in the Congo during the last twenty years. In deference to our neighbours, however, our sector of the mountains has at length been proclaimed a Gorilla Sanctuary. And yet the Belgians continue to press for a National Park status for the area.

Why this insistence? Because a National Park status implies that there shall be no interference with nature, and it is nothing less than this for the whole range which will content them. More specifically, it is because of an actual interference now in progress—the cutting of the mountain forests for firewood by the natives living in the plains below. This was proceeding at a great rate along the slopes of the whole range. It is now nominally stopped, and actually much reduced, in all the Belgian part. And it would, they point out, be a great pity if it were allowed to continue in the British area until the forest limit was pushed right up the mountain—both for the sake of the forest, and because interference with the forest means very direct interference with the gorillas.

.   .   .   .   .

With East Africa's natural resources, it should not be hard to plan a National Park system which would bring visitors from all over the world to her shores. First and foremost, the alpine zone of the three great mountains, Kilimanjaro, Kenya, and Ruwenzori, should be made National Parks, together with a considerable section of the forest zone, leaving the rest of the forest as Forest Reserve; and Mount Meru perhaps deserves the same dignity. One or two sectors should be developed for the convenience of mountain-lovers; but in each case considerable amounts of the remoter areas should be set aside as Sanctuaries. With Ruwenzori, no effort should be spared to make the whole mountain a joint Anglo-Belgian National Park—a lasting monument of international co-operation for supernational ends.

There are other spots where international co-operation could take place, but on a smaller scale. I have spoken of one in the Virunga volcanoes; another would be in the plains south of Lake Edward, where a fine game region belonging to Uganda abuts on the northern sector of the Parc National Albert. To erect this at all events into a Game Reserve,[1] but preferably into a true National Park, with a Sanctuary occupying the frontier region, would be a graceful act.

Then there is the Victoria Nile from Murchison Falls to Lake Albert. This, with a strip of country on either side, is eminently suitable for raising (much of it is already Game Reserve) to National Park status, with its beautiful scenery, its incredible swarms of hippopotamuses, its herds of elephants which reveal themselves so obligingly to travellers on the river steamer.

In Tanganyika, the existing Selous Reserve, near the Rufiji river, should clearly be raised to the dignity of a National Park Sanctuary. It, too, possesses abundant elephants and huge numbers of hippopotamus (a creature that is becoming sadly reduced elsewhere in the Territory). And it should have loosely attached to it a region on the Kilambero River, further west, to bring in that rare and interesting buck, much in need of protection, the Puku or water-cob. Not much provision would need to be made here for the recreational side (unless the projected railroad to the south-west should pass near this region).

[1] Since these words were written, I hear that a Game Reserve has been proclaimed in this area.

The chief National Park of Tanganyika, apart from Kilimanjaro, would be concerned with game and volcanoes. It would include part of the famous Serengeti plains (where lions, as we all know from Colonel Marcuswell Maxwell's marvellous pictures in the *Times*, can be photographed, whole family parties of them, with no more *apparent* difficulty than rabbits at home). It would also include some of the volcanic area to the eastward, between Lake Eyasi and Lake Natron: without question this part of the Park should comprise the amazing and unique Ngorongoro, one of the largest craters in existence, whose floor, rich in succulent clover, is pastured by unbelievable herds of game. Unfortunately, not only did the German Government permit half of this wonder of the world to pass into private hands, but we have allowed this arrangement to continue. There can, I think, be no question that the interest of the place is so extraordinary, its potential value to the Territory so great, that the alienated area should be bought back and the whole incorporated into a National Park. The Park would then presumably consist of two regions, separated by ten or twenty miles; but this arrangement holds for the two sectors of the Parc National Albert, and there works perfectly well. Here again, part of the Serengeti, and without doubt part of Ngorongoro, should be reserved as Sanctuary.

In Kenya the Lorian Swamp should surely be made a National Park instead of merely a hunting-ground; there is a great deal to be said, too, for some of the Marsabit area, with its marvellous crater-lakes and rich forest life isolated in a desert region; and also for converting some of the Forest Reserve on the Aberdares into a National

Park for the health and pleasure of the white upland areas round about.

I have left the great southern Game Reserve of Kenya to the last, because it presents special problems. With our genius for compromise, we made this huge area a reserve not only for the game but also for the Masai tribe. This dual purpose arrangement has worked reasonably well up to the present; but it cannot continue indefinitely. Unless we take steps to plan ahead, only two solutions are possible. If the efforts of the Government are successful, the Masai will be supplied with water by borings and dams, educated to utilize their cattle by turning their milk into ghee and cheese, by selling the beasts' hides to traders and the carcases to a meat-factory, perhaps even persuaded to grow a few crops to supplement their unbalanced protein diet. If so, they will become both more prosperous and more sedentary; there will be more conflict between their cattle and the wild game; and automatically though gradually the game will go. The other alternative is that the Government will not be successful, and that the Masai, caught by the strange psychological disease, a sort of racial melancholy or tribal *spleen*, which affects so many primitive tribes who cannot adjust themselves to contact with white civilization, will dwindle and die out through gradual excess of deaths over births. And in that case the wild creatures will presumably remain sole heirs of the Reserve. But even if the Masai develop towards a settled life, there is an alternative: to set aside one part of the area as primarily Native Reserve—Masailand; and the rest as a National Park—the Masailand National Park. In the former, the Masai would be encouraged in every way to develop into dairy-farmers and eventually into settled agriculturalists; their interests would be paramount, to use a word much in fashion in East Africa at the moment, those of the game wholly secondary. But in the latter, the interests of wild life and wild nature would be paramount; the Masai might still wander through it nomadically with their herds, but would be discouraged or prevented from settling, and their interests would here have to give way to those of conservation.

It will at once be said that this is impossible, owing to the solemn treaty into which we have entered with the Masai, whereby the whole of this area is made over to them and their tribe for ever. This is true, but a way out might be found. The scheme could be put through if the Masai would consent to it; and they might well do so if the National Park were still regarded as part of their tribal area, if admission fees and camping dues were charged to visitors, and if the proceeds, after deducting some reasonable commission, were paid over into their tribal funds.

It might be difficult for them to see any point in the transaction before they had developed a little further and could think in terms of money and the advantages it brings, not merely as now of head of stock, however undersized, and area of land, however barren. Meanwhile it would, I think, be quite legitimate for the Government to plan ahead, work out what would be the best boundaries for game and native areas under a hypothetical scheme of division, and then concentrate all their work for native development—water-borings, dams, schools, demonstration farms, and the rest—in the "native" area, while deliberately keeping the other as untouched as possible. By the time these works had borne fruit, the Masai should be ready to see the advantages of intensive development in a limited area, aided by an agreeable revenue from the National Park; if they did not, and the plan for a National Park fell through, no harm would have been done, and the Government could proceed with native development in the other area.

Meanwhile, let East Africa remember what a difficult time South Africa had in establishing the Kruger National Park, but what a success it has been since its establishment. It took more than twenty years to overcome opposition and reconcile all the conflicting interests; but in its four years of existence it has exceeded almost all expectations as an attraction both to visitors and to the inhabitants of the Union. East Africa should find the preliminary task less hard, the success equally immediate.

Wherever practicable the National Parks should be surrounded by strips of Game Reserve, elastic buffers between the sanctuaries within and the claims of sportsmen or of cultivation without. And small Game Reserves to act as wild-life reservoirs should be dotted about the country. There is no reason why the course of events in East Africa should follow those in West Africa, where over huge areas all or most large animals have been exterminated. In spite of the needs of agriculture, there will be much of the country in which for one or perhaps two centuries it will be quite reasonable to keep a certain number of big animals to gladden the eyes and kindle the sporting instincts of the inhabitants.

Finally, may we hope that the policy of wholesale extermination of game, save in a few sanctuaries, in order to eradicate the tsetse, will not be pursued in East Africa as it is in certain territories further south? For one thing, we quite definitely do not know enough to say that the experiment would be successful. Certain results seem to show that even when tsetse are reduced to very small numbers, they still can spread disease in a quite disproportionate way. We might kill all the big animals, and yet find ourselves almost as badly off as ever with tsetse-borne disease. There is also the possibility, which Duke is now working on, that, as regards sleeping-sickness at least, game acts as a reservoir in which the parasites become less virulent to man, so that they may be a help instead of a hindrance to human health.

And for another thing, Swynnerton's work in Tanganyika is pointing the way to a method by which large areas, and the game in them, may be cleared and kept permanently free of tsetse. At least half of all tropical Africa is infested with tsetse of one beastly sort or another: the problem is enormous and will be solved only by patient work, by accumulating and applying knowledge, not by hasty and isolated experiments based on insufficient evidence.

But enough of detail. The salient facts are simple. In her large animals East Africa has a unique possession; if she allows them to be destroyed, they can never be replaced. That is one fact. A second is that her wild animals and her scenery constitute, from a purely commercial point of view, one of her most important assets. And a third is that if she has a purely selfish interest in developing these natural assets, she has also a duty towards the rest of the world. Humanity does not live by bread alone; in East African wilds a stream of men and women down the generations may find quickening, refreshment, inspiration.

Chapter XXIV

VOLCANOES AND FLAMINGOES

Oct. 17*th.* This last forty-eight hours has been very agreeably varied. After a hectic last morning in Nairobi and a train journey spent mostly in sleep until the spectacle of the Rift commanded my vision and my thoughts, I landed at Kenton College, three-quarters way up the escarpment, in a lovely bay of the hills. Before the war it was an hotel; now it has been turned into a private school for European boys. The headmaster took me up a hair-raising road he had made with the aid only of unskilled native labour (three miles of it at an expenditure of ten pounds!), up and up to the crest. Beyond this, a meadow fringed with woodland—fresh and northern. But the forest when the road plunges into it turns out to be all bamboos, most un-European of forests. I personally find these woods of great poles, with their thick, dank atmosphere, a most depressing environment. Those sportsmen who come here to hunt the Bongo or forest antelope (a remarkably big beast to be able to slink about through the stems that interlock at every angle) have my sympathy. De Watteville camped for weeks in these glooms before he secured his beast.

The crater of Longonot dominates the scene as you look out from this school over the Rift floor. After I had been cajoled into talking to the assembled boys, it was decided that I should go up it next day in company of one of the masters. It was only an hour and three-quarters from the railway to the rim—a most rewarding climb. The crater floor, flat, scrub-covered, quite circular and over a mile across, is nearly a thousand feet below you; the sides are so precipitous that only at one spot did there seem even a possibility of descending. At one place a jet of steam half-way down reminds you that the fires are not long extinct. We made our way round to the highest jag, another hour's going. The gullies in the tufa were like those near Camel-dole and in other craters of the Phlegraean Fields behind Naples.

The view from the top is astonishing. No peaceful land-scape of gentle foldings and slow erosion as in England. Nothing is visible that is not a reminder of enormous dis-locations in the earth's rind or violent belchings from her bowels below. Even on top of this peak you are impris-oned within the enormous Rift, unable to see over its edges; and in the Rift nothing is visible but volcanoes and their products.

We were back before two; and at three I was on my way to the Leakey's archæological camp at Elmenteita.

The camp—a couple of huts and some tents—is set over against the far scarp of the Kenya rift, in wildish country. Coming hither you must pass close to the southern end of Elmenteita Lake. As we came in view of it, I could not help exclaiming at its strange likeness to the English lakes —dark grey-blue waters hemmed in by low hills, regular north-country fells on which grew yellowish grass and patches of bushes and small dark trees among the rocky scars. (I later found this same yellowish grass, so like the moor-grass of our northern hills, combining with the hill shapes to give to the north end of the neighbouring Lake

Nakuru a delusive, derisory likeness to Capel Curig or other North Welsh scenery.)

A little bay, charming in the extreme, irregular with promontories and rock knolls crowned with scattered trees, ran in towards us. It might have been transplanted from Windermere, after having been commemorated by Wordsworth in one of his innumerable sonnets. But the final touch was most un-Wordsworthian. Not daffodils bordered it, but flamingoes. At first sight they too had a flowerlike air, as of enormous lotuses or lilies thrusting themselves out of water to burst into bloom. But then the lotuses raised sinuous necks from their subaqueous browsing; they looked at us with suspicion; they began to walk. Flamingoes, supreme combination of the grotesque and the beautiful: Windermere, with its shores bordered by great rosy birds! Then suddenly I saw that the far shore, four or five miles away, was bordered with pink. Surely this could not be birds?—it must be some geological deposit, some incrustation. But the glasses insisted on the fantastic truth—it was all birds, battalions of birds, massed in a pink continuous army.

Oct. 19th. Lake Nakuru presents the same spectacle of flamingoes as does Elmenteita; but the lake's pink border is much bigger. You can see it clearly from the top of Meningai, the mountain above Nakuru town, though the far end of the lake is ten miles off. I know something of estimating the numbers of birds or animals, and how easy it is to overestimate (the same is true for all objects—how many people realize that the total of stars one can see with the naked eye on a light night is only some two thousand?); and I have a perfectly good conscience in asserting that the flamingoes I saw on Nakuru were to be numbered by the hundred thousand: I should hazard that they were over half a million.

Ten minutes in a car gets you down on to the mud border of the lake; and then you begin to realize the numbers. You get out and walk towards the pink regiment. The whole shore smells with the smell of an enormous, not very clean, poultry-yard. A pinky-white window runs the length of the shore, a foot or so wide: it is all made of moulted flamingo feathers, washed up by the waves. Most of the birds are busy in the shallows; they walk out as you approach, and finally fly up. With wings closed they are all pure pink, but in flight the deep red of the wings is revealed, bordered heavily with black.

There are two kinds of flamingoes here; the commoner is smaller and brighter pink. The other, paler, more roseate and less salmon, is not only larger but has relatively longer legs and neck: it is adapted to feed in deeper water.

The flamingo is the only animal, so far as I can recollect, which feeds with body right way up but head upside down: in this position the lamellated beak, nuzzling through the mud or water, sifts out the material on which the birds feed; it is the same sort of action by which a duck or a whitebone whale sifts out its nutriment. One is usually told that flamingoes feed on small shellfish and crustacea; but Miss Jenkin, a zoologist recently out in these parts, found nothing in their stomachs but the tangled microscopic threads of blue-green algae, those very primitive plants.

Unfortunately, there were no quite young flamingoes here; they begin life with shorter necks and less bizarre beaks, and have to feed in the ordinary way. I should have liked to see some at the transition stage when they were just changing to upside-down meals. But these flamingoes breed elsewhere, in Lakes Baringo and Hannington to the northward, and only visit Nakuru and Elmenteita when the young are well grown.

However, I learnt something which was new to me—that flamingoes may feed while swimming. Here and there a long file of apparently headless birds drifted past out in the lake. They were paddling slowly, and their heads were busy three feet below the surface.

Towards sunset, most of the birds gather (or gathered the two days I watched them) round the north end of the lake. The air was full of flocks, a few hundred in this one, ten thousand in that. The bird-forms outlined against the sky, with their queer big heads, their enormous sinuous necks, and long legs trailed out behind, were redeemed from grotesqueness not only by their glory of colour, but by a certain arrowy quality of flight, a natural wildness. As with so many other creatures (though not all), the flamingo is only grotesque in captivity.

As I came back just at sunset, an apparent piece of drift-wood resolved itself into a family of hippos. I approached across the mud to within thirty yards; there were four—two grown-ups, one half-grown, and a little fellow, all waiting for nightfall to come out and feed. Only the tops of their backs showed besides their eyes and their nostrils; as the water was only a foot or eighteen inches deep, they must have been embedded in deep mud.

That this was quite possible was practically demonstrated to me the next moment. I tried to get still closer. The entire family of river-horses reared up, snorted, and plunged heavily away; and I went in above the knee with both legs into jet-black mud smelling strongly of the fowl-house.

One can see the pink bird-border of the lake from the town, and from the train even. Yet I was told that there are settlers at Nakuru who have never been down to the lake to get a close view of the sight. If this is true, I can only say it is as astonishing as the spectacle of the birds itself.

In the afternoon I went to see the second of Nakuru's two notable sights. Driven in the Provincial Commissioner's hospitable car, by the Provincial Commissioner's jewel of a native chauffeur, up the two thousand vertical feet of the road which the Provincial Commissioner has had constructed, I climbed to the top of Meningai.

The road ends among the long, dry grass. Turning back a moment, you see the lake and its fantastic pink bird-borderings spread out below, among the jumbled anfractuosities of the Rift landscape. Then a few yards forward, to find yourself on the rim of the crater. And what a crater! The inner wall, sharply defined, slopes down always at an uncomfortably steep angle, sometimes in rocky precipices, a thousand feet to the scrub-covered floor below. The opposite point of the wall is about eight miles away, and the rim is a perfect circle. From the centre of the floor rises a dome, at about the same gentle angle as the outer walls of the mountain; its summit is a little below you as you stand on the rim. All is concentric, regular, enormous.

These giant basins are a special form of crater; several more of them occur near the Kenya-Tanganyika borders, forming a group which has been christened the Giant Cauldron Mountains. Geology does not seem certain as to their origin. They may perhaps be volcanoes which have blown off their heads and most of their bodies in a vast explosion, and then in some cases built up a new cone within the huge cauldron. The peak of Vesuvius to-day is such a new cone standing within the rim of the old cauldron of Monte Somma, which blew its flanks out over Pompeii and Herculaneum; but the diameter of the crater here at Meningai, and in others of the Giant Cauldrons such as the famous and still larger Ngorongoro, is far greater than that of Monte Somma.

The other theory is that they owe their present form not to eruption but to collapse. After a broad low cone had first been formed, some withdrawal of pressure from below caused the whole central portion to crack away like a gigantic apple-core, and subside.

In any case, Meningai is a remarkable spectacle, and nowhere else in the world can such a crater-cauldron be seen so easily, with rail and road to bring you to its very lip. Everyone who can afford twelve hours should break his journey at Nakuru to see its birds and its volcano.

Chapter XXV

EARLY MAN IN EAST AFRICA

Africa is a continent almost without a history; but it is rapidly acquiring a surprising pre-history.

I had been invited by Mr. and Mrs. Leakey to spend the night with them and see the remarkable results of their excavations near Elmenteita. We had a long drive, during which our car too often progressed in that distressingly crab-like fashion common in cars on Kenya roads after rain. At one place the track led through a big cattle-farm; we stopped to ask the way of an attractive young woman, in broad hat, bright neckerchief and blouse, and buff trousers. It is pleasant that the wives of Kenya settlers can and do so often keep so fresh and look so well turned out. Finally we came upon a little signpost bearing the legend "Archæological Camp."

It is unfortunate that the word Archæological has such a forbidding sound. I was told that the Prince of Wales, when last in Kenya, had been asked if he would like to see the Leakeys' work in Archæology, and had replied with *God forbid*, or some other forcible negative. It was his loss—and the fault of *archæological*. In point of fact, it would be difficult not to get interested and even excited over the cave, the bones of its long-dead inhabitants, their implements, and all the ideas that flow from them.

It was pleasant, after an excellent meal in the Leakeys'

263

reed-roofed cabin, to enjoy the luxury of a good talk—discussions on the genesis of the Rift, the correlation of geological events here with the Ice Age and its subdivisions, Leakey's own discoveries of fossil man and his implements; and then switching over to the things of to-day, the Kikuyus and the Government, missions and native education, problems and personalities of all sorts. And so to a late bed in a tent, and a sound sleep in the cool night, under a coverlet of antelope skin.

The camp itself is right in the bush. A dewy walk in the cool dawn air took me through bird-haunted scrub and aromatic glades where red aloes bloomed, to the foot of the scarp. Here a gorge emerged from the hills. On the right was a rocky cliff dotted with shiny dark-leaved xerophytic shrubbery. Across its face occasional baboons of various sizes and ages strolled and climbed. Nature, African nature, baboon nature, not man, was master of this little bastion.

> But O that deep romantic chasm which slanted
> Down the green hill athwart a cedarn cover!
> A savage place!

Yes, the gorge had something about it as of Xanadu, but an African Xanadu. Steep-sided, almost a canyon, it wound away into the escarpment. Where it debouched, along a little stream, a group of noble "fever-trees"—the green-stemmed acacias that love water—rose in the valley. On the left a rocky slope broke down to the valley. But in place of cedars, it was covered with a forest of those astonishing and purely African vegetables, Candelabra trees. Even in the bright sun of early morning they were alien and fantastic. And if there be love-making there, it will not be by women, however black, not by demons, however autochthonous, but by the hordes, unhuman and unspiritual alike, of African baboons.

But we must return to our archæological muttons. The cave which has been the Leakeys' chief site is close below the rift-scarp. When found, it was almost full of débris—nearly thirty feet of it. It was not abandoned till the sheddings of its inhabitants had pushed the floor twenty feet up towards the roof. Some of the débris was wind-blown sand and droppings from the roof, during periods when it was uninhabited; but the bulk is human leavings—ashes from fires that perhaps (one would like to think it, and it may well have been so) burnt for millennia, each kindled from its predecessor; huge numbers of bones (mostly broken to get at the marrow) from a secular succession of meals; bone beads; and obsidian implements, in quantities unbelievable to any one familiar only with European sites. The Leakeys have collected over 45,000 perfect specimens, rejecting many more than this number as imperfect, in a single season's work; and the cave is perhaps half excavated. While we were there, three basketfuls of material were sifted for our benefit, and yielded over thirty implements, a couple of nice beads, and dozens of bones of antelope, fish, hyrax and what not.

As material for tools, obsidian has a striking property; it looks as fresh now as it did the day it was chipped—a beautiful, shiny, black surface. And the tools preserve their edge. Among the implements are beautifully-fashioned knives, up to five or six inches long. Lady Hall, who was also visiting the camp, was rather sceptical when Leakey told her they would cut as well as a steel knife. So a test was arranged; and after Lady Hall herself had cut real drawing-room slices off a by no means stale loaf, she admitted that the maker of these tools, though dead perhaps fifteen or twenty thousand years, knew his business.

One of the commonest implements is a little half-moon-shaped flake, sharp on the straight side. Leakey has convincingly shown that these were arrow-barbs, and that they could be fashioned in a few seconds with the aid of another common tool, which he styles a fabricator. Their astounding abundance he would explain by supposing that the cavemen poisoned their arrows, and that, when the game was brought in, the inedible area containing the arrow-head was simply cut out and thrown on the fire, it being less trouble to make new barbs than to pick out the old. Then, besides the fine knives, there are rough blades for chopping up meat, scrapers admirably adapted for shaving down and softening hides without tearing them, sinew-frayers to fray down animal sinews into thread for sewing, and spokeshaves, with the aid of which Leakey found it easy to make a good arrow-shaft.

The beads are interesting. They are of shell, bone or ivory, perforated and flat; one side is almost always rubbed smooth, the other not, so that they must have been sewn on to skin garments as decorations.

The culture is obviously of the type called Aurignacian. In Europe this is the product of the earliest known men of our own species, *Homo sapiens,* and supervenes on the Mousterian culture, which was the work of that extinct kind of creature Neanderthal Man, *Homo Neanderthalensis,* bow-legged and prognathous, lower-browed, poorer-brained and altogether more primitive than we.

In the Elmenteita cave have been found the remains of some of the people who made these Aurignacian tools.

ABOVE, THE SNOW DOME OF KILIMANJARO AT SUN-
SET, FROM OLD MOSHI, FOURTEEN THOUSAND FEET
BELOW IT.
BELOW, A PROOF OF THE SKILL OF PREHISTORIC
AFRICANS. LADY HALL CUTTING BREAD-AND-BUTTER
WITH AN OBSIDIAN KNIFE OF THE AURIGNACIAN
PERIOD, AT MR. LEAKEY'S ARCHÆOLOGICAL CAMP.

View from the Edge of the Crater of Mt. Longonot, in the Kenya Rift. A Small, Subsidiary Crater is Seen in the Foreground. The Dark Area to the Right of This is a Lava Flow Extending on to the Rift Floor. In the Background is Lake Naivasha, with the Western Scarp of the Rift Beyond. (*This beautiful photograph I can only acknowledge anonymously, having been stupid enough to mislay the name of the taker of it, who sent it to me and generously gave me permission to reproduce it.*)

But though they are, as was expected, men of our modern species, they are of a distinct type. By no means negroid, they were of great height, running to well over six feet, with huge faces, and primitive in possessing an enormously thicker brainbox than any existing man, with a relatively smaller brain inside it.

Aurignacian man seems to have entered Europe as the last of its four coverings of ice began to retreat, about 20,000 years ago. These Elmenteita people, it is probable, are not older than this, and may date from still more recent times, which would indicate that both they and their European colleagues in the new culture had spread from some other centre of human evolution, presumably in Asia.

But there are two points of special interest about these Kenya finds. It is usually laid down as a definite doctrine that no pottery existed in the Old Stone Age: man, it is asserted, did not think of making it until he began to settle down to more agricultural ways. But here, in definitely Pleistocene deposits, in an obvious Old Stone Age culture, Leakey has found pottery. That is a radical upset of our current notions. (I understand from him, however, that as a matter of fact some pottery has been found in European sites of similar age, but that to save the No-Pottery doctrine it has been called Baked Earth and not pottery. Truly the love of dogma and the hair-splitting ingenuities in defence of it are not confined to theologians!)

The other novel fact is that while in Europe the Aurignacian culture succeeded to the Mousterian, at Elmenteita the two are contemporaneous. Here the Aurignacian tools are found mostly in caves, while those of Mousterian type are scattered over the plains. We know that the African Aurignacian was a modern *sapiens* man. Though unfortunately no remains of the local Mousterians have yet turned up, there can be little doubt that they, like the Mousterians of Europe, belonged to another and more primitive species. Thus it looks as if the cleverer *sapiens* had succeeded in taking possession of all the best dwellings, leaving his inferior *neanderthalensis* relative to wander about in the open, perhaps making branch shelters for himself.

The co-existence of the two races, and the fact that Elementeita man was of very un-negroid type, raises other questions of intensest interest. Was there intermarriage between the two races, and is the true negro type—full-lipped, prognathous, and kinky-haired—a result of the cross? This, in the present state of knowledge, is a mere floating note of interrogation; but it needs to be considered.

Besides these comparatively modern implements, whose age is certainly to be reckoned only in tens of thousands of years, there are in various parts of Kenya (and in Uganda) abundance of much older man-made stone tools, of Acheulean and Chellean type, dating back hundreds of thousands of years. And later we get types apparently comparable with the familiar European cultures of Solutré and la Madeleine. So that Africa has had the same general human succession as Europe and Asia. Finally, a site near Nakuru has linked African archæology with world history, by yielding, together with stone hut-circles, beads which can only come from Egypt or the Near East, and must have been brought by traders not earlier than about 4000 years ago.

On Lion Hill, a prominent bluff that overhangs Lake

Nakuru, there is a series of deposits which to the eye of scientific imagination reveals the drama of a long-dead community. Lion Hill, during the last pluvial period, stood out of the waters of an enlarged Nakuru, as an island; and it was inhabited by early man. In the lowest and therefore earliest deposits there are a few bones of good-sized game like buck. Later, no more large creatures are represented, and the rock-rabbit or hyrax is found as the chief food of the people. Later still, even the rock-rabbits disappear, and fish and snails become the staple. And finally there is a layer without trace of human occupation.

These early hunters, thus it seems, gradually exterminated the game on their restricted home: first all the big game, then all the small game, until, after existing wretchedly on water animals for a time, they either migrated elsewhere or died out.

Besides the tools and skeletons, the geological discoveries at Elmenteita are of great interest. Wind-blown sand and water-born debris tell the story of alternating periods of dry and wet. It seems that there were in Africa two prolonged rainy pluvial periods, the earlier one probably corresponding to the first two of the four ice-advances of the European Ice Age, the later to the last two; and that they were separated by a long dry period. And even after the second main pluvial, there have been marked oscillations of climate.

In wet periods, of course, the rift trough fills up with water; in dry times, the lakes shrink, become salty and may dry up. There was an age when water probably extended from Rudolf to Manyara—one huge lake about half as long again as Lake Tanganyika to-day; there were other ages when the rift-floor boasted nothing but dried lake-beds, sheets of salt and perhaps a few small and saline waters. And early man witnessed and had to adjust himself to all this violence of change.

In passing, modern man too may have to make up his mind to such changes. Lake Nakuru, for instance, is only a few feet deep; in 1929 it had shrunk beyond the recollection of any white man, and there seems little doubt that its shrinkage has been progressive during the last half-century. It may quite well be that the rift is in for another cycle of aridity.

Early man also had to submit to changes wrought by tectonic forces. Leakey has found a deposit, one half of which is on top of the rift-scarp, the other half down in the trough, over a thousand feet below; and embedded in the portion in the rift-floor, tools of early man have been found. Along the rift-edge the earth has cracked and one side of the crack has been thrust up, the other down, a process not unaccompanied by earthquakes, subsidences and eruptions. Luckily for the prehistoric Africans, however, the displacements of faulting would rarely have been more than a few feet at a time, any more than the lakes would have dried out or flooded the rift in a generation; so that man could always have adjusted his life in gradualness. None the less, there must have been fearful times. Longonot, for instance, and several other volcanoes of the rift, are new products, erupted almost entirely since man's advent in Africa. There is every probability that we owe the tale of Sodom and Gomorrah to the violent outbreak of rifting in the Dead Sea Valley. The African Wraths of God, though unrecorded, cannot well have been less portentous.

Chapter XXVI

RIFTS AND RIFTING

We English over most of our country are used to little-disturbed strata, folded or tilted but gently, well covered with vegetable life, slowly eroded to give mild green scarps like those of the Chilterns or the Cotswolds, pleasant river valleys like Thames or Severn, undulating plains like the Midlands, baby plateaus like that of Salisbury. More northerly, we encounter the effects of the great glacial ages —deep-scooped valleys, moraine-dammed lakes, corries and coombs hanging on the mountain-sides.

Many other kinds of country have a formation or origin so different as to surprise and excite us at first sight of their unfamiliarity. There are deserts, waterless and wind-eroded; canyons; volcanoes; badlands; salt-basins; true plains in their level vastness; and there are Rift Valleys. These last are so striking in appearance and so peculiar in function that the exotic geological thrill which they produce (I am speaking for myself) is only rivalled by the effect of a large and active volcano.

Let me begin by an attempt to evoke a couple of such pictures. In Kenya the road towards the southern and western Masai country climbs slowly out of Nairobi over undulating land towards the serrated crest that is called the Ngong hills. From woodland it passes into lovely park-like country. Then with an abrupt sweep to the right it leads you to a dip in the ridge—and suddenly you are in another world. You are at the top of a steep scarp, descending in two or three abrupt steps to a plain (scrub-covered, haunt of zebra and antelope, ostrich and giraffe) some fifteen hundred feet below. The country is cut through as by a knife. These Ngong hills to the south of you are only half a range; they rise gently from the east, but have no western half, because the scarp happens to slice right through them. Forty miles across to the west, the plain is bordered by another scarp, the mirror, as it were, of that on which we stand. In front of you, in the middle of this broad ribbon of plain, is an extinct volcano. It rises above the plain half as high as does Vesuvius above the sea; its crater is far broader than Vesuvius'. But so gentle is the slope of its sides, so worn its rim, that only after a time do its volcanic nature and its great size dawn impressively on you. Far to the north is the more obvious crater peak of Longonot, with the lake of Naivasha; and other volcanoes rise from the valley floor to southward, with just a glimpse of the white dead shores of the soda lake Magadi.

Some five hundred miles to the westward, on the hills overlooking the Belgian post of Ruchuru, the view repeats itself in its essentials. You stand on a scarp: below you is a plain extending north and south; beyond the plain rises another scarp, a formidable wall of mountains. Nor are the volcanoes and lakes wanting. To the north shimmers Lake Edward; to the south rises one of the most extraordinary chains of volcanoes in the world, eight of them, ranging from ten to nearly fifteen thousand feet in height, right across the valley in a single transverse row.

Here again there are two kinds of country—the uplands extending east and west for hundreds of miles, and the trough that is cut through them from north to south. The uplands are rolling country with systems of streams gathering together to make big rivers; it is in the trough, steep-sided and flat-bottomed, that the lakes lie and the volcanoes rise.

The impression on the eye is remarkable enough; but when knowledge and imagination are called in to aid, the effect is overwhelming.

These two rifts, eastern and western, are part of a single enormous African rift system, extending nearly two thousand miles, from south of the Zambesi to the Sudan and Abyssinia. Single in the south, the rift forks north of Lake Nyasa, and its two branches enclose Lake Victoria. Save for this great sheet of water and its satellite Chioga, all the East African lakes, great and small, lie in the main rifts—Nyasa, Tanganyika, Kivu, Edward, Albert; Rudolf, Baringo, Nakuru, Naivasha, Natron—or else, like Lake Mweru, Lake George, or Lake Eyasi, in what one may call tributary rifts, small branches divaricating from the main trough. Nor does the matter end there. There is no doubt but that the Red Sea and the Gulf of Aden, enormously broader though they be, have something in common with the African rifts; and from the Red Sea there runs northwards a typical rift valley, comprising the Gulf of Akaba, the Dead Sea, the Jordan Valley, and the Gulf of Galilee.

Some notable authorities, such as J. W. Gregory, maintain that the Dead Sea and the Red Sea system of rifts is connected by a diagonal rift-trough across Abyssinia with Lake Rudolf, and so with the eastern African rifts. And if so, this strange system of cracks extends for six thousand miles, girdling a quarter of the earth's circumference.

. . . . .

But what is a Rift Valley, and how is it formed? It is, though a trough, many miles wide, with flat bottom and steep parallel sides, and it generally has little or no connection with the main river-drainage of the country.

An ordinary valley is essentially a drainage furrow. Its precise position may have been determined by some geological fact—a fault, or a contact between two different kinds of rock. But it is a valley because water runs along it now, or has run along it in the past; its shape and its history depend upon the carving, soil-removing, and soil-depositing action of running water; it is combined with other valleys into a regular system, a branchwork of conduits that drain the country.

A rift valley, however, has no primary connection with water. Once formed, it cannot help but be moulded in minor details by rain and the action of streams; but water did not carve it out. The steep sides are due to faulting. That is to say, the bottom of the trough was once on a level with the tops of its sides; the crust of the earth cracked along the edges of the future trough, and the slice of crust between the two parallel cracks sank relatively to the bits of crust on either side. (Note that word *relatively*. The same effect could be produced by the collapse of the central strip of crust, or by the forcing upwards of the two sides; and it is precisely this point that is at the present time in dispute among the geological experts.) Naturally, this faulting will not take place all at one time; even the greatest earthquakes of which we have knowledge are not accompanied by faults more than a score of feet high. The fault-cracks must rather be thought of as lines of weakness along which accumulating tensions and pressures in the earth's crust are periodically released by a few feet of faulting; and so in the course of ten- or hundred-thousand-year periods the huge scarps are gradually built out of the little recurrent faultings.

Formed thus, the rift-troughs will have no organic connection with the drainage system of the country. They may acquire one secondarily, but this will often be of a peculiar nature, as when the Nile runs into and out of Lake Albert almost at the same spot; or when Lake Tanganyika, instead of having its exit north or south along the rift, is connected westwards with the Congo by a small side river. And many parts of the rift floor are closed basins. The rain that falls over them never escapes in rivers to the sea, but accumulates in lakes without exit, gradually evaporating into saltiness. Among such are most lakes of the eastern rift, such as Rudolf, Baringo, Nakuru and Magadi.

As to the formation of rifts, there are two main theories. The one has as its protagonist Professor Gregory, who embodied the results of his journey of 1893 in that classic of combined exploration and science, *The Great Rift Valley*; and after a second visit to the country in 1919, gave us a second book on the subject, *The Rift Valleys and Geology of East Africa*. (It is narrated that in 1919, as he was descending the rift escarpment in the train, a fellow-passenger asked him when he first knew the country. "1893," answered the professor, doubtless with a recollection of his first view of the great rift, a solitary white man with his long train of porters, the country on either side full of hostile Masai or equally hostile Kikuyu. "Did you say 1903?" countered his questioner. "No, 1893," answered Gregory; upon which the other, indignant at having, as he thought, his leg pulled, retreated behind a newspaper.)

He believes that the rift is a trough that has fallen in. First, by slow compression, an arch was raised in the earth's crust (it is noticeable that the rifts almost always run along a stretch of high land, the country sloping gently from the scarps on either side). Then the arch sags, some lateral support having given way, and the keystone gradually falls in, forming the floor of the trough. There is evidence that land once stretched across the Indian Ocean from East Africa to India—or at least that there was some land connection between the two continents, and Gregory thinks that the foundering of this land, the collapse of this bit of crust to far below sea-level, weakened the eastern sides of the rift-arches and caused the collapse of their keystones.

Others connect rifting with the fascinating theory of continental drift proposed by Wegener. According to this, the continents are not necessarily fixed on the earth's surface. They are protruding bits of upper crust. Below them are deeper layers of a heavier material; this heavier material lies naked, save for water and the deep-sea oozes, at the bottom of the great ocean basins. Sometimes this deeper material is solidified, and holds the continents fast; but at other times, as the heat due to the earth's inner radio-activity accumulates, it liquefies, and then the continental crusts float in it like bits of wood in tar, or toast in treacle. When this is so, they would be free to move, albeit with extreme slowness, over the earth's surface; and one can deduce that if they could move, they would, on account of the earth's rotation, tend to drift slowly westward. Sometimes one side of the crust is tight stuck while the other is free to move; and then the free bit may crack and rip off from the other.

This in brief is Wegener's theory. By it he seeks to explain the extraordinary correspondence between the west coast of Africa and the east coast of South America— the New World has simply split off from the Old; the strange resemblances that existed in late coal-measure times between the plants and animals of South Africa, Southern India, South America, Australia—these regions, according to him, were not connected by enormous land-bridges, as others are forced to believe, but were all parts of a single land-mass, now cracked and drifted away in pieces; and so on.

And on a Wegenerian view, the rift valleys are incipient splits in the continents due to the tension and drag of a huge drifting block of crust; Africa would thus be showing the first signs of division into two sub-continents. Enlarge a rift, and you would have a split like the Red Sea. Enlarge it still further, and you would have an ocean.

Of late years, however, a precisely opposite view has been propounded. Rift valleys, say the upholders of this view, are not formed by the dropping-in of a keystone under an arch left unsupported at the side, or actually exposed to tension. There was never an arch at all, nor any sideways pull; on the contrary, it is compression which has done the trick, terrific pressure from both sides fracturing the crust and forcing up the margins of the rift-trough. If a brick or a stone be subjected to enormous compression, it will often give in this way, the three resulting bits now taking up less space from side to side than did the intact brick. Our block of crust could also yield to pressure by bending up into an arch; whether it shall do this, or shall fault and fracture, seems to be determined mainly by the kind of rock of which it is made. Ordinary stratified rocks usually bend; so you get the folds, the anticlines and synclines, so familiar in such districts as the Weald or the Isle of Wight. But certain kinds of ancient rocks, metamorphosed by long baking and the pressure of overlying strata, tend to break instead of bending; and it is of such rocks that the plateau of East Africa consists.

Support for this view has come from various sources. Deposits whose shells show them to have been laid down in a lake-bed are found cut through by the rift faulting, so that part of them are on the bottom of the trough, part on the heights beyond the top of the scarp. And these high-lying lake deposits are often now in positions where water would have run off instead of being impounded to form a lake: these deposits must have reached their present height by being pushed up, instead of the low-lying deposits having been pushed down.

There is, then, the interesting fact that in Uganda there exists a system of faults and lines of weakness of earlier age than the rift itself: and these do not run parallel with the rift, but at a slight angle with it. If the rift were due to tension and collapse, the crust would surely have split along these old lines of weakness. And there are a number of other more technical bits of evidence.

Whatever be the truth, there is no doubt that formidable displacements of the crust have taken place, altering the whole structure of the country. With the aid of a map, a few photographs, and some exercise of scientific imagination, one can reconstruct the course of events, and see the topography of Africa melt and change as the geological periods pass.

Round Kampala, and indeed in all the belt bordering Lake Victoria on the north, you see flat-topped hills with valleys between. The flat tops represent the original level of the country after the rains of ages had slowly denuded it to what geographers call a peneplain—an all-but-plain, nearly level, gently sloping seawards, low-lying, with sluggish streams and broad mature valleys.

For new valleys to be cut into this monotonous landscape, the country must have been upthrust to give a greater fall to the streams and confer new power on running water. Now comes a strange fact. If you look on the map at the region of the north-west corner of Lake Victoria, you will see a river which seems obviously to be running away from the lake, for its tributaries converge regularly towards the west. But as a matter of fact, it is flowing *into* the lake. The water in the tributaries all begins its course in the opposite direction, then turns round a sharp bend as it enters the main stream. At a point about a hundred miles from the lake, there is a swamp on the river's course; and beyond this, the flow is in the other direction, to the west. Other rivers, like the Kafu entering Lake Chioga, show the same curious characteristics. In addition, the shores of Lake Victoria and Lake Chioga are bordered by bays and deep channels which a glance at the map shows to be drowned river-valleys, linking up with the valleys of the drainage system on dry land.

What do these facts mean? They can only mean that, when the low peneplain was first pushed up, there was a bulge of high ground where Lake Victoria now lies, and that from this higher ground the streams radiated outwards to dissect the peneplain and cut the valleys that we now see. But this state of affairs could not have lasted. Later, there was a tilt of the crust, warping the original bulge downwards to make a shallow basin, and warping the country on the west upwards. In the basin, water collected to form the lake, great in extent, though nowhere deep; the head-waters of the original rivers are drowned below its surface, leaving their valleys as testimony; and other parts of the rivers have had their flow reversed.

This warping, Dr. Wayland of the Uganda Geological Survey suggests, was due to the first formation of the great rift to the westward. A large section of the earth's crust was bodily tilted, turned as on a pivot: as its western edge was forced up along the fault-crack to make the rift's eastern scarp, its eastern part, a couple of hundred miles away, was inevitably depressed, giving birth to Lake Victoria.

In deposits laid down by Lake Victoria we find the bones of the strange creature Dinotherium, related to the early elephants; and we know that he existed in early Miocene times. Thus Lake Victoria had been formed by the Miocene; while, from other evidence, the upthrusting of the peneplain must have happened in the period before, the Oligocene.

Lake and Rift had their first origin together. But the forces that lead to rifting did not cease with this: they continued to act and to accumulate until further relief was afforded by further faulting and additional deepening of the rift-trough (or heightening of the rift-scarps, whichever you prefer). From certain lines of technical evidence, this violent rifting seems to have happened three times, each time on a grander scale than before. And before the last great disturbance, man was already inhabiting the land.

The approximate dates in our history are thus as follows: Central Africa a low flat peneplain in the early Tertiary, about fifty million years ago. Twenty-five or thirty million years ago, in the Oligocene, uplifting of the plain, establishment of a new drainage system radiating from where Lake Victoria now lies. About twenty million years ago, at the turn of Oligocene and Miocene, the first rifting, the formation of the Victoria basin. Later, perhaps about ten million years ago, second rifting. And finally, in geologically very recent times, probably less than 100,000 years ago, in the Pleistocene, the last and greatest outbreak of rifting and tilting.

All this travailing and groaning of the earth could not be accomplished without cracks finding their way to molten reservoirs below, and pressure being released by the squirting of lava, the belching of ash. The Central African volcanoes are all associated with the rifts. Sometimes they are in the very rift-troughs; often they rise along nearby faults, old wounds of earth, which the new violence of rifting has reopened.

The most extraordinary manifestation of volcanic action in Africa is perhaps that of the Virunga mountains, in the Kivu district of the western rift. I say "perhaps," for Kilimanjaro and Kenya Mountains are not to be despised. Kilimanjaro is the highest volcano in the Old World. Kenya, a much older mountain, must in all probability have been higher still, for its jagged peak is the remains of the lavaplug that once filled its throat below the crater: the crater itself, floor, sides and rim, has long since disappeared, eroded by frost and wind, sun and water, and carried down to the sea and to Lake Rudolf. Both these mountains are enormous, countries in themselves. They both exceed two

hundred miles round the base, and have whole tribes inhabiting their foothills. Above the foothills is an enormous
forest-zone, and above that again wide alpine meadows,
miles of them, before the rock and ice are reached.

However, these Virunga volcanoes are more spectacular.
There is a chain of them right cross the rift-trough; and
although the base-line of the chain is no larger than the
diameter of Mount Kenya, yet in this space there rise no
less than eight peaks, four of them really magnificent
mountain-forms. In addition, the floor of the rift is studded
with tiny craters, a few hundred feet high. There are
scores and scores of them. The view down upon this crater-
studded plan from the escarpment would be like a lunar
landscape, were not everything green, plain and craters
alike covered in rich grass, and the crater slopes often cultivated in little patchwork fields. Out of this plain and its
craters, towering high above the edges of the rift-scarp,
rises the chain of major volcanoes. Most of this chain is of
very recent date. Two peaks are old enough to have lost
all traces of their craters through erosion. Three, though
extinct, have such perfect craters that they cannot be long
spent. And two are still active.

This mountain barrier, nowhere less than seven thousand
feet above sea-level, has completely blocked the rift-trough.
To the west, you can see the lava slopes of Nyamlagira,
the latest of the eight, banked against the rift-wall, so that
less than a thousand feet of steep scarp stands clear, instead of the three-thousand-feet bastion fifty miles to the
north. Originally, it seems, there was a water-shed north of
Lake Tanganyika, and all the water north of this flowed
down to Lake Edward and Lake Albert. Then the valley
was blocked. The water from the south of the barrier

could no longer escape, and accumulated to form a lake. This was the origin of Lake Kivu, last formed as well as last discovered of all the great lakes of Africa. The level of the water rose and rose against the volcanic dam; to-day, you can see the original lava-flows plunging deep below the water. It rose until its surface now stands the highest of the great lakes; and finally it rose until it overflowed to the south and discharged into Lake Tanganyika. This lake, in its deep and narrow rift, with bottom actually below the level of the sea, is even now slightly saline: evidence that it was once a closed basin. The new access of water from the north raised its level too, until finally it brimmed over to the west, and from a closed basin became tributary to the great Congo system, a change which seems to have been fully accomplished only in historic times.

The difference between the two lakes' history is seen in their animal inhabitants. Kivu is poorly populated—no crocodiles, no hippos, comparatively few fish. Tanganyika has a rich fauna, with an extraordinary number of fish and mollusc species peculiar to itself, proving long isolation from the rest of the freshwater system of Africa.

I mentioned in passing that during the last great outburst of rift-faulting (one speaks geologically of an "outburst," but it must have been spread over tens of thousands of years) man was already in existence in these regions. Until recently this conclusion was based only on indirect evidence—on the recent look of the steep scarps, and on various local legends which pointed to the memory of some great cataclysm. Now, however, we have definite proof of this. Leakey has found a layer containing implements fashioned by man, cut right through by the rift-fault, one part down near the floor of the trough, another part hundreds of feet above, on the scarp.

Various volcanoes, such as Longonot in the Kenya rift, and at least two of the active mountains of Kivu, seem undoubtedly to have been thrown up since man's arrival on the scene. Little wonder that tales and legends of the earthquakes and the lava-flows survive! Nor do they survive only here: the story of Sodom and Gomorrah is in all likelihood the memorial of the simultaneous workings of the crust and the fires below, along the Jordan Rift.

The question presents itself, at once and forcibly—is this unpleasant activity at an end, or may there at any moment be a recurrence of rift-faulting and violent volcanic outbreak? But to this, Science can as yet give no answer. Each outburst of rifting lasts over many millennia; there is no reason to suppose—geologists are agreed on this—that the last outbreak is yet at an end. Doubtless the process goes by jerks and starts, the crustal forces alternately piling up and being released in paroxysms of earth-movement; and the inhabitants of Central Africa may be living in the fools' paradise of one of these short intervals. Or they may not; the outburst may be really over, and peace due to reign over the rift for many years to come.

What we can say is that the peace, even now, is not entirely peaceful. The steam jets on the hillside south of Nakuru are one of the sights of the Kenya railway. Doenyo N'gai, on the Kenya-Tanganyika border, has a red glow over it of nights: so has Nyamlagira, by Kivu. In 1904 Nyamlagira discharged from one of its subsidiary vents a huge sheet of lava to the north; in 1912 it threw out another to the south, which entered the lake and changed its geography. Mount Meru, on whose slopes most of the white coffee-planters of Tanganyika Territory are settled, is said to be showing signs of activity after long quiescence; what if Arusha is destined to be the Pompeii of Africa, its new hotel preserved for future ages to wonder at?

Nor are earth-movements lacking. Sometimes rails have to be relaid on the railway. In 1928 there was a serious earthquake in Kenya that would have done much damage if it had struck an important town. The establishment of the seismograph at Entebbe has shown how exceedingly frequent are minor shocks.

At Nakuru I was given a remarkable photograph; it shows a chasm perhaps fifty yards long, fifteen feet wide, and twenty feet deep. The chasm lies right across a road. One day many vehicles had crossed the road. Next morning the first car was faced with this fissure, which had opened in the night.

Until our knowledge increases, we can only wait. Perhaps, as the seismograph records accumulate, we shall be able to say whether earthquakes are growing more or less frequent, and to learn how to foretell major shocks. Meanwhile East Africans can comfort themselves with the thought of Naples, of Messina, of Japan, and all the many other regions where, in spite of eruptions and earthquakes all through history, civilizations have not only existed but prospered.

There is much else of interest about rift valleys. There is the presence of huge lava-flows round the Kenya rift, their all-but-absence round the western rift. There is the fact that rifts have often been upheaved along their length, so that the originally level trough-floors are now tilted. There are the subsidiary rifts that run out from the main troughs, a whole branchwork of cracks across the half-continent—the Pangani valley, the Nandi scarp, the trough between Pemba island and the mainland, the Lake Eyasi valley. There is the occasional one-sidedness of the rifts, the trough having but a single steep scarp (always, I believe, the western), and sloping gently up on the other side; this is so, for instance, south of Arusha, where the Mbulu escarpment towers over the Mbugwe plain, but has no answering eastward scarp. There is the fact that the rift-faults are by no means always single: often the scarp breaks down to the rift-floor in a series of gigantic steps, as notably where the main Nairobi-Nakuru road passes down the scarp: or there are miniature riftlets within the main rift, little troughs perhaps a quarter of a mile across, as in the Kenya rift below the Ngong hills.

All such are details; but I must give a moment to the strange phenomenon of Ruwenzori. Ruwenzori, unlike all the other great mountains of East Africa, is not a volcano. It is a "block mountain," a block of the same material as the general country, standing isolated in the middle of the western rift, which is here deformed and bulged out to the eastward to accommodate this huge mountain structure. Ruwenzori is, it must be admitted, rather difficult to explain on the subsidence hypothesis of rifting. For one thing, what supports it, with its top far above the sides of the rift-arch, if the lateral supports have given way? For another, if it were an exceptionally high part of the original arch we should expect traces of ice-action from its glaciers to have been left on the rift-scarps to right and left; and there is no such trace. The compressionists, on the other hand, would explain Ruwenzori as an upthrust block, held in place by the great sideways pressure. It is, if you like, a rift valley upside down. The factures are reversed, and so the middle of the rifted area has been forced up, the sides let down.

But I have said enough, I hope, to show the intense interest of rifts. With the aid of telescope and spectroscope we have learnt a great deal about the constitution of stars fantastic distances away; but we know singularly little about the interior of our own planet. The study of rift valleys cannot but help to throw light upon the nature and working of the hidden forces beneath earth's thin rind.

Chapter XXVII

THE HEART OF UGANDA

Uganda. If the heart of Tanganyika be enormous plains and rolling dry bush, and that of Kenya be high cool uplands, the heart of Uganda is an intense tropical greenery, clothing an endless succession of little hills.

The hills have been carved out of an ancient peneplain. You can see the old level in the flat tops of so many of the hills; if you prolonged their planes, they would all meet, just as would the straight table-tops of the hills round Thursley and Churt on the north side of Hindhead.

After millennia of stability, the crust of Uganda was tilted—downwards in the centre of what became the Lake, upwards all round its borders; the change of levels set the forces of denudation hard at work, and the network of valleys and slopes is the result.

And everything, as I say, is green, a deep spinachy green, not a bit like the pale cool green of the Kenya heights. The ubiquitous banana-groves set the tone, and then in the valleys there are winding strips of true tropical jungle, remains of the original rain-forest, palms and big evergreen shiny-leaved trees and lianas, meandering snake-like along the stream-courses. The eternal green, the repetitive succession of similar hills, is monotonous and a trifle oppressive.

Round the lake-shores this monotony is broken. There

288

are huge papyrus swamps, in which the Situtunga, the water antelope, lives secure; there are land-locked bays, and broad expanses of blue water with islands on the horizon. All round Entebbe there are grassy swards, which have been cleared of all but a few great trees, sloping down to the water's edge.

Less than twenty-five years ago, Mr. Winston Churchill in his *African Journey* called Entebbe a death-trap. "Behind its glittering mask," he wrote, "Entebbe wears a sinister aspect." And he concludes that "there seems to be a solemn veto placed upon the white man's permanent residence in these beautiful abodes." He may have been indulging his propensities to rhetoric a little. To-day, at any rate, with a little care you may live for years in Entebbe without catching anything very serious, and the European community, women as well as men, seemed just as cheerful and as healthy as a similar body of men and women at home.

There is indeed a good deal of loose talk about tropical diseases. There are, of course, some diseases, of which sleeping-sickness is a notable example, entirely confined to the tropics. But there are others, like malaria and plague, which are really not tropical at all. A few hundred years ago they were just as prevalent in temperate as in tropical countries. Think of all the references to ague in Shakspere; and ague is malaria. Malaria was a serious cause of death as far north as the lowlands of Scotland right into the nineteenth century. It is still a grave burden over enormous stretches of the United States.

There is no reason why diseases like malaria and plague should not disappear from Africa as thoroughly as they have from northern Europe. Civilization has killed them there: it can do so here. When a disease is insect-borne like malaria, it will be a little more difficult in Africa, because insects, being "cold-blooded," multiply faster and are active all the year round in the tropics. However, modern preventive medicine has in effect given up the idea of controlling malaria by getting rid of mosquitoes. It is only in special cases, as in the Panama Canal zone, that anything of the sort can be done. As is emphasized by a recent League of Nations Report on malaria in Europe, as well as by the Report of Colonel James, the expert who was sent out to advise on anti-malarial measures in Kenya, the prime cause of malaria's diminution has always been and will continue to be the general raising of the human standard of life, which results in better houses, less contact with mosquitoes, more drainage, greater resistance, readiness to call in a doctor, and readiness to take more trouble about sanitary matters in general.

First raise the standard of African life: then use our knowledge of the rôle played by the mosquito to inculcate a hatred of the insect until a housewife (black or white) would as soon have it known there were mosquitoes in her house as she would bed-bugs, and malaria will become negligible in Africa.

Meanwhile, civilization sometimes begins by aggravating instead of ameliorating disease. There seems no doubt whatever that it was the opening up of the country which brought the sleeping-sickness parasite into Uganda, with what ghastly results we all know. There is no doubt that the introduction of the motor-buses has facilitated the spread of plague. In the crowded bus, fleas leap easily from one passenger to another, and thus plague readily gets transferred from village to village.

THE HEART OF UGANDA

In any case, although tropical diseases are bad enough, so are those of our zones. Influenza, to take but one example, is a comparatively rare and mild visitant to Africa; it does not kill its hundreds of thousands every year, as with us.

Kampala, October 22nd. My host, the Director of Education, is a great swimmer; indeed, he affirms that if he had the choice of a reincarnation he would like to inhabit the frame of a hippopotamus. Every morning before breakfast we go bathing—either in the King's Lake or the swimming-pool built by the C.M.S. The pool, though pleasant enough with its grassy borders, is the less amusing. It has, however, one feature of interest: by it stand two palm-trees, which look as if they were bearing a crop of enormous nuts, so beset are they with weaver-birds' nests. The black-and-gold birds chatter and scold, falling silent now and again all together. One flies up with a strand of fibre; another is busy weaving; and below the entrance to many nests in which the female is sitting, the cock birds hang upside down, flapping and fluttering, and chattering to their mates within.

The King's Lake is a bigger bit of water; an earlier Kabaka of Buganda made it by damming up a stream. Cormorants fish in it, and rest on the bathers' raft; and round its borders you may see the delightful Lily-trotters. They are a kind of jaçana, birds of the rail family, about as big as a coot, chocolate-brown with a white bib and waist-coat; their toes are enormously enlarged, spreading their weight (on the principle of skis) so that they can run over the surface of the lily-pads and other floating vegetation. Round tropical lakes the fringe of such floating plants is often so thick that swimming birds cannot penetrate it; and yet an ordinary land-bird above a quite small size would be in constant danger of submersion; so that the simple expedient of toe-lengthening has enabled the Lily-trotter to avail itself of a rich zone almost untapped by other birds.

Many people maintain that bathing in the tropics is unhealthy. My host, who has bathed there regularly for over ten years, is proof to the contrary.

.   .   .   .   .

Kampala, like Rome, is built on seven hills. Law and Order crowns one, in the shape of the Jail; Religion, too, with rival Cathedrals; Medicine, a fourth, with the Hospital; two I fear I have forgotten; and Education with Makerere College claims the seventh.

Makerere was started in 1923, as a technical school. Since then a proper technical school with five workshops has been founded. All the apprentices go there, and Makerere has become a College. Its chief work for the present is vocational; it trains boys for the various posts open under Government or in private employ. Last year it had 127 pupils; 33 were in training to be clerks, 30 to be schoolmasters. Of those going in for more specialized studies, 31 were still in their first year, 14 were definitely specializing for engineering or survey work, 13 as agricultural or veterinary assistants, and 8 as medical assistants.

The course at the College for clerks is two years, for all other lines of work three years. After this the more specialized vocations demand a further year's training in their respective Departments; and for medical work, two years more in the Hospital.

The medical programme is the most ambitious. Some of the lads are being trained for senior medical assistants, who will have a status almost similar to sub-assistant surgeon—a grade now filled exclusively by Indians. If this works satisfactorily, the College will aim higher, at the production of fully-qualified medical men; but that will be a matter of decades yet. However, a remarkable beginning has already been made.

It was very striking to see boys whose parents had lived the immemorial tribal life dissecting a cadaver, and to hear them give quite intelligent answers, in good English, to my questions about the functions of the liver or the meaning of reflex action.

The buildings, of stone, long, low and cool, are well planned, comfortable without sacrificing simplicity; and the young men look pleasant and upstanding, and seem to work keenly.

Makerere, like all institutions aiming at any but technical education for the East African, has come in for a great deal of criticism. It is perhaps worth recalling that it is still so young that it will be another year before any product of its new, revised curriculum will have graduated, so that criticism is a little premature.

And its doors are not open to Uganda boys only; any young East African, if he reach the proper standard, can enter, and there is already one boy from Kenya in the College. As the educational systems of Kenya and Tanganyika catch up with that of Uganda—which has had a quarter of a century's start—the number from other territories will increase; and in due time, I think there can be no shadow of doubt, Makerere will become a true university, the University of East Africa. It is difficult to prophesy; but I would put this time about forty or fifty years hence, after two more generations of education.

Oct. 23*rd,* A.M. To see the White Fathers' higher (intermediate) school at Kisube. Here are two big dormitories for forty boys each; specially-trained Teaching Brothers give the instruction; all is orderly and efficient. None of the Teaching Brothers are English; and it is a little curious to find a French Canadian or a Dutchman giving an English reading lesson to Baganda lads. As a result, the boys' English accent is not very good; on the other hand, they write the language excellently. I was intrigued, looking at some of their essays, to see the systematic treatment. First comes *"Subject"*; then *"Skeleton of treatment,"* with heads one, two, three; then *"Development,"* where the essay really begins.

Indeed, the whole establishment breathes this scholastic systematization. You feel in the presence of a machine which has been in successful operation for centuries. It is now applying its formulae to black material as it has elsewhere and in other times applied them to white; and judged by examination results it is eminently successful.

. . . . .

After visiting the school we called on the Father Superior of the Mission, Father Walters, a distinguished-looking and learned Dutchman, with a beard of Smutsian cut. He is one of the greatest authorities on the Luganda language, and my host had come to consult him about its orthography. At the moment there are two orthographies: one Protestant, worked out by the Church Missionary Society; the other Roman Catholic, due to Father Walters. The Government, notably its Department of Education, is concerned to establish a single standard orthography; but the question is in danger of being complicated by religious feeling: round the practical and linguistic issues hangs a faint odour of Scarlet Woman. However, a compromise is at last in sight.

The debate on this curious subject was attended by curious incidents. The good Father hospitably proposed a glass of white wine; which was duly poured out, and with fitting politeness swigged off—to be discovered, at the expense of much choking and subsequent politenesses, as neat cooking brandy. After this (but quite definitely *post hoc*, not *propter hoc*), other odd things began to happen. Both doors of the little white room were open to the midday light. Through one of them the roof of an outbuilding was visible. On it was an object which I had casually noticed and put down as a weathercock of rather striking design. Suddenly, however, the weathercock began walking down the tiles, and revealed itself as a heron.

A few moments after, the debate was proceeding, far above my head, as to whether certain Luganda sounds should be represented by the Catholic method of double letters, or the Protestant one of prefixing the letter with a dot above the line. I happened to turn my head towards the door behind me, and there on the threshold, still and alert, looking as if it were giving the subject its full but ironic attention, was a large lizard, at least two feet long, grey-brown with green-blue thighs and a shiny azure head. I rubbed my eyes, but it was quite real. The discussion grew heated, and it made off.

The same afternoon, the better to make comparisons, I went to the King's School at Budo, a Church Missionary Society School corresponding to Kisube, but comprising younger boys as well. This school interested me for three main reasons. First and foremost, I thought it the best school I saw in Africa; second, it was such an interesting contrast in atmosphere and methods to the admirable Catholic school I had seen that morning; thirdly, it was a testimony to the power of a headmaster to make or mar a school. When Mr. Ormsby-Gore's Commission visited East Africa in 1924, they thought the school far from satisfactory. Since then, Mr. Grace has been appointed headmaster, and by his broadmindedness, energy, and uncanny power of persuading the best type of young masters to come and work under him, has put a new spirit into the place.

We all know that the English Public School system is not ideal; but there are many things in its atmosphere which are pleasant and good—the independence of the boys, their feeling that in some intimate and enjoyable way they belong to the place and the place to them, the delegation of discipline to the senior boys, the companionship and co-operation. At Budo I had the impression of such an atmosphere. This fellow, one of the prefects, for all his black skin and bare legs, had the air of a prefect at home as he strolled in his blazer and shorts across the playing-fields, unconsciously and amiably lordly in his little domain before going out into the world. That little lad of the Watusi tribe, with his thin aristocratic features (the nose almost semitic, not in the least negroid) looked like any clever but shy boy just finding his feet in an English public school. The boy-scouts, doing various feats of scoutcraft with ropes and ladders under the supervision of one of the European masters, were enjoying it all as thoroughly and behaving in as friendly and cheerful but respectful a way as a party of boy-scouts at home. (In passing, one might have thought that the African boy, brought up in what to us would seem a perpetual round of "camping" discomfort, would not appreciate the joys of boy-scouting, a movement designed primarily for the town-bred or the over-civilized; yet he seems to take to it very kindly indeed.) Later on I witnessed the end-of-term performance given by the boys—songs, plays, recitations and the rest; the whole atmosphere of an English school entertainment was there.

Yet of course the differences are immense. The primitiveness of the kitchens and plainness of the food was one difference; great cauldrons full of cooking bananas were simmering as sole preparations for the evening meal. The dormitories were equally simple; but of course they must have been equalled in this respect by the dormitories of English schools in earlier centuries, such as Long Chamber at Eton; and naturally there were dozens of subtler and more important differences. None the less, imposed on all the differences was the resemblance in vital atmosphere; and this seems to me a remarkable achievement.

The contrast with the White Fathers' School was interesting. The Catholic institution probably stood higher in pure academic achievement; but here you felt a much greater freedom, more give-and-take, a system that perhaps thought less of souls and brains but more of human beings.

One excellent institution at Budo is that of hobbies. Each boy is free to choose one of a number of hobbies to which, under supervision, he devotes so much time every day. Most of these hobbies are utilitarian, like tailoring or shoemaking, carpentry or knitting or metal-working. There is also "general utility," which consists in keeping the school tidy, adding coats of paint where needed, and undertaking special jobs of improvement from time to time.

Printing is an interesting hobby; the boys can learn to be quite good compositors, and set up all sorts of programmes and what not. The only non-utilitarian hobbies are the collecting of wild plants and insects. I was much interested to see the extent of the collections that had already been made, and the way in which almost all the specimens had been named. For the scientific names the help of authorities in the laboratories at Kampala had often to be sought; but it was remarkable to see that almost all of them had a native Luganda name affixed. It is often asserted that the African does not concern himself with what is not of direct use or harm to him, and is not easily interested in natural history for its own sake. I made a point of asking about this at every opportunity: and there was general agreement among those who knew the natives really well that this was not true. They have an enormous vocabulary for plants and animals of the most varied kinds, useless as well as useful, and for their parts and organs. While it is true that their scientific understanding of natural phenomena is not at a high level, they most of them seem to have a real and spontaneous interest in such things. Certain it is from the results obtained at Budo that interest both keen and scientific can be aroused in natural history; though here as elsewhere such an experiment can only be a thorough success if it is organized by someone who is himself keen. At Budo they have not only an excellent European science master, but a native teacher who has a real and unusual devotion to natural history, and has learnt to find his way about stiff textbooks of botany and entomology. In the course of time their collections should be of as considerable scientific interest as the making of them is of educational value.

Each boy chooses his hobby for a year, and must stick to it for that space of time: at the end of the year he can go on with his original choice, or change to another. The system seems to work very well, and, with the introduction of one or two other hobbies, both utilitarian and non-utilitarian (one thinks of bee-keeping, chickens and rabbits, flower-gardening, painting and modelling), should cater for all tastes and aptitudes.

At nearly all African schools fees are almost nominal; but here in Uganda a good many natives are quite prosperous through cotton and other crops, and the Budo authorities felt it was time to make the parents pay something more substantial for what the boys were getting. A few years ago, in the face of a good deal of opposition, and gloomy prophecies that attendance would fall off, they raised fees to the sum, very considerable for Africa, of £25 a year; and the applications for entrance are more numerous than ever. It seems to be as true in Africa as at home that people value more highly what they have to pay for.

I went home inspirited by the high standards of which I had been witness; and also reflecting that it was lucky my itinerary took me to Tanganyika first, and last to Uganda. The Uganda schools are the fruit of thirty years' missionary work, the most intensive educational effort in East Africa. Had I seen Uganda first, I should have been disappointed in the Tanganyika schools. As it was, I was able to see them in their true light, as parts of a very youthful but very vital system, to be judged not by their present standards but by the future towards which they are rapidly moving. Education in Tanganyika is merely in the bud stage: in Uganda, the blossom has opened.

Kampala, Oct. 27th. So far I have said little about this

place and its people. But this has only been because I have
been so concerned with what I have been seeing from day
to day; for if one had to name the three most interesting
towns in East Africa, Kampala would undoubtedly be one.
Zanzibar would rank among them as centre of the old
Arab civilization, as a place full of historical associations
and remarkable Oriental buildings; Nairobi as representative of the new civilization brought by European settlement; and Kampala as centre of the most civilized native
people of East Africa.

Walking down the main street, you receive a wholly
different impression of the native Africans from what you
get in Nairobi or any Kenya town. Here are no glorious
savages like the Masai or Nandi, half-naked, smeared with
ochre, and carrying spears; here is no one still wearing a
primeval dress of skins and bangles, like the Kikuyu
women in Nairobi streets.

It is the native women of Kampala who attract most
attention. They walk abroad leisurely and dignified, their
glistening and beautifully-shaped shoulders rising bare
above a long robe, gathered at one side, that falls from
breast to feet. In old days the robes were as modest as now,
and of the same general pattern, but made of dark cloth;
to-day, however, the women wear cotton prints, or, if they
can afford them, the most radiant silks or even velvets. It
is an unforgettable sight to see a Baganda woman, with
her soft rounded features and close-cropped head, advancing towards you, her chocolate skin in perfect contrast with
a blue velvet or daffodil silk.

On their heads the women carry what they have to carry,
from really heavy burdens down to trifles like match-boxes
or medicine-bottles. This undoubtedly gives them poise of

body and grace of gait; but Dr. Cook of Namirembe Hospital told me that it was not without serious consequences. It bends the end of the spinal column in a little, in such a way that it may interfere with child-birth; and quite a number of abnormal and difficult deliveries are due to this cause. The Kikuyu woman, with her perennially bent back and enormous burdens on it secured by a strap passing over the head, has not the same grace; but she only deforms her cranium a little, and this seems not to interfere with her health.

Many of the Baganda men wear European clothes, often a little ragged; but a considerable proportion, one is glad to find, go about in the white khansi, the long robe whose introduction into Africa is due to the Arabs; and this, if it is modelled on the pattern of a nightdress, does in fact have much of the dignity of a toga.

The general impression given by the Baganda is of a pleasant, kindly and rather sensitive people. This last quality I found exemplified in the school-children too. Most African boys, if asked to read aloud or drill or in other ways to show their attainments in class before a visitor, rise to the occasion with the gusto of little monkeys. It was only in Baganda that I came across boys who manifested the shyness and diffidence one so often meets with at home on such occasions.

The common people are of a rather different type from that of the aristocracy: these retain more or less pure the Hamitic strain of the invaders who not many centuries ago came in from the north-east and imposed themselves on the country as a ruling caste. For the kingdoms of Uganda are amongst the most elaborately organized in tropical Africa. A full account of them is to be found in Sir Harry

Johnston's big book on the Uganda Protectorate. For our present purpose, the most important fact to remember is that, under the agreement by which we assumed our protectorate, we preserved most features of their organization and delegated to the King and the officials of his kingdom a great part of the duties of administration: an early example of indirect rule.

There is a hierarchy of Chiefs and Headmen, with several grades, looking after districts of various sizes; there is a native Parliament which meets at Kampala, to discuss the affairs of the kingdom; a native Court of Appeal, presided over by the King, also at Kampala; and a small Council of Ministers who advise the King.

I was present at a tea-party given by the District Commissioner to the King and various chiefs assembled for the Parliament; a number spoke English, and their courtesy and intelligence made a very favourable impression. My favourite was old Ham Mukasa, the Sekibobo of Buganda; in features, bearing and expression he might have been a good-looking heavily built Englishman—save for the one fact of his black skin. He told me that he had been to England (what struck him most there, he said, was the Forth Bridge), and had written a book on his impressions; I replied that I knew he had, and that I had just got a copy and was going to read it. "You will be much interested," he said. "I am sure I shall," I answered. And I was.

Certain difficulties have arisen in Uganda. When establishing the Protectorate, we "confirmed" many of the chiefs in a right which they never possessed—freehold possession of land: as result, there has grown up a not wholly desirable landlordism. And the local functionaries of the native kingdom have occasionally abused their trust, and become

A Lake View in Uganda. Among the Sese Islands, on the Victoria Nyanza.

Another Uganda Lake. Our Baggage Being Ferried Across Lake Bunyoni in Dug-out Canoes.

extortionate or tyrannical after the fashion of those entrusted with power, whether white, black, brown, or yellow,
when the checks of inspection or control, or their own
characters, are not strong enough.

None the less, the country has made a great deal of
progress. Many Baganda are no longer willing to live in
huts, but build nice little thatched houses, with sparse but
decent furniture. You may catch a glimpse through a door
of a family at table, with a bicycle leaning against the wall.
Bicycles, indeed, are very widespread; the possession of a
bicycle in Baganda is like the possession of a small car
in England. What is more, they are one of the not too
common importations into Africa where British manufac-
turers have not only a pre-eminence but virtually a monopoly. Some years ago a German firm tried to undercut the
British, but its goods were not up to the natives' standard,
and they soon came back to their old love. The Raleigh
Company have the bulk of the market; their two famous
advertisements of the lion pursuing a black man on a
bicycle, and then giving up the chase, have sold thousands
of machines for them in Africa.

Cotton has been the great export crop grown by natives
in Uganda; but since the disastrous slump of a few years
back, caused by over-production, strenuous attempts are
being made to introduce other export crops as well.

Whatever the future has in stock, life seems pleasant
enough in Uganda now. The native cultivator will never
starve while he sticks to bananas as his staple diet; and
he can generally be sure of making some money as well.
The land itself might undoubtedly be made to increase its
produce by more efficient methods of cultivation; but it is
doubtful if the net profit would be greater if white capital

and white plantations, with their high overhead costs, could be substituted for the native cultivator.

The native is beginning to have his little luxuries—bicycles, clocks, furniture, cutlery and china, pretty stuff for dresses, books and even gramophones; he can speed about over the excellent roads of his country in motor-buses; go to market and enjoy himself in the capital. Plague is the chief horror in his life; though the possibility of a recrudescence of sleeping-sickness hangs like a spectre in the background for those few who are aware of it.

Some observers wonder whether the Baganda will maintain their progress, or whether they may not be content with the level to which they have already attained. Their pre-eminence at the moment is doubtless due largely to the historical accident that intensive missionary effort has been longer exerted round Kampala than anywhere else in East Africa. Other tribes, like Wanyamwezi and Kavirondo, are now catching up, and may eventually overhaul and surpass them.

It is obviously important for the Baganda that progress should not cease at its present moderate level. Nothing succeeds like success; and nothing is more damping to enthusiasm than stagnation after preliminary advance. It is to education more than to any other single factor that we must look for the continued advance of the Baganda. Fortunately, the Uganda Departments of Education and of Agriculture are both of them far-sighted and energetic; and the experiments they have recently started ought to ensure that what improvability the Baganda people possess should be taken advantage of in the fullest way.

Oct. 29*th.* Last night I again showed my three E.M.B. educational films to a native audience. But this time the

show was in a large, well-built cinema instead of a tin
shed, and invitations had been sent out to all kinds of educational institutions. Contingents arrived from the C.M.S.
schools, the boys' school at Budo and the girls' school at
Gayaza; from the Roman Catholic schools, both White
Fathers' and Mill Hill Mission; from the Government
workshops and the teachers' training school; a fine looking
body of girls from Mrs. Cook's training centre for maternity workers; young men from Makerere College, and
mere children from various elementary schools. The floor
of the hall grew packed; space had to be found in the
gallery, which was to have been reserved for Europeans;
and even so a number had to be turned away. Of these
several hundred boys and girls, certainly three-quarters and
probably more had never seen a film before.

Two young men, in very smart European clothes, who
had just graduated from Budo School, were allotted to
translate into Luganda the captions and any remarks I
chose to make; and the show began.

I started with the simplest film, of the Nigerian cotton
industry. At first the audience was obviously puzzled.
After a minute or so, however, they adapted themselves
to the new medium, and then the fun began. Each new
incident—the entry of a group of natives, the passing of
a string of pack-camels, the process of weaving or dyeing—
was greeted with applause. And when the film showed
anybody doing a good job of work, the applause rose to
fever pitch, stamping of feet, roars of laughter and shouted
comments being added to mere hand-clapping. As for the
furore which greeted a sort of mannequin parade of Nigerian girls in really lovely cotton dresses, it was fanatical.
The mixture of interest, excitement, and naïve, high-spir-

ited enjoyment was irresistible. I lay back in my chair and laughed to exhaustion.

Here, too, I asked for essays from my auditors, and comments from their teachers. Without exception, the latter said that the films had made a very great impression and aroused much new interest in geography and natural history. And many of the essays showed a very thorough comprehension as well as a remarkable command of the English language. Again I append one or two of the most interesting. My reader should refer back to those by the Tanganyika schoolboys, remembering that those were younger and had begun school later, and that the general standard of native education in Central Uganda is, for historical reasons, far higher than anywhere else in East Africa.

Here is the essay of A. B. K. Muchira, from Makerere College:—

"By 7.0 P.M. of the 25th.10.29, the theatre hall was compact mass with the school boys and school girls of the various schools in the country. Electric lamps were flashed and the bell was rung to warn the chatting people that the speech was at hand. At that very moment Mr. Huxley the Professor of biology appeared at the platform and started to give a short speech about what he was going to do and it was translated into Luganda by Mr. Kironde owing to the fact that quite numbers of girls and boys who were unable to hear [understand—J. S. H.] what he talked. When this had just been finished an electric beam threw a picture on the south west wall of the hall which was of the busy Nigerians picking up cotton.

"The proceeding film showed us the zeal of the Nigerians at picking up cotton and at a short interval we saw groups of Donkeys, Mules and Camels taking the cotton barrels to the cotton markets where weighing and buying take place. The remarkable thing I noticed to the Nigerians is strength because I saw how quickly and strongly they load and off loading the weighing balance.

"From the cotton buying centers cotton is taken to the ginneries where seeds are separated from lint and soft cotton is packed into big barrels weighing 400 lbs.

"After this has been done soft cotton is taken to the railway stations by means of lorries or carriages which take it to the harbour and then another arrangement of transporting is arranged by means of ships to Europe.

"Besides this cotton which is taken to the cotton markets, Natives reserve for themselves a certain amount of cotton which they gin by means of their native custom of ginning and women spin from it hundreds and hundreds of yards of threads from which beautiful chintzes are made. The last film showed us how the native women dress in these stripped [sic] clothes. The Nigerian women are more like the Nubian women in dressing and they differ from the Baganda women in Dressing.

"The second subject was more complicated than the former to those who never learn at all Botany of the Plant physiology. The first film showed us how a seed germinates and how the top part afterwards becomes a stem goes out pointing upwards and how the radicle goes into the ground when the ground is soft and how it dies when it meets the rock or stone. When the radicle gets big it separates itself into many other branches. From these branches grow very fine hair roots which absorb water and fertile the plant. The top part also separates itself in many branches and on these branches grow leaves which take in the plant oxygen and take out from the plant carbon dioxide.

"The last subject was the most complicated subject of the lot. This subject showed us the objects which live under water. I did not know before that moment that there are many objects under water until it came to my notice that under the Deepless oceans, many living things are seen.

"With my surprise I began to question myself how they take pictures of the under water objects. Turning from my surprise from the living objects which jumped like monkeys in the branches I saw how under water plants grow and how they eat the very minute substances. I offered my thanks to the photographers who took great trouble to take these pictures.

"I humbly offer my best thanks to our kindly visitor who gave us his expensive time and let us see these wonderful things. My best thanks do not miss the Honourable the Director of Education in Uganda and Staff who permitted us to be present at the speech and who hired the Theatre hall for us. This day will take a long time in the hearts of the Uganda children."

Then an extract from S. N. Lameka, age twenty, training for a medical assistant at Mengo Central School:—

". . . The method of growth of cotton in Nigeria in the first stage is almost alike of ours in this country, but from harvest to made-up lint or even to a garment in the hands of the natives themselves became gradually differently when compared with of ours. . . . They themselves dress in their own European-made looking clothes, manufactured every inch in their own land, with their own hands and brain. While the Cotton Industry in Uganda is grown by Natives themselves and shipped for foreigners, *and that is all.*

"The second section on the screen—The *Protista* and its being was in two parts. The first was about the Life in far deep water: The lens illuminated the very first scene in my life to the dwellers in the beds of the Sea. Some protophyta, which I knew very little from study in books and moveless pictures, for more or less than a year, were all; as now I can say; in my sight and at that time I was almost on the bottom of the great ocean, as well as on a well sunlighted shore.

"I was very delightful [*sic*] when I first saw the rolling waves and then down the bottom of the sea. I was very surprised with the breathing of the human-looking Cephalopoda—the octopus. The invisible Protozoa were almost visible. . . ."

Here is a short essay by A. K. S. Mukasa, Standard VI.:—

"I think everybody who attended the cinema on Friday was surprised to see that there is an African nation which has such knowledge of using cotton for itself.

"The people of Nigeria are very clever in growing cotton. There are so clever that they can reap it very quickly and clear off the seeds in it by quite a good means.

"They have a great number of cameras [camels—J. S. H.] on which they load cotton bags after collecting it in the fields. These cameras take it to their own cotton markets, where tremendous cotton is gathered, and perhaps if you were there for a day you might note that one hundred thousand pounds of cotton can be brought to one market. These people have good machines for ginning cotton and from it they can make clothes by themselves."

And finally the sprightly conclusion from a Budo boy's

composition:—". . . Before leaving the Hall Mr. Morris
the Director of Education said 'It is the time now for the
Educational Department in Uganda to have a cinemato-
graph for the schools of Uganda, as it is one of the most
leading feats before the civilized countries, but not the
sticky [stick-up—J. S. H.] collars us most young men use
in Kampala.'" I don't think Mr. Morris used quite these
words; but you can deduce what he did say, and it was
quite opposite.

Government House, Entebbe, Oct. 30th. Uganda Government House itself is too fantastically incongruous. It might
be a mansion built about 1895 near Woking by a rich
stockbroker, and transplanted by some misguided magician
to the Equator. But you pardon all this, or rather you just
forget it, in delight at the surroundings and the view. In
the distance, the horizon of the great lake, with the Sese
islands disappearing over it. Nearer, the green and lovely
coast-line, the rising lawns, and then a garden which trees,
flowers, birds and view combine to make a jewel of beauty.
It is never too hot here, and never in the least cold; the
sunshine and the flowers bloom all the year round. And the
birds! Glossy starlings with long fanlike tails hop down to
dispute the tea-table crumbs with the bulbuls, trim little
creatures, dark above and white with a touch of sulphur
below. The cossypha, handsome relative of our robin and
nightingale, sings in the bushes—the only really beautiful
bird-song I heard in Africa; high in the palm-tree rattles
a bush kingfisher, lovely pale azure on his wings, as big as
a missel thrush, ready to swoop like our kingfisher at home,
but into the grass for insects, not into the water for fish.
There are golden and black weaver-birds, a modest thrush
or so (unspotted), orioles, barbets, crimson-breasted and

with big white beaks halfway to woodpeckers'. There is an amazing shrike, deep but lustrous indigo above, vermilion all below—such good taste, and so well tailored! He and his mate give a duet—two notes only, the cock bird first, the hen on a different note directly afterwards; it needs ocular proof to believe that the two notes are not produced by a single bird. And you may see a crested crane fly over, or a troop of little egrets, or even a pair of grotesque horn-bills. Strangest of all, I heard a willow-wren, all the way from Europe, singing his delicate, pensive cadence in a palm-tree.

Finally, there is a little swimming-pool, in which you can make up for all the bathes in the lake of which the crocodiles have deprived you. Entebbe is without question the most beautiful capital in East Africa, and Government House the most beautiful spot in Entebbe; and if you pine never for a change of seasons, life there should be very agreeable.

Chapter XXVIII

THE EDUCATION OF THE AFRICAN

Education is usually regarded as a dull subject. This is not without some reason; the ponderous technicalities of pedagogics are copious and not inspiring. But in Africa it ought to be more difficult to be dull about education; for education in Africa is 'so vital, so controversial, so charged with fate. To the primitive tribal native, Western education is a sort of magic; we can hardly hope to grasp his state of mind about it. We are so cluttered up with books and machines that we can hardly imagine the thrill with which the mere learning to read and write, or the comprehension of a motor-car engine, must be experienced by an imaginative African.

Then there are religious and political controversies which rage round education in East Africa with a violence, or at any rate an extreme divergence of view, unknown at home. And finally there is the simple fact, which may not even have occurred to most people, but has been stressed by all who have brought their imagination to bear on Africa, that education could be the most important factor in the future destiny of the continent.

With education, as with all else in a new continent like Africa, the first essential is to make up your mind about principles and general ideas; otherwise you will have scrappy, self-contradictory systems.

THE EDUCATION OF THE AFRICAN

The first principle is no longer in dispute—it is that Africans should receive some education. When I say that it is not in dispute, I mean that it is not in dispute in responsible quarters. There are, however, a great many people who still believe that it would be better to leave the African as uneducated as possible. These disbelievers in native education belong to two types. One is the type which thinks of black men solely as labour-fodder, and believes that education interferes with their inclination and capacity to work. It should not surprise us that this attitude is often met with among employers of labour in East Africa, since it is by no means uncommon at home in Britain. It is, however, more than usually rampant in Africa. At my single visit to the Kenya Legislative Council I gleaned the dictum (from one of the settler members) that all native education which was not strictly technical and practical was "always useless and usually harmful"; and this was no isolated viewpoint. The other anti-educational type is the sentimental pro-native, the believer in the noble savage, who sincerely thinks that African natives should be allowed or even compelled to continue as far as possible in their original way of life. There might be something to be said for this point of view—if it were but practicable! Here and there it may work reasonably well for a moderate time, as with the Tanganyika Government's handling of the Masai, or the treatment of some of the more primitive Uganda tribes. But it cannot last. The mere presence of the white man in Africa makes it impossible for the primitive condition of things to continue. He has altered the way of life of every tribe in three fundamental ways—by preventing inter-clan and inter-tribal war, by imposing taxes, and by providing, through his mere presence, a new realm of ideas for them to think about. Every motor-car, every mission, every packet of cigarettes or yard of cotton print, every book to be read, every black man who can write—these and a thousand other things are altering the conditions in which and the ideas by which African natives live.

Before the white man came they had educational systems of their own, usually connected with the rites of initiation into adult life. These were doubtless crude, full of gaps, based on tradition and magic rather than on science and independence of thought; but in their way they were definitely adapted to the people's existing mode of life, and were inculcators of important virtues like bravery, tribal solidarity and respect for social authority.

We should not neglect these educational systems, which in large measure still survive. But in so far as they were closely adapted to the old African way of life, they will not be closely adapted to the new; and we must accordingly supplement them by other systems which fit the changing conditions.

I agree entirely with Mr. J. H. Oldham when he says that "the fundamental business of government in Africa is education." However, granted some educational system, what should it be, what goals should it have? It is astounding what different views are held by educated people as to the function of education in general, whether in England or in central Africa. Some see in it a means of training the leaders of the country; if education is to be given to the masses too, its aim should be to teach them to know their place, or, as it is often more unctuously put, to be content with the station in life to which it has pleased God to call them. This point of view, it will be seen, envisages two quite distinct kinds of education—one for the classes, the leaders, the other for the masses, the workers, the contented-with-their-appointed-lot. You may wish to provide both kinds of education for natives (as in Tanganyika, where Tabora caters specifically for the sons of chiefs); or you may wish to restrict native education to the second type.

Closely allied with the station-in-life school of thought is that which would teach the natives (or the working classes when there are no natives about) nothing but trades and useful arts. The one view, in fact, is the obverse of the other. The one maintains that the station in life to which the lower classes or races have been called is cheap production for the benefit of the rest of the world; the other is more concerned with the inner life which, while cheaply producing, they should cultivate.

Linked on to the leadership view, on the other hand, is the idea that an education—a real education—is something which stamps one as a member of the upper classes, a superior person. There is, of course, genuine truth in this; the man who is lucky enough to be endowed with a mind that can profit fully by education, and to have enjoyed an education by which his mind has been truly profited, he *is* a superior person, though by no means in the sense in which that phrase is ordinarily employed. But the idea is usually falsified by being applied in an esoteric way, as if education were an initiation rite, and the facts imbibed in the class-rooms of superior schools constituted an arcanum of knowledge denied to the vulgar. It would not be hard to argue that this intellectual snobbery, this attitude as of initiates in a secret society, has contributed materially to the prestige of classical learning in our modern unclassical world, and has accentuated the warmth with which pure scientists and philosophers defend studies without utilitarian aims, knowledge for knowledge's sake. And of course there are plenty of cheerfully-ignorant men and women who rather like to think of others vicariously bearing the world's burden of mysterious but heavy knowledge. If, for instance, the sonorous technical terms of medical phraseology, the pseudo-Latinity and illegibility of prescriptions, are, like their counterparts the stuffed crocodiles and semi-magic recipes of mediæval medicine, the buttresses of an esoteric knowledge which is power, it must be confessed that the mass of the lay public like it so.

It may be expedient that a few men should know for the people; the danger comes when a considerable number of men think that they can provide their sons with the prestige arising from knowledge by giving them the opportunity—denied to the children of poorer parents—of spending several years imbibing a special brand of rather useless information.

Then there is the religious theory of education, which holds that the primary duty of an educational system is to bring up children in a particular faith, and that, this being so, secular subjects should be taught in conjunction with and subordination to religion, as a safeguard against their being taught by others in a secular or irreligious atmosphere; or as a bait to attract souls to be saved into the religious schools. This idea dominated European education for centuries; it is now gradually being replaced by the idea of education for education's sake, with religious instruction on an equality with instruction in any other subject. But in many African territories where Government Departments of Education are still feeble, it still plays an important and sometimes a dominant rôle, since it is the idea accepted by many missions.

There are the theories that education is to develop the intellect; that it is to provide a store of knowledge or to form character. In regard specifically to native education there is the theory that it should Westernize, civilizing by making a break with the past; and the opposed theory that it should eschew too many new ideas, and civilize by slow development out of the past. Indeed, in some brands of native education these two apparently incompatible ideas have been combined. Many missions are Westernizers as regards religion and ethics, and attempt to break with all pagan customs and ideas bearing either on theology or on morals; but discourage Western science or literature or liberal thought, and favour gradual development in agriculture and useful arts. Many Government schools, on the other hand, are Westernizers in regard to skilled trades and even to applied science, but in other respects tacitly or explicitly prefer the mind and habits of the natives to remain as little altered as possible.

And finally, in regard to native education again, there is the dispute as to language. Should native boys and girls be taught English or whatever is the language of the European power concerned with their education; or some local *lingua franca*, such as Swahili for East Africa; or be restricted to their own vernacular? If English or Swahili are to be aimed at, are they to be aimed at for everyone or only for a few? and at what stage should the teaching of them begin?

At the expense of being somewhat dogmatic, it is perhaps worth while running over some of the principles and ideas that are beginning to emerge now that the chaos in which the theory and practice of native education has inevitably found itself at its inception, has been submitted to a decade or so of organized criticism and thinking.

In the first place, then, education is a problem of human development. You are not framing curricula *in vacuo*, as it were, for ideal beings with unlimited time at their disposal. "Had we but world enough and time . . ."; but we have only a few short years, crowded with the physical and emotional difficulties attendant on growth and adolescence; and we are dealing not with intellectual angels, but with human children, possessed of imperfect minds, limited capacity for attention and retention, restricted interest. Nor indeed in education should we be thinking solely or chiefly of minds. We are dealing with organisms, body-minds, or mind-bodies, as you prefer; to try to deal separately with only one of these two aspects of their reality is fatal.

The first thing to consider is not what the teacher would like to teach; not what the ideal human being ought to know; not a curriculum framed to cover the range of human knowledge and activities, in relation to which children are so many examination candidates. The first thing is what the child can profitably learn; what is suited to the needs and desires of limited human organisms in a particular environment; a curriculum framed to promote the development of individual growing boys and girls. This is the modern biological idea of education, which you will find held wherever people have really thought out their ideas on the subject, and are not carrying on by inertia or merely putting their prejudices forward in the guise of ideas.

Then there is the double principle that education should

be adapted to the local environment of time and place, and yet give the opportunity of transcending that environment. This is the "dual mandate" of education. It recognizes that men and women have to be prepared for earning their livelihood and doing the work of the world, but recognizes equally that they should be introduced to those ideas and activities—in literature, history, science, religion, art and other forms of self-expression or self-realization—which will enable them to reach a level of existence above immediate drudgery or anything of purely practical scope.

Working out the application of these principles, we arrive at some such conclusions as the following. Education for the African boy and girl should have its practical aspect, but should also concern itself with ideas and activities of no immediate practical value. In both these aspects it should include handwork as well as headwork, nor should activities concerned with self-expression, such as singing and dancing, games and acting, be neglected. It should not be too ambitious at the start, but should at first aim at making the children understand their own African surroundings in a new way, later linking this knowledge on to broader themes. It should aim both at giving sound elementary education to the many and at providing opportunities for the few of outstanding ability or keenness to continue up to a high standard. It should not attempt a rigid programme from the outset, but, realizing that any system of native education in Africa is a novelty, should encourage experiment and variety among different schools. Realizing, too, that school education is only half the battle, and that the native child has no home background in the least comparable to that of European children, Education Departments should concern themselves with the back-

ground as well as with the school, with adult education as
well as with the education of children, with anything that
will raise the native standard of life and thought, and not
only with education in the narrow, formal sense.

In fact, as one Director of Education said to me, his Department ought not to exist; it ought to be a Department
of Native Development. This, which seemed to me a wise
but Utopian saying, I quoted in a newspaper article. Some
months later I was surprised but delighted to get a letter
from the Director of the *Department of Native Development* in Northern Rhodesia, explaining that he had read
my article, and thought I might like to know that the local
Department of Native Education had been thus transformed, in title and in scope, the previous year. This was
indeed welcome evidence of an open mind and forward
spirit in educational affairs; and I hope the example will be
followed elsewhere.

Perhaps the chief dangers of native education in the past
have sprung from what I may call the Academic Fallacy.
This issues in many ways. It produced the old-fashioned
classical education of Europe, whose rigours the younger
generation can hardly imagine, though many older men
still living have submitted to them (I think, for instance, of
Mr. H. W. Nevinson's amazing account in his autobiography of the education he received at Shrewsbury); in the
same way it produced the old-fashioned classical education
of pre-war China. It has produced the Babuism of Bengal.
It is in our own country giving us a secondary education
which aims first and foremost at preparation for the University (whither only a few of its victims will proceed)
instead of being rounded off and satisfying in itself. It
fosters the idea that education produces a superior caste,

irrespective of what knowledge it imparts and how it is applied.

‘ This danger is ever present. It can perhaps never be killed, for it is so much easier and simpler for the less gifted teacher to make his children learn something by heart than to be sure they have enthusiastically made a fact or an idea part of their mental being; much less trouble to give lessons out of books than by means of practical activities in the field, the laboratory, the school garden, in the acting of real plays, or the making of real objects in the workshop. Something can be done to avoid it by insistence on a proper apportionment of time between class-room work and other activities, but most of all by making sure that the teachers are trained along the right lines.

With regard to the details of the curriculum, everyone would agree, I think, that in addition to the three R's you need in Africa a good deal of agriculture and hygiene, practical as well as theoretical; you need some further language beyond the local vernacular, some acquaintance with geography and history, some games and drill, and something in the nature of skilled handwork.

This is a heterogeneous collection of subjects, dictated some by practical, some by academic, some by pedagogical considerations. A unifying principle is lacking, and is badly needed. We need not make the mistake of thinking that a course of work constructed *a priori* round some particular subject—be it classics, or history or science—is ever going to be really satisfactory; such ideas have been repeatedly tried by over-schematic minds, and have never succeeded. The main reason for the inclusion of a subject in a child's education must be its intrinsic importance for the growing

human organism. On the other hand, continuity and coherence are in themselves important for the human organism; mere eclecticism will not work (as shown at
another level of education by the abandonment, in American colleges, of the completely free elective system, under
which students took any subjects they fancied, however
heterogeneous). The intrinsic value of separate subjects
may decide on their suitability for inclusion in the curriculum; but there will not be room for everything, and
what shall be left in, and how it shall be emphasized, may
rightly be decided with reference to some central core deliberately chosen as part of a logical scheme.

What is such a central core to be in African education?
Assuredly not classics: hardly literature or modern languages; religion, even if desirable, which it is not, would
be impracticable owing to the multiplicity of creeds; purely
practical activities cannot provide the necessary background
of ideas. There remain history, geography and science. History is probably not suitable as the key subject, the core.
It is more remote from life, and in the teaching of it the
book-learning attitude and the pitfall of academic handling
are more difficult to avoid. Further, in hygiene and agriculture—which are included in the curriculum of every
African school—you have subjects which cry out for a basis
of pure science. It is being found out, for instance, that
hygiene without a good deal of general biology is an empty
and vain subject. Its methods almost inevitably tend to
approach those which Mr. Squeers, if reincarnated on a
slightly higher plane, would have adopted: "T-O-O-T-H,
B-R-U-S-H, Tooth-brush: go, dear child, and use it."

For these and other reasons it seems that biology and
geography make the best central core for the academic

side of native education. The biology will begin with nature study, not merely the nature study of familiar animals and plants, but also the nature study of the human body, and will never, I hope, become very abstruse or advanced save in the rare high schools or colleges.

The geography will be largely physical and social geography; and thus much of it will, if you like, be part of, or at least the complement to, biology. For a plant or animal or man does not exist *in vacuo*, but only has meaning in relation to its environment; and geography can be treated largely as the study of life's environment.

History, which will begin with tribal and African history, can spring naturally enough out of social geography. The elements of physico-chemical science, so important as "anti-magic" studies and as introducing the child's mind to the idea of order and natural law and to accuracy of thought and method, are soon found necessary to understand biological facts, and then can be developed as seems best. And the work in hygiene, in agriculture, in economic geography, and in citizenship, will all take on new vitality for having a basis or a background of biological ideas.

We have dismissed literature as a possible candidate for central subject; but this does not mean that we want to turn our backs on it. In point of fact, in any curriculum which is not purely practical, you cannot avoid some literary education. What the children read is literature, even if, alas! often of very poor quality; there must be some standard according to which they are made to write their compositions, and this again involves literary values.

People do, of course, exist who assert that native education should definitely eschew literature; but all this means in practice is that they provide bad or inadequate or colourless literature for the boys and girls they are educating.

We do not want belles-lettres in the African school; but we can aim at three objectives. One is that the readers provided are well written and, when possible, should contain apposite extracts from good authors; another is that the children should be so taught that they can write clearly and really express themselves freely on paper; and the third is that at the end of their school career they should realize that in books there exists the chief repository of the world's thought, and that they should be able if they so desire to draw upon this heritage of ideas and beauty by reading.

There are difficulties in the way of any such development of the curriculum, to be sure. There ought to be in East Africa at least one trained biologist and one anthropologist at the service of the Education Departments. It will probably not be easy to obtain sanction for their appointments, nor to find the right men once they are sanctioned; but they ought to be appointed.

But the greatest difficulties are the shortage of properly-qualified teachers and the shortage of suitable textbooks, readers, and teachers' handbooks. In the matter of teachers the education authorities are between the devil and the deep sea. They are urgently in need of more native teachers, hundreds of them; they are equally in need of a higher standard among the teachers; and yet to set your standard too high means delaying the release of your teachers-in-training, and also the cutting down of the percentage of successful candidates. They have therefore wisely adopted a policy of going slow. The standard is being gradually raised, but not enough to cut down the number of teachers passing out. On the other hand, they do not want a too rapid increase of the number of teachers, for this would fix a low standard of teaching on the system for years to come. On strictly academic grounds, the standard still seems very low to those accustomed to home conditions: certificates for teaching in the bush schools, are issued to men and boys who in their school work are nowhere near completing the curriculum of a child in an elementary school in England. They have, however, to take certain professional subjects; and of course they are mostly of quite advanced years, so that the subjects mean more to them. And even these apparently minimal qualifications are a great advance on those of many natives actually teaching, especially in mission out-schools. Some of these know how to read and write in the vernacular, to do very simple arithmetic, the catechism, some hymns, *et voilà tout.*

As to books, the difficulties are legion. Sometimes the choice is not a good one. A distinguished German missionary in Tanganyika exclaimed to me upon the queer English authorities who had chosen, as the first English book to be translated into Swahili for a school reader, one dealing with piracy, drunkenness, robbery and murder. After a little reflection, I was able to recognize this as *Treasure Island*; and had to confess that it was really not suited to the growing native mind in its present transitional state.

The chief difficulty, however, comes from the total absence of books adapted to local conditions. Readers are chosen which contain passages describing an English winter; or fairies; or town life; although the unfortunate African child has rather less idea of a large town than of fairies, and no idea whatever of snow or ice.

You cannot begin teaching native children history through the history of England; you need a primer of East African history. Neither is it much use beginning your lessons in geography or agriculture or biology, save with Africa as background and source of all your illustrative examples.

However, something has been done to tackle the question. In East Africa, for instance, sanction has been given to the setting up of an Inter-territorial Language Committee, which shall have as one of its main duties the selection and preparation of school-books and their translation into native languages. The British Social Hygiene Council has just embarked on the preparation of an annotated list of the school-books in use in our tropical colonies, dealing with hygiene, biology and agriculture. There is an official journal called *Overseas Education*, in which experiments in book preparation can be noted and criticized.

Here, again, the man at home needs to use his imagination to realize the difficulties of the man overseas. Many of our school-books in England may be poor, but at least they exist. And our teachers have to come up to some reasonable standard before they are qualified. But in Africa the books are often just not there; and without them, especially without good teachers' handbooks, the poorly-prepared native teachers are in many subjects almost helpless.

These difficulties, however, will slowly right themselves. I must spend a little time on another problem which contains germs of graver because more political difficulty—the problem of a second language. There are over 400 different languages (not mere dialects) spoken in Africa; and they are not merely as different as English from Italian, Greek from Norwegian, but belong to several different families of language, with altogether different principles of construction. To learn Swahili, an Englishman has to learn not only a new grammar, but a new kind of grammar. Another Bantu-speaking African would be familiar with this kind of grammar; but a Masai, for instance, would be as badly off as the Briton.

It is clear, therefore, that some second language beyond the local vernacular must be taught for the sake of easy communication and to provide access to a larger literature. This at once raises two questions. First of all, what shall this second language be? Shall it be a European language, the language of the European power in control of the territory; or shall it be an African language, chosen because it is already more or less of a *lingua franca* in the region, or quite arbitrarily because you want to make a *lingua franca* out of it? And once you have chosen your second language, are you to begin teaching it in the earliest stages, or wait until after a few years of school life?

There are many who are much opposed to the teaching of a European language to natives. Some think it will facilitate the spread of Bolshevism, Trade Unionism, Socialism and various other -isms of the left wing. Others simply dislike the idea of their black servants understanding what they say; others again believe that the African mind will only develop properly through the medium of an African language; and so on.

But to all these objections there is one overwhelming answer. The African wants to know English; as education spreads, he will want it more intensely; and, like the little boy in the Pears' Soap advertisement, he won't be happy till he gets it. Any attempt to keep the progressive African from European languages is doomed from the outset to create friction and to end in failure.

Furthermore, there is the fact, which seems undoubted, that most African languages, including Swahili, the only rival to English in East Africa, are deficient in abstract terms. To be able to use abstract ideas and to generalize are necessary for Africa if education is to take her far along the path of progress. It would seem that the adoption of an African language would retard or even prevent this advance.

As a result, it is universally agreed that English should be taught in the more advanced forms. In all East African schools of intermediate standing and non-technical character, English is taught, and in the highest forms the instruction in all subjects is given in English.

For the other end of school life, too, there is general agreement. With few exceptions, it is agreed that quite young native children should only receive instruction in one language, and that that language should be their local vernacular or some very closely allied tongue. For one thing, they have to be taught to think and express themselves; they will not do this easily or readily save through the medium they have imbibed unconsciously since infancy. And for another, recent studies in Wales and elsewhere have shown conclusively that to attempt bilingualism or even a second-language subject too early is a definite handicap to the majority of children.

The African child will thus begin his educational career through the medium of his own mother-tongue. He will end it, if he sticks to the academic side and goes far enough in it, through that of English. But what of the intermediate stages, and of the technical side of education? It is here that controversy is still rife. One school of thought wants to embark on English quite early, and make it the only other medium of instruction beyond the vernacular. The opposing school wants to insert Swahili as an African *lingua franca* to be used as a medium of instruction in the stage between the multiplicity of vernaculars and the final European language.

This latter is now the orthodox procedure insisted upon by the Government Education Departments over the four East African territories, in spite of opposition from the protagonists of early-begun English or late-continued vernacular, the latter especially powerful in regions like Buganda or Kikuyuland, where missionaries have long been at work and have translated the Bible and many other books into the local language.

In favour of Swahili, its advocates remind us that in respect of the area over which it is understood (though not in respect to the number of those who speak it as their mother-tongue) Swahili is one of the dozen major languages of the world. With its aid you can make yourself understood over almost the length and breadth of East Africa (save perhaps the barren Northern regions), and far across into the Congo. They also claim that it is much easier than any European language for an African to pick up.

This latter point is doubtless true for all Bantu-speaking peoples; but by no means true for Hamites and Nilotes and those who speak true Negro or Sudanic tongues. For them a Bantu language is every whit as difficult as English or French or German.

On paper this insistence on Swahili would seem very difficult to justify. The study of an extra language confers relatively little educational advantage to set off against the enormous expenditure of time and mental energy needed to master it; and the insistence upon Swahili can be construed by progressive Africans as a means of heading them off their natural ambition to learn English.

And yet at the moment the educational authorities are, I think, in the right. There is one obstacle, insuperable for the time being, in the way of the early and widespread teaching of English, and that is the absence of teachers competent to teach it. For a hundred native teachers who can teach adequately in Swahili there are perhaps ten or a dozen who could make some sort of a showing with English, and three or four who would make a good job of it. The only result of immediate insistence on English as second language would be to encourage the most appallingly bad English.

On the West Coast a fearful brand of pidgin English has grown up which it will take decades of hard work to reform. There may be a superficial picturesqueness in phrases such as "little beef what live in tin" (meaning, of course, sardines), but I don't think any one would deliberately wish to encourage such pidginry in East Africa.

And if English is impossible, then the authorities are undoubtedly right in insisting upon some *lingua franca*; nothing will do so much to facilitate communications and the spread of ideas. The Government publication *Habari* ("News"), written in Swahili, already has a wide circulation through East Africa and is doing a great deal to disseminate new ideas on health and agriculture, as well as providing the educated native with reading matter for his leisure. Such publications can be most potent in bringing about a better understanding between Government and governed; and as a common language spreads, their influence will be multiplied.

(In passing, think too of the influence which could be exerted by Swahili talking films, Swahili gramophone records, Swahili talks over the wireless, as the mechanical possibilities of their use become more widely spread in Africa.)

There is, however, one obvious danger in the present policy—the danger of making it permanent. It should be the avowed aim of the Education Departments to push English gradually back in the curriculum *pari passu* with the increase of teachers capable of teaching it, until it has either ousted Swahili altogether, or at least reduced it to a very secondary position. This may quite well take two or three more educational generations. None the less, policy in this matter should be declared from the outset, for, if not, there is the risk that the mere machinery of Swahili teaching—the number of native teachers who will be reluctant to see it go because of the hard work they have put into learning it, the number of books written in or translated into it—will hang like a dead weight round the neck of change, and help crystallize into permanency what should be a transitional phase.

Another point worth stressing is the need for freedom of experiment in such a new field as that of native education. There has been a notable amount of such freedom in the young Education Department of Tanganyika, resulting in an extremely interesting variety of Government schools—from Malangali, which is seeking to develop on a foundation of native ideas, through straightforward scholastic efficiency like that of Moshi, to Tabora which combines an aristocratic idea of education with deliberate and rapid advance towards Westernization. And besides these there are, of course, Technical Schools and also the many Mission Schools, all now with common minimum standards but great diversity of method. Such variety cannot but be fecund, and every effort should be made to avoid levelling it down by regulations from headquarters, until a half-century of such experiments has enabled us to see the lines of greatest progress.

Equally important is the need for relieving the unfortunate educationist of the fetters of red tape and the burden of forms which often prevent him devoting his energy to his real job—and sometimes, indeed, reduce the total of energy which he has. Would Governments spend more by not bothering about occasional waste in nibs or blankets, than by wasting the highly-paid time of head-masters in checking the precise number of nibs and blankets in their possession and filling up detailed returns on the subject? I understand that a policy of minimum forms and maximum trust has been tried in the Survey Department of one of our West African territories, and has thoroughly justified itself.

But enough of more or less technical details. The main thing to remember for the Englishman interested in or concerned with the problem is that education in Africa at the moment is a great adventure—*the* great adventure, indeed. Villagers listening to officials of the Medical Department and learning of new ways to avoid old diseases; boys at a Government school being introduced to new tools which they can use at home, like the plough, being inoculated with new ideas such as those of scientific order and control, or the progressive development of nations; tiny creatures in a remote bush school growing up with the idea that reading and writing and arithmetic are part of the normal human heritage, not esoteric, nor alien to their African life; girls imbibing the ideas of cleanliness and hygiene, ventilation and healthy diet, at a mission school; technical apprentices learning trades that will enable them to hold their own in the economic life of the world; most striking of all, grown men sitting round after their day's work on a plantation, poring over the spelling-books which contain the magic key to knowledge;—in all of them the ferment is stirring which, more thoroughly than any mere political or economic changes, is destined to transform the continent.

Africa for thousands of years has remained in a state of arrested growth. But, just as the arrested development of a cretinous child can be set moving again by the chemical magic inherent in desiccated thyroid glands, so Africa's development can be resumed under the stimulus of the intellectual hormone administered through education.

I can indeed think of no better outlet for the energies and aspirations of young men (and perhaps soon young women too) who, though possessed by the missionary spirit, have no zeal for a particular sect or creed, than the educational service in Africa. Here is a whole continent demanding fuller life, and to satisfy that demand will need all the resources of energy and imagination of which our educational missionaries are capable.

Chapter XXIX

MISSIONS AND THE LIFE OF AFRICA

The Mission field is dangerous ground for an outsider to tread: yet missions have been, are, and will continue to be such important elements in the development of changing Africa that it would be merely cowardly to omit all mention of them in a book designed to give an impression of African variety.

First and foremost let us recognize to the full the virtues and the achievements of the noble missionaries of the pioneer period. Without the missionary spirit we should never have had Livingstone: without Livingstone the exploration and opening-up of Africa would have been long delayed (perhaps with beneficial results: one thinks of the Congo atrocities—Livingstone begot Stanley, Stanley begot the Belgian Congo): without Livingstone the ghastly crime of the slave-trade would have lasted many decades longer. The early missionaries were undeterred by tropical diseases in days when even the bare facts about their transmission were not known and tropical hygiene was yet unborn. They were undeterred by physical hardships or by the very real dangers from savage and hostile negroes. I myself have met men, and women too, who have walked the eight hundred miles from Mombasa to the shores of Lake Victoria—a *safari* of nearly three months.

In the unsettled conditions of those early years they

played a vital rôle. Then the country was just being opened up. Many tribes were still unsubdued, hostile, dangerous. Arab slavers and equally unscrupulous white traders were eagerly exploiting the natives. There was no British administration, no central governments at all, no transport faster than a string of porters, no hospitals, no safeguards against insidious disease.

In that early stage the missionary was the much-needed antithesis to the slaver and the unregulated trader-adventurer. Even when settled government began, the missions for a long time supplied a large number of the administrations' defects; any education or medical service which the natives got was provided by them; they imported useful plants and trees, and taught useful arts.

The mission stations often provided havens in which the victims of primitive barbarity could take refuge, where the savage could escape from cruel, unmeaning custom into a serener air, a fuller life. Without them, it is perfectly clear that the unregulated first phase of Africa's new life would have been different, and would have been worse.

But conditions change rapidly in Africa. Could Livingstone come back to-day, or Sir John Kirk, or Bishop Tucker of Uganda, to revisit the lands they knew, they would assuredly not at first credit the change that has taken place within two human generations.

To-day the various African dependencies, governed by an admirable staff of administrators, are rapidly becoming organized states with their own patriotisms, their own life. Slavery (save in Abyssinia and perhaps in some remote parts of West Africa) and tribal war are no more; alien trade and settlement are carefully regulated; there are State medical, agricultural, forestry services; scientific discoveries, unknown in their pioneer days, are being requisitioned to build the foundations of health and prosperity; railways, steamers and motor-buses speed up transport; the natives themselves are anxious for education, and the breath of ideas is stirring among them.

The period since the war has been characterized by a new spirit in African affairs—the desire to find and lay down principles of native policy which shall be acceptable to the general conscience of civilization and shall promote both the development of African material resources for world use and that of the African peoples towards a fuller life. The exact issue is not yet decided; but we can safely prophesy that the history-books of the future will record as one of the special characteristics of the present half-century the fact that it fixed the broad lines along which the destinies of Africa were to develop.

What part are the Missions to play in this new, stabilized Africa? That is the question at issue. They are a powerful body. For one thing, they have organized themselves. The World Missionary Council of 1910 introduced a new spirit of co-operation which has since added markedly to the unity and efficiency of the non-Roman-Catholic bodies; and the Roman Catholics on their side have also consolidated their position. Missionary effort is now better organized than many businesses. Then they control considerable sums of money. The income of the various Protestant Missionary Societies has risen steadily from about 2¾ million pounds in 1895 to nearly 15 million pounds in 1925. In the latter year they had over 7000 ordained ministers in the field, and claimed a total of over 8 million converts, with over 3½ million communicants. Figures do not seem to be available for the income of Roman Catholic

Missions, but their effort is of the same order of magnitude, since in the same year they boasted over 8000 European priests in the mission-field, and about 7½ million native converts.

Taken at its face value, the transfer of less than 1 per cent. of the total population of the world (15 out of 1800 millions) to Christianity may not seem a result commensurate with the labour, devotion and money involved. But in reality the effects of missionary work cannot be judged in this crude way. Its efforts are concentrated especially in the primitive regions of the globe. We should leave out of account the great religions; then the number of converts made from primitive paganism would amount certainly to over 5 per cent. of its total. And the influence of missions in such countries is far greater than can be reckoned in terms of converts. It is subtle and pervasive. The missionaries are often the chief or only source of the light of Western learning and ideas; their converts play a disproportionate part in the life of the country; missions are usually entrusted with all or the major part of education in primitive regions, and entrenched in their privileged position by sanctions and subsidies from the local Governments; in backward territories, where the natives have as yet no real power, they may constitute one of the three estates of the realm, on an equal footing as regards influence with the personnel of Government and the unofficial white community of commercial men and planters.

The chief difficulty in discussing the rôle of missions is the enormous difference between them. Not merely will one missionary body base itself on quite different ideas from another—what could be more different than a typical White Father, devoted and hardworking, limited yet tolerant, an earnest and learned German Lutheran, and a representative of corybantic Fundamentalism from the United States?—but two stations or sections of one and the same Missionary Society may be as different as chalk from cheese: one may be dominated by old-fashioned ideas and narrow, bigoted minds, the other by the most humane and modernist temper. This last phenomenon attracted my attention especially with certain Protestant missions; but even with bodies whose ideas are not in such a transitional state, such as the White Fathers, very considerable divergencies, for instance in the attitude adopted towards native customs, may be found between different stations.

Then again there are all grades of devotion and sacrifice. At one end I think of saintly-faced French nuns who have come out to Africa knowing that the regulations of their order will never permit them to see their own land and people again, of men working for native health and happiness as hard as the hardest-driven Government servant, but with a far lower standard of living and far less leave. At the other I think of men I have met who obviously found in missionary life in Africa a much freer, ampler and more comfortable existence than any they could have looked forward to at home—lords of their own little domain, with abundance of black men and women to wait on them and labour for them, no more work than they cared to do, and with a mild spice of adventure thrown in. One of them in conversation quite frankly acknowledged the immense advantages, to him, of missionary life.

None the less, there are some general or fairly general statements which can reasonably be made. The first is that medical missions, almost without exception, are accomplishing first-class and indispensable work. The C.M.S.

Medical Mission in Uganda is the outstanding East African example. To be shown over the hospital at Kampala by Dr. Cook is a revelation. This big place, admirably run, would never exist but for the rare combination of missionary zeal, medical skill, pioneering spirit, and practical ability of this one man. And his wife's accomplishment is almost equal to his. She has organized a system of maternity clinics far and wide over the country, and trained the Baganda girls to act as midwives and nurses in them. So reliable are they that though the outlying clinics, for lack of white staff, can often not be visited for weeks or months at a time, the girls can be trusted to carry on and cope with the work unaided. I saw a class of them in the hospital at Kampala, learning the elements of gynaecology— a pleasant sight, with their soft-modelled, kindly faces and trim uniforms. I have already spoken of the wonderful single-handed work, along similar lines, of Mrs. Maynard in Tanganyika.

Then there are the immense services of the Missions to native education, on its practical and technical as well as its academic side. Do not let it be forgotten that missions have been so long in the field that they have had time to spread a network of schools all over the country. If the Government Departments of Education had had to start from scratch, they would have taken decades to build up as extensive a system. But even if, for the sake of argument, the Governments could have somehow bought out the Missionary School system, they could not have utilized it as fully as it is now utilized, because Mission education costs less than Government education. I am not speaking of the inefficient Mission schools, of which there are still many, but of Mission and Government schools of comparable standard. The reason is simple—on the average, white missionaries are paid lower salaries and get less leave and fewer allowances than officials in the Government service. They are content to do this, and the native benefits accordingly.

And good missionary schools are very good. The best school I saw in East Africa was to my mind the King's School, at Budo in Uganda, run by the C.M.S. And I saw Roman Catholic schools which equalled it in every way save that they seemed more formal, less free and modern in spirit.

In general the missionary bodies have shown great willingness to co-operate with the Government Education Departments, although these must seem to them upstarts and often imbued with strange notions. There have been difficulties, but on the whole the system works well whereby the missionary bodies receive grants, and in return are subject to Government inspection and must teach according to the Government syllabus; and some such arrangement is likely long to continue.

Then no one can see the two great cathedrals outside Kampala (both fine, and one a really striking building, full of dignity and cool simplicity), can visit them and listen to the choir sing Bach or plainsong, see the thronging attentive congregation, almost entirely native, hear a fiery sermon preached by a Muganda, without realizing that the missionaries have not only brought to Africa a religion which does most definitely suit many Africans, but have done much more to introduce the African to beauty, whether of architecture, of music, or of thought, than all the rest of the white men on the continent put together. Unfortunately, the beauty is sown very sporadically; most churches in East Africa are still ramshackle affairs, most church music goes no further than a harmonium and atrociously nasal hymn-singing. But there are a fair number of exceptions, and they are increasing; you feel it must have been a little like this in England about 1100, when Norman cathedrals were springing up, dwarfing the rude Saxon churches, and new ideas from across the sea were spreading in the land.

Then the missions are often the disseminators of new and healthier ways of living. In the Kikuyu Reserve, mission-trained girls are generally not content to live in a dirty, unventilated beehive hut: they insist on their husbands building them nice little houses, two- or even four-roomed, with windows and a door. These, with their tin roofs and bare-looking wood walls, are lamentably less picturesque than the old huts, but palaces in comparative comfort, and infinitely healthier. Nor are most of these Christianized women willing to go on with the time-honoured methods of bringing up children; they wash them, knit them little garments for the cool evenings, give them food which will not swell their unfortunate little stomachs to bursting-point. And the same is true among many of the Baganda and other tribes.

Again, the mission stations may still provide much-needed refuges for native girls threatened with a husband they dislike or with the enforcement of some tribal custom that is cruel or repugnant. The African is charmingly good-natured and indulgent to little children; but he can be cruel enough to them when they grow up, with the frank and unpleasant cruelty of the barbarian.

That is the credit side of the balance; and it is impressive enough. There is, however, a debit side. Even those two great cathedrals at Kampala have their discouraging aspect. For there are two of them, only because they are rivals. They are visible memorials of the fact that Uganda was the scene of the last religious war between Christians. They are symbols of the fatal disunion of Christianity, which invades Africa divided into dozens of separate sects, each assuring the black man that it alone holds the secret of his eternal salvation—and implying if no longer openly asserting damnation to the rest. What wonder that the natives become a little bewildered at the sectarian divisions in the white man's religion?

It is an interesting fact, but one which may make white Christians blush, that the first school in East Africa where both Protestant and Catholic teachers worked together was founded by a native chief in Uganda, himself a Christian convert, who refused to believe that sectarianism could be good. The only other schools of such a nature are not Mission but Government institutions, and even in them the Catholics have sometimes tried to get the native Catholic teachers away from this sinful association. At the Government training-schools for teachers and other higher institutions, attempts have been made to set up common hostels for everyone; these attempts have always broken down owing to the opposition of the Catholics, who will not tolerate the notion of undenominational services or to close mixing of the sects.

Then, of course, you have to face the fact that if most of your education is going to be given through the Missions, most of your education will have a strong religious bias. The principle of secular education, established for half a century all over Western Europe, has not yet found much foothold in Africa. In Kenya, even though there is a Government Education Department, the right of inspection of Mission schools by Government inspectors is only recognized when the schools are in receipt of a grant, and the Roman Catholics have chosen to do without grants so that they enjoy complete freedom to teach what they like, of whatever standard they like. This is an anomalous situation, which should not be allowed to continue.

By the principle of secular education I mean the principle that education has value in itself and is itself a sacred task, in which specifically religious education has only a minor rôle to play. With few but notable exceptions, missionary endeavour puts conversion far above education, concentrates as much as possible on religious teaching, and often—though this attitude is decreasing—sees in secular knowledge merely a bait with which to angle for souls. (That being so, one can hardly blame those among the natives who, being astute enough to see this, manage to secure the bait without swallowing the hook.)

I shall not easily forget the impression I got at one large mission in the Kikuyu country. An official of the Education Department and I were being shown over the school by the head of the mission, a charming and saintly man who has devoted his life unsparingly to this work. He is a great believer in keeping to the local Kikuyu language in preference to Swahili, the East African *lingua franca*. In the school, however, a good deal of Swahili was being taught. When asked why, he answered, "Because *the whole* of the Old Testament has not yet been translated into Kikuyu." I was staggered: I had not envisaged a state of mind which would make a man willing to insist on his boys grinding away at Swahili, against his own educational convictions, in order that they might have the privilege of reading Deuteronomy or a few of the minor prophets. It all seemed so wrong-headed, so astonishingly out of proportion.

This attitude also encourages, or at least permits, a low standard in non-religious subjects. There are still hundreds and hundreds of bush-schools in which hymns and catechism take the lion's share of the curriculum; while the rest is devoted to exceedingly sketchy instruction in reading and writing, a little arithmetic, and rarely geography or history.

Combined with the natural desire to score as many conversions as possible, and the need to impress subscribers at home, this tendency is doing no good to native education. A missionary body likes to be able to report that it possesses so many hundred schools and is educating so many thousand little heathens. But the people who drop their pennies in the missionary-box at home would often be astonished enough if they could see the miserable huts that serve as schools, still more if they could hear the limitations of the teaching, and most of all if they realized the extremely casual attendance at such schools. I should imagine, from inquiries I made, that only between thirty and forty per cent. of the children put down as attending mission schools in East Africa were getting an education worth calling an education.

It may be argued that in the present stage of African evolution the barest grasp of reading and writing, or even the grasp of their being possible, is an education worth having. That may be so; none the less, the present state of affairs cannot be regarded as satisfactory. It is gradually being remedied by Government inspection—in other words, by the recognition of the secular principle in education.

When conversion is the prime aim, it is almost inevitable that many valuable native customs will be lost in the process. Conditions vary a great deal in this respect, but it is not unfair to say that through the missionaries there has been a widespread discouragement of tribalism and the customs associated with it, just because it is pagan. The average tendency is strongly disintegrative. Converts often come to despise all their own customs. They throw the baby out with the bath, and abandon respect for tribal elders and tribal traditions. Yet they almost inevitably fail to imbibe our Western traditions properly—how could they in a few short months?—and so usually fall between two stools. I may quote an actual instance. The Government of Kenya are making a determined effort at the Jeanes School to teach native handicrafts, songs, and tribal history to the teachers-in-training. I was told there that one of their greatest difficulties was the reluctance of many Christian native teachers, and of the white missionaries under whose instruction they work, to countenance such "evil practices." Here I may perhaps quote the well-known Phelps-Stokes report on native education in East Africa on the subject (paragraphs 33, 34): "It is notable that native ministers are often the most emphatic in their opposition to native amusements. . . . Their convictions are sometimes the result of their intimate knowledge of the degenerating influence of native amusements, but often have their source in the narrow conception of recreation imparted to them by the missionaries."

Then we must not forget that natives do not always embrace Christianity for the reasons the missionaries would desire. Christianity is the white man's religion, and in many regions it definitely confers social prestige. When this is so, the convert tends to look down on his unconverted brethren. As a result of these two tendencies, it is unfortunately often the fact that in Africa certain types of Christianized "educated" native, if put into a position of responsibility, tend to treat their own people very harshly.

Then there is the grave question of religious intolerance. Intolerance is to be expected among half-educated converts who have been assured that Christianity (or rather one particular branch of it) means salvation, while all other religions mean damnation. In a district of Western Uganda which I visited, there was considerable trouble a year or so ago owing to the fanaticism of a native Christian who was going about inveighing against, and sometimes deliberately destroying, the little shrines outside the native huts. These are really miniature models of huts where a simple and innocent ritual of ancestor-worship is carried on. But as certain of the local missions have given them the name of "devil-houses," it is not to be wondered at that zealous converts who pursue their lead set out to extirpate these "abominations."

One must confess that there is still a good deal of narrow-mindedness among missionaries in the field. But there has been a notable change in this respect of recent years. For instance, owing to the efforts of the British Social Hygiene Council, and of the more enlightened of the missionary bodies, special courses for missionaries have now been held for the last two years in England, where they can hear from the lips of experts of the latest discoveries and ideas as regards biology and anthropology, sex, education, and psychology, and discuss the bearings of all these subjects on their work. This is bound to have a potent effect in the long run; but meanwhile it has only affected a small minority of mission workers. And I do not think it unfair to say that at present the proportion of men and women with at all liberal or modern ideas about religion is lower in the mission-field than in religious circles at home.

Let us also remember that missions in Africa are in a position to exert more power and influence than religious bodies at home. In England there are other currents of thought besides the religious—literary, scientific, artistic, philosophical—which help to mould the country's ideas and action; but in the tropics missionary notions on theology and moral values can exert their influence starkly with scarcely a competitor.

There are two unfortunate results of this strong influence of any missionary narrow-mindedness. In the first place, much to the bewilderment of the native, a gulf seems to yawn between the standard ideas of the two kinds of white men with whom they are chiefly brought into contact— the missionary and the administrative officer. Most men in Government service in Africa have the standard of ideas of the average middle-class Englishman. They do their job to the best of their ability, they devote a good deal of attention to tennis, golf, and other forms of sport, they are always playing bridge, and they dance whenever they can find an opportunity. They regard alcoholic refreshment as an essential part of the day's routine. In missionary circles, however, I was astonished to find how many people still regarded cards as the devil's bible, the theatre or the cinema as wicked, and dancing or the least trace of alcohol as deadly sin. And in place of the usual tolerance of the official, I was horrified to see the amount of hostility, veiled or open, between the official representatives of different Christian sects.

Several times I was told the story of a certain wealthy supporter of one of the missionary organizations who threatened to withdraw his subscriptions if the daughter of a prominent dignitary of his church insisted on going to a ball at Government House to which she had been invited. Perhaps one should give no credence to such mere gossip. On the other hand, there is no smoke without fire, and I must confess that after my own experience I am quite prepared to believe it. It is certain that the admirable attempt made by the authorities in Nairobi, of regulating the supply of beer to the natives by starting a municipal brewery which brewed pure beer, and a beershop where natives desirous of quenching their thirst could do so decently and in comfort, was met with definite hostility by certain personages in the local religious world.

When missionaries are narrow-minded, their narrow-mindedness has other unfortunate results. It tends to make them intolerant of, or even hostile to, any manifestation of beauty in art. Too often art, like secular knowledge, is regarded either as a mere handmaid to religion, or in some cases as definitely hostile to it. It will be a long time before the idea that art for art's sake and knowledge for knowledge's sake are two great liberating forces for the human spirit, neither of which is inferior to religion proper, will have taken root in missionary circles. Here again there are exceptions; but it is undoubtedly the fact that in many cases the effect of missionary influence and missionary education has been to break down the traditional native ideas, and their mode of expression, without putting anything in their place. Or what is put in their place is too often inferior. Art and beauty are regarded as of very secondary importance, and therefore only a perfunctory attention is given to them. Here and there I have seen fine designs of traditional native work being copied, but in many other places all this has been scrapped. To often you will find native girls, for instance, turning out basket-work worthy only of a place on a table of knick-knacks in a suburban drawing-room. In drawing, the tradition of copying from models, followed by elegant water-colours, is only too usual; the idea of encouraging the children really to express themselves with pencil or paint is usually not at all envisaged.

Quite pleasant songs are sometimes taught, but on the other hand music is often confined to hymn-singing. And what hymn-singing! I shall never get out of my ears the sound of the hymns at one big mission church in the Ki-kuyu country. The church was packed to overflowing, the mere odour was overpowering. The hymn was given out; the congregation threw themselves upon it. A volume of sound broke forth which you could have heard a mile away. Determined, strident, metallic, it pierced one's very vitals. The hymn continued, always *fortissimo*, verse after verse. I did not dare raise my eyes to look at my com-panions. At the end I felt battered to my soul's recesses. And yet the wonderful results achieved in places like King's School, Budo, show that the East African only needs proper training to love good music and to sing it well.

And finally there are clothes. At some places, like the White Fathers' Mission where I stayed, at Lulenga in the Belgian Congo, they have given up trying to make their converts wear European clothes, because they have realized that the natives' traditional costume of skins is healthier, even if it does leave a good part of them uncovered. But in most places, either on the score of health, or usually on the score of propriety, missions encourage, or even insist upon, the wearing of European clothes, especially amongst the boys and girls actually in their schools. The unfortunate thing is that these costumes are almost invariably so much less becoming than the old native traditional clothing, and much less so than they have any need to be. In some cases also, although they cover up all of the body, they often do so in such a way as to reveal or to accentuate the form, thus becoming a good deal more sexually provocative than the old frank semi-nudity.

Then one must say that some missionaries appear to imagine that they should be allowed to enjoy certain privileges denied to other mortals. This is seen especially in their attitude toward work for the benefit of the mission. At many stations, much work is done for the benefit of the mission station and the missionaries themselves, by native labour which is definitely underpaid even in relation to the low standard elsewhere prevailing in Africa. Some of this is doubtless given freely and willingly. But there can be little doubt that the prestige of a creed which lays claim to a control over man's eternal fate contributes, consciously or unconsciously, to this result. And in the commandeering of porters, or of foodstuffs, the missionary will often find that the end justifies the means. In Western Uganda I was myself witness of an illuminating incident. The District Commissioner was seeing us off on our way towards the Belgian Congo, when a nice-looking native came up and spoke to him. He was complaining of the local mission. He had been in possession of an island in the lake and had been growing coffee and bananas on it. The mission had then obtained a permit for temporary occupation of this island. They had dispossessed the man and cut down his bananas and were profiting by his coffee-plants; but they had up till now refused to pay any compensation to him whatever. So far as I could understand, they were letting the island and the cottage they had built on it to settlers who wanted a holiday, and thereby making considerable profit, although by the terms of their contract sub-letting was not permitted. I do not know what was the upshot of the case, but the District Commissioner thought the man's story was in all probability true.

There remains the most fundamental question of all—the suitability of Christianity, and the suitability of mission methods of Christianizing, to the African. Here, again, a great deal depends on the particular case. A Martian observer would, I imagine, find an ironical humour in studying some of the more fundamentalist creeds that are being pressed upon the Dark Continent. For, after all, if judged by the consensus of educated thought, they are in many respects little more advanced than those they are attempting to oust. What!—we attempt to wean the negro from his addiction to magic, and yet allow him to be preached at and converted by people who solemnly believe in prayers for rain, the literal inspiration of the Bible, the historical truth of Genesis' account of Creation, and all the rest of it! Over and over again I was warned as to the difficulty of introducing biological ideas into native education—because biology implied evolution, and evolution (although admittedly the greatest and most illuminating single new idea which we owe to the nineteenth century) was anathema to large sections of Protestant and Catholic missionaries alike.

I wonder if people of this stamp realize that their ideas seem exactly as barbaric, crude, and wrong to a considerable and influential section of civilized people as do to them the ideas of the primitive tribes among whom they are working? Do they at all grasp that there exists a large and growing body of men and women, brought up in the new conception of the universe which science is revealing, familiarized with modern ideas on religion, who find religion a way of life, an attitude of mind, not a body of dogma or a system of salvation, and who believe that religion can only live if it abandons its primitive certitude and learns to change and grow—and that to them the theology which was orthodox up to the late nineteenth century is completely obsolete, as obsolete as feudalism, bows and arrows, or the divine right of kings? I will quote one instance of what I mean. The following extract from a letter was in a copy of *Ruanda Notes*, a Central African missionary journal, which I happened to see. The pious gentleman is describing some of the horrors of a famine. "As I walked down the hill from the hospital my blood boiled because of the cruelty of it all, but the answer came to me. Sin was written across these withered bodies. Satan had dragged them down, and given death and disease as his reward." This is white enlightenment and Christian charity! The letter concludes, 'We badly need a box-body car."

Fortunately, there is a strong broad-minded minority among the missionaries. But it is beyond dispute that outworn theological prejudice has retarded, and is still retarding, the enlightenment of Africa; and will continue to do so until the enlightened minority becomes a majority.

Relevant here is the grave question whether conversion may not do as much harm as good. Even if, as undoubtedly often occurs, it helps individuals, it may do social harm by rotting the framework of native tradition and tribal ideas without succeeding in putting anything adequate in its place. This is especially true with the converts of bodies which believe in the efficacy of sudden conversion. For how can you expect a primitive negro mind by a few weeks or months of religious instruction to acquire a complete new background of all the ideas which alone give significance to nominal Christianity? Especially when his old background of ideas has been almost non-existent? Incautious proselytization runs the risk of producing intolerance, disintegration of social solidarity, disrespect for tradition. Administrators and anthropologists can produce scores of instances in which the new ideas have had unfortunate and sometimes entirely unforeseen results. Here again Professor Malinowski's books on the Melanesians may be cordially recommended as a source of dispassionate information.

Then there is the radical difference between the points of view of the missionary and of the other white men in the country. This difference often has its admirable side: it is highly important that in a new country there should exist an influential body of men whose attitude is coloured neither by the incentive of personal gain nor by the outlook and restrictions of Government service. But it has its faults as well as its merits. As illustration, I will content myself by setting down an incident which was narrated to me by a European education officer. A boy at a Government school, a non-Christian, met with a nasty accident and was taken, unconscious, to hospital. There he was seen by a charitable Roman Catholic missionary, and baptized—while still unconscious. He recovered, was informed of his baptism, and came in some perplexity to

my informant: was he really a Christian, would he have to
go to church, believe all the things the missionaries told
him, and behave as they bade under penalty of damnation?
His idea seemed to be that, having come under the control of the Christian God by the rite of baptism, he would
now be subject to that God's power. He was told that as
the rite had been administered without his knowledge,
he was perfectly free to do as he liked. However, he appeared to feel that some magic compulsion lay upon him,
went to church to see what it was like, as he put it, and
has thus drifted into Christianity. To the orthodox Catholic the missionary's action seems not only legitimate but
highly praiseworthy; it was done to make quite sure that
if the boy died his soul might have a chance of being saved.
To my informant, on the other hand, it seemed a wholly
unfair way of gaining influence over the unprepared mind
of a young native.

The view of some of the more liberal of the younger
missionaries is that the theological aspect of Christianity
should be reduced to a minimum in mission work, and
that the stress should be laid on its ethical side, and also
upon the general raising of the native's standard of life
and thought, irrespective of whether he become formally
converted or no. They point, with some reason, to the impossibility of supposing that tribal Africans can be brought
at a bound to appreciate in any adequate way the theological elaborations of Christian religious thought—how
can they do so, for one thing, through the medium of
languages in which words for abstract ideas are sadly lacking? And they object to any such idea as the verbal inspiration of the Bible, preferring, again with reason, to see
in it the history of a religious evolution from a barbaric

stage scarcely more advanced than that of many African religions to-day up to a high level of ethical monotheism finally illuminated by the ethical insight of Jesus and his spirit of sacrifice. They are also quite alive to the danger I have already mentioned, of inducing mental and social chaos by insisting on new and unassimilated ideas, and would accordingly do everything in their power to keep as much as possible of customs like initiation which lie at the root of tribal organization and native psychology, of the dances which are the African's most cherished recreation and his chief emotional outlet, of local art and music, crafts and folklore, which embody the soul of the people. And they would give the greatest possible autonomy to the local churches as they developed.

With regard to the last point, it is an interesting fact, not perhaps generally known, that the affairs of the Anglican Church in Uganda are looked after by a body on which natives are in a majority, and several cases have occurred in which black opinion has been opposed to white and has outvoted it. Not long ago, for instance, a proposal was made to put up a stained-glass window in the Cathedral to the memory of Bishop Hannington, who was murdered, forty-five years ago, by the Baganda because he persisted in trying to reach the capital by the forbidden route from the east. The European clergy were almost unanimously in favour of this. But unfortunately the language difficulty cropped up again: the Luganda phrase for *stained glass window* included a word also used for *graven image*; and as graven images are forbidden in the Old Testament, the proposal was rejected by the black majority, and the subscriptions had to be returned.

Further to the south in Africa there is a strong move-

ment in favour of an autonomous African Church, and
it is at least arguable that the best thing for the African
will be to let him work out, with large latitude, the types
of religion best suited to himself—even should this here
and there involve such patriarchal doings, on the whole
well suited to African conditions, as the marriage of more
than one wife, for instance.

Here again let us remember that there can be no question of shutting off the African from religious progress
any more than from economic or intellectual progress.
There is, it is true, one region of British Africa (in Northern Nigeria) in which Christian missionizing is actually
prohibited under the treaty by which the country was
taken into the Empire, but this is already under the sway
of an advanced religion—Islam. In regions where the original primitive religions still prevail we can no more suppose or hope that the people will cling to their primeval
crude beliefs than to their illiteracy or their insanitary
huts or inefficient methods of agriculture. Progress in any
one department of life will react on the rest.

If Christian ethics, humanist ideals, and non-sectarian
services and beliefs, based on some simple monotheist creed,
could be universally given in Government schools, it might
be that the African would build up for himself a Christianity so highly modified as to be a new religion. Meanwhile, however, the choice lies between educated paganism,
Christianity, and Islam. Educated paganism may become
a force to reckon with in East Africa; at the moment it
is negligible. Remain the two Western world-religions.
There are a great many people who stoutly maintain that
Mohammedanism is the best religion for the African, that
it encourages in him greater stability, more self-respect as

well as more respect for authority, less restlessness and less hypocrisy, than does conversion to Christianity.

It would seem that there is something in this. And yet it is very difficult to believe that in the long run Islam would be better for Africa than some form of Christianity. Wherever Islam has made headway in Africa, it has led to a definite and real progress, true, but to a progress which has then been arrested. This seems to be the all-but-universal opinion of those in a position to judge. It takes the pagan so far and no further.

This is doubtless due to the fact that the profession of Islam, in practice if not in theory, means chiefly the keeping of certain rules, the practice of certain ritual observances, the recitation of certain words; while Christianity, even in cases where it is strictest in the matter of rules of life, ritual or credal efficacy, does invariably insist on the importance of the inner life and of high standards in regard to it. The standards of Christianity are often described as impracticable and impossible, leading inevitably to hypocrisy or a divorce between precept and practice. This may be true in its degree, yet it seems undoubted that it is the very impossibility for the Christian of living up to the standards of his religion which has given Christianity its real vitality. It is impossible to live up to any standard of perfection, in matters intellectual or artistic as well as ethical. But the fact that it is cherished impels to further effort.

On the other hand, belief in the efficacy of external things, be they words or deeds of a practicable instead of an impracticable standard, will tend to moral and intellectual stagnation. It may, if the prescribed rules be well chosen, help markedly at first towards a raising of level of life and an increase of self-respect; but after a time this will almost inevitably cease.

As between Islam and Christianity, then, it would seem that, although Islam may secure greater immediate progress, the improvements due to Christianity are likely to be in the long run more considerable and more continuous. If we desire a progressive development for the African native, we are more likely to get it through Christianity than by either encouraging Islam or safeguarding paganism. But we should attempt to make the Christianizing progress a gradual one, and to temper it with that combination of science and humanism which is the new spirit of the post-war age, and may one day form the basis of some religion as yet unborn.

And our conclusions? It is no good merely reciting merits and faults, apportioning praise or blame. The missions exist, firmly rooted, in Africa; they are a part of its system. The most bitter opponent of missions could not seriously suggest abolishing them, for he must know this would be wholly impossible. But their most enthusiastic adherents should agree that they ought not to lay claim to any privileged position, and should guard against developing too solid vested interests; and he would probably agree also that the system had many faults.

The chief remedy, as it seems to me, is to take the missions more seriously, as an integral part of white activity in the tropics, not merely as evangelizing agencies to be tolerated by an embarrassed administration, nor as organizations to be utilized, because they happen to be there, by Education Departments in a hurry, nor as bodies whose medical activities present ways of saving expense in the budgets of the Department of Medicine and Public Health.

They are *de facto* a Third Estate of the realm in almost all African territories; let us recognize and regularize the condition.

What would such recognition mean? It would mean that the relation of the missions to the State and the Government would become regularized in regard to all their activities, as has already been done with their educational work. Their present complete or almost complete freedom would be diminished, but in return their rôle as co-partners with Government in the development of the natives would be enhanced.

But even if this proposal, which doubtless savours of Erastianism, were not acceptable, much could still be done. Perhaps the missions will not become more closely linked with Government Departments. Even so, now that stable and efficient Governments with a continuous policy have been set up, the recognition by the Governments of the missions' value to the country, and of their right to continue their work there, involves certain corresponding recognitions from the missionary bodies.

And by far the most important of these is the recognition that, since to be a missionary in a primitive and changing country is a great responsibility, a definite and high standard should be demanded from would-be workers in this field, just as it is from candidates for the Administration, the Agricultural Service, or any other Government Department.

A missionary in Africa is a man who sets out to remould the immemorial life of whole peoples. He sets out to convert them to a new religion, to alter their morals, their social customs, to educate their children in a radically new way, to teach them new ways of doing old

things, and things which are new altogether, to cure their
diseases and make them live healthier lives. Now this is
a very responsible, not to say ticklish job to undertake.
And one surely has a right to demand that the men who
intend to undertake it shall submit themselves to as
definite training to prepare themselves for it as do candidates for any other professional career.

Missionaries who intend to take up highly specialized
careers like medical work or advanced teaching will obviously need specialized preparation: but I am speaking of
the rank and file who, like the administrator, will be concerned with all the aspects of native life. Their own religious bodies will demand that they receive a specialized
religious preparation; practical needs will see to it that
they learn the language of the country once they get
there. But is it too much to ask that they should prepare
themselves beforehand by passing courses in the history
and geography of the country where they intend to go;
in psychology; if possible in science, notably as regards
elementary physiology and the biology of reproduction and
sex; and very definitely in social anthropology, so that they
may understand the meaning and value of the institutions
and beliefs they are setting out to alter? I do not think that
it is. And Governments of African Territories could ensure
its being done by giving notice that, after the lapse of a
certain time, missionaries would only be allowed to enter
the country if they could produce a certificate showing
that they had passed through such a course of training.

And many of the missions themselves, it seems, would
be likely to agree. At least, a beginning has been made.
I have spoken of the courses organized by the Protestant

missions, in conjunction with the British Social Hygiene Council, for missionary workers in the tropics. These have proved so successful that it is proposed to hold them annually and to enlarge them as much as possible.

It is a notable step, and one symptomatic of the spirit of progress now to be found in almost all the more active missionary bodies. The only difficulty is that missions are primarily dependent upon voluntary subscriptions, and that it is apparently much harder to get contributions for the slow work of what I may call anthropological missionizing than for the more spectacular business of quantitative conversion. We can only hope that this will change as the increase of public enlightenment grows at home.

The missionary spirit is a vital thing, productive of much self-sacrificing activity, much potential good to the world. The problem is how to harness it to the best effect for the good of the world—in our particular case, for the good of Africa.

At the moment there is one great source of wasted energy. Many people with the missionary spirit do not belong to any Church; as a result there is at present no outlet in the missionary field for their enthusiasm. If it were possible to organize a non-sectarian mission, a large new supply of energy and devotion would be put at the service of native peoples. Any such body, though unsectarian, would have a truly religious aim—to work so that Africa-to-be should have more life, better and richer life, and enjoy it more abundantly.

But even without such dreams, much can be done. And it would seem that the most important things which the missionary spirit could do at the moment are to co-operate to the utmost with Governments in the general task of native development, even if this means sacrificing some of its independence; and still more, to submit itself to discipline and training, thorough and scientific, for the work it wants to carry out.

Chapter XXX

SOME AFRICAN ANIMALS

This chapter is not intended as a fragment of a technical zoological *opus*; nor as a recital of the detailed adaptations or strange life-histories of a few of the continent's hundreds of thousands of animal species; nor yet as a bit of popular natural history concerning the larger mammals and other prominent creatures, already almost too well and certainly too much described. It is merely an attempt to set down some of the most striking facts of animal life observed by a three-months' traveller who happens also to be a biologist, and some of the trains of thought to which they give rise.

In the first place, Africa is the continent most remarkable for the number and variety of its large mammals. Where else can you see a hundred great aquatic beasts like hippo in one glance; find creatures, like giraffe, as tall as watch-towers; see herds of a thousand head, zebra, gnu, gazelle, and all the other various buck; or hear the roaring of lions so often and so readily? Where else can one still discover big animals new to science, like the okapi, the giant forest-hog, or the strange hyaena-like creature only this year sent back from Uganda? Africa boasts the largest of all living land animals, the largest fresh-water mammal, and two of the three lone survivors of man's nearest kin, the higher anthropoid apes.

Many have marvelled at this abundance of large life, so spectacularly displayed before his train windows to the traveller arriving from the coast: but why is it so?

We can marvel, partly because at home we have killed off all the big creatures until there is little left to marvel at in temperate countries. Partly, too, because Africa is tropical; for though in sheer numbers of animals temperate regions may rival the tropics, yet the tropics, with their richness and their permanent luxuriance, will always excel in variety. And partly because East Africa, though tropical, is largely dry.

Where the tropics are not dry, all the solid ground in them is covered with forest. And forest is bad country for seeing game. Game there may be in abundance, but it will not be in large herds; nor will it ever be conspicuous. But Africa east of the Congo basin and the western Rift is largely a dry country, with broad arid plains, three to five thousand feet above sea-level. Here you can see any game there is to be seen. And though the grass may often be scanty, and much of it dries right up in the dry season, yet the extent of the country is so vast that the great herds can simply migrate from one plain to another, from open plains to river-banks, from river-banks to foothills, as the need arises.

The Pampas and other plains of eastern South America might show us a fauna almost equally amazing; but during the last Ice Age some strange fate overtook the great majority of its members, and the horses, the tank-armadilloes, the giant sloths, the toxodonts and other queer ungulates of many types no longer found upon the earth, were all mysteriously extinguished, at most a few hundred thousand years ago.

But if climatic changes in other parts of the world have helped to leave the African zoo unique, man has also helped. He has cleared the lions out of the lands north and east of the Mediterranean, the elephant out of the North African littoral, the wolves out of England, the bears and urochs out of Central Europe, the bison out of the great American plains. And he has been at it since the old Stone Age; it is quite likely that the extinction of creatures like the mammoth and the woolly rhinoceros is due as much to human destructive skill as to change of climate.

Whatever the multiplicity of causes, the East African fauna of large animals is unrivalled. May man at last turn preserver instead of destroyer and keep it in its full glory!

But in many ways the birds and small creatures of Africa are more remarkable than the large mammals, and certainly less well known. I will begin with a fact about flowers which links on to animal life. Even the most casual observer in East Africa must be struck by the abundance of red flowers—not pink like our temperate campions or thrifts or pinks, nor mixed with blue to give a purple-red like our foxgloves or milkworts, knapweeds or dead-nettles, but real red, pure scarlet or pure flame. The Erythrina tree lights innumerable hillsides with its tufted fires of scarlet, all the more conspicuous because every leaf is shed before it blooms. Then there are the Flame-trees and the Flamboyants which in their season make Dar-es-Salaam so violently bright. There are the Leonotus, common plants of the wayside, tall herbs with a series of round balls of flame-orange flowers; there are scarlet frizzy-headed lilies in Uganda woods; there are the magnificent Hibiscus, big red trumpets with stamens and pistil protruding far and proudly like the trumpet's jet of sound made visible; red-hot pokers; orange-red aloes; and many other red-flowered plants.

I had been struck by this riot of red, but had not troubled my head to ask myself why. However, I suppose the habit of looking for reasons gets so ingrained in the scientist that I had asked the question subconsciously. Anyhow, one day the answer flashed into my mind unsought. It is because of the many flower-visiting birds, the abundant members of the family Nectariniidae or sun-birds, which get most of their nourishment from nectar, supplemented by the insects they find in and by the corollas. Now, bees have eyes which are sensitive to some of the ultra-violet rays invisible to us: but to red they are not attuned—it is no colour to them at all, but merely blackness. Birds, on the other hand, are sensitive to red; and whether they actually prefer it, or whether the flowers that set out to attract birds have developed a colour invisible to insects so as to remain unvisited by creatures to which they are not adapted, and by which they cannot be fertilized, it is certainly true that, just as the generality of moth-flowers, destined to be visited at night, are white and scented, so the generality of bird-flowers are red.

And this scarlet of the bird-flowers, forced on them by natural selection, is in itself further dependent upon tropical conditions. For birds to exist whose staple of existence is provided by flowers, you must have a land where flowers can bloom all the year round. Not only that, but birds small enough to make a living out of flowers must be inhabitants of a warm climate, for in a cold one the relatively huge amount of surface which they expose would make it very hard for them to keep up their temperature.

The Ease of Seeing Big Game in East Africa. This Picture Was Obtained Without a Telephoto Lens Just before Sunset, Twenty-five Miles from Nairobi. We Left the City at Four, and Were Back Soon after Seven.

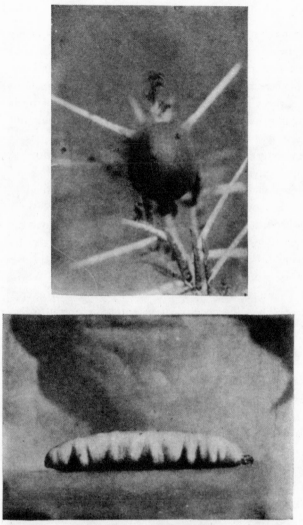

ANTS, WHITE AND OTHERWISE.
ABOVE, THE GALL OF A GALL-ACACIA. IT IS INHABITED BY A
COLONY OF ANTS, SOME OF WHICH HAVE RUN OUT TO
ATTACK THE INTRUDER WHO HAS JUST SHAKEN THEIR
HOME.
BELOW, A QUEEN TERMITE (WHITE ANT). HER HEAD AND
THORAX ARE ON THE RIGHT; ALL THE REST IS BLOATED
ABDOMEN, FULL OF EGGS.

SOME AFRICAN ANIMALS

If tropical warmth is one of the chain of causes which gives rise to sun-birds, honey-eaters, humming-birds, and the red flowers with which their existence is bound up, it has other more direct and more serious consequences. It encourages reptiles and insects at the expense of birds and mammals. Birds and mammals share a peculiarity which is one of the triumphs of evolution: their tissues are no longer subjected to the varying temperature of the outer environment, for they live in an internal environment whose temperature is constant. They not only possess their own heating system, but it is one whose heat is regulated. It is on this account that mammals and birds can penetrate far up into high latitudes, while reptiles and amphibia cannot. To take but one example, the British Isles possess three species of frogs and toads, and all North Central Europe under a dozen; East Africa, well over a hundred. The difference of mean annual temperature between North Europe and Central Africa is about 20° C.: and as a result the mean annual activity of a cold-blooded animal is about six times as great in Uganda as it is in Yorkshire. Thus it is no wonder that mammals and birds, while pre-eminent in temperate latitudes, have to share their supremacy with reptiles and insects in the tropics.

It is perhaps the insects that impress one most of all in Africa—the mere numerical quantity of them (where but in the tropics could you have lights put out by insects and run the risk of suffocation by them, as is narrated of the lake-fly?); their appalling variety (the layman perhaps does not grasp the fact that the number of kinds of African insect is to be reckoned not by mere thousands, but is of the order of magnitude of a hundred thousand; nor that dozens of new species are being discovered and described

367

every year); their ceaseless activity all the year round (for there is no winter, and the dry season is only a very relative check to their activity); and the number of them that are engaged in spreading disease, attacking crops, or otherwise damaging man and his property.

Africa's big animals have been photographed almost *ad nauseam*. I endeavoured to get pictures of some of these small creatures. One should, of course, have a great deal of time and patience for any sort of nature-photography but with a fixed programme I had no chance of searching for subjects, and could only take the rare opportunities that presented themselves. And even these I sometimes missed. I bungled a fine chance of five dung-beetles making themselves balls of dung out of a single piece of excrement; and owing to sheer laziness (no one who has not walked a long way under an equatorial sun knows the distaste for further expenditure of energy which one can thus acquire in Africa!) I failed to walk a quarter of a mile to get my camera for a picture of a river—there is no other word—of driver ants; and another day another quarter of a mile for about two hundred butterflies of about twenty different kinds, all drinking at one little patch of wet mud. But a very large praying mantis having flown into the rest-house one night, I secured him in a glass and made a portrait of him next morning. The mantids are among the relatively few carnivorous insects—a fantastic epitome of miniature but cruel voracity. And later I got a photograph of a large caterpillar still crawling about though covered with the white cocoons of ichneumon-flies, and therefore eaten out inside to little more than a walking shell—another horrible product of Nature's amorality, confutation in itself of all the sentimentalism about a purposeful and beneficent Creator.

It is, however, the ants and the termites which are the most wonderful small creatures of the tropics; and I secured one or two pictures of these. One of the most familiar sights in East Africa is gall-acacia scrub. Gall-acacias grow in dry, barren country; they are pretty when in leaf, and still more when covered with their little scented flower-balls; but for most of the year they are nasty little trees, anywhere from three to thirty feet high, armed with formidable spines an inch and a half long, and dotted over with peculiar black swellings the size of a large chestnut. These swellings are the galls, and they are almost invariably inhabited by living colonies of ants. Tap a gall, and out of the little entry-hole which they have gnawed there swarm a couple of dozen little black ants, to rush about angrily, with abdomen stuck straight up in air, looking for the intruder. There must be many millions of gall-acacias in East Africa; each acacia will bear scores or even hundreds of galls; and most of the galls will harbour dozens of ants.

There seems little reason to doubt that the ants help in protecting the plant. The thorns keep bigger animals from the leaves, while the ants deal with lesser enemies. There is also no doubt that the ants take on the rôle of guardians merely because they find convenient houses provided for them in the shape of the galls. But nobody knows for certain whether the acacia grows these structures unaided, or whether some irritation or secretion of the ants is needed to set the plant proliferating the gall, as that of other animals is needed for other galls. In favour of the latter alternative is the fact that now and again you see a gall-

acacia without galls, though growing in the midst of
gall-bearing trees.

Termites are more essentially tropical than ants; one has
no idea of their prevalence till one goes to a hot country.
Coming back from the Congo through Western Uganda,
we came round a corner into view of a plain extending
several miles and apparently covered with corn-stooks.
Corn-stooks—on the Uganda plains . . . it gave one a queer
feeling of unreality; but then suddenly we tumbled to the
fact that they were all termite-nests, hundreds upon hundreds of them, five or six feet high, spaced over the plain
at regular intervals of about thirty yards.

These were comparatively small nests; other kinds of
termites build nests fifteen feet high or more. One biggish
nest was dug open for me. It was exciting to see their
little underground gardens, chambers filled with the white
mass of the special fungus which they cultivate. And most
exciting of all was the royal chamber in which lives the
bloated queen, repulsive beyond all belief in her flabby
pink-whitishness. Her stretched skin is so translucent that
you have sight of tubes and strings floating about in the
liquid interior: one thanked God for the opacity of the
human abdomen. By her side is the king, her spouse, not
a hundredth of her bulk, but yet bigger than any of the
other misshapen specialists that make up a termite nation.
The natives call him the *askari*—the policeman. I took the
queen out and put her in a soap-dish for the night. She is
so tuned up to egg-production that she cannot restrain
herself; before morning well over a thousand eggs—little,
long-oval whitish things—had been laid by her.

Another peculiarity of ant and termite life in the tropics
is that with the intensity of competition many species have

taken to the trees, where they make compact nests either of rammed earth or of carton—chewed wood-pulp. None of the tree-termite nests that I examined had any of the typical soldiers, huge-jawed and massive-headed, which defend the ordinary ground nests. In their place there swarm out as defenders the most fantastic creatures, their heads swollen and drawn out into a neck like a phial. In point of fact, their heads *are* phials. They are filled with glands which secrete a horribly adhesive material, and their method of fighting is to squeeze some of this out at the hole at the tip of the phial-spout, thoroughly gumming up their enemies. They thus share with a few other insects, some sea-snails which use acid to dissolve the shells of their prey, modern men, and skunks, the distinction of having invented chemical warfare.

All worker termites—another fantastic and rather horrible fact—are white and pigmentless and cannot stand the light of day. In order not to waste any working time, however, they build tunnels of wood-pulp down the trunk of the tree so as to get at decaying wood and other food on the ground below. Break open one of these tunnels and you will see the double file of these wretched gnomes hurry away into safe obscurity.

Then protective coloration and mimicry, with the greater intensity of competition in the tropics, runs to a pitch beyond what one is accustomed to at home. Grey-brown grasshoppers pulled out to look like sticks, green grasshoppers striped like grass-leaves, brown grasshoppers with their bodies and legs all distorted to give them the semblance of a dead leaf on the ground, bugs modelled to seem like thorns or like seeds, spiders like bird-droppings, spiders mimicking ants, with their one pair of legs too many held out to simulate the antennae which they lack—the most casual search reveals wonder after wonder.

It is a matter of great surprise that more people in Africa do not take up some branch of natural history as a hobby. If you have the collector's instinct, there are still thousands of new species waiting to be discovered and described. There is always the chance of enduring fame— *aere perennior*—in having a new animal baptized *Smithi* or whatever your name may be. If you are more interested in the habits of living things and the meaning of natural phenomena, the unexplored field is much more vast and rich. And yet ninety-nine out of every hundred white men and women in Africa neglect all this, prefer to spend their superfluous energies on golf, tennis and bridge, and when not pining for their next leave home make their lives as faithful a copy as possible of what they would have been in a London suburb or an English county town, instead of taking advantage of the unique opportunities which Africa spreads before them.

Chapter XXXI

BIOLOGY, EMPIRE AND EDUCATION

I suppose a biologist can hardly help trying to apply his subject to the problems under his nose. Here in Africa to me the application of biology looms up second only to native policy in importance. Yet to most people biology has still a somewhat *outré* connotation. As a school subject it calls up visions of a few eccentric boys dissecting worms, frogs and other "types," making drawings of rabbits' bones, messing about with pickled specimens of odd appearance in a strong atmosphere of spirits, and looking through microscopes at the inhabitants of drops of dirty water. As a pure science it is often thought of either as a wilderness of monkeys and other organisms plastered over with Latin names, or as an elaborate system of knowledge and jargon concerned with a comparison of the more useless attributes of the more exotic animals and plants. Even in the sphere of evolution, where it has touched the popular imagination, there is plenty of misconception. The school-boy's celebrated *Short Essay on Evolution*—"Mr. Darwin said that the first monkey was a kind of jelly"—is a statement of the subject masterly in comparison with some current ideas; and the interest of most people begins to wander when the supposed relation between man and "the monkey" has been dealt with. And as an applied subject, the man in the street seems firmly convinced that biology begins and ends with insects.

Whatever mild justification there may have been for such an attitude thirty years ago, there is to-day no more foundation for it than for the older attitude, now happily a thing of the past, which preferred to sum up physico-chemical science in the one word "stinks." Biology is now no longer a group of subjects, but one closely knit and unified subject in which advance in any one branch means advance in every other. The working of animals and plants, their chemistry and their classification, their present distribution and past evolution, their individual development and their natural history in the field, their sexuality, their heredity, and their diseases—all are part of the one discipline.

And in applied biology the change has been equally great. Medicine, while never ceasing to be an art, has become largely the science of applied physiology. Mendel's principles are being applied in plant and animal breeding. You cannot grow crops, or keep yourself or your beasts healthy, especially in the tropics, without a knowledge of insects; and this knowledge demands not only central museums where the specialist can classify and identify the many hundred thousand kinds of insect, but also elaborate studies in field and laboratory of the life-history of insects, their enemies and parasites, of their interdependence with plants and soil. The study of the cycles of animal population which give us occasional vole plagues or lemming migrations is proving useful to the fur trade, to medicine, to the study of the weather, to protection of crops from pests such as locusts. The principles of heredity and evolution, it is just being realized, are important in human politics, and must be applied to man if his stock is not to de-generate. The future of fisheries depends upon the progress of our knowledge of the microscopic organisms that float near the surface of the sea. And so one might continue: there is not a field in which man is concerned with plants, animals, his own health or his own future, in which ap-plied biology has not a rôle to play.

In Africa this need for biological knowledge thrusts itself forcibly upon one: you cannot escape from biology. Here, for instance, is an area as big as Great Britain which is closed to human settlement because the tsetse-flies kill all the cattle; here is another, not quite so big, but big enough, in which other tsetse-flies are giving sleeping-sickness to human beings. Some of the best grazing coun-try is unavailable because of ticks which spread deadly disease. Without a knowledge of these creatures' life-his-tory and habits you will never be able to throw open these areas to cattle—and so relieve the pressure on the over-grazed tick-free areas where grass has been browsed away to nothing and the bare earth is showing. The most care-ful studies are needed to tell us whether some native meth-ods of agriculture are not better suited than ours to the peculiar conditions of the tropics. Native crops and native beasts have their merits; to raise them to their full possi-bilities, instead of merely importing other crops and other creatures, hit or miss, from other countries, is a pressing task.

What might you not do with the wild animals of the country? The patience and enthusiasm of the Belgians have demonstrated that the untameableness of the African elephant was a myth. But why can we not domesticate the zebra and the eland? Both are immune to tsetse; the zebra could take the place of the horse, the eland of the ox (in passing, elands are about twice the weight of good native cattle). People will tell you that the experiment has been tried; that the zebra is intractable, and that the eland, though readily tamed, has hooves too small to be of use as a draught-animal. But to modern genetics these are inconclusive objections. Given a well-endowed and permanent research institution, in which research could be pursued for generations, it should be readily possible through selective breeding to modify the zebra's temperament and the eland's toes.

Then preventive medicine in Africa is largely a matter of biology. Intestinal worms and malaria—every native has one or the other (or both); if you could clear them out of the majority of the population, you would have a new Africa, with a new outlook and new possibilities. Biology has given us the life-history of the hookworm and the malarial parasite; it remains to apply the knowledge. True that the application in practice is not simple; but without the foundation of biological knowledge we would be wholly impotent.

There there is the game question. Game in East Africa is already important as a financial asset, and will become increasingly so as more people come from all over the world to see the unique spectacle. Yet some would have the game destroyed as carriers of sleeping-sickness and cattle trypanosomiasis, others as destroyers of native crops and competitors with native cattle. To deal with the first difficulty, we need more knowledge of the behaviour of tsetse-flies or the parasites which they transmit—knowledge of the type which Dr. Duke is amassing at Entebbe; and we also need field experiments like that of Mr. Swynnerton in Tanganyika, to see whether game in a fly-free country can be kept from migrating to infested areas by game-proof fences. As regards the second point, we need the most careful studies of the food-habits and migrations of game (the Uganda Game Department in its dealings with elephants is beginning to set a standard, with its data on the size and movements of every herd in the country) and of their periods of abundance or decrease, which seem to run in cycles of about thirty years.

We jump to education, only to find that biology comes in here too. If we are to educate African children into being citizens of the world, we can only do it properly through making them better Africans. The first requisites here are the applied biology of agriculture and hygiene, the pure biology of African animals and plants in relation to African soil and climate, and the human biology of local village life expanding into geography and history. Not only that, but we need the educators themselves to have a background of biology so that they can think of the children for whom they are responsible, not merely as examination candidates, or as so many brats, tiresome or attractive as the case may be, or as eternal souls, but as so many growing human organisms.

Physics and chemistry, so vital to industrial countries, will long be subordinate sciences in a country where agriculture and human health are the two great problems. It is primarily on biology that the future of Africa depends; and the same is true of the rest of our tropical possessions.

What are we doing about it? The answer is, a good deal, but not enough. And the reason we are not doing enough is not in this case the much-abused Government, but the lack of men qualified to do what needs doing.

When I was in Africa I was asked if I could recommend anyone for an absolutely first-class research post just fallen vacant. I did my best, and so doubtless have many others; but after eight months that post is still vacant. If it had been in chemical or physical or medical work, it would have been filled in a few weeks. That is symptomatic. There is a shortage of biologists of all kinds, and an intense shortage of biologists of the first class. People seem so ignorant of the openings available for biologically-trained men in the Colonial service that it is worth while giving some figures. In each year from 1924 to 1928, over sixty new appointments were made of men with some biological training; and the numbers were increasing at the close. This is, of course, quite independent of the demand from the Dominions and the Sudan, and takes no account of biologists in the medical service. The chief demands are for agriculturalists, foresters, and veterinary officers. To secure a supply of these men, the Government has initiated various scholarship schemes, which again seem to be little known. About fifty of these are now given every year in agriculture, veterinary science, and related subjects like entomology and mycology, usually for two years at £250 a year; and the number of these awarded has been increasing steadily since the inception of the scheme in 1925.

These are bare figures; but the background of them is worth remembering. The agricultural or veterinary officer in Africa has not the same restricted scope as he would have at home. If he is engaged on research, the problems that open out before him are so varied, so untouched, and so numerous that he has much greater chance of arriving at results of striking practical importance; should he, beyond his work, make a hobby of some branch of botany or zoology, he has unlimited opportunities for indulging his taste for pure science. If he is on field-work, he will be thrown in contact with the natives, and every quality of insight and leadership which he possesses will be called into play. This is perhaps most especially true of veterinary work. Unfortunately, the veterinarian in Britain is still too often looked down on as a mere cattle-doctor or dog-surgeon. In Africa the prosperity and indeed habitability of enormous areas hangs upon his success or failure in research, and research along the broadest biological and medical lines. And to get his ideas carried into practice he must understand the natives' minds and their attitude towards cattle as the highest form of wealth. To be a good veterinary officer in Africa you must be a first-class biologist, and you must be a knowledgeable and sympathetic anthropologist as well.

It is not so many centuries since the surgeon was classed with the barber; it is within living memory that dentistry rose to the same professional status as medicine; it is now the turn of veterinary science to achieve its rise. Last year's report of Lord Lovat's Committee on the veterinary services abroad may well initiate the change.

Further, there are the openings in education. I can imagine no better career for a young man possessed of the missionary spirit, but untouched by the claims of orthodox religion or dogmatic creeds, than the African educational service. But a marked biological tendency is invading the African curriculum. Posts are being advertised for trained biologists to help the Departments realise the new ideas; and there is a demand for specialists to teach agriculture and hygiene.

It might be thought that a few years of propaganda would bring the stream of specialists for whom the colonies are asking. But pro-biological propaganda has been going on for years, and little or nothing happens. The school curriculum is too rigid, the university scholarship arrangements too unaccommodating.

But in any case, the provision of specialists would not be enough. Besides the biological specialists, we need some appreciation of biology on the part of the administrator and educator. Wherever I went in Africa I found such men lamenting that they had not been given a chance to learn something of biology at school, so that they would have some solid background against which to see what the specialist was after, some personal understanding of the broad problems involved.

This can only come about through making biology a part of general education, a cultural subject with whose facts and ideas, as with those of physics and chemistry, every boy in a public or secondary school must make acquaintance before he is sixteen and begins to specialize.

Nor is this a Utopian dream, fathered by a biologist's natural love of his subject. Schoolmasters to whom you broach the subject shake their heads and talk of overcrowded curricula. They appear to be entirely ignorant of what happens in other countries. A committee of the British Association recently prepared a report on biology in education. They found that Great Britain was one of the few important European nations where biology was *not* part of a general education!

Of course the thing can be done—but only by striking at the tyranny of early and excessive specialization, and by destroying the superstition which has tacitly arisen that "science" means physics and chemistry, and that biology is a sort of extra. Science is science, and biology is the half of it.

We might make a little progress if the school authorities would get it into their heads that the boy who is good at physics, mathematics and chemistry will, if he has not an active distaste for biology, be able to beat most of his competitors if he changes over to that subject, and will be entering an understaffed instead of an overcrowded profession.

There the matter lies. One would not have thought that the labours of the gentlemen who frame school certificate regulations and allot university scholarships were intimately connected with the future prosperity of Africa and the health of its native inhabitants; yet so it is. Meanwhile, until the ponderous educational machine gets adjusted, it is worth remembering that there are these posts crying out to be filled, and that to fill them adequately will be a service to the Empire, and to the native races under its flag.

Chapter XXXII

THE NATIONAL PARK OF THE BELGIAN
CONGO

As you follow the western of the two great Rift Valleys of Africa northward from Lake Tanganyika, you pass into strange country which was only penetrated by white men a generation back. Lake Kivu, highest and loveliest of the African Great Lakes, was not discovered until 1894. Lake Kivu lies at the south end of the territory I shall describe; Lake Edward at the north. Between the two the barrier of magnificent volcanic peaks which I mentioned in Chapter XXVI runs across the Rift—the Virunga volcanoes, which are fellow-claimants with Ruwenzori to be Herodotus's Mountains of the Moon. The lava-streams which they have thrown out are traceable below the present water-level of Kivu, and extend for thirty miles or so down the much longer stretch to Edward. Kivu is deep, clear, and lovely, but on the whole bare of life; Edward is low-lying, shallow, muddy, but teems with beasts, birds, and fish. Between Edward and the northern end of the lava-beds is a dry, hot plain, home of enormous numbers of buck, pig, buffalo, and other game.

The whole is enclosed between the two great fault-scarps of the Rift Valley, rising steeply from the plain to heights of seven, eight, and even ten thousand feet, but far overtopped by the great volcanoes between.

THE NATIONAL PARK OF THE BELGIAN CONGO

It is in this area that the Belgians have created a wonderful nature reserve, the Parc National Albert. As long ago as 1915 M. Hemeleers, the present (and first) Conservateur du Parc, urged that the Lake Edward plains should be made a game reserve. Shortly after the War, Carl Akeley, the American naturalist, was so struck by the beauty of the volcanoes and their forests, and the interest of the gorillas which inhabit them, that he made representations to the Belgian Government about the creation of a gorilla sanctuary; and the idea was favourably received. In 1926 he again visited the district with Dr. Derscheid, now Secretary of the Bureau International pour la Conservation de la Nature at Brussels, and they drew up a scheme for a national park. Akeley died of dysentery, and is buried up in the mountains he loved so well. But his work bore fruit, and the park is now an accomplished fact. Within its boundaries animal and plant life are safe; a bit of primeval Africa, with all its astounding wealth of contrast, is here preserved, let us hope for ever.

There are three foci of interest in the park. The central volcanoes are the first; they comprise the highest mountains, nearly 15,000 feet high, with their enormous forests, their gorillas and pigmies, their open uplands with fantastic African-alpine vegetation. The eastern volcanoes are the second. They are still active; in one of them a boiling cauldron of lava can be seen. The third is the southern end of Lake Edward; here, besides interesting fishermen tribes, there is a wonderful multitude of plains game, vast numbers of water-birds, and more hippo than anywhere else in the world, save perhaps near the Murchison Falls.

To reach the foot of Nyamlagira, where the lava-cauldron boils, you have to cross an appalling plain, made of successive lava-flows from the mountain. The latest flow is only twenty-five years old, and over it progression is laborious in the extreme; the lava is harsh and jagged, and you jump from block to block, with always the danger of twisting your ankle in the cracks. There is but one path available—the sole track, for thirty miles north of the volcanoes, which crosses the plain to the western hills —and this path involves a considerable detour. In addition, the path, like all native paths, winds about in the most maddening way, and so makes your journey at least half as long again as it need be. You see nothing, as you are always in woodland. But the place would have a great interest to ecologists. For the various lava-flows are of different age, and are in different stages of colonization by plants. The twenty-five-year-old flow has only scrub on it, others have immature woodland, while the oldest ones boast true forest.

Our porters were appallingly slow, and we, overtaken by night and a real tropical downpour in a place where it was impossible to drive a tent-peg into the lava, were forced to use the tent as a bivouac over a pole. Next morning Russell, my companion, was unwell; it turned out to be still eight hours merely to the foot of the mountain, and we had to be at our base again the day after. So we resentfully turned back, for six hours' lava-hopping in the rain.

For the gorilla-mountains we had four days; this time my wife was of the party too. The first took us to a village at the base of the real ascent. A party of pigmies armed with their queer little bows and arrows met us on the path. On the second day we made camp at 10,000 feet in the middle of the mountain forest. We rose through successive belts of vegetation, spending a weary two hours

EAST AFRICAN NATIVES.

LEFT, A KIKUYU GIRL; BRONZE HEAD BY DORA CLARKE. (*By courtesy of Miss Clarke.*) RIGHT, A HEADMAN AND HIS ATTENDANT AT KINANIRA, IN WESTERN UGANDA. THEIR SLIM BUILD IS DUE TO ADMIXTURE WITH THE ARISTOCRATIC WATUSI STOCK.

MORE EAST AFRICAN NATIVES.
ABOVE, TWO SOMALI CATTLE-TRADERS IN THE NATIVE MARKET,
NAIROBI.
BELOW, AN EDUCATED CHIEF FROM CENTRAL UGANDA. (*By
courtesy of Mr. R. E. Parry, Inspector of Schools for Uganda.*)

Transport on Lake Edward. Russell and the Belgian Game Warden in a Native Canoe. The Canoes Are Made of Bits of Bark and Are Punted. Hippopotamus Skulls Were Provided as Seats for the White Passengers.

GOOD-BYE TO THE WESTERN RIFT. A SUNSET VIEW OF MUHA-VURA (13,500 FEET), THE EASTERNMOST OF THE VIRUNGA VOLCANOES, FROM THE ESCARPMENT (8,000 FEET) ON OUR HOMEWARD JOURNEY.

in the mysterious but dank and gloomy bamboo-zone, slipping in the mud, scrambling over the stems which elephants had broken down across the path. Spoor of buffalo, elephant, lion, and leopard was everywhere; but we saw no life save a few monkeys. The monotony was relieved by patches of lovely pink orchids, and occasional white flowers, richly and muskily scented, which had dropped on to the path from unknown trees above.

Our camp was just above a rocky gorge which comes down in splendour from the peak of Mikeno. (Mikeno is the Matterhorn of the range, rising in forest-clad precipices to a rock peak which has only twice been climbed.) As we explored the gorge after tea, we heard a squealing grunt and a crash: a gorilla had seen us and was off. Next day, leaving our men to pitch camp at 11,000 feet, close to where Akeley is buried, we pushed on to the plateau on Karissimbi, where, at 12,000 feet, forest gives place to alpine meadow. On our way we saw the tracks and the dung of numerous gorillas, and found four or five groups of their "nests"—hollows on the ground, usually between the roots of a big tree lined with vegetation.

The ultimate forest-zone is extraordinary; as on all the great African mountains, you come first to tree-heather, rising gracefully to thirty feet or forty feet, and finally to a fantastic vegetation as of some other planet—tree-groundsels (*Senecio*) and bush-lobelias. A huge and solitary buffalo here lay chewing the cud; we got to within fifty feet of him, but he made off before we could take a photograph. At the foot of the final cone of Karissimbi we sat in the sun and watched the superb bell-like peak of Mikeno free itself of cloud, and Lake Kivu, pearl-grey in the distance, play hide-and-seek with the mists. Then (with how much regret!) we turned downhill. The evening of the next day (a very long one) we were back at our hospitable base, the White Fathers' Mission.

Lake Edward demanded at least six days. M. Hemeleers, the warden of the Park, kindly made this unforgettable trip possible. After leaving the road and passing some remarkable streams and jets of nearly boiling water, we emerged on to the game-plains. Here, in a little village, we camped. It was close to the Ruchuru River, which, like Lakes Kivu and Edward, is crocodile-free, and Russell and I found a delightful spot to bathe.

Next day, after a long and broiling march across the hot, dry plains, relieved by the sight of huge herds of topi (a relative of the hartebeest) and the beautiful Uganda cob, with reed-buck and wart-hog and monkeys thrown in, we reached a tiny village of fishermen on the shores of Lake Edward. Buck grazed within a hundred yards of our tents. A quarter of a mile away was a pond whither I repaired whenever I had a few minutes to spare; if you sat quiet there, even without a hide, the creatures would come down to drink. And at night the lions roared from far and near, as nightingales answer each other in Surrey.

But the lake is the fascination of the place. You are punted about in canoes which make dugouts seem liners. They are made of bits of wood or bark sewn together with vegetable fibre; somewhere or other an irregularity in the bark is sure to reduce the freeboard to a few inches; in most of them you have to bale at least half the time.

Leaving the village, you pass down a narrow arm of lake fringed by broad reed-beds. Malachite kingfishers—like ours, but smaller and deeper-coloured—fly past, pelicans swim majestically along, egrets and enormous goliath herons stand fishing in the reeds, terns hover and call. You pass the natives' fish-traps, and then out into a stretch half-overgrown with Nile cabbage and other weeds, upon whose precarious surface the jaçanas or lily-trotters run and the paddy-birds stand and fish. And then you turn a corner into what I named Hippopotamus Reach—a shallow bit of water, sheltered from the outer lake, stretching for almost a mile, and dotted in every direction with the heads of hippos. I did my best to count them. One day I counted 120, the next day 140, all in view at one time; but as they are always submerging, the real number must be well over 200. To see these delightful, plump, but active beasts—snorting and diving, yawning like huge pillar-boxes, fighting, playing, leaping half out of the water—is a revelation after the somnolent sausage-creatures of our zoos.

We landed on a bit of solid beach. Russell and I stripped, and with nothing on but our spectacles waded in up to our armpits towards a herd of twenty-five or thirty hippos. They let us come to almost a dozen yards, and floated there inquisitively gazing and puffing; further approach meant that the nearer ones dived and re-emerged at the back. It is a blessing that they are protected here: on Lake Albert, farther to the north, they are, I was told, being massacred in quantity to supply meat for native labour. These great creatures feed by night, and entirely on land. In the country round the lake their trails are everywhere, often leading half-a-dozen miles from water; you are reminded of the network of hare-tracks on an English chalk-down—but enormously magnified.

There are only two bits of open hard beach for miles among the mud and reeds; and here birds congregate in vast numbers. One is on the shore of Hippo Reach. As the canoes approach it, wave after wave of birds flies out—thousands of cormorants and darters, egrets and spoonbills, ducks and geese, several kinds of small wading birds, majestic pelicans. A few birds tolerate your landing; most lovely among these are the pied fantastic-legged stilts that the French call *chevaliers*.

And so, back—six days' hard walking and one of canoeing—to our car and civilization. My wife had the distinction of being the first white woman to walk to the south end of Lake Edward and back, instead of being carried in a litter.

The Belgians are building a big road all down the Edward-Kivu rift. It will link up with the Nile steamers in the north and with Lake Tanganyika on the south. They are planning a commercial town at the south of Lake Kivu, and a pleasure city, with huge hotel, casino, and the rest, at the north end. In five years' time, perhaps, the international rich will be arriving by road and air. But the pygmies will still be living their immemorial life; from their virgin forest fastness the gorillas will look down on the motor-boats and golf courses by the lake; the buck will graze within sight of the motorists; and the hippos, though within earshot of the traffic of the great road, will continue to browse and snort and bask in peace. For no shot may be fired in the Parc National, no man may enter without a permit.

Chapter XXXIII

RACIAL CHESS

I remember reading in one of the numerous books on Kenya and its problems that Sir Charles Eliot, High Commissioner for what was then a Protectorate, wrote in one of his despatches to the Secretary of State that now the Protectorate was thrown open to European civilization, we ought to face the eventual issue, which was that "White mates Black in a very few moves."

That was a quarter of a century ago. Sir Charles Eliot was responsible for initiating the process whose results he prophesied in these somewhat cynical words. But though he welcomed the white farmer on the spot, he could not stomach the idea (which would obviously tend to reduce the number of moves necessary in the check-mating process) of syndicates in London making money out of land speculation and absentee landlordism in Africa; and it was largely over this question that he was driven to resign.

But, one naturally enquires, is it really necessary to think in these terms? Are White's interests really inimical to Black's? Must the contact of two races result in the subjection of one?

This is the sort of question which one cannot help asking oneself as one travels through tropical Africa. Perhaps I should not be so sweeping. Judging by the books

which they write when they get home, many of those
who go to Africa (generally Kenya) for a more than usually exciting holiday, or for big-game shooting, never ask
themselves such questions at all; or if they do, they fail
to find them troublesome, since they seem incapable of
thinking of any status for the native but the *status quo.*
I should thus amend my sentence: I should have said
that no one who uses his imagination, and reflects on what
he sees, can fail to ask himself such questions, especially
if he has any historical background to his thinking.

What are we really in Africa *for?* Have we any clear
idea, as a nation, of what we think or hope the country
will be like in fifty or a hundred years' time? I am not
at all sure that we have. Some of us have not got any
ideas at all on the matter; and the ideas of those who have
them are so diverse that they cancel out.

There is one point which needs mention before getting
to the main issue. The usual view of most administrators
and practically all settlers is that you should trust the
man on the spot. He knows, by arduous experience, what's
what; the stay-at-homes of Whitehall and elsewhere don't
know, and even if they bestir themselves to come out and
see for themselves, their visits are so short and superficial
that they still don't know the real inwardness of anything.
Unfortunately, however, when you try to erect the trusting
of the man on the spot into a principle, you find that it won't
work. It won't work, simply because it isn't a principle
at all. The men on the spot differ a great deal in their
ideas according to individual temperament, and still more
according to profession; administrators, settlers and missionaries, though all on the spot, tend each to have their own
very distinct set of ideas. Even when there exists some

quite general consensus of opinion, a very little perusal of history will show that this too may change, often with surprising rapidity.

The man on the spot has his unique fund of experience, which must, of course, be drawn upon and taken into account, together with the ideas which arise out of his experience, when policy has to be framed. But just for the very reason that he is on the spot, you must not expect principles of long-range policy from him. He is too much concerned with practical adjustments in a makeshift changing social order; he is immersed in the troubled waters of On the Spot, and inevitably finds it difficult to get his head out and take a general survey. If the greater world of home cannot have his advantage of detailed knowledge of local problems, neither can he, save in the rarest cases, have the balanced and general view of principles to which dispassionate observation from nearer the centre of things may help a man. When business on hand is so pressing, he must in the nature of things always find it hard to think in long-range terms, and his great difficulty is not to take things for granted.

Even the casual visitor like myself finds it difficult to escape the *genius loci*; the intellectual climate enfolds him, and because almost everyone he meets tacitly makes the same general assumptions, he very often falls into the current way of thinking. It is only when he gets away again and finds that other people live in other intellectual climates and have quite other ideas on the subject, that many of the local assumptions are seen to be really assumptions, and that he begins to try to think in terms of fundamentals instead of principles of minor scope—or rather, that what he had thought to be fundamentals now turn out to have other foundations below, which too need examining.

There are, of course, very different ideas at the back of policy in different parts of East Africa—in Kenya and in Tanganyika, for instance. In Kenya, policy is coloured by the presence of several thousand private white settlers, for whom the black man exists primarily as a source of labour-supply, a mere adjunct in the business of European profit-making. It is, I think, quite fair to say that well over nine-tenths of the non-official European population of Kenya think that as many as possible of its black population should be directly or indirectly compelled to work for the white, and that when not so engaged they should be encouraged to live their immemorial life in Reserves set apart for that purpose; and that they should be discouraged from growing crops in competition with their white neighbours, from all political aspirations, and from all but utilitarian and technical education.

In Tanganyika, on the other hand (and the same with differences of detail applies to Uganda) there are no Native Reserves, since the whole territory is regarded as essentially a native country, with a few white settlers allowed in here and there. The natives are encouraged to produce all kinds of crops for export, but the authorities are not particularly worried if some of them prefer simply to support themselves, so long as they pay their tax. And they are encouraged to take over as much self-government of the local sort as they can manage. In the one territory the first place is occupied by the natives and their affairs; in the other (whatever may be the pronouncements of visiting Commissions as to "native interests being paramount") it is as a matter of hard fact occupied by the Europeans and their affairs, although there is only one non-official European to every three hundred or so natives.

But even where, as in Tanganyika, the administration is taking most seriously, the idea of white trusteeship for the native population, the full implications of the idea are veiled and obscured by various current assumptions which are felt rather than thought out, and felt as so self-evident that they are hardly ever questioned. The chief such assumption is that black men are in their nature different from white men and inferior to them. The second is that since white men know how to do a great many things of which black men are ignorant, they therefore know what is best for black men and are entitled to lay down what they ought to do and how they ought to live. The third, continuing the second, is that natives should develop "along their own lines"—their own lines being those on which there is the greatest possible taking on of European useful arts; the least possible taking on of European ways of dress or ways of general thought; the least danger of their claiming or obtaining political, social or intellectual equality with Europeans; the greatest chance of perpetuating the gulf between the races. The fourth is economic: it is that production for export is virtuous, while production merely for your own local consumption is not—and is, indeed, rather reprehensible.

It is, of course, the first of these assumptions which is the most fundamental. The second is really a *non sequitur*; the third, if partly inspired by a recognition that our own social order is not such an unqualified success that we wish to inflict it upon others, is for the most part a device, perhaps unconsciously adopted, to prevent our superiority from being mocked by imitation or even threatened by real attainment. And the fourth has behind it the idea that, Britons being Britons and natives being natives, it is better that natives should moil and toil if by so doing more Britons are kept busy making cotton print and bicycles to be exchanged against this native surplus of food, rather than that the natives should be self-sufficing and have more leisure; and of course it is also linked with the idea that a native should have as little leisure as possible.

But they are all really corollaries or consequences of the first and greatest assumption, of black's considerable and inherent inferiority to white. And this in its turn is based on something more fundamental still—race and class prejudice, and the all but universal human tendency either to exploit or to patronize those who have less power and less knowledge than ourselves.

It is, I repeat, exceedingly hard to resist making these and similar assumptions. But are they true?

It is very difficult to think dispassionately where one's feelings are aroused; and major racial differences certainly can arouse feeling. I remember once, in central Texas, arriving by car in a little town whose streets were crowded (it was market day), and crowded almost wholly by negroes; there were hundreds of black men to tens of white. I am bound to confess that this first experience of mine of being in a small minority among human beings of another colour and another physical type gave me an emotional jolt; and I began, without any process of ratiocination, to understand why white men living in such circumstances generally took to carrying revolvers and developed a race-complex. One could doubtless get over such feelings; but the point is that they arose unbidden.

Again, the abolitionist North in America has always

decried the South for its discrimination against the negro on colour grounds alone. But when, after the Great War, crowds of negroes poured into the Northern states, racial feeling was at once aroused. To take but one example, coloured gentlemen who presumed to take houses in the respectable residential quarters of Chicago were reminded of their complexion, and their presumption, by the arrival of bombs through their drawing-room windows. Southern cynics could hardly be expected not to smile.

It is difficult to think dispassionately; but we ought to try. In the first place, let us sedulously remind ourselves that "native" in Africa is an omnibus term, embracing the most diverse racial types. Leaving out of account the pigmies and the bushmen, there is at least as much difference between a typical Bantu and a typical West Coast negro as between a typical Scandinavian and a typical Sicilian; and between either and a typical Hamite such as a Masai there is a much greater difference. It is a commonplace of anthropology that many single territories of tropical Africa, such as Nigeria or Kenya, contain a much greater diversity of racial type than all Europe.

Let us also remember that "race" is in any case a term of mere convenience to help in pigeon-holing our knowledge of human diversity. The term is often used as if "races" were definite biological entities, sharply marked off from each other. This is simply not true. In a community like that of the human species, in which interbreeding is possible between each and every variety, and migration has been the rule since the earliest times, long before the beginning of recorded history, such entities cannot exist. In their place, modern views of heredity set the idea of a collection of genes, as Mendelian inheritance-factors are now generally called, which changes as you pass over the world's surface. Any given "race" is characterized by containing within its boundaries a certain assortment of genes. One racial assortment will differ from another in the nature and proportionate abundance of the different kinds of genes of which it is made up, and every race will share some genes with many other races, probably with all. Through Bantu, semi-Hamite, and Hamite there is every gradation between negro and full white. Through the importation of slaves to Greece and Rome, the cosmopolitan nature of the late Roman Empire, and the Saracen invasions, the Mediterranean "races" of Europe contain many genes imported from Africa during the historic period, just as many "white" genes are drifting through the population of Africa as a result of the commercial and military penetration of North Africa by Europe at various stages of its history, and of the unions of Arabs and Europeans with native women all over the continent.

However, the *average* differences which do exist between races are real enough, and have often a definite biological significance. Negroes are black or dark brown, have wider nostrils and more sweat glands than Europeans; and all these characters are adaptive in that they fit their possessors to a tropical climate. Be it remembered, though, that even average racial characteristics may be and usually are slowly changing.

But, finally, there is no reason whatever for supposing any existing race to be the last word in adaptation or evolutionary progressiveness; and the science of heredity makes it clear that out of the crossing of two distinct types we shall obtain numerous new combinations, some doubtless poorer than what we had before, but others quite possibly more efficient either in local adaptations or in more general ways. If improved types come into being at all, selection can see to it that they will increase at the expense of others during the generations.

Race, in fact, is a complicated subject. To pretend that it is simple and clear-cut is self-delusion, and leads among other things to the unfortunate dissemination of much pseudo-science, of which the great Nordic myth, so sedulously propagated by Houston Stewart Chamberlain and various American authors, is the most obvious example.

Coming back to Africa after this digression, we find that, quite apart from any racial or inherited differences, there exists enormous diversity of social organization. Side by side in one territory may be found three of the primary ways of human life—the hunter, the nomad herdsman, and the agriculturalist; and among the agricultural tribes are to be found all varieties of social organization from the most primitive up to strong monarchies like those of the Bahima in Uganda, the Watusi in Ruanda, or the Bushongo in South Congo, with graded hierarchy of rank, a copious and elaborate court ceremonial, and a strong flavour of feudalism. Here again the diversity is at least as great as in Europe, and in some ways greater.

Among this heterogeneous collection, some certainly look of lower type than others. I have seen negroes as low in forehead as Blake's "Man who built the Pyramids," and with huge prognathous faces on which the squat nose projected scarcely more than an ape's; physically at least these were a good deal more primitive than anything to be seen in Europe, and the presumption is that they are primitive mentally too. Some tribes, both Bantu and true Negro, have

397

a much higher proportion of men with primitive build of face and skull than others; and then there are races like the pigmies and the bushmen, who are generally acknowledged to be descendants of earlier and more primitive buddings of the human stock. But all that concerns us in thinking broadly of Africa is the average, and the average among the more widespread and successful tribes.

In East Africa, for instance, it is the average man among the Kikuyu, Masai or Wakamba, Kavirondo, Baganda or Wanyamwezi, on whom we must concentrate our attention. Is he, or is he not, inferior in innate capacity to the average Italian or Scotchman, Serb or German, Greek or Russian? and if so, is the difference great enough to warrant his being treated permanently as a creature on a different level?

The answer is unfortunately that we do not know; and we shall not and cannot know until and unless we have observed and experimented for several generations. There are, however, a number of arguments on both sides; and if we spend a little time considering them, we may be able to reach some provisional conclusions, strong enough to support policy in the immediate future.

The most telling count against the African is perhaps that of history. It is a striking and really rather depressing fact that he has never discovered written language, the use of the plough, or the art of building in stone. To the latter statement Zimbabwe is the exception which proves the rule. It is true, as the latest investigations clearly show, that Zimbabwe and the other similar Rhodesian stone buildings are products of the native African, and only a few hundred years old; but it is probable that the stimulus to their erection came from Arab and other traders, and certain that the art died out without leaving any trace.

Against this it may be said that we do not expect so many inventions in a tropical country. When scratching the ground with a hoe gives quite good results, there is not the same urge towards the invention of ploughs; where the climate is always warm, there is not the same need for better methods of building. Further, even if we do not agree with the extreme diffusionist school of anthropologists, it seems abundantly clear that major inventions are rare in early stages of human culture, and that there is no particular reason to suppose that even the most intelligent peoples would have made all the important inventions had they been kept isolated from the rest of mankind. Some might have failed to think of ploughs, others of an alphabet, others of wheels, and so on. And finally, even if negro inventors had arisen, or outside inventions had penetrated into Africa, the country itself is against progress. The excessive luxuriance of nature, the heat of the climate, the prevalence of insidious and chronic disease, combine with the ease of gaining some reasonable livelihood with very little effort, and the uniformity of the seasons, where no winter forces men's thoughts in upon themselves. The sum-total of these influences makes it less likely for inventions, even were they made, to be seized upon and spread, than in more temperate regions.

Relevant here, too, is the statement, often made, that the negroes in the United States have not made contributions to the national life proportionate to their number, and that those American negroes who have attained distinction almost invariably possess an admixture of white blood, though ranking as "negro" to the inflexible race prejudice of America. The first part of this criticism must be largely discounted owing to this very fact of colour prejudice, which makes it far harder for a negro than for a white man to rise to wealth or eminence. There would appear to be more truth in the second assertion, though here again it is hard to know how much to ascribe to the restlessness and "divine discontent" generated by racial discrimination in the minds of those who are in a measure outcast from both parental stocks, without any racial spiritual home.

In any case, the point is really not relevant to our consideration of Africa, since the Bantu, and still more the Hamatic peoples, have a considerable proportion of more or less "white" and quite definitely Caucasian blood in their make-up.

Then there is the general impression, reinforced by the positive testimony of men who have lived for decades in close contact with the native African, that he is on the whole irresponsible, improvident, and lacking in the higher ranges of intelligence. This is largely offset by the equally impressive testimony of the same men in favour of the negro's loyalty, his cheerfulness and gaiety even under trying conditions (General Smuts speaks of the negroes as the only happy race in the world), his fine physique and physical courage. But in so far as the accusation is true, it would obviously keep the negro back from the higher achievements of civilization, to attain which a combination of foresight, intelligence, and pertinacity is needed.

The evidence of intelligence tests has been adduced to support the assertion of negro inferiority in brains; but no intelligence test has yet been devised which will discount really large differences of home environment and early training. The only such tests I know of which begin to be scientifically admissible are those of Davenport, who in the West Indies tested various poor whites, negroes and mulattoes all living under closely similar economic and social conditions. His findings were that the negro average of pure intelligence was definitely but slightly below the white, and that the negro was rather more emotional and excelled in certain tests indicative of artistic appreciation. In every test, however, both races showed a wide range of variation, and over most of the ranges the members of the two races overlapped.

On the other side may rightly be adduced the fact of the negro's extraordinary vitality in Africa, in spite of disease, in spite of enervating tropical climate, in spite of slave-raiding and alien denomination. This inherent vigour, expressed visibly for all to see in the magnificent physique of so many tribes, is a first-rate asset of the race; and it is not merely vigour in general, but vigour in the trying conditions of Africa. Besides this, there is the fact that in very various tribes there do arise men of high distinction and intelligence, whose foresight and will enable them to achieve remarkable results. In addition to the well-known examples from Zulu history, one may mention Lenana, the celebrated medicine-man of the Masai, or Rindi, the prince who united the Chagga. And besides these outstanding personalities, there are plenty of others possessed of very real character or ability, above the average for any race whether white or black, to be found scattered among the tribes. Powys, in his *Black Laughter*, mentions a Kikuyu strongly endowed with artistic impulse and talent; the present Sekibobo of Buganda is a distinguished orator with a fine and balanced character; I have seen a native teacher

with a passion and genius for teaching which would have
satisfied the heart of Sanderson of Oundle; I have spoken
of the little Kavirondo hunchback with an innate gift for
machinery; the mere existence of the Colour Bar Bill in
South Africa proves that the Bantu are sufficiently able to
learn skilled occupations to compete on terms of reasonable
equality with the skilled white artisan;—and so one might
go on.

Then it is very frequently stated that the African is incapable of profiting by education to the same extent as
the white. He is said to acquire patchy and unrelated bits
of knowledge, to lack determination and intellectual initiative, and in spite of marked intelligence in childhood to
fall off gravely at puberty. On this last question I made a
point of asking for information; and the general and indeed almost unanimous consensus of opinion among those
who were concerned with teaching was as follows: A fall-
ing-off of intelligence among native boys at puberty does
exist, and is widespread. But it is not universal; and it is
not inevitable. In the existing state of native culture, sex
looms large, and at puberty comes to occupy the focus of
life. If you can provide native boys with a different background of thought and practice, their intellectual development can continue through puberty with no more break
and disturbance than overtakes the average white child,
and can continue and mature as with us. Gandhi in his
autobiography speaks of the obsession of sex which overtakes Indian boys as a result of marriage soon after puberty,
and how it is only the practice of sending the girl-bride
home for several months of the year which releases the
young husband's thoughts and energies for work and
thought; and the point is relevant to our purpose.

The evidence seems clear that in Africa the difficulty, though real, could be surmounted, wholly or in part, by a changed background.

Similarly the criticism that the African acquires only a patchy knowledge and a patchy character as the result of European methods of education is very insecurely grounded. Such results are undoubtedly produced; but they are produced by an educational system which is itself patchy. The two great difficulties of education in Africa at present are, first, the difficulty of getting children young enough and educating them continuously enough; and secondly, the extraordinary gulf between the mental outlook of the untouched tribal native and that which dawns upon him through education. At the risk of tediousness, it needs reiterating that we Europeans can hardly imagine the extent of this gulf. In Europe even the poorest slum-dweller or the inhabitant of the remotest country village is brought up in an atmosphere which simply assumes reading and writing, books and newspapers, cinemas and wireless, steam and petrol, centralized government, scientific enquiry, an organized tradition of development through the centuries. To the primitive African this is all new, startlingly and often indeed almost meaninglessly new. It is a violent invasion of his mental country. His atmosphere had been unreflective, unprogressive, local, both in time and space. The true idea of science, whether as spirit of free enquiry or as controller of nature for man's use, is alien to his thought. He has no history; and his tradition, instead of being an organic body of thought, is crystallized into a body of rules and observances extraneous to his inner life. Reading and writing still can appear to him in full freshness as a magic key to new realms and powers.

The gulf is so great that it is extremely hard to bridge. To change the metaphor, the educated African is generally riding two horses at once; and we all know how hard that is. It is for this reason that in their education they should be caught young and kept long; for only so can we reasonably hope to build up a coherent inner life related to the new information, new ideas, and new power we so recklessly pour upon them. It is only when boys can be put to school as early as we put ours, and kept under some civilizing influence till well after puberty, that we have the right to expect a unified product with no dislocation of the soul. And when that happens, we often do get the expected result. But before we can expect the result to be general, the cleavage between home background and school outlook must be diminished; and this can only happen when a couple of generations of education have provided a new background, in the shape of educated parents.

As we have passed from one argument to another, we have found pros and cons more or less balanced; and we are back at general principles and probabilities. The net result is that we cannot appraise the African's capabilities in any accurate or scientific way until he has had several generations in which to demonstrate what they are. Meanwhile we need some provisional view on which to take action. We shall at any rate not go wrong if our conclusions are along the following lines.

In the first place, we may grant to the believers in negro inferiority the possibility of being right. Human beings do differ very considerably in inherent mental capacities and potentialities, in spite of the sentiment of Rousseau and the Perfectibilists, the political prejudice of certain left-wing theorists, and the nonsense talked about heredity by some psycho-analysts and the whole Behaviourist school. And there is not the least reason why races should not differ in the average of their inborn mental capacities as they do in their physical traits. In fact, there is every reason to suppose that such mental differences do exist. On biological grounds they *should* exist. As Huntington has lucidly pointed out in his book, *The Human Habitat*, every big change in way of life, every mass migration, every partial migration such as that from Southern Ireland to the United States, from the country to the towns, that of the Huguenots to England, or of the Pilgrim Fathers to America, is selective in its action, and will change the average composition of the populations concerned in regard to mental qualities such as temperament and initiative.

There is also a certain amount of evidence that the negro is an earlier product of human evolution than the Mongolian or the European, and as such might be expected to have advanced less, both in body and mind, than they. And in the tropical countries to which he has been restricted during thousands of years, there seems to be little driving force of selection to push the level of mental qualities upwards. Popular belief and the few properly-conducted mental tests point in the same direction.

I am quite prepared to believe that if we ever do devise a really satisfactory method of measuring inborn mental attributes, we shall find the races of Africa slightly below the races of Europe in pure intelligence and probably certain other important qualities.

But—and the but is a big one—I am perfectly certain that if this prove to be so, the differences between the racial averages will be small; and that they will be *only* an affair of averages, and that the great majority of the two populations will overlap as regards their innate intellectual capacities.

How they will prove to overlap one cannot say. It might be that the overlap was symmetrical, so that five per cent., say, of Africans were below the European minimum, five per cent. of Europeans above the African maximum. Or both might start at the same minimum, but the European reach further upward. Or it might even be that the arithmetical average for the two was the same, and the Europeans extended both further downwards (through possessing a larger proportion of mental defectives), but also further upwards; even in such case, however, their possession of a small number of exceptionally-gifted minds would more than compensate for the extra quantity of defect, and they would be inherently the better race.

But if there is this broad overlap and the bulk of African people are, as there is every reason to believe, just people, no better nor worse than the bulk of white or yellow people, though perhaps rather different in average quality, than they can be transformed by education, by social environment and tradition in ways so radical as to be beyond the imagination of their detractors, and perhaps beyond that of their well-wishers too. It is a hackneyed parallel, but none the less a salutary one, to remind ourselves of Julius Caesar and the Britons and Teutons with whom he fought. Their organization was not quite so primitive as that of the ordinary African tribe; none the less, it is more than doubtful whether Caesar, seeing their barbarian ways, ever dreamt of their rising to found great world-powers, pre-eminent in war, government and every attribute of civilization.

There are people who will admit the aptness of the parallel, but insist that to effect a corresponding change with the Africans will take a corresponding number of Millennia. This, however, is a fallacy. Man does not owe his culture to his physical heredity, nor does civilization leak slowly into the hereditary constitution. He owes his culture primarily to his upbringing. True that he imbibes a great part of it unconsciously, but this soaks into his individual being from his social ambience. It does not take generations of culture to make a man capable of appreciating Shakspere or Plato: how many evidences to the contrary have there not been among poor and uneducated workers in this country alone? And there have already been numerous examples in Africa of native chiefs possessed of unusual talents and foresight who have greedily sucked in Western ideas and imposed them, often very successfully, upon the people under their charge.

Rare Africans of exceptional ability may indeed profit so fully by the education they can now pick up, that they will step from barbarism to civilization, both in thought and practice, during their own single lives; but most natives either do not start their education early enough or have not the requisite mental freshness (most white people in similar circumstances would find the same difficulty), and so only arrive at a half-way stage. This halfway stage is doubtless very unsatisfactory and trying in itself. But at least those who are in it have some background of Western ideas; and thus their children have their baby minds formed in relation to this and not to the background of untouched tribal life, wholly alien to what they will meet with in their education. Thus they grow up without that breach of continuity, that necessity to bridge an all but unbridgeable gap, which is the lot of the first generation of natives exposed (I used the word advisedly) to education; and it is only among *their* children, of the third generation, that you can expect a reasonable stability of mental life.

Those are considerations affecting the single family; when it comes to the population as a whole, quantity comes in too. If the present state of affairs continues, in which only about ten per cent. of native children get any education whatever (and perhaps two or three per cent. any education worthy of the name), we shall naturally not arrive at that general background of changed ideas from which alone a new social tradition can spring. Unless at least half the parents have been educated, you cannot expect the new generation to be able to profit fully by its education and to grow up in stable inheritance of the new traditions of thought and life. And when I say parents, I mean parents of both sexes, mothers as well as fathers. The education of the native women of Africa is in many ways more important, as it is in many ways more difficult, than the education of African men. And if boys' education, though well started, has only touched a fraction of the future fathers of Africa, girls' education has scarcely been envisaged on a systematic scale.

Thus, while three generations is the minimum time which must elapse before we have a right to expect an answer to our experiment of educating the African, in actual practice the expansion of the educational system to cover the majority of the population, female as well as male, will take so long that four or five generations will certainly be needed. It is thus that the transmission of human thought simulates the inheritance of acquired characters.

It may be that at the end of that time we shall find the experiment has not worked. There may be in the African races some little defect or kink of temperament which will prevent them utilizing the new ideas as another race could have done—some unadventurousness of spirit, some lack of continued purpose, some mental laziness, some failure to achieve the higher reaches of thought. If that should be so, the problem of their future relation with the rest of the world will be a difficult one and will need to be considered afresh. But we need not think of crossing bridges before we come to them—especially if we do not know whether they exist. And in any case, two things are certain. One is that, as we have embarked on the experiment of educating the native, it is our business to push on intensively and get an unequivocal answer from it. The other is, that if we do push on with it, and if we do not nullify our efforts at providing the natives with a stable background of thought and idea by political or economic policies leading to racial bitterness, the result, whether African civilization and thought achieve the heights or remain mediocre, will be remarkable enough and will astonish all but the most visionary and sanguine of the present generation.

In passing, the proviso in my last sentence is important. You cannot expect a people to make a really good job of becoming civilized if while you proffer Western ideas with one hand you take away the fruits of them with the other. If Europe thrusts disabilities upon Africa, she cannot expect Africa to develop with that fullness or serenity which might be hers if there were no bitterness to rankle in her soul.

But there can be no point in prolonging such speculations about the future: sufficient unto the day . . . Looked at in a long perspective, our racial chess is seen to be very different from the simple game of white versus black which it appears to the eye of immediate exploitation. The question of the inferiority or equality of black to white sinks for the time into the background. Because what most believers in African inferiority mean is the inferiority of the untouched pagan or the present disoriented detribalized native to the civilized European; and what most believers in equality mean is something unreal, based on mystical ideas about the soul or the brotherhood of man. What concerns us at the moment is the improvability of the black; and this is an undoubted fact. When we have seen how far it can lead, it will be time to debate the older question afresh.

Chapter XXXIV

POLITICAL ISSUES

The visitor to East Africa is so struck by the diversity of the tribes and their way of life, as well as by the difference in the history, status, and administrative practice of the separate territories, that he wonders whether any formulation of a native policy for the region as a whole, which has often been proposed as a prerequisite to federation, is possible in the immediate future. Would it not be better, he thinks, should federation be decided upon, to lay on the Governor-General as one of his primary duties the task of surveying the field, and at the end of five or ten years, during which he would naturally have been endeavouring to adjust differences and apply principles, of reporting on the detailed lines of a joint native policy for the federation?

Here, again, escape from the local atmosphere conduces to a change of mind. Why should this grave responsibility be laid on the shoulders of one man? Too much would depend on the accident of the appointment. Nor would he be in the least likely to evolve any brand-new principles of policy. These principles have been fully discussed in books like Lord Lugard's *The Dual Mandate in Africa*, and various works by French and Belgian administrators; in the histories of different territories we can read the effects of this or that policy or lack of policy. In the matter of principles, in fact, London already has at its command all the resources of knowledge and experience needed to come to a decision. A decision has to be arrived at, and ought to be arrived at soon. And if there is to be federation, the Governor-General will have difficulties enough without being called on to make decisions for which the real responsibility lies after all with the people of these islands.

The difficulty, of course, with decisions of principle is to keep them elastic of application without leaving them so vague in interpretation that they can be stretched to the degree of meaninglessness. We need a golden mean between detailed prescription and mere general sentiments.

For example, the assertion that "native interests must be paramount," which was first used, I believe, in the White Paper of 1923, and has figured prominently in all subsequent discussions of East Africa, or the statement embodied in the League of Nations Covenant whereby the Powers agree that the "well-being and development" of the population in Mandated Territories "form a sacred trust of civilization"—these are principles of the utmost importance, and yet so vague as to be of little more than negative value.

Their observance will, it is true, make it impossible for white civilization to repeat some of the abuses which have sullied its past dealings with races at a lower level— the battues by which British settlers exterminated the Tasmanians; the shooting-out, in quite recent years, of the Tierra del Fuegians by white flock-masters; the forced labour imposed by the Spaniards on the conquered Indians to work the mines of Peru; the slaveries, real or virtual, and the cruelties attendant (within living memory) on the commercial exploitation of Africa by Belgians, Portuguese and Spanish; the sending of the United States soldiers to shoot down bison in order to force the Red Indians into the reserves, where degeneration was their usual fate.

Direct enslavement, exploitation, and massacre are ruled out. And something positive is implied—some attempt at peaceful and orderly administration, some provision for improved public health, some sort of education. But, beyond this, individual interpretation can have full play. If, for instance, the principle of paramountcy be interpreted merely in terms of vague and general benevolence, it amounts to nothing. If, on the contrary, it be taken to mean wherever white interests and native interests conflict the latter shall always prevail, it inflicts a real injustice on the white population (and, rightly or wrongly, the white population of our African dependencies have got it into their heads that this is what the present Government means by the phrase). But if it means that since in tropical Africa there are hundreds of blacks to one white, and since the blacks are the original inhabitants and must continue to make up the great bulk of the population, therefore, while the interests of both races should always be taken into account, those of the natives should have a prior claim,—then it inflicts no injustice, but acts as a useful general principle, which may be argued about but should not arouse any bitter feeling. But, even so, a more detailed interpretation will still be necessary before it can be put into practice.

There are many people who quite sincerely believe that the most valuable lessons which natives can learn come from their association with white men and their methods, and that accordingly the real interests of the natives are most paramountly served by setting more and more of them to work as labourers on European estates. There are others who, again quite sincerely, believe that natives will be on the whole less happy if they learn to read and write, grow civilized and think politically, and who therefore would make native education severely and solely practical. In the same way the "development" of native peoples can be interpreted in a hundred different ways to suit current ideas and prejudices. And further, in many cases these vaguely benevolent principles are interpreted on the fatal assumption that the white man always knows what is best for the black man, that the native must not be allowed to make experiments in case he makes mistakes, and that benevolent European guidance should prescribe the exact course of the natives' development even if what it prescribes is by no means always what they want.

The Hilton Young Commission (pp. 39-41 of their Report) seized upon this phrase concerning the paramountcy of the interests of the natives, and saw that it needed defining. "It might perhaps be argued," they write, "that the phrase attempts no more than to indicate the general spirit in which the policy is to be applied, and that it is a mistake to endeavour to define too closely what it means. It appears to us, however, that nothing is more important than that there should be a clear idea now and at each stage of development what British policy both as regards natives and immigrants is to be, and that this policy should be affirmed not merely as that of one political party, but with the concurrence of all." This is a weighty pronouncement, and in what follows I have tried to trace out its implications in my own way.[1]

[1] This chapter was written before the publication of the recent Colonial Office White Paper on Native Policy in Africa, which sets out to define

It is on this account that further and more detailed principles are needed. We have one of them already to hand in the League Covenant, which expressly envisages the Mandatory Powers exerting their authority until, and indeed in order that, the native population shall become capable of self-government. I am perfectly aware of the fact that a great many people regard this as "mere eyewash." But we have put our national signature to the treaty which embodies the promise, and it lies upon us as a solemn obligation. Those on the spot, especially those unconnected with Government, are indeed preponderantly against the idea, and against the possibility of its realization (a regrettable cleavage here opening between colonial opinion and home opinion, which on the whole—though doubtless rather vaguely and with some scarcely conscious reservations—accepts the principle).

The usual shift for avoiding the obligation is a simple and natural one. It is to assert that it will be an extremely long time before native people are even approximately ready for self-government (somewhere about the Greek Kalends, it is often hoped and hinted), and that meanwhile the best thing is merely to go on governing them by the methods that have been found effective in the past for keeping subject races in their place.

It is precisely here, however, that we need to make our vague general principles more precise—to work out their consequences and set them down in official black-and-white. Throughout we can, and indeed must, make the

---

the detailed principles of policy very much as here suggested. As the question is of such importance, and as in many ways the treatment of the subject in the White Paper differs from that adopted here, I have thought it best to let the chapter stand as it was written, save for a few minor additions.

415

assumption that the language of the Covenant about Mandated Territories expresses the best opinion of the nations upon the treatment and the future of native populations under white control, and that accordingly we should endeavour to apply it to all other similar territories that happen not to be mandated (where they are administered as protectorates or colonies or under chartered companies).

The points on which dispute is now most violent and practice most divergent, and on which guiding principles are therefore most urgently needed, seem to me to be as follows:

First, which is more important—the profitable investment of outside capital, or the development of a prosperous native population with its own economic basis and its own stable social system?

Wherever capital has been poured into an African territory, it naturally, though often unconsciously and automatically, seeks to answer this question in its own interests. It is a commonplace of electioneering for the Legislative Council in Kenya, for instance, for candidates to ask what would happen to the millions sunk in European estates if natives were to be allowed to plant coffee, or encouraged by Government to grow cotton. Mr. Leys, in his book on Kenya, quotes from the speech of one successful candidate in 1924: "You may be sure," he said, "that once the native had tasted comparative luxury from his cotton-growing, he would not be prepared to come back to work on our farms at the present rate of wages when the [cotton] boom was over."

The question is made even more pressing when chartered companies administer large areas, as in parts of Portuguese territory, or when, as in the Belgian Congo, special bodies are organized, under a certain degree of Government control but primarily as instruments of private capital, to exploit the resources of particular areas, be they the ores of Katanga, or the minerals, the agricultural possibilities and the scenic beauty of Kivu. Enlightened self-interest may often see to it that excellent labour conditions are enforced, as in the Katanga mines; but what I may call population interests get little chance of being heard as such.

The second point is this. Should native production for export be discouraged or encouraged? This is often bound up with our first question, but there are many remote areas where it needs to be answered on its own merits.

The third concerns the destination of money derived from direct native taxation. When the appropriate deduction has been made for general administrative services, should any of the proceeds of native taxes be devoted to any purpose save the direct advancement of native interests? (In Kenya, for instance, it seems clear that native taxation contributes to the education of white children and the financing of agricultural and medical advice to white settlers, as well as to administration and the needs of native education and native agriculture and health.)[1]

The fourth is educational. Are we to aim at widespread or universal education for the native peoples? If so, are

[1] My constant references to Kenya must not be taken as implying any hostility to the hardworking, hospitable and pleasant people who make up the majority of its white settler population. Kenya cannot help being the storm-centre, because it is the only country in tropical Africa where intensive white settlement has taken place. As a matter of historical fact, I should imagine that the European settlement of the Kenya highlands has taken place with less cruelty or injustice to the indigenous peoples than has the European settlement of any other country in historical times, be it Canada or Peru, South Africa or the United States. But this does not make it any the less necessary to try to work out principles and safeguards for the future.

they to be given a mainly technical education, or are all the resources of Western knowledge, thought and skill to be thrown open to them, for those to profit who can? This, too, is by no means an idle question. We might expect the mass of settlers to want native education to be merely technical and useful; this has almost always been the attitude of property-owners in bulk to an uneducated labouring class, irrespective of all differences of colour or race. But even the Phelps-Stokes Commission, which was sent across to look at African education through American eyes, in spite of its disinterestedness and of all the benefit and the raising of standards which it secured, did not escape the prevalent idea. Its recommendations have in some quarters been criticized as recalling the methods of Mr. Squeers; and even if this be unjust, it remains true that its constant stressing of the need for "community adaptation" and the rather elusive "character-training" can, unless these terms are properly defined and amplified, be interpreted as meaning that native education should recall the brands of education so familiar in Europe in the early and middle nineteenth century, designed to "fit the labouring classes to their station in life," to "train them in habits of industry and piety," as Hannah More put it, and in fact to increase their docility and their output in the God-appointed *status quo.*

The fifth point is political and administrative. In a country with a great numerical preponderance of natives, should questions involving native interests ever be decided by the votes of an elected assembly on which natives are not adequately represented? (This would obviously be the case, for example, were Kenya to be granted self-government. In a modified form the question presents itself wherever private white interests are powerful and vocal enough to influence the decisions of a legislative council, even though the constitution puts the unofficial members in a minority in the council; this, I think it is fair to say, has been the actual state of affairs of Kenya since the War.)

The sixth also concerns administration, but primarily native administration. Should native chiefs and councils be given a generous degree of responsibility and freedom in regard to local administration; or should they be kept as far as possible in leading-strings, with very little power to act save as cogs in a prescribed train of Government machinery, and with the minimum of financial, moral and intellectual responsibility?

The seventh concerns land. Should there be some principle irrevocably reserving certain areas or amounts of land for native occupation; or should it be in the power of Governors or of the Crown to alter the amount or the boundaries as they think fit?

The eighth also concerns land. Should the system of native land tenure be such as to make it possible for an individual cultivator to profit himself and his descendants by the improvements he has made? At present most tribal systems of tenure make this impossible; while mere grants of freehold land, even if safeguarded against transfer to men of other races, may produce a system of native land-lordism under which the tenant gets all the worst of the bargain.

And the ninth concerns labour. Is it justifiable to employ any form of forced labour? and if so, is it justifiable to employ such labour on private estates, or solely for governmental or communal purposes?

A native policy, to be a policy and not a pious senti-

ment, should make some definite pronouncement of principle on each of these points.

My own reactions to these questions (which are here
volunteered simply as the logical consequence to my mind
of the facts and impressions which came my way during
my four months in Africa) are somewhat as follows:—

1. The first question, as to the possible conflict between
the claims of native development and of white private interests, I should answer as follows: In tropical areas where
there is a large preponderance of natives over whites, the
development of a stable and prosperous native social system is the prime duty of colonial powers.

This implies that the recruitment of labour to satisfy
immigrant settlers or outside capital should never be permitted to dislocate the social life of the native areas by
withdrawing too great a proportion of the able-bodied
men, as the demands of the settlers' farms have admittedly
done in parts of Kenya, or as the demands of the mines
appear to be doing in parts of Rhodesia. Attempts are
being made to put this principle into practice in the Belgian Congo by laying down that in each village or district
a certain proportion of able-bodied men shall always be
left behind to get on with their own work. I do not know
to what extent it has proved possible to carry out the regulation in practice.

Another way of ensuring the continuity of native social
life is to transplant whole villages, men, women, and children, to the neighbourhood where labour is required. This,
too, is being attempted in parts of the Congo; the Dutch
have adopted the principle in order to colonize under-
populated Sumatra from over-crowded Java; the squatter
system in Kenya, whereby natives can occupy and cultivate

parts of settlers' estates on condition of giving at least six months' labour in each year to their white landlords, is a move in the same direction, and could be developed so as to give a full realization of our principle.

One great difficulty, of course, is the African tribes' obstinate attachment to their own area and the spirits of their ancestors therein resident; but the widespread migrations which have occurred in the past, and still occur now, are evidence that this is by no means insuperable.

2. Both as corollary of this, and as an answer to my second question, I would have it laid down that every encouragement should be given to natives to raise their agricultural production, including production for export. There are a few crops which for some time to come, or perhaps for all time, will be unsuitable for native production, chiefly on account of the need for great capital outlay, long years of waiting for returns, and large-scale organization. Such, for instance, are sisal and tea.

The level of skill and foresight needed to grow certain crops may also be above native reach. This is the plea put forward in Kenya to prevent coffee-growing by Africans.

It may thus be necessary to discourage or prohibit the growing of certain crops by natives; but no body of local opinion, liable to pressure from all kinds of vested and speculative interests, should induce the Secretary of State to abstain from exercising his powers of control in these matters, since no native policy can be adequate which does not take full account of native production.

For one thing, the growing of produce for export by natives is desirable, since with most crops the experience of Uganda and the West Coast shows that this is the quickest way of utilizing the country's agricultural possibilities to supply the needs of the world, and also the way involving least overhead charges and least waste of energy and capital. In Nigeria, for instance, most natives grow food crops for their own use, and in addition some crops for sale. Even should the market slump, they are self-supporting, unlike the European planter, who in like case is ruined. It is also desirable since increase of general native prosperity is essential for the development of any proper social system for Africa, any permanent rise in the natives' standards of health and housing, education and general living. It should thus be encouraged as a general factor in social improvement, as well as for purely economic reasons.

3. My third question related to the allocation of native tax. In regard to this point, I believe that financial statements should always be so framed that not only the amount of money raised by direct native taxation should be immediately ascertainable, not only the total amounts spent on different services, but also the amounts, within each service or department, spent in native areas and for specifically native purposes.

In the second place, the system in force in Tanganyika and Nigeria should always be adopted, of returning to the local native authorities a certain considerable proportion of the tax collected, to be spent by them (after paying the salaries of the chief and other members of the native administration) for such purposes—schools, roads, agriculture, water-supply or what not—as they think fit. This is far better than the plan usually adopted in Kenya of having local cesses for special purposes like native education.

Thirdly, the principle should be laid down that the proceeds of direct native taxation should not be employed for any purposes save administrative expenses and the direct advancement of native interests.

At the moment, for instance, in Kenya direct native taxation is in the form of a hut-tax of 12s. per hut (*i.e.* 12s. for each adult man *and* for each of his wives), or for detribalized natives a poll-tax of 12s. Europeans pay a poll-tax of 30s. and an education tax of 30s.—£3 in all. The Government's expenditure on native education in 1925 is stated to have worked out at about 2¼d. per head of native population, while that on white education was over £2 per head of white population. This is a proportion of 200 to 1, which is raised to over 400 to 1 if we take the cost per child of school age. It seems obvious that the natives are being made to contribute to the education of settlers' children. While it is, of course, true that many settlers find it to their interest to establish native schools on their estates, this contribution of theirs to native education is not compulsory. If the figures were available, we should undoubtedly find that the natives were also contributing one-sidedly to the superior medical facilities and agricultural research and advice available to the Europeans in the colony.

4. My fourth question concerned native education. To it I can see only one answer. It should be laid down as a fixed principle that the development of native education should rank with the development of native health and material prosperity as the prime charges on the Colonial Powers; and equally definitely that all educational facilities, general and liberal as well as technical and utilitarian, should, in due proportion, be provided for natives. A general all-round education should thus be the basis, and both

specialized vocational training and a higher liberal education should be available for those who can profit by them.

I have already spoken of various special problems of native education. There is no need to go into further detail here, especially as in British colonies the principles I have just outlined are in general clearly recognized by the powers that be, however violently they may be criticized by settlers and others of the powers-that-would-like-to-be. But it is worth while remembering that the Phelps-Stokes reports made it clear that there exist various other parts of tropical Africa where these principles are either not recognized or not acted upon by the Governments concerned.

5. The fifth question to be answered concerned the control of native interests by local bodies of other races. On this it should be laid down that native interests should never be at the mercy of the majority vote of an elected body composed wholly or mainly of non-natives.

Within the tropical African possessions of the British Empire, the only difficulty that is likely to occur in applying this principle in its straightforward form would be if "self-government," in its proper sense of responsible government, should be granted to Kenya Colony, or to its "white" highland area. This is the aim which the bulk of the white settlers have in mind, and it is the natural end-point towards which all extensions of parliamentary institutions *via* the stages of unofficial majority and representative assembly must inevitably tend. In Southern Rhodesia there has been an attempt to combine incompatibilities by granting to the white settlers what is virtually responsible government on the ordinary elective parliamentary plan, but superposing upon it the check of a representative of the Crown with powers of veto on certain subjects. It may safely be prophesied that within a few decades these powers of veto will have lapsed into desuetude. Responsible government by a white electorate means in fact the handing over of native interests out of the care of Whitehall into the hands of the local white settlers. (When, as in Kenya, an Indian electorate exists too, the question is complicated but not essentially altered.)

There remains as palliative of this the granting of the franchise to educated Africans as well—equal rights for all men of equal civilization. But this, if we penetrate far enough into the future, will eventually mean a large majority of native voters and presumably of native members of the assembly: and a parliament of whites, browns, and blacks is hardly calculated to promote peaceful interracial development.

The Hilton Young Commission, recognizing these difficulties, and concluding definitely that "there can be no question of responsible government in these territories until the natives themselves can share in the responsibility," throw out suggestions in a different direction. They first point out that parliamentary systems are really alien to the native mind, and that advisory councils are much more likely to be representative of native opinion than the men of professional politician type whom an ordinary electoral system would bring to the front; this suggests that political institutions for natives should be developed along lines of their own.

Secondly, they remind us (p. 87) that "responsible government, as understood in the light of British experience, depends on representative institutions which are founded on the basis of a single homogeneous community." And since it is exceedingly unlikely that European, Indian, and

African will, within the next few centuries at least, blend into a homogeneous community, they do not envisage the granting of responsible government to the immigrant population, nor, consequently, the lifting of the Secretary of State's control over native policy. This would mean that the white settlers must be content to see in an unofficial majority, without representative executive institutions and without full self-government, the utmost goal of their hopes. And it may well be that it is along lines quite other than those of traditional British parliamentarism that there will be found the best solution for the problems confronting white settlers in these tropical areas, where they must always be in a marked minority.

At the moment, however, the real difficulties crop up where a legislative council exists whose powers are nominally only advisory to the Governor, but on which the elected unofficial members can actually exert a strong influence. The tendency in such a case has been two-fold. There has been a tendency towards losing sight of the advisory function of the assembly, in which most subjects are debated on party lines between official "Government" and unofficial "Opposition." And there has been a tendency for the unofficial members, as the interests which they represent become more powerful, to influence the Administration on important questions of policy almost as definitely as if they possessed a voting majority. A striking instance of this was the holding-up of the Kenya Native Lands Trust Bill in deference to the hostility of the unofficial members of the Legislative Council. It seems clear that this bill, so essential to the allaying of native unrest and suspicion, would never have found its way on to the statute-book unless the overruling powers possessed by the Colonial

Office had been looming in the background. The remedy for such *de facto* changes in the function of advisory bodies would seem to be not only to retain the salutary powers of final decision now enjoyed by the home authorities, but to increase on the legislative councils the number of members representative of native interests, and perhaps in due course of time to give representation to elected or selected natives.

6. The sixth question concerns the responsibility of native chiefs and councils. Here liberal opinion at least is unanimous. The local native bodies should be given as much responsibility as they can stand. They should be made to feel that they are truly responsible for law, for order, for the details of local administration; and they should be encouraged, though never forced, to embark on progressive schemes for improving the health and prosperity of the community, such as hospitals, roads, experimental farms, seed-stores, etc.

But for the time being at least there must be careful if tactful inspection by the European administrator, and the fullest possible machinery for allowing appeals from native courts to the district officer or to white courts.

The principle is not the principle of dyarchy, with its two sharply-separated categories of "transferred" and "reserved" subjects. It is the principle of allowing to native councils the maximum possible amount of responsibility over all subjects, but reserving a certain degree of control over all of them in the persons of the European administrators. It is the principle of learning through your own experience and efforts, even at the cost of making mistakes.

7. The seventh question concerns the delimitation of white and native areas. In a succeeding chapter I shall

discuss various principles according to which land should
in the first instance be assigned to white settlement or
native development. The question which concerns us here
has rather to do with the carrying out of these broader
principles; but it is none the less essential. In most parts
of Africa we are irrevocably committed to the dual policy
of encouraging some degree of white settlement *pari passu*
with native development. The universal experience, wherever any land is alienated to the private ownership of
Europeans or other immigrants, is that suspicion and unrest
are eventually engendered among the natives unless the
area reserved for native occupation is definitely fixed in
some way, either by delimiting boundaries once and for
all, or by making a proviso that not more than a certain
total amount of land may be alienated. This principle, too,
should be formally asserted.

In regard both to this question of land, however, and to
the preceding question of white self-government, Kenya
provides a special problem, by virtue of the comparatively
large numbers of private white settlers and the compact
area of the colony's land which they occupy. On general
principles it is inevitable that this area will come to enjoy
an increasing measure of self-government. Indeed, there is
always the possibility that the territory may be split into
two parts—a native Protectorate, organized and administered after the fashion of Uganda or Tanganyika; and a
Colony consisting of the alienated lands and some of the
unalienated Crown land, in whose affairs the white settlers
would have a preponderant say.

The problem of natives within this "white" area, whether
it becomes officially separated or no, will of necessity be
a special one; it seems to me impossible to envisage a

whole territory or special area of government where natives would have no rights in land, and it would be in the interests of the settlers as well as of the natives to regularize and extend some type of squatter system. Accordingly, for this and any other similar exceptional areas of white preponderance—or I should say predominance, for natives even here would still be in a great numerical majority—some such exceptional principle as regularized squatting should be enunciated.

8. The next question concerns the method of land tenure. It would seem quite impossible, as Lugard points out at some length, to find any single method which would be universally applicable in theory, or could be universally enforced in practice. However, there appear to be three principles which could justifiably be laid down, and the adoption of which would materially help towards solving the problem. The first would limit change at one end. It is the general and obvious principle that any change should as far as possible take existing native customs as its basis, and grow naturally out of them.

The second limits it at the other end. It is that absolute freehold is undesirable. In the first place, no system should permit natives to sell land to Europeans or Indians, or to any natives not subject to the local native jurisdiction; and in the second place, we should make it impossible for land speculation and unrestricted landlordism to arise in Africa after we have experienced in our own civilization the evils that are inherent in them.

The third principle prescribes the general direction in which development should move. It is that we should aim at reasonable security of tenure to the cultivator, and at securing to him and his heirs the advantage of any improvements which he may make. Only so can we discourage the wasteful system of shifting cultivation, while at the same time encouraging individual enterprise and preventing exploitation by the owners of land rights, with the resultant growth of a class of landless labourers. Systems of this kind have already been introduced with marked success in various parts of Africa, such as the Transkei.

9. Finally we come to the question of labour. All are agreed in principle that slavery and forced labour are wrong and must be prohibited. The difficulty arises in applying the principle. To recruit men at the point of the bayonet and make them work, whether for wages or for nothing, is clearly intolerable. But what of imposing a native tax in money, when conditions are such that the money can only be earned by natives leaving their own villages and crops to work for hire under Government or private employers? Is this not a method of forcing labour, none the less efficient for being indirect? Sir Harry Johnston, in imposing a tax in Uganda, frankly recognized that fact. And in Kenya it has in the past been repeatedly underlined by those in authority.

A Governor of the Colony has publicly asserted that "we consider that taxation is the only possible method of compelling the native to leave his reserve for the purpose of seeking work"; and at one period after the War, instructions were sent from Nairobi to all District Officers that "moral suasion" was to be used to get people to leave the reserves for private estates, and chiefs (who were merely salaried employees of Government) were "encouraged" to increase the labour supply, and "repeatedly reminded that it is part of their duty [sic] to advise and encourage all unemployed young men in the areas under

their jurisdiction to go out and work on plantations"
(1919). The forcibleness of this moral suasion and encouragement is attested by the fact that the heads of the Anglican and Scottish Missions in Kenya were driven by this
development of public policy to publish a manifesto in
which they asserted that a frank application of the principle of compulsory labour, if limited in amount and
demanded equally from all tribes, would be preferable to
the results of the so-called voluntary methods in use. "This
'moral suasion' exerted by Government officials to secure
black labour for white farms has now been abandoned by
explicit command of the Secretary of State, but the demand
for labour is still a crying one, and still exerts its pressure
in one way or another throughout the colony." As a matter
of fact, in many parts of Uganda the old tribal custom was
that men should engage on communal work for one month
in the year; and in various districts it is still in force.
Settlers in Kenya are wont to remark ironically on the fact
that this system arouses no comment, whereas anything of
the sort in Kenya would, they say, at once provoke a storm
of questions in Parliament.

The problem is a difficult one; but here again it would
seem possible to lay down principles which will safeguard
all interests. Where motor roads do not exist, one form of
compulsory labour—namely head-porterage—is necessary
for the bare existence of administration. This is now in
most territories carefully regulated, and will gradually
dwindle with the improvement of road communications.
There is, further, no fundamental objection to labour
being demanded in place of money as a form of taxation.
But, if so, there must be some moderate maximum fixed,
say one or at most two months in the year; and labour

must not be called out during the "rush" seasons of native agriculture—planting and harvest. Further, the system should be applied all round, and no discrimination made, as was done in the Compulsory Labour Regulations in Kenya, which only decreed compulsory work for Government as the lot of those who had not worked for private employers during at least three months of the preceding year. Either compulsory work should be entirely for Government; or else a choice should be possible between work for Government and work for private employers, on the same scale of wages. The complete failure of the compulsory labour sections of the Glen Grey Act in South Africa should be a useful warning to other territories.

Secondly, there is work on special undertakings of benefit to the native community. As instances of these may be cited the clearing of bush in tsetse areas in Tanganyika, or the work on the extension of the Uganda Railway from Jinja to Entebbe.

Both of these schemes have the full approval of the native authorities; but both have been criticized in certain quarters as involving "forced labour." It is true that in neither case would a great number of the natives have come out to work if orders had not been expressly issued, and doubtless some pressure exerted, by the local chiefs and headmen. But then neither should we, most of us, pay our rates if the local authorities had not power of enforcing us under penalty to do so. It would seem that whenever exceptional schemes which are urgently necessary for native development can only be carried through by the aid of an exceptionally large labour supply, and the native authorities are so convinced of their utility as to volunteer to make themselves responsible for getting the men, we shall not be infringing any sacred principle of liberty in embarking upon them.

There remains the subtler problem inherent in the indirect forcing of labour by means of taxation. Here the remedy against possible injustice is to lay down as principle that so long as the tax is paid, there shall be no one-sided pressure on men to earn it as wage-earners on white estates rather than as producers on their own lands (a point stressed by Lord Lugard); and, as corollary of this, that adequate facilities shall be given to natives to earn money by their own efforts on their own lands.

There seems no reason why principles of this degree of detail should not be laid down by Parliament or by the Colonial Office.[1] If they could be, they would ensure that native policy in our different African territories would always be moving in the same general direction. At the moment, it is trending in one direction in one territory, in a quite different direction in another. This may not seem serious at the moment, but it has two grave disadvantages. Federations may be desirable—and it makes federation dif-

---

[1] The volume of protest which has been raised by white communities in Africa against the Colonial Office White Paper of 1930 is really very curious, considering that (as the Uganda authorities pointed out) it merely amplified the details of a policy which had already been in force for seven years. It must be confessed, however, that the phrasing of the White Paper was not always conciliatory, and that its tone rather than its matter may have been responsible for the anger undoubtedly, but very unfortunately, aroused in various African territories. Anger makes people say silly things. For instance, the report of the East Africa Women's League meeting on the subject of the White Paper makes the chairman say that the policy of the Colonial Office "could only lead to the ultimate destruction of the native races"—a statement which if not meaningless, is stupid. And anger makes give-and-take more difficult, and overrides the claims of reason, just at the moment when reasoned policy and generous give-and-take are most needed. The only remedy is to get back to principles.

433

ficult. Much more serious, it means that one day, sooner or later, as education spreads and political self-consciousness grows, the natives will begin to ask themselves and to ask us, their white trustees or masters, why within a single region of the Empire there exist such differences in the status and the treatment of native Africans. And we shall not be able to give any satisfactory answer.

Chapter XXXV

LAND, POPULATION AND GENERAL SMUTS

There is one aspect of policy which demands separate consideration, for it immediately concerns white as well as black; and that is the apportionment of African land between white settlement and native development. This in turn is inextricably bound up with questions of population; and since without a proper perspective on population we are liable to go off the track about land, I propose to begin with this.

It has often been argued, for example, by white settlers in East Africa, and by those at home who favour intensive white settlement, that reserves should be demarcated on the basis of the existing native population, and that the rest of the land should be made available for white occupation. Some go further and claim that natives have no right to possess land of which they are not now making adequate economic use. In other words, if white men can make better use of it, white men are morally entitled to possess it.

This criterion, it will be readily seen, would be fatal to the economic future of a country which is seriously under-populated and whose perennial cry is for more native labour; and it is manifestly unjust in that it allows for the expansion of the whites, but not for that of the blacks, and ignores the proved capacity of the blacks to improve their methods of production under proper guidance.

More just was the principle advocated by the Hilton Young Commission, who urged that the extent of land reserved for native occupation should be conditioned by the needs not only of the existing native population, but also of the probable increase in the next generation. Clearly, however, this was only intended to cover the immediate future: the Commissioners themselves recommended further enquiry with a view to the discovery of more fundamental principles on this as on other questions; and it would be a thousand pities if this compromise of theirs, valuable as it was as a deliberate temporary expedient, should become erected into a permanent guide for policy.

The perspective we need is that of the biology of the growth and decline of populations. For the last quarter of a century most native populations in equatorial Africa seem to have been stationary or going slightly downhill (though there are salient exceptions); and this seems due to the combined effect of indigenous and introduced diseases, of various native customs and tabus, and quite possibly to the strange distaste for living or conferring the gift of life which has seized upon various primitive peoples, notably the Melanesians, on being brought under the influence of an alien and incomprehensible culture. There is, however, every reason to suppose that, by an improved public-health service, by education, and by providing incentives to a fuller life, we shall be able to counteract and overcome these destructive tendencies and set native population on the up-grade again (as has, for instance, just been achieved in Uganda). And if so, it will not be long before the available spaces fill up. In South Africa the pressure on space has already begun. This is partly due to the insufficiency of the area reserved to natives, but at least equally to the fact that in the Union a fair rate of increase of native population has been maintained.

In point of fact, the sufficiency of an area for the needs of an existing population, or of its estimated increase in the next generation or so, is in the long, biological view a principle of secondary importance. Population density must tend towards a final equilibrium, and on its way thither will halt in various positions of comparative stability, each adapted to the general mode of life at the time. But when a relatively stable phase of life is upset, as African tribalism is being upset by white impact to-day, the stability of numbers is upset too, and we shall find population either growing until it puts pressure on the available land, or else shrinking until it is inadequate to the land it occupies. Shrinkage is a comparatively rare phenomenon, and the empty spaces can always be filled up from the surplus of more expansive peoples; thus the general tendency, as Malthus saw a century ago, is for populations to "press upon their means of subsistence"—unless, as the Neo-Malthusians soon pointed out, deliberate steps be taken to keep the population at a lower density, before the pressure has become painful.

The consequences of this for our problem are obvious enough. The principle of reserving land which is adequate for the needs of this or the next generation is a minimum principle whose observance will ensure that the canons of humanity and fairness are not violated at the outset; but it is entirely irrelevant when we consider the future and the definitive adjustment of populations which we would like to see eventually established.

I have in what follows deliberately avoided consideration of the Indian question. It is a grave complicating factor, but need not be more. Since racial problems bring such peculiar difficulties, I personally should welcome the gradual disappearance of Indians from Africa—not from the least hostility to them as Indians, but because their presence at once trebles the number of racial problems. At any rate, I cannot conceive any responsible person in the present position of the world advocating intensive settlement of Indians in Africa.[1]

We Europeans happen to be responsible at the moment for Central Africa. If we genuinely believe that the presence of Asiatics introduces extra complications there, and that we can educate natives to fill the Indians' place in the economic scheme, we have not only the right but the duty to try to prevent extra complications.

When we begin thinking of these questions (which are none the less urgent because their final solution lies a few generations further off), we see, if we are frank with ourselves, that the sole criterion for action is one of racial and social aspirations, not of population needs. There is a limited area of the world's surface—Africa—to be filled with people. With the suppression of wars and slave-raids, and the encouragement of health and agriculture, population pressure will fill it in what, biologically speaking, is a very short space of time. We are at present going on the assumption that over much of Africa the filling process could be equally well accomplished, merely as a physical fact, by whites or by blacks. The only question of long-

[1] Since this was written I find that Professor Thompson, who is certainly a responsible person, has advocated this very thing in his recent book, *Danger Spots in World Population*. He would seem to be so much obsessed by population pressure that he shuts his eyes to the biological perspective of the matter, and therefore puts a temporary adjustment of Indian pressure above the more lasting achievement of a true African civilization.

range principle in apportioning areas for native occupation, therefore, is this—how much of the surface of Africa would we like to see reserved for the growth of an essentially black civilization, how much for the growth of one which is primarily white? And in deciding this we have to take into account a number of factors. First there is the existing native population and its present requirements in land. As I have said, however, these are minimum requirements, and there are many areas which are to-day grossly under-populated. The next is the suitability of a given area for white settlement. There are some regions in which it is difficult or impossible for the white human organism to live permanently; and there are many others in which he *could* exist, work and reproduce, but where the black organism could exist with much more comfort, work with much greater efficiency, and reproduce with much greater free-dom. Such areas should be reserved for the growth of native civilizations; if white planters are to be allowed to settle there at all, they must be few, and they must recon-cile themselves to being strangers in the land, as they would if they settled in China or the country of any other alien civilization. Within tropical Africa there remain the highland areas, in which both white and black can live and work on more or less equal terms, and those few very high areas to whose temperature, it would seem probable, the white man is actually better adapted than the native Afri-can (though the altitude may be bad for the hearts and nerves of both). The die is here cast, and the principle of reserving some of this land for white settlement is now recognized. What is not decided, however, is the propor-tion of such areas to be reserved to Europeans, and the density of the white settlement which is envisaged. The only rights which Europe has in the matter are those of conquest, occupation and superior power. What she proposes to do in detail will depend upon how she tempers those rights derived from power with the principles of corresponding duties, and with considerations of long-range efficiency.

For instance, Western civilization seems to have tacitly accepted the general principle explicitly laid down in Lugard's *Dual Mandate*, that colonial Powers have a double duty, not only of protecting native populations and promoting their development, but also of making available the resources of the country to the world as a whole.

Policy must thus often be a compromise, for the two duties by no means invariably point in the same direction.[1] Where the world has need of African crops or minerals and cannot get them without white settlement, or can get them better with white settlement, then white settlement is, to our present view, legitimate. However, there may well be cases in which, though legitimate, it might not be desirable. For instance, if the area suitable for whites was small and was in the middle of a larger area where native production and native development were being pushed forward, it might legitimately be felt that the difficulties created by a white island would overshadow the possible cultural and economic benefits. This is the situation in parts of Tanganyika to-day. The influence of extensive

[1] The antagonism between the two parts of our "dual mandate" may be serious, as is pointed out forcibly by Professor Malinouski in two very able articles (*Africa*, January 1929; and *The Listener*, July 16, 1930). I must leave my readers to pursue the subject further in his pages, merely pointing out that the idea of the dual mandate does not provide a simple and glorious reconciliation of all difficulties, as is sometimes assumed by enthusiasts, but is a compromise, and, like all compromises, has to be operated with the greatest care and discretion.

white settlement on native social life must also be considered. If it disorganizes tribal life by withdrawing the majority of able-bodied men from their villages for large parts of the year, is this not a grave disadvantage, economic as well as social, to set against the advantages it confers? Parts of Rhodesia are said to be now almost bare of men owing to the magnet of highly-paid employment in the Rhodesian and Congo mines.

Then are you to restrict the white man in tropical Africa to supervisory functions, so that, even in the "white" areas, natives will always be in a very great majority? Or do you wish to have a civilization in which the numbers of whites are not overwhelmingly disproportionate to those of the blacks? In the latter case, of course, you must envisage white men engaged in various quite subordinate kinds of work, including skilled if not unskilled labour, and therefore in competition with natives; and you must face the terrifying possibility that a "poor white" spectre may arise in tropical as in temperate Africa to haunt and mock the civilization which has given it birth.

Further, from the point of view of the world at large, are you going to exploit the resources of tropical Africa more efficiently if you bring in a large population of white men, whose standard of living is high, or if you rely as much as possible on the labour of independent native producers?

At the moment we do not know for certain if white men can continue to live and reproduce without impairment of health or efficiency in tropical Africa, even in the highlands. Though we can foresee that white immigration on a large scale might easily lead to grave difficulties, such as a "poor white" section of the community, economic friction between white and black, or excessive demands for native labour, we find it much harder to see how such difficulties could be effectively guarded against. And we have no reason to suppose that a large white community would be more efficient than a small but picked one for promoting the material prosperity and development of the country as a whole. In the circumstances it would seem wise to go slow, and to envisage the white population of tropical Africa, settlers and traders as well as Government servants, as a limited and selected body of men on whom devolves the duty of acting as the agents of Europe in the dual task of supplying the rest of the world with what they want from Africa, and of helping Africa to develop along the lines best suited to her own people and her own conditions.

I have so far refrained from discussing General Smuts' very definite ideas of land and settlement policy in East Africa, as set forth in his recently published Rhodes Lectures (*Africa and some World Problems*). His conclusions, however, are so different from mine, and seem to me to lead to such a curious and undesirable compromise, that they demand a detailed consideration.[1]

With regard to the actual areas reserved for white settlement, the geographical considerations so forcibly put forward by General Smuts must clearly weigh with us— namely, the existence of a more or less continuous belt of

[1] As it was published while I was still in Africa, I did not happen to hear of Mr. J. H. Oldham's excellent criticism of General Smuts' lectures, *White and Black in Africa*, until after this chapter had been completed. It is perhaps interesting that a distinguished representative of missionary organization and a heterodox professor of biology should independently have come to almost identical conclusions on the subject. Mr. Oldham's book should be read by any one desiring a rather fuller treatment of the subject than I have had space for.

high land, much of it suitable for white settlement, from Kenya through Tanganyika and Nyasaland to Rhodesia and South Africa. The idea of a new area of continuous white civilization from the Cape to north of the equator has undoubtedly a potent attraction, and should dictate the broad outlines of any policy of territorial segregation as between white and black. But that is a dream for the future; while it is desirable that nothing immediate we do in the way of encouraging native development should prevent its possible realization later, for the present other factors should dictate the actual allotment of land to white immigrants. The desirability of going slow is one; and the other is the need for giving white communities the best possible chance of success. This cannot be done by scattered or haphazard settlement. Definite areas of reasonable but restricted size should be opened up in succession, and some trouble should be taken to plan each venture and to guide its development as a single whole; each area can then be enlarged as circumstances allow. In this way we shall get experimental cultures, so to speak, of white civilization in different parts of Africa, and find out what white settlement can do under various conditions. If they work satisfactorily, we can gradually encourage their extension until they join up into a more or less continuous area of white settlement, or at least white predominance. If they do not, we can relinquish the "white backbone" idea without too much disappointment, and without having prejudiced other methods of helping Africa's development.[1]

In any case, a consideration which ought *not* to weigh

[1] General Smuts writes as if lands above 4000 feet were always, or usually, suitable for white settlement. This is hardly the case; in certain regions much of this land is mere dry scrub, barren and hot. The "white backbone" could not, as a matter of hard fact, be really continuous.

with us is the possibility (envisaged by General Smuts on p. 64 of his book) of using the "vast empty spaces" of Africa in the attempt to reduce unemployment in Britain. In the first place, the remedy is in itself not a remedy but a mere palliative; problems of population can only be solved biologically, and not by such mechanical means. But in this particular case the palliative would not even palliate appreciably. The total white population of Kenya, Uganda, Tanganyika, Zanzibar, Nyasaland, and Northern Rhodesia in 1926 was about 25,000. To-day it appears to be rather less than double that figure. The most intensive schemes of settlement could not hope to add much more than 10,000 a year to this white population without dislocating the region's whole economic life; and this quantity is often exceeded in the monthly fluctuations of our unemployed, who now amount to well over two million. In other words, we could not hope to reduce unemployment even by 1 per cent. by dumping unemployed men in tropical East Africa. Further, unless General Smuts envisages the presence in Central Africa of large numbers of white artisans and clerks as well as of settlers, which would enormously increase interracial difficulties, the most prolific sources of our unemployment would hardly be touched. As the population of Great Britain will within a decade or so be either stationary or declining, and as this fact and the practice of birth-control will alter the whole problem as far as it concerns later generations, we are justified in dismissing from our minds emigration to Africa as having any real relevance to unemployment. It is, if I may be Hibernian, a fleabite in an ocean, and a temporary ocean at that.

Apart from drawing attention to geographical facts, General Smuts lays down two principles. One is that any enduring or desirable African civilization can only be based on rather intensive permanent white settlement in all areas where permanent white settlement is possible; for East Africa he would include in this area roughly all land of over 4000 feet elevation. The other is that there should be territorial segregation of white and black. All areas not reserved for white settlement should be reserved for natives, and they should be there encouraged to develop along their own lines, with the maximum amount of responsibility for their local self-government. But the fewest possible number of natives should be allowed to live in white areas, and *vice versa*.

I may quote a few of his own words to illustrate the meaning which he attaches to his first principle. On p. 67 he says that, as foundation for the future civilization of Africa, "a large white population seems to be a *sine qua non*"; and it is difficult to imagine a white population which shall be large and not contain many skilled workers, clerks and technically-trained men, who would then compete quite unnecessarily and very unpleasantly with the natives we have been laboriously educating to take up just such work. On p. 55 he says that "the wasteful character of native production is being realized," even, I understand him to mean, in West Africa; and on p. 51 writes that "the white settler is the most effective and expeditious means of pushing forward the economic progress of the continent." And finally (p. 50) we read: "Granting in principle that native interests should rank first, I still submit that white settlement under proper safeguards remains the best means to give effect to that priority"—in fact, that it is always better, as a means of fostering native development, to have natives working for white masters than for themselves.

General Smuts, in fact, quite definitely regards native production as a *pis aller*, a second-best to white settlers producing with the aid of native labour; he lays stress on the *rapidity* of white exploitation of African resources, without discussing whether this will conduce to ultimate stability or no; and he quite definitely prefers that the future civilization of Africa should be dominated from the start by the ideas of an immigrant white community rather than that it might develop along lines of its own, though, of course, profiting by Western ideas under the guidance of administrators and missionaries.

It is impossible not to sympathize in many ways with the idea of the "white backbone." The ample grandeur of Rhodes' ideas has captured the imagination of General Smuts, and this is the form in which he sees them realizing themselves in the future. But he goes too fast; he takes too many things for granted; and he fails to envisage the essential differences between temperate and sub-tropical Africa on the one hand, with abundant areas as suitable for Europeans as for natives to live in, and tropical Africa on the other, where much of the area is definitely unsuited to white settlement, and the bulk of it better suited to black than to white. As a minor detail, he also overrates considerably the amount of fertile land at low levels. When he states (p. 56) that in addition to the highlands over 4000 feet, which he would reserve for white settlement, there are "immensely larger areas of fertile lowlands and river valleys," this is simply not true for some of the territories concerned. In Kenya, for instance, the greater pro-

Two Uganda Flowers.

Above, a Large Orchid, Its Flowers Daffodil Yellow
with Chocolate Throat, from the Western Rift.
Below, One of the Blue, Scented Water-lilies Which
Border the Shores of Lake Bunyoni.

TREE-GROUNDSELS (*Senecio*) BY A CRATER-LAKE NEAR THE TOP OF MOUNT ELGON. ON THE NEAR SIDE OF THE LAKE IS A BUSH-LOBELIA. (*Photo. by Mr. W. Soundy, Department of Agriculture, Uganda.*)

portion of such land is desert or semi-desert, as little suited to native agriculture as to white.

He very airily dismisses native production as wasteful, and therefore a second-best to white settlement. This is not, however, the general view in Tanganyika and Uganda; and from what I can gather is quite contrary to the facts in West Africa. We need take but two illustrations. Most of the world's cocoa is raised in West Africa by native producers. And the natives of Nigeria buy more, per head, from Britain than do the inhabitants of the United States; as there are over twenty million natives in Nigeria, this is a biggish item in our trade. General Smuts, I believe, has never been in the Gold Coast or Nigeria; perhaps a visit to these countries, which are prosperous in spite of the alienation of any land to white settlers being virtually prohibited, except for certain limited purposes, would cause him to modify his views.

But the real weakness of General Smuts' position appears when we follow out the effect of his two policies, white and black, upon each other.

He definitely lays down (pp. 98-99) that we should force the native wage-earner to retain his home in the native areas by compelling married native women to stay permanently in the reserves, and prohibiting men from being engaged by white employers if they are accompanied by their wives and children. This, he admits, will be difficult, since many white men prefer (not unnaturally!) their house-boys to be leading a normal married life, and since the general experience of employers of native labour, including such important bodies as the Kenya and Uganda Railway, is that the men are more contented, work

447

better, and stay for longer spells if they are encouraged to bring their families.

Personally, I cannot imagine any proposal more calculated to hinder the development of a stable African civilization than a system which would always ensure that a large proportion (for with intensive white settlement it would be a large proportion) of married native men would be separated from their wives and homes for six or even three months out of every twelve, and that the native villages would always contain a large proportion of grass widows.

Even if you adopt the principle of intensive settlement of a "white backbone," this state of affairs could still be avoided, but only by encouraging squatter settlements and model native villages in the white area. Not only, however, would this sacrifice General Smuts' cherished principle of territorial segregation, but such mixing of the races in close proximity clearly contains the germs of many grave difficulties for the future—as regards land, for instance, or racial discrimination. And the greater the extent of the white area and the more intensive its settlement, the more acute will every such difficulty become. General Smuts' solution, to my mind, is no solution at all: it is the setting up on an equal basis of two principles which are both admirable *in vacuo*, but which cannot be prevented from interacting and by their interaction producing a crop of highly undesirable results. One of them must relinquish its claim to equality; in the tropical parts of Africa, as I have tried to set forth in a previous chapter, this must be the principle of white settlement and white production.

And by this I emphatically do not mean that there should be pro-native favouritism, whether in law, in the allocation of grants, or in any other respect. I mean that in planning and executing the broad lines of policy, we need this simple rule of the road. It is not in the least necessary that the development of white settlement and white production should clash with the development of native population and native production: but if there should be a clash, then the interests of the white tens of thousands must give way to the interests of the black tens of millions. We are committed by the facts of history and by official promises to some degree of white settlement in East Africa; and for some purposes, both economic and political, white settlement is necessary, or at least very desirable. But, if we accept the conclusions of preceding chapters, white settlement should, as regards the interests of the country as a whole, be not equal but subordinate to native development and native production. And if it is definitely regarded as subordinate, the violent clash and wholesale difficulties inherent in General Smuts' scheme would be avoided. This is not to imply that difficulties will not arise under any scheme, or that white settlement, even on a small and carefully-regulated scale, will not involve compromise. All government involves compromise; and all contact of markedly different races and cultures brings peculiarly difficult problems. But at least, if white settlement is not regarded as an end in itself, but as subordinate to the general progress of a country in which the social and economic development of the native population is the first aim, then difficulties can be adjusted as they arise. Compromise is the oil of the social machine; but if the machine incorporates two antagonistic principles of equal driving power, no amount of oil will ensure efficient working.

449

Chapter XXXVI

EPILOGUE

Africa view. . . . Is there a single view to be had of the vast of Africa? If there be, can a flying visit attain to the view-point? What approximation to it have I achieved in my short four months? Here, in most un-African surroundings, I sit and reflect upon what I saw and felt and thought in Africa. Outside are people on the pavements, men going into the City on their business, women shopping, tradesmen's boys on bicycles, children off to the Heath—a minute fraction of our immense and overgrown London. This one little suburb contains more white people than all East Africa. From my window I see the spire of Hampstead Church over the horizon of the Heath, hear the bells of trams, and feel the cold air of a northern spring. For as far as I can see in the dingy, smoky air, and for miles beyond, all the land save a few patches of imprisoned greenery is covered with cement or asphalt or stone, bricks and mortar, steel and concrete, is honey-combed with pipes and tubes, meshed with wires.

It is against this background that I think of Africa, and in my mind's eye see enormous lakes, horrid expanses of dry scrub, surprising mountains, little villages of beehive huts, herds of zebra and antelope, tall black men with spears who do not think of hiding the nakedness of their magnificent bodies, laughing chocolate-coloured women in beads and skins, the farms of lonely white settlers and the golf courses and clubs with which they relieve their loneliness, little schools far in the bush where black children learn the magic of reading and writing, whole tracts of country gone out of use because of tsetse fly or tick, laborious cultivation that yet but scratches the face of the land, volcanoes big and small, strange saline lakes, rifts that scar the continent; I feel the wicked power of the equatorial sun and the effort and strain of altitude; I hear the distant reverberation of lions roaring, the ear-splitting noise of cicadas and mole-crickets, the native drums at night where a dance is being danced; I am conscious of the presence of lurking disease in air, earth and water all around, of the existence of crocodiles and beasts of prey and pachyderms, of African ways of human life entirely alien from the ways of Europe; I am aware of change, invisible, often unwanted, stealing in upon the land with white men and their ideas and inventions—Capitalism and Christianity, books and motor cars, science and cinemas, law and cheap trade goods.

Yet something coherent does begin to emerge from all this procession of images and impressions and contrasts. The view of Africa which organizes itself in my brain is of a continent equal in importance and variety and interest to its sister continents, but with its destiny still fluid, the lines of its human future not yet laid down. It is the one continent which is not yet set in its ways. It could develop a civilization of its own unhampered by the forms and traditions and preconceived ideas which are part and parcel of our Western civilization whether it is continuing in old or spreading in new lands—and indeed part and parcel of all established civilizations, Chinese or Hindu as much as Western.

We who belong to an old civilization have many things to be proud of; but we cannot be very proud of the state, or, to put it bluntly, the mess, at which our civilization as a whole is now arrived. We can be proud of our scientific and technical achievements, our knowledge and art, our organization and our wealth; but we cannot, I hope, be proud enough of them to wish to give them to another continent if this also involves the gift of the other concomitants of our civilization, including slums and overgrown cities, gross inequalities of wealth and opportunity, class discontent and chauvinist nationalism, the over-multiplication of the unfit and the horrors of modern war. I see Africa chiefly and most thrillingly as the one part of the world of continental magnitude in which (without the destruction or degeneration of an old civilization) there could arise a new civilization, consciously planned or at least consciously guided from its beginnings.

That is the central part and foreground of the view. But there is an ambience, a perspective, and a background to fill in too; and they have power to alter the picture very radically.

We can try to avoid fixing the shackles of past custom or present prejudice on to a new civilization; but we cannot anticipate the future, or go beyond the enlightened thought of our own time for guidance. If I were asked to sum up in a phrase the main trend of post-war thought, I would say that, in so far as it was not merely pessimistic or destructive, it was in the direction of science tempered by humanism. Theology was queen of the sciences in mediæval times; but this pre-eminence of religion came to an end with the Renaissance, and the distinction between sacred and secular emerged sharply in practice and ideas. Then science grew up within secularity; and a new orientation revealed itself. Science appeared as an independent menace both to religion and to secular humanism, while these had by no means reconciled their antagonism of worldly versus other-worldly. But the very triumphs of science recast the parts again. The greatest burst of new activity is now in the human and social sciences, not in natural science; and our main search now is not merely for new scientific achievements, but also for a scale of values. The aim of any humanism can, I suppose, be summed up as *more life.* This modern brand of humanism is distinguished by the place which it allots to science. It sees in science, its method, its results, and its general outlook, the only means for realizing its aim, in matters of social organization or systems of government as much as in the control of nature. But its aims and values are humanistic, and it does not intend to let these be controlled by science, any more than by any other sort of intellectualism, or by theology, patriotic ambition, or commercialism. You will not want what you ought to want without the humanistic spirit: you will not get what you do want without the scientific spirit.

But besides her practical and concrete benefits, science can help by giving us a broad, dispassionate view, unclouded by any supposed need of apportioning moral praise or blame. At the moment we are inclined to lose our perspective by being in a hurry, to look down on other races if they have not achieved civilization as quickly as we Westerns, to grumble if we do not achieve our aims in a generation or two. Let us restore our sanity with a little science. To think about Evolution, even about human evolution, we need 10,000-year periods as our units of time, for centuries are too confusingly small. Both agriculture and civilization seem to be confined to the last one of such periods; and our modern species of man to less than ten. To reach the earliest living creature that could possibly be called human, we need about 100 of these time-units; but to the earliest known fossils—which were already quite complicated organisms—some 5000. Man, in fact, is an extremely late product of life, and settled civilization an extremely late product of man. It may possibly mean a great deal that the Africans to-day have not advanced beyond the state in which our ancestors found themselves a few thousand years back. But it may quite well mean very little; at least the lag is, on the biological scale, a paltry one.

Again, natural science combined with archæology and anthropology is putting the recent history of Africa in a new perspective. Africa as we know it is not immemorial, even by human standards of time; it has been the scene of changes as recent and as unceasing, if not so progressive, as those of Europe and Asia. Not only was it subject during the Ice Age to changes of climate as important as those of higher latitudes, but during this period, even when man of modern type was already in the continent, a last and violent outbreaking of rifting and volcanic action changed the very face of the land. The only men so far discovered from those times were, though *Homo sapiens*, of a different type from the modern Negro or Bantu. A few thousand years ago, the pigmy races must have been far more widespread than they are now, and have only been gradually restricted through the pressure of new human waves that forced their way into Central Africa. As for the tribes of to-day, in many cases we know that their present distribution and sometimes their present mode of life are extremely recent, dating back only a few centuries. The Kikuyu seem only to have been in Kikuyuland for about four centuries, and during that time to have changed over from hunting to agriculture. The Lango have been in northeast Uganda an even shorter time and have changed their habits equally radically. The scattered native kingdoms which possess a comparatively high political organization, such as Buganda or Toro in Uganda, the Watusi kingdom in Ruanda, or the Bushongo in the Southern Congo, have all taken their rise from the immigration of a conquering race; and these immigrations seem all to have taken place well within the last thousand years. The Bantu were behind the whites in reaching the southern parts of South Africa. Tribes like Galla or Masai or Zulu can rise to be the scourge of their neighbours in a few decades, and in some cases may fade into insignificance again with equal rapidity.

Nor, in the times of which we have actual record, let us forget what has been the effect of contact with more advanced races. Up till the middle of the nineteenth century the outside world had exerted three chief influences upon equatorial Africa. First, on the credit side, the introduction of various useful animals and plants; and, to debit against this, secondly, a number of parasites and diseases, and, thirdly, the slave-trade. Let it never be forgotten that Europe and America were for centuries the chief organizers of the West Coast slave-trade, and were just as bad as the Arabs on the East. Many worthy merchants in English cities, and many planters in America and the

West Indies, were made rich by slavery; but the effect on Africa was not merely to make the negro countries poor— it changed their outlook on the world. There seems little doubt that the violence and the unpleasant superstition of the West Coast negro were in large part a direct reaction to the ghastly business of the slave-trade, just as the chaos of behaviour and thought which followed the Black Death was due to the terrors of the plague, or the crop of irresponsibility and superstition which grew up in 1919 was a reaction against the four beastly years of war. If horror be sown, horror will be reaped, even if in changed or attentuated form.

And even when we come to our own times, the process continues. We have made many tribes suspicious and intolerant of change, simply by the vacillations of our land policy. In 1914 we Europeans could have pointed with some pride to the fact that we had for all practical purposes suppressed the constant violence of inter-tribal war in Africa. But by 1919 that boast seemed a little empty. In four years, more African natives had been killed or had died of disease or even of starvation as the result of a white war than in forty years—perhaps a century—of the old primitive warfare of the blacks. And the reaction to this experience has been definite enough, and on the whole not pleasant, either for black or white. The native has lost his childlike belief in the white as an inherently superior being. He has become more critical and more restive; but we are to blame for the new spirit, not he. Let us not forget, in fact, that some of the qualities which we are apt to dislike in the customs and mentality of Africans are directly due to our own interference with Africa.

Then there is the future. If science can provide a background for past and present, humanism must help point the way into the future. Humanism, reiterating her demand for more life, can keep us on our guard against false directions. It can guard us against substituting one drab uniformity for the rich potential variety of social organisms and their achievement. It can make us refuse to regard any country, however backward, as a mere appendage of the world whose prime aim shall be the production of food and raw materials and wealth for other nations; it can make us discount mere quantitative expansions, whether in population or wealth or anything else, and see in these only a means to an end. It can, in fact, help us to remember that a real civilization for Africans is the only comprehensive end for which we can possibly work in Africa.

But if Africa is to develop her own civilization, she and her peoples will pass through many phases which cannot but rouse our distaste or our antagonism. Let me take a parallel from family life. There are plenty of parents who treat their children as pets. They find them delightful so long as they remain childish—playthings which have the unique advantage of being alive and able to talk. But they have forgotten that the little darlings are real human beings like their elders and betters; and when the children grow up, show signs of thinking for themselves, and demand to be dealt with on the adult plane—why, then there is trouble. The trouble comes from two sides at once. For one thing, the parents want to keep their pets as long as possible, and unconsciously resent any move in the direction of independence; and for another, the boys and girls are, of course, very young and inexperienced, they do make mistakes, they are crude and callow and unbalanced, and

irritate both by their awkward diffidence and their un-
teachable obstinacy.

But the children *will* grow up—that is how they are
made, that is why they were brought into the world, and
it is doubtless very irrational of parents to feel aggrieved
at it. But aggrieved they often feel, and will do so unless
they discount the change beforehand with the aid of a
little reason and a little imagination.

It is much the same with the contact between a high
civilization and the more primitive peoples under its
charge. As long as natives can be treated as children,
aggravating and yet charming creatures who must just be
told what to do and what not to do, and attempts at
argument can be cut short by some authoritarian gesture,
they will inevitably be popular with their white guardians.
But when they begin to develop and to demand a share
in the same world of thought and life in which we white
people live, matters are different. The black children are
growing up. They are no longer children. But the adolescence of a people is more prolonged and more difficult
than the adolescence of an individual; its half-bakedness
and crudity will be more pronounced. And an adolescent
people is bound often to irritate those who have stood *in
loco parentis* to it, and set their teeth on edge.

It is indeed remarkable to see how widespread (though by
no means universal) and deep-rooted (though often unconscious) is the feeling of white men against the euro-
peanized, educated, or even progressive black. And the
feeling is often strongest in those who have a whole-hearted
liking for the unsophisticated native. It is remarkable, because, after all, the white man's very existence in the country involves change and introduces new standards; the

assumption underlying government of black by white is that white ideas and methods are superior to black; and the aim of the control and the education we thrust upon them is to give them Western ideas, skill, and individual self-reliance, and, in the case of mission education, Western religious beliefs and ideals as well. Yet if they really begin to put these new ideas into practice and try to live up to the new standards Europe has brought into Africa, the first reaction of Europe, in the persons of the local Europeans, is hostile. There are administrators who frankly prefer Mahomedan to Christian natives, Islam to Christianity as a religion for the "inferior race." There are settlers who will not engage a native if he can read, and will even dismiss their most skilled men if they are discovered guilty of this crime.[1]

Many white men seem to regard it as their duty to "keep the black man in his place," a process which chiefly consists in snubbing educated natives on principle. They are in favour of increasing the efficiency of the natives, but when the natives profit by their efficiency to become economically independent they run the risk of being denounced as selfish, and when a well-to-do chief builds a stone house and furnishes it in European style he is liable to be laughed at as a mere ape of Europe.

Europe cannot have it both ways. If we rule in Africa by virtue of some white superiority, we must expect the natives of Africa to take our ideas and methods as worthy of imitation; if we educate them to think for themselves

[1] V. Murray in his *School in the Bush* (Appendix 2) draws an interesting parallel between this attitude and that of the upper classes in this country, a hundred years ago, to the education of the masses. Francis Place, the notable reformer, lost many customers (he was a tailor) "owing to their learning of his habits of study."

about their agriculture and their trades and their local administration, we must remember that the different parts and activities of mind are by no means thought-tight, and must expect them to use their brains on other and more general topics; if by granting special facilities to Christian missions we give it to be understood that Christianity is the religion of which Europe approves, we must expect native converts to take us *au pied de la lettre*, to try and puzzle out the application of Christian principles to their twentieth-century African problems, and to put pressing questions concerning the Christian doctrine of the universal brotherhood of all men. When you have encouraged the child to grow up, you must not expect him to remain a child.

The parallel between the unreflective parental attitude to children and the unreflective subconscious white attitude to natives comes out with extreme clearness in regard to native administrations. The commonest criticism of indirect rule by the unofficial white community is that it will lead to peculation by the chiefs and the oppression of their native subjects; the greatest obstacle to the full application of the principles of indirect rule in practice is probably the reluctance of white administrators to see their charges expose themselves to criticism by making mistakes, with a consequent tendency to keep them in leading-strings. Just so do we reiterate the command to be a good boy upon our sons, just so do we shrink from allowing them to make the experiments and errors which alone can lead them to a true maturity.

It is only too true that natives can caricature Europeans in a most irritating way and grow into a patchwork of incompatibles. You cannot achieve civilization in a few years, not even by means of sudden conversion, or a complete suit of European clothes. But these difficulties are the inevitable difficulties of adolescence, and may be discounted by a sympathetic imagination, and minimized by a proper system of indirect rule. To British India we have given what is probably the most honest and self-sacrificing administration that any Empire has had to show. But it is essentially a direct administration; the organs of native self-government atrophied through disuse; and now that we are trying to put in European methods of government from the top, with the aid of Indians educated along purely European lines, we find chaos below the surface.

In India we have been driven to the principle of Dyarchy; the principle of indirect rule is single, not double, and in it the native administration, whether its powers are large or petty, is an essential part of the unitary machine.

To give the people of Africa a share in the administration of their own territories, and a responsible interest in their economic and social development, is what is wanted. The native chiefs and their councils of tribal elders; the native sanitary inspectors and agricultural assistants; the clerks to native courts; the village schoolmasters and teachers under native administrations—if such men exist, properly trained, and interested in their work, they will be of infinitely more service to the future of their continent than any quantity of University graduates, turned out as in India by an essentially alien system of education, with few roots in their native world of thought, little chance of obtaining the kind of posts which they would like, and little aptitude or liking for the kind of posts which are available. The transformation of a continent must begin at the bottom, not the top; and if the native's energy and interest are once caught and held in the concrete business of developing Africa, he will not have much to spare for merely imitating the ideas of Europe. If he is organically growing, out of his own soil and the increased health and prosperity he has achieved there, into a better African, he is a real being and cannot irritate as he can if he develops as a mere appendage, economic or religious or intellectual, to an alien system.

And if Africa should develop along these lines, what might she become? No one can foresee in the least to what our present confusion of thought and practice may bring the world. Our economic system seems to be a Frankenstein monster which may destroy its inventors; nationalism may smash the nations; humanitarianism may well unnerve Western Europe and America before it has tempered the raw violence of new powers like Russia or China; the uneven practice of birth-control may upset all the balance of power among peoples; science and knowledge may outrun goodwill and capability. A hundred things may happen to throw the world back into chaos. But if order has it and no new dark age or period of war should supervene, I can envisage a real African civilization growing up in the next century or so. It would be based on agriculture. Black yeomen and peasants would form the bulk of the population, cultivating their own land, living in decent houses in pleasant villages. Dotted over the country would be numberless small towns, thronged for weekly markets, seats of local administrations with their courts and hospitals and schools, centres of trade and amusement for the country round. The sharp tribal distinctions would have gradually faded away, leaving agreeable local patriotisms and differences of manners, accent or dress such as with us divide Highlander from Devon man, or Wales from Yorkshire. Abundance of roads, with abundance of motor-cars and motor-buses on them, would connect all the towns; the people as a whole would be literate, and would have their newspapers and their wireless as we do at home, while sport would undoubtedly fill a great part of their leisure.

By then, the world will have had time to reflect upon the problems of population that are now just looming grimly into its consciousness. We may suppose that, through rational schemes of conception-control directed by the public health service, populations then will be self-regulatory in size; and that it will no longer be considered an axiom that the maximum possible number of people is also the optimum for a country, or that total quantity of trade, irrespective of the number of people who engage in it or what opportunities they may have of enjoying its fruits, is the first criterion of a country's success.

If these ideas have penetrated the world's skull in time, then we shall see great areas of Africa still set aside as game sanctuaries and native reserves, even though some of them could be turned into agricultural man-supporting land by the applications of science. All of the great mountains of Africa, and many of the lesser ones, with names hardly known yet to the world outside Africa—Hanang, Essimingor, Agoro and Debasien—will be reserved from exploiting hands, either as forest sanctuaries, as absolute nature reserves, or as national parks. Kenya will still greet the newcomer with the authentic African thrill of herds of buck and zebra, gnu, ostrich and other game, seen from the train-window. Big-game hunters, if one may read the signs of the times, will have dwindled, and their place will have been taken by naturalist observers and photographers and lovers of wild life who, on paying their fee, will be able to camp in remote corners of the game sanctuaries and for once realize what the world was like before man came among the beasts.

Man does not live by bread alone, nor by machines alone. Some men at least need the beauty of nature, the interest of nature, even the wildness of nature, the contact with wild animals living their own lives in their own surroundings, the temporary release from civilized routine and elaboration into the immediacy of camp and travel. These wants Africa can provide abundantly for the world, if only the world takes things in time, and does not, as in England, only begin a desperate saving of a country-side when much of it is spoilt beyond saving, a precipitate rescue of already tarnished amenities.

And it is not only the preservation of nature that we may work for; we may also work for her embellishment. Often, as one walked or drove through the tropical scene, the eye would miss what it might have found in Europe—the hill crowned with a little house, the church spire in the distance, country-houses among trees on the fertile lands, castles or monasteries on their perches, beautiful bridges old and new, the comfortable look of a market-town glimpsed in a far valley. Africa, too, will grow its towns and houses—but will they embellish the landscape? There is no reason why they should not, and one prays it may be so. There may not be any African monasteries or castles, but there will be schools and laboratories, town-halls and libraries, shops and factories and Government offices; any and all of these can be beautiful, and buildings like the Indian School or the Railway Offices at Nairobi have already set a standard.

. . . . .

Pessimistic observers suggest that England is past her zenith, and British commercial prosperity condemned, by the economic changes which have come upon the restless world, to inevitable decline. Even if this fate should be hers, she may yet remain great if she can but retain one of her present attributes—the faculty of turning out men with a gift for the administration of primitive peoples. She may sink to second-rateness as an industrial power and yet remain great as the director of an Empire.

And that Empire will be centred in Africa. The old Empire has evolved into a federation of Dominions, a society of autonomous nations whose members have already achieved a status of almost complete equality with the mother-country and each other and, whatever the precise form their association may take in the future, will always remain each "master of its own destiny." India, if she remain British at all, can only do so by ultimately evolving into a Dominion, though doubtless a Dominion of a new type. Remains the Colonial Empire: and the Colonial Empire consists of two parts—huge and coherent areas of Africa: and scattered outliers dotted about the world in the East and West Indies, the Pacific and Atlantic, South America and Malaya.

The only other power with an extent of African territories comparable to those of Britain is France; and her African possessions differ from ours in two salient ways—a large part of their area is taken up by the vast Saharan waste; and they begin on the Mediterranean, so that there is a continuous gradation of culture between Paris, through southern France, the North African littoral, the Sahara and the semi-Arab civilization south of it, to the tropical recesses of French Equatorial Africa. There is no such bridge between London and Lagos or Entebbe; the British possessions in Central Africa are by far the largest territory in that continent which has the opportunity and the prospect of developing a civilization of its own without organic connection and continuity with the civilization of Europe.

My Africa view ends here. Looking back, I see my crowded and random impressions, from my first tourist sensations on landing to the ideas I dug out of books on my return, all converging to the future and this thought of it.

I see Central Africa as the one continental bulk where the step from barbarism to civilization has not yet been taken; the one major region of the world still free to achieve a new civilization without destroying an old. And I see England as the country which has the greatest opportunity of helping Africa towards such a future.

Index

INDEX

INDEX

INDEX

INDEX

INDEX

INDEX

INDEX

White Man—(*Continued*)
tendency to dominate, 389
unreflective attitude towards native, 460
White Papers, 412; 433, *note*
on Native Policy in Africa, 414, *note*
Women, childbirth made difficult, 301
"circumcision" harmful, 203
initiation rites, 202

Women—(*Continued*)
results of carrying burdens on head, 300

Zanzibar, 33, 34
bazaar, 38
geographical formation, 39
museum, 37
Zebra, 72
Zimbabwe, 398
Zulus, 455